# Developments in West German Politics

# Developments in West German Politics

*Edited by*
**Gordon Smith**
**William E. Paterson**
**Peter H. Merkl**

MACMILLAN

First published 1989

Published by
MACMILLAN EDUCATION LTD
Houndmills, Basingstoke, Hampshire RG21 2XS
and London
Companies and representatives
throughout the world

Phototypeset by Input Typesetting Ltd, London
Printed in Great Britain by
The Camelot Press Ltd, Southampton

British Library Cataloguing in Publication Data
Developments in West German politics.
1. West Germany. Politics
I. Smith, Gordon  II. Paterson, William E. (William
Edgar), 1941–  III. Merkl, Peter H. (Peter Hans)
320.943
ISBN 0–333–47367–1 (hardcover)
ISBN 0–333–47368–X (paperback)

# Contents

## Part Two: Politics and Society

## Part Three: Economic and Social Policy

## Part Four: Germany and the World

# List of Maps, Illustrations and Tables

# Preface

*Developments in West German Politics* is intended to bridge the gap that exists between the approach adopted by texbooks and the material that is often available only in journal articles or in German-language publications. In this book we have sought to give the reader up-to-date assessments of key trends and issues in the Federal Republic with sufficient background analysis to make the treatment of the various topics accessible to those without detailed prior knowledge of German politics.

A distinctive feature of this venture is the cooperation of specialists in German politics from both sides of the Atlantic. We should like to thank our contributors for their commitment and cooperation and our publishing editor Steven Kennedy for the enthusiastic encouragement he has given to this project throughout. We are also grateful to the secretarial staff in the Government Department of the London School of Economics for the generous help they have given.

Gordon Smith
William Paterson
Peter Merkl

# Notes on the Contributors

**Christopher S. Allen** is Assistant Professor of Political Science, University of Georgia, specialising in political economy and comparative European politics. He is co-author of *European Politics in Transition* (1987), and he has contributed to *Industry and Political Change in West Germany* (edited by P. J. Katzenstein, 1989) and to *The Political Power of Economic Ideas: Keynesianism Across Nations* (edited by P. A. Hall, 1989).

**Gerard Braunthal** is Professor Emeritus of Politcal Science, University of Massachusetts, Amherst. He is the author of numerous books and articles on West German politics, including *West German Social Democrats, 1969–1982: Profile of a Party in Power* (1983).

**Simon Bulmer** is a Senior Lecturer at the University of Manchester. His publications include *The Domestic Structure of European Community Policy-Making in Germany* (1986), *The Federal Republic of Germany and the European Community*, with W. Paterson (1987), and he is the editor of *The Changing Agenda of West German Public Policy* (1989).

**Russell J. Dalton** is Professor of Political Science at Florida State University at Tallahassee. Among his publications are: *Germany Transformed: Political Culture and New Politics* (1981), *Electoral Change in Advanced Industrial Societies: Realignment or Dealignment?* (co-editor, 1984), and *Citizen Politics in Western Democracies* (1988).

**Kenneth Dyson** is Professor of European Studies at the University of Bradford. Besides writing on German politics, his publications on European affairs include: *The State Tradition in Western Europe* (1981), *The Politics of the Communications Revolution in Western Europe* (1987), and *Combatting Long-Term Unemployment in Western Europe* (1989).

**Eva Kolinsky** is a Senior Lecturer and Director of German Studies at Aston University. She is the editor of *Opposition in Western Europe* (1987), and she is the author of *Parties, Opposition and*

*Society in West Germany* (1984) and *Women in West Germany –
Life, Work and Politics* (1989).

**A. James McAdams** is Professor of Political Science, Princeton
University. He specialises in the politics of the German Democratic Republic and inner-German relations. He is the author
of *East Germany and Detente: Building Authority after the Wall*
(1985).

**Steen Mangen** is Lecturer in European Social Policy, London
School of Economics. His recent publications include *Mental
Health Care in the European Community* (1985), and 'The Politics
of Reform: Ten Years of the Italian Psychiatric Experience',
(forthcoming).

**Andrei S. Markovits** is Assistant Professor, Department of Political
Science, Boston University. He is the author of *The Politics of the
West German Trade Unions* (1986) and has written widely on trade
unions and social democracy, including *The West German Left:
Red, Green and Beyond* (forthcoming).

**Peter H. Merkl** is Professor of Political Science at the University
of California, Santa Barbara. His extensive publications on
German and West European politics include: *Political Violence
and Terror: Motifs and Motivations* (1986), *When Parties Fail . . .
Emerging Alternative Organizations* (1988), with K. Lawson, and
*The Federal Republic of Germany at Forty* (editor, 1989).

**Stephen Padgett** is a Lecturer in Politics in the Department of
European Studies, Loughborough University. He is the co-author
of *Political Parties and Elections in West Germany* (1986) He has
a number of publications on the West German SPD and European
social democracy; and he is currently conducting research into the
West German electricity supply industry.

**William E. Paterson** is Reader in German Politics at Warwick University. Besides his writings on German politics, he also specialises
in aspects of European politics. Among his recent publications,
he is co-editor of *The Future of Social Democracy* (1986), and he
is co-author of *The Federal Republic of Germany and the European
Community* (1987), as well as *Government and the Chemical Industry: A Comparative Study of Britain and West Germany* (1988).

**Peter Pulzer** is Gladstone Professor of Government and Public
Administration and fellow of All Souls College, Oxford. He is the
author of *The Rise of Political Anti-Semitism in Germany and
Austria* (1988) and *Political Representation and Elections in Britain*
(1967). In 1988 he was Eric Voegelin Visiting Professor at the
University of Munich.

**Gordon Smith** is Professor of Government, London School of

Economics. He is co-editor of the journal *West European Politics*, and he has written extensively on comparative European themes, especially *Politics in Western Europe* (1989). Among his publications on German politics are *Democracy in Western Germany* (1986) and, as co-editor, *Party Government and Political Culture in Western Germany* (1982).

# Glossary of Party Abbreviations and Political Terms

## Party Abbreviations

| | |
|---|---|
| AL | Alternative Liste (Alternative List) |
| CDU | Christlich Demokratische Union (Christian Democratic Union) |
| CSU | Christlich-Soziale Union (Christian Social Union) |
| DKP | Deutsche Kommunistische Partei (German Communist Party) |
| FDP | Freie Demokratische Partei (Free Democratic Party) |
| KPD | Kommunistische Partei Deutschlands (Communist Party of Germany) |
| NPD | Nationaldemokratische Party Deutschlands (National Democratic Party of Germany) |
| NSDAP | Nationalsozialistische Deutsche Arbeiterpartei) National Socialist German Workers' Party) |
| SED | Sozialistische Einheitspartei Deutschlands (Socialist Unity Party of Germany) |
| SPD | Sozialdemokratische Partei Deutschlands (Social Democratic Party of Germany) |
| SPV | Sonstige Politische Vereinigung (Alternative Political Association) |
| SRP | Sozialistische Reichspartei (Socialist State Party) |

## Other Abbreviations

| | |
|---|---|
| APO | Ausserparlamentarische Opposition (extra-parliamentary opposition) |

BBU | Bund für Bürgerinitiativen und Umweltschutz (Federal Association of Citizens' Initiatives and Environmental Protection)
BDA | Bundesvereinigang der Deutschen Arbeitgeberverbände (Federation of German Employers' Associations)
DBV | Deutscher Bauern-Verband (German farmers' association)
DGB | Deutscher Gewerkschaftsbund (federation of German trade unions)
FGDO | Freie Demokratische Grundordnung ('free democratic basic order')
FGR/FRG | Federal German Republic (West Germany)
GDR | German Democratic Republic (East Germany)
MdB | Mitglied des Bundestages (member of parliament)
SDS | Sozialistischer Deutscher Studentbund (German socialist students' federation)

## Political Terms

| | |
|---|---|
| Bund | Federation |
| Bundesbank | Federal Bank |
| Bundesland | Federal constituent state |
| Bundespost | Federal postal service |
| Bundesrat | Upper house of Federal parliament |
| Bundestag | Lower house of Federal parliament |
| Bundeswehr | Federal armed forces |
| Deutschlandpolitiēk | Inner-German Policy |
| Kaiser | Imperial ruler |
| Land (plural Länder) | Federal constituent state |
| Landtag (plural Landtage) | Land parliament |
| Ostpolitik | Policy towards the East |
| Reich | Imperial (or Nazi) state |
| Reichstag | Imperial parliament |
| Statistiches Bundesamt | Federal Statistical Office |
| Verfassungsschutz | Office for Protection of the Constitution |
| Westpolitik | Policy towards the West |

MAP 1 *The Federal Republic of Germany and the Länder*

# Introduction

*Developments in West German Politics* is designed to provide an accessible introduction to the key issues and changes in the political system of the Federal Republic during the 1980s. The dominance of the government of Helmut Kohl in this period means that its policies and problems constitute a central theme of the book, but our intention has been to relate them to longer-term trends and underlying structural features.

Each chapter is written by a leading authority on German politics writing in an area of particular expertise. The editors have not sought to impose a single approach or ideological standpoint, preferring to allow new insights to emerge through the juxtaposition of different perspectives. Nonetheless the book does provide a coherent and systematic picture of how the West German political system functions and of its key challenges and preoccupations which will be as interesting and useful to students approaching the subject for the first time and those who already know it well.

An appropriate point of entry to a discussion of contemporary West German politics is the subject of Chapter 1: the ever-recurring theme of German cultural and political 'identity'. Peter Merkl analyses this mainspring of German political concerns which more than anything else sets the Federal Republic apart from her West European neighbours, and he demonstrates the various ways in which the question of identity has a continuing political relevance.

In Part One on 'The Governmental System', Gordon Smith first reviews the leading structural features of the Federal Republic (Chapter 2). Of particular importance is the dispersed nature of political authority – 'the state without a centre' – and the essentially static nature of the constitutional order; both these features help determine the course of 'developments'.

Simon Bulmer in Chapter 3 then examines the federal system and its special features. He argues that, with the intermingling of federal and Länder powers, there is a drift towards greater centralisation. Two kinds of pressure are at work: the international pressures, especially those resulting from European integration, and financial

1

pressures, with regional imbalances and a greater dependence on the federal government.

The question of political leadership (Chapter 4) focuses on the constitutional and political position of the federal chancellor. Adenauer is a natural point of reference for an evaluation of West German leaders, and they have differed considerably in performance judged on a number of criteria. Gordon Smith argues that Helmut Kohl has abilities keeping him in office, but not those promoting integration or innovation.

Part Two on 'Politics and Society' opens with an analysis by Peter Pulzer (Chapter 5) of political ideology, especially in relation to the anchoring of liberal democracy in Germany: the meanings that may be attached to 'democracy' and how various movements have sought to exploit the term in the demand for 'democratisation'. The German right, in rejecting the 'excesses' of radical reform, has tried to reinvoke the appeal to traditional national values – and that is reflected in the *Historikerstreit* (historians' debate). But Pulzer concludes that, despite these two alternative ideologies, neither can erode the broad, moderate consensus.

Russell Dalton (Chapter 6) examines the causes and possible consequences of the basic changes in electoral behaviour that became apparent during the 1980s. These changes have been caused primarily by changes in socio-economic structures, and they have led to a weakening of party loyalties and to increasing electoral volatility. Dalton takes two alternative explanatory models – realignment and dealignment – both with fundamental implications for future development, but he finds that, although both account for the diversity of voting patterns, neither can as yet shown to be conclusively correct.

Following this examination, Stephen Padgett in Chapter 7 first traces how the party system evolved prior to 1982 and then makes the contrast with the later 1980s. The former pattern of a 'two-and-a-half' party system may, if the Greens consolidate their position, be giving way to a two-bloc system. This development would have numerous consequences for the parties, and they already have problems relating to inner-party democracy and their finances; the party system in the Länder also gives rise to complicating factors.

Part Three on 'Economic and Social Policy' concentrates on two leading areas of public policy. Kenneth Dyson (Chapter 8) takes the major themes of the 1980s and with a wealth of illustrative material shows how the economy and industry have fared in this period. Although the underlying consensus and continuity of policy have not been weakened, structural problems have created uncertainty and led to demands for new approaches; new ideas have been forthcoming mainly from the left. Dyson analyses the decisive factors in the policy process – the bank-industry nexus, the role of the Bundes-bank and the Länder – and concludes that the forces of consolidation outweigh other influences.

Steen Mangen (Chapter 9) in 'The Politics of Welfare' examines the problems of the Kohl government in securing cost-containment and retrenchment in the provision of welfare. Mangen argues that the German 'Social State' (not a welfare state) is based on devolved responsibility, a rigid legal framework, and a large bureaucracy – all features that make reform difficult. After detailing government policies and the party positions on welfare, he takes two current issues – health services and the crisis in the financing of pensions. Both are affected by the unfavourable demographic trends and neither problem has been satisfactorily resolved.

In Part Four on 'Germany and the World,' William Paterson (Chapter 10) first sets out the security priorities of the Federal Republic and then focuses on the issues surrounding the INF debate before considering the options in security now facing the governing coalition. In foreign relations, the Gorbachev initiatives have altered West German thinking about the Ostpolitik. Paterson argues that changes in the parameters of security and foreign policy necessarily cause greater uncertainty in West German relationships.

West Germany's external relations are further explored in Chapter 11. Simon Bulmer shows how large the European Community looms as a factor in the foreign policy of the Federal Republic as well as in domestic policy-making. Bulmer argues that the Federal Republic has moved from being an exceptional member of the EC to becoming an ordinary one. There are contradictions and ambiguities in West German policies towards the EC; to explain them it is necessary to look at structural factors such as federalism, departmental autonomy and the high degree of sectorisation. He concludes that despite the favourable view taken of integration there are negative features relating to these structures and to German attitudes.

In Chapter 12, on inter-German relationships, James McAdams concentrates on the changes in West German party positions, in and out of government, over the past two decades, noting the contrast for the CDU when in opposition throughout the 1970s as against its policies in government during the 1980s: from a negative stance towards the GDR to a surprisingly conciliatory position. McAdams suggest that the reason for the change was the CDU's wish to pro-mote a more moderate image, and the CDU was able to go further than the SPD would have dared. The party positions are now sub-stantially similar, and in the present era of renewed detente there is only limited scope for the two states to make more of their special relationship except in the international sphere.

Part Five of the book on 'Current Issues' concentrates on a number of issues that were of major public concern during the 1980s. Eva Kolinsky (Chapter 13) deals with the political implications of 'generation and gender'. In the Federal Republic, generational differences have a greater political salience than in most other countries, and Kolinsky shows how they have affected the understanding of democracy at different stages, in the most recent of which the drive to nonconformity has had a strong political consequence, although the form of political participation is greatly influenced by an individual's socioeconomic circumstances. Kolinsky also traces the generational factors that have affected women's political orientations. Of critical importance in recent years in raising the political awareness and the demands made by women have been the Greens; their effect has been important in changing the outlook and policies of the other parties. She argues that, important as the Greens have been in promoting equality for women, too much emphasis on 'self-realisation' and protest action leaves the initiative for making substantive policy changes to the established parties.

William Paterson (Chapter 14) in first showing that initially environmental questions had a low priority in the Federal Republic looks at the reasons for their rather sudden emergence: the expansion of the nuclear-energy programme coincided with a failure of the left within the SPD, and this led to widespread, extra-party protest. Against this background, Paterson gives an extensive casestudy of the politics of nuclear energy. The issues surrounding the chemicals industry illustrate a different combination of factors, since early on they were taken up by the parties (Greens and SPD). Paterson concludes that the costs involved in protecting the environment affect competitive efficiency less than the rigidities associated with the 'old' politics.

Chapter 15 by Andrei Markovits and Christopher Allen examines the problems of West German trade unions in the 1980s. Many of these problems are common throughout Western Europe, but German unions have experienced less than the United States or Britain the impact of government anti-union policies. After detailing the different periods of the post-war era and how unions fared in each, Markovits and Allen proceed to identify the specific problems now faced by German unions. This 'decalogue' of problems – structural, legal, technological, social and political – can be grouped under two heads: 'attacks from above' and 'attacks from below'. They conclude that German trade unionism faces considerable challenges if the unions and the political left are to be able to mobilise sufficient support and regain a leading position in progressive politics.

The fourth area of 'current issues' concerns public order and civil liberties in the Federal Republic. Gerard Braunthal (Chapter 16) bases his analysis on German historical traditions, especially the tradition of the 'strong state' which set tight limits on personal liberties. Despite the numerous rights and freedoms set out in the Basic Law, the concept of a 'militant democracy' can be applied in an intolerant way. Braunthal reviews the saga of the 'Radicals Decree', government surveillance practices, and anti-terrorist legislation to show the problems of achieving a proper balance in a liberal democracy, especially considering the experience of political confrontation and terrorism in West Germany. A related issue involves the question of immigration and political asylum which has now become a live political issue. The relatively liberal policies pursued by the Federal government means that there are considerable problems, both in assimilation and in economic pressures which are particularly felt by the Länder governments.

Finally, in Chapter 17 William Paterson and Gordon Smith take up several of the themes that have been raised elsewhere. They start by looking back to the 'plateau of stability' that the Federal Republic seemed to have reached in the 1970s and then examine what changed – and what did not change – in the 1980s. The problems already faced by the established parties – internally and externally – are now magnified by the reappearance of the extreme right, and the party system is poised between an old and a new form. The same sense of flux is apparent in the foreign perspectives of the Federal Republic – although they may transmit back into domestic politics more than they affect West Germany's international position. Political 'stability' is not really in question, but – returning to Peter Merkl's opening chapter – the question of the German 'identity' still has a peculiar dynamic.

# 1

# The German Search for Identity

PETER H. MERKL

More than most other nations, Germans have suffered from uncertainty, even recurrent crises, regarding their identity as a modern people. In one form or another, in fact, the German search for identity has gone on for two centuries and, therefore, can hardly be considered a new or startling revelation. Such agonies of the mind and the soul are not unknown among other nations. There are concrete reasons, nevertheless, why the Germans appear to have far more of such agonies than a reasonable share, in fact so much that prominent foreign observers, from Madame de Staël in the early nineteenth century to allied leaders and critics in the 1980s, have tended to associate German identity crises with typical German national traits and even with Germany's fateful struggle against the West from 1914 to 1945. Some contemporary critics blame the German identity crisis for neutralist stirrings against NATO or for the deeply-rooted sense of alienation among the Greens. Most reasons for the uncertain identity of Germany and the Germans are easy to enumerate, even though some aspects may be rather controversial. First if not necessarily foremost are the uncertainties of geographical boundaries, of what populations or parts thereof are part of the claim of nationhood and which are not. Secondly, and perhaps most painfully, Germans have suffered from uncertainty about their cultural identity and image of themselves: Between the resurgent memories of an earlier German culture and allegedly Americanised visions of modernity they wonder just who they are or who they ought to be. Finally, there is a kind of identity that arises from the goals of political action and from the institutional patterns of liberal democracy. This could give them a secure sense of who and what the Federal Republic is, if only they could come to a consensus on it. All three of these notions of identity were raised again in the German historians' debate of the late 1980s, which attract much attention abroad. It is doubtful, however, whether the proverbial man in the street in Germany or abroad or even German youth have been vitally interested in the often dubious alternative postures laid before them in learned articles and books.

## Geographical Uncertainties and Dilemmas

From the very beginnings of a German national consciousness, in the aftermath of the French Revolution, there has been an astounding uncertainty about exactly where the German nation was located, who belonged to it, and where a future German nation-state might pitch its tents. As a result of earlier migrations, German-speaking populations were scattered and interspersed with other nationalities from the Rhine to the Volga rivers and down to Northern Italy and Romania. Some states of kindred tongue (Netherlands, Switzerland) had long achieved separate establishment, a path eventually followed by Austria and the East German republic (GDR) of today. The two largest German states vying for the leadership of German national unification in the mid-nineteenth century (Prussia and Austro-Hungary) each included large non-German populations (Poles, Czechs, and other Eastern European nationalities) who soon developed a desire to establish their now respective nation-states. The borders of the prospective German nation-state were most uncertain in the north (Schleswig-Holstein), west (Alsace-Lorraine), and in the south where the formation of the Italian nation-state required the cession of large, formerly Austrian territories including German-speaking South Tyrol. The eastern borders were the most difficult to draw amidst scattered and interspersed nationalities under the Hapsburg and Prussian flags and here the final *de facto* settlement was not achieved until the 1970s when Mutual-Renunciation-of-Force treaties between Bonn and Moscow, Warsaw, and Prague, confirmed the (until that time unrecognised) borders prevailing at the end of the Second World War. The scattered German ethnic minorities, including the Sudeten Germans and Polish Germans (whose alleged mistreatment had been the immediate pretext for starting the war in 1939), had already been expelled to East and West Germany in the late 1940s.

The German nationalists of the last century and a half rose to the challenge of these geographic uncertainties in changing fashions. In the early days, they still argued over whether to seek a Greater German (including Austria) or a Smaller German (Prussian-led) nation-state. Otto von Bismarck fought off Denmark, France, and Austria (in league with several south German states) to establish a Smaller Germany, which was economically and militarily secure and seemingly without further nationalistic ambitions. After his death and with the next generation, however, German nationalists took a much more expansive view of German power on the European continent, on the high seas, and among the colonial empires of the day. Most ominously, Pan-German writers proposed to enlarge the Bismarckian empire to include all areas where German-speaking minorities played significant roles, such as in Eastern Europe where German ethnic minorities frequently constituted the bourgeois, urban elites ruling over large awakening Slavic nationalities.

The defeat in the First World War not only brought the German aspirations to be a European hegemonial and 'world power' for the time being to an end. It also freed the new Polish, Czech and other East European nationalities each to establish a nation-state of its own which could not but diminish the dominant German social and political position under the pre-war empires. Some German ethnic minorities from Eastern Europe sought refuge in Weimar Germany and the rump state of German Austria where many of them became enamoured with the National Socialists who in turn sympathised with their plight and promised to help them return to power in their Eastern European homelands. The National Socialists were indeed the successors and executors of the Pan-German legacy who, once they had attained power in Germany, not only renewed the German struggle for European hegemony but launched a vast crusade for a German racial empire in Eastern Europe. Their solution to the geographic challenge of German dispersion was clearly the most expansionary one. It failed catastrophically, drawing into its collapse the expansion of Soviet power over nearly all the Eastern European successor states and over the eastern half of pre-Second World War Germany. Since 1945, the Soviets have been standing at the Elbe river, signalling the end of all German eastward expansion. East Prussia and a fourth of German pre-war territory is gone forever – the German population fled or was expelled – and there is a new border through the heart of Germany: a Communist satellite regime is firmly ensconced in the heart of Brandenburg-Prussia, the German Democratic Republic (GDR).

The new West German government, for its part, has foresworn all attempts at the pursuit of European hegemony or reconquest of the ethnic German Eastern homelands by force of arms. The first post-war chancellor, Konrad Adenauer, in fact, was an avowed antinationalist who preferred to lead his country into the arms of Catholic 'Little Europe' (Italy, France, and the Benelux countries) instead. He saw to it that there would be no independent German national army (by placing German troops under NATO) and no German coal and steel industry (by establishing the European Coal and Steel Community, ECSC) to serve future German nationalistic ambitions. He sought to base the future of the Federal Republic on close friendship with France, the old enemy, and was even willing to accept French annexation of the long-disputed Saar – although the Saarlanders decided otherwise – just to cement Franco-German reconciliation. With regard to the lost areas beyond the Oder-Neisse line, the Sudentenland, and East Prussia furthermore, the Adenauer government and assorted refugee organisations simply cried out periodically as an amputated man might express 'ghost pains' in the limb he no longer had. Finally, Adenauer thoroughly tied West German security to American power and NATO and the resurgent West German economy to the European Community (see Chapters 10 and 11), further emphasising that even the small remaining German rump state ought to be firmly integrated with its European neighbours, and not off on its own.

If these policies anchored West German geographic identity more firmly with the West than it had been under pre–1945 regimes since Bismarck, the East German GDR was just as firmly planted in the East, the Warsaw Pact, and Comecon, the Communist equivalent of the European Community (EC), The two 'hostile brothers' have glared at each other for decades across fortified borders and death strips, seemingly oblivious to the ritual calls for German reunification in the early years of both German states. Since the beginnings of Ostpolitik, their separate geographic identities, the western liberal democratic one of Bonn and the Eastern-oriented Communist one of the GDR, have gradually begun to move towards each other again though they may never again coincide (see Chapter 12). East-West polarities are too strong to be overcome with assertions of a 'common fate' (*Schicksalsgemeinschaft*) with regard to exposure to nuclear war or, from less moderate quarters, of the desirability of Germany's equidistance from both superpowers. Most West Germans, according to public opinion polls, are not ready to cut the umbilical cord to NATO, and the East German population is unlikely to have a choice between reunification and the Warsaw Pact. Nevertheless, among the opposition Social Democrats, there is some talk about a 'second phase of Ostpolitik' which would further intensify West German interaction with the East at some point in the future.

## Agonies of German Cultural Identity

If West Germans suffer from the uncertainties of their geographic identity, they agonise even more over their cultural identity, their self-image of who they are and who they ought to be. After several decades of profound modernisation in life-styles of prosperous, urbane cosmopolitanism, a pervasive malaise has set in among the educated middle class that questions the 'soullessness' of this modernity and the 'loss of meaning' in modern existence. The days when small-town and rural houseowners would plaster over the exposed half-timbered exterior of buildings to make them look more modern are long past. Now they are restoring old façades and spending vast sums for projects of authentically historical preservation. The great passion for expanding *Autobahnen* (motorways) and bridges, cross-town freeways and airport facilities has given way to stubborn resistance to nearly all major public building projects by local citizen initiatives and by the mostly bourgeois Green party (see Chapter 14). Even the decennial census, a measure as essential to planning and modern management as it is symbolic of modernity, came under such determined fire of criticism and threat of a Marcusean 'great refusal' to cooperate that it was scrapped in 1983 after the forms had already been printed and an army of census-takers mobilised.

After decades of relative silence and conformity to the modern trends, the voice of German bourgeois culture has come to the fore again with overtones familiar from earlier eras of *Biedermeier* (roughly 'homely' – an early nineteenth century bourgeois life-style) sentimentality and cultural pessimism. Elements of bourgeois *Totalkritik* (total rejection of everything the Bundesrepublik stands for) have appeared among Green apostles of environmental doom and among pacifists not far from the bourgeois pietists of the nineteenth century. As in past German bourgeois generations up until the 1930s, it has become fashionable again to blame it all on Western versions of modernity, especially on the Americans and their alleged lack of soulfulness. The nature romanticism of the early nineteenth century and of the twentieth century bourgeois Youth Movement has sprung back to life throughout German society, as concern for the (acid rain-induced) dying of the forests makes a timid stand against the epitome of modern life, the love affair with (fast) automobiles gobbling up kilometres on the *Autobahn*. Educated women who only yesterday were battling the establishment for freedom of abortion and for public funding for women's shelters are rediscovering a new *Innerlichkeit* (subjective awareness) and femininity shrouded in the subjective nature of personal relationships. Subjectivity – indeed irrationality – is 'in' and causes are 'out'.

## The Great Historians' Debate

While these new trends have divided cultural sensibilities rather than bringing about a widely shared new consciousness, they have clearly affected West German views of politics and of the nation's history. A new political romanticism – not necessarily of the conservative hue of its nineteenth century and Weimar predecessors – has set armies of young, educated Germans on the march (see Chapter 13) through such new social movements as the Peace Movement, ecological protests, and attempts at an alternative, counter-cultural economy in the big cities of the north. Socialist utopian dreams are once more blooming in the midst of the chilly, anti-utopian head-winds blowing from the Soviet Union and China. In some quarters there is also a new attitude towards the political use of violence, non-utilitarian and non-purposive, and less related to the ethics of a century of the labour movement than to the aesthetics of modern German poets and to the 'propaganda of the [violent] deed' of the latter-day anarchists. Urban squatters' confrontations with the police have become exhilarating happenings while lusty *Chaoten* and *Spontis* (those who cause chaos and those who act spontaneously) will travel all over the country and abroad to participate in the big battles over the construction of fast-breeder reactors, nuclear missile sites, and airport runway expansions. Violence and getting arrested have become expressive rituals that no longer seem to require success to appear worthwhile.

Since Germany – notwithstanding Michael Stürmer's famous phrase – is anything but 'a country without history', German attitudes toward the country's recent past have been drawn into the agonies over the German identity as well. There have been grassroots movements of community volunteers and history enthusiasts who have created local history workshops that, for example, attempted to reconstruct and present to the public what repression of union activity or free speech may have occurred on a certain factory floor in the early days of the Third Reich, or how the neighbours looked on in cowardly silence when Nazi thugs burned synagogues, smashed Jewish shops, and brutalised Jews on 9 November 1938, on the so-called *Kristallnacht* (night of broken glass). In some places, syna-gogues have been rebuilt as a pointed reminder of the past, in at least one case even in the absence of a Jewish community that might use it and so really as a memorial to the dead and persecuted. Some of the recent historical orientation was clearly heralded for decades by the large volume of serious historical scholarship on the Nazi period and the holocaust, and the more recent turn to local histories of the Nazi takeover and to the history of little people and everyday life in that fateful period, the *Alltagsgeschichte* (everyday history) of the Third Reich and its reflection in television drama documentaries, factual documentaries, and in popular periodicals from *Der Spiegel* to *Der Stern*.

But if there are pointed reminders of a shameful era of German history, there has also been a popular straining towards a self-image of historical continuity, such as in the many sequels of the television drama serial *Heimat* (Homeland), the story of a family and small town through several generations, ranging through most of the period of social modernisation in Germany from long before the Third Reich to the present. There are no categorical or ideological judgements in *Heimat*, just friends and relatives over time, some foolish, some criminal, and very few of notable wisdom. Involvement in the Nazi party or the Second World War simply *happens* to people, compelled by circumstances and facilitated perhaps by personality. In similar fashion, prominent conservative politicians and historians have urged the public not to view German history 'as if it only consisted of the twelve years of Hitler' (Franz Josef Strauss). In 1988, Bundestag President Philipp Jenninger (CDU–CSU) awkwardly, if not unreasonably, tried to explain the euphoric German reaction to Hitler by saying that the dictator's had 'created an atmosphere of optimism and self-confidence' among Germans after the deep malaise of the Great Depression and, presumably, of the defeat in the First World War. Jenninger's poor choice of words in this instance, at the commemoration of the *Kristallnacht* pogrom, led to a public uproar and his resignation. Prominent historians, however, have presented far more provocative themes of continuity: Andreas Hillgruber, for example, suggested that the collapse of the German nation-state and of the historical barriers against the intrusion of Soviet power in Eastern and Central Europe should simply be bracketed together with the holocaust (without explaining that the latter was the deliberate intention of Nazi Germany whereas the former were only unintended consequences of the Nazi crusade to conquer Europe) as 'two kinds of catastrophe '(*Zweierlei Untergang*). Ernst Nolte (1987) somehow managed to blame Hitler's genocidal actions on the bad example given earlier by Stalinist terror and concentration camps (*Der Europäische Bürgerkrieg, 1917–1945*). At a more transparent level, spokesman of the New Right in the Federal Republic proposed simply 'decriminalising' the persecution of the Jews by comparing it to other contemporary or recent horrors, such as the Allied air raids on Dresden or Hiroshima, the expulsion of ethnic Germans from Eastern European countries, American actions in Vietnam, or the era of slavery. According to them the holocaust was not a unique event but only a tragedy among many occurring in various countries.

The historians' challenge to the prevailing interpretations of recent German history called forth the critical voices of other historians, who dissected this line of reasoning and sharply attacked its spokesmen and lines of argument. The great 'historians' debate' was joined, and has been carried on in the pages of books, periodicals, and newspapers for the last several years, and there is no end in sight. Many of the questions raised are so fundamental that they cannot really be answered in an objective manner. They are questions of guilt and atonement, individual and collective responsibility, and of hidden agendas and intentions. The educated public has participated in the historians' debate only in a limited way, for example in readers' letters in newspapers. University students also express opinions on the subject, but there is nothing to suggest that these concerns are shared deeply and widely among German youth, or by the public at large. Historical continuity, after all, can be understood in many different ways and the generations that grew up since 1945 have little reason to identify with the nationalistic zealots of another age, and their opinions, pro and con.

The generation that went through its formative period (i.e., was 15 to 25 years old) in the Second World War or earlier amounts to only about one-fifth of the West German population today, and it does acknowledge the problem of collective responsibility either positively or by the violent rejection we might expect from the millions of ex-Nazis and a few neo-Nazis. The other four-fifths who grew up (1) after the war, (2) in the late 1950s and 1960s, or (3) since the early 1970s are divided by a different alignment: A majority takes the position that the great crimes of the Nazi era belong to the past, that their responsibility lies with the present and future, and that a *Schlusstrich* (or final line) ought to be drawn under the whole Nazi business – two-thirds of all West Germans believe this. A minority, differentiated by shadings between these three generations and by political leanings, still shows a vital concern with Nazi crimes – supporters of the Greens and the SPD often associate many Christian Democratic attitudes and practices with survivals of the old Nazi authoritarianism. The vast majority of people outside of Germany is probably similarly indifferent to whether or not the crimes of half a century ago are duly remembered – except, of course, for the survivors of the victims.

## A Patriotism of the Constitution?

Identity and political obligation need not be tied to a given geographic configuration or identification with a certain historical period anyway. Citizens of the Federal Republic in the 1990s could just as well define their identity in terms of the successful political and economic enterprise they have built up over the four decades since 1949. As the sociologist Jürgen Habermas argued in the course of the historians' debate, why not centre the Federal German identity in a patriotism directed at the constitution, a commitment to Western-style constitutional democracy, and perhaps even to the social contract underlying West German labour-management relations and economic policies?

At first glance, this call for a 'constitutional patriotism' may recall the struggles during the Weimar Republic when republican governments introduced an annual public holiday named 'Constitution Day' (on which schoolchildren could stay at home). This was in reaction to the local German Day celebrations staged by veterans and patriotic right wing associations who would wave the flag and stage demonstrations against the government's policies of 'fulfilment' (of the demands of the 1918 Treaty of Versailles) in their fateful struggle for the hearts and minds of pre-Hitler Germany. The black-red-golden flag of the republic also triggered extensive constitutional disputes because it was quite different from the black-white-red imperial flag, and the choice of the colours of the bourgeois 1848 revolution for the republic rather than those of the Empire was quite deliberate. Such a comparison, however, breaks down when we consider the length of time that the Federal Republic has been a going concern as compared to the fourteen years of Weimar. There may still have been some doubt about German dedication to Western-style constitutional democracy in the first two decades of the Republic when many political appraisals routinely suggested that West German democracy was no sounder than its 'economic miracle'. If the latter should ever be in danger, so would be the former.

Although earlier measurements of the West German self-image, for example, in the 1950s showed a great deal more pride in West German economic achievements than in the political system of Bonn, this situation has changed for the better since the 1960s (see Chapter 6). The more recent generations have developed a good deal more identification with the 'basic democratic order' in the Federal Republic than their predecessors exhibited. There has also developed a general rejection of the idea of the German political *Sonderweg* (different route from other Western countries) in the past. This *Sonderweg*, historians decided at a 1988 conference at the Munich

Institute of Contemporary History, clearly ended with the dramatic disaster of the Second World War and the events, such as the holocaust, that took place during that time. Today's Germans are not looking for a *Sonderweg*.

## The Political Relevance of Identity

'Germany? But where is it? I do not know how to find the country', wrote the eighteenth century poet, Friedrich von Schiller, one of the first of a long series of Germans agonising over the question of German identity. In an age of national movements and new nation-states, the German quest for identity may not at first glance have seemed to be a wild goose chase, or a quixotic pursuit of the impossible. The geographical perplexities and the catastrophic results of the German campaign for European hegemony and racial empire alone, however, have brought the Germans back to far more limited and pragmatic visions of a divided rump Germany or, more precisely, two rather incompatible German states within as greatly reduced national territory, each tied to opposing superpower blocs. The Pan-German idea of bringing the ethnic Germans in Eastern Europe '*Heim ins Reich*' (home into the Reich) grimly succeeded but without much of a Reich to which to come home. The nationalist hubris of fifty years of German history, the blinkers which tragic delusion put over the eyes of most Germans in the first half of this century have fallen off and the survivors have made a new life for themselves in two political systems constrained by the international environment. For the West Germans it has been no mean achievement to have created this Federal Republic, with its conspicuous stability and adaptability which easily outshines all its predecessor Germanies on nearly every count relating to the well-being and dignified life of its citizens.

One need not be beholden to a socialist utopia or be a social historian to know that earlier Germanies by comparison were lacking in many vital respects. Prior to Bismarck, the mass of Germans were living in repressive small states, in rural squalor, and under the social oppression of an uninspired aristocracy. Their lives were marked by ill-health, illiteracy, poverty and a general lack of opportunity for individual self-realisation that only a social romantic can ignore. While these conditions may not have prevented great music, poetry, and philosophy from flourishing, average people must have led depressing lives, and probably vast amounts of talent among the people were lost or never developed. With national unification, the lives of average people began to change and yet their progress towards a dignified life was agonisingly slow and repeatedly set back by waves of major nation-wide depressions.

Once the great slaughter of the First World War had ended and the Kaiser and other princes had fallen, the parties supporting the Weimar Republic held out the hope of 'a beautiful life of dignity and freedom', but social realities and the political polarisation of Germany decreed otherwise. There are grim testimonials of the miseries of unemployment, bankruptcies, and rural poverty in pre-Nazi Germany, and the easy manipulation of the masses of Germans by the Nazis and others before and during the Second World War set appalling standards of political commonsense and democratic maturity. Even without the immense death toll and destruction of the war, the Germans of 1945 in East and West were in a sorry state and, beyond reasonable doubt, had shown themselves incapable of intelligent self-government.

It was this context, along with the post-totalitarian disillusionment of the immediate post-war period, that makes plausible the contention of the post-war utopias, democratic socialism, communism, Christian socialism, and liberal democracy for the most reluctant souls of the '*Ohne mich*' (without me: count me out) generation. The actual choices made by the Germans in divided Germany, of course, were constrained by the presence of the victorious powers that saddled East Germans with a communist dictatorship that at first could claim, not unreasonably, to have established the first Germany of workers and (prior to collectivisation) peasants, free from the domination of Junkers, Prussian militarists, and exploitative capitalism.

The West German rump state, nevertheless, soon turned out to be by far the better German successor-state in nearly every respect, and most of all with regard to individual freedom. This is not to deny many imperfections and justified complaints and, least of all, the fact that many West Germans and especially German youth have tended to deny vociferously that theirs is, by and large, a good and free life which has allowed them to escape most of the pitfalls and constraints of the past. It is not clear how or whether this pervasive malaise may be related to their flawed or uncertain sense of German identity. But it is hard to imagine the sense of puzzlement in the minds of many a foreign student from a Third World Country when they first encounter the extraordinary pessimism and negative national self-image current among West German academic youth. One could also mention the curiously low birthrate of West German society which, aside from reflecting the changing self-image of women's role, appears to express the German lack of faith in a normal future for the nation.

Let us attempt more specifically to relate the debates over German identity to the politics of the Federal Republic. First of all, a look at other modern nations may not be amiss. While there may be some doubt about comparing the memories of German misconduct under the Third Reich with whatever actions, say, Britain or the United States may regret in their respective pasts, the presence of such an agonising debate alone is worthy of comment and, perhaps, a reason to admire the self-critical attitude of today's West German *bien pensants* (right-thinking people). The closest analogy to the soul-searching – some observers call it 'an obsession with guilt' in Michael Stürmer's phrase – might be the American debates in the Vietnam era when all the dirty linen of the nation from the treatment of racial minorities to a century of foreign policy was spread out for all to see. No imperial nation was ever so publicly convulsed about its past wars and colonial exploits.

The West German preoccupation with the German past has obviously played a major role in restraining Bonn from engaging in power politics and national aggrandisement and perhaps even from excesses of domestic repression. Even such transgressions as the *Berufsverbot* (ban on employment in the public service) for radicals or the hysterical reaction to the German terrorist challenge have been mild deviations from the canons of liberal democracy as compared to, say, the era of McCarthyism in the United States. As old German radicals used to say grudgingly about the political climate of the Adenauer era – which was dominated by fear of communism at home and of the USSR – '*Es hätte viel schlimmer kommen können*' (It could have been so much worse).

To understand the role of the identity debate over the full life of the Federal Republic, we have to fit it into its distinctive generational eras. In the first decade of the new republic, the shock of war, destruction, and defeat, and the fear of a vengeful Soviet Union were so great that the Germans mostly left all political decisions to their self-appointed political elites. The liberal democratic course and institutions of their leaders and the Western allies were simply accepted by the people as a small price to pay for external security from the Soviets and domestic reconstruction. Adenauer's 1951 commitment to pay restitution to Israel and to Jewish survivors was popularly accepted as part of the deal with the Western allies, which is not to denigrate its intrinsically moral character. When West German post-war politicians adopted a resolute anti-Nazism, debated the question of collective guilt, or shame, and took specific steps to suppress neo-Nazi revivals (while neglecting the prosecution of some old Nazis), there was little public response. The call for *Vergangenheitsbewältigung* (mastering the past) by the first president of the republic, Theodor Heuss, left little imprint upon a populace suffering privation and not a great deal on the *intelligentsia*. Even notable historians such as Friedrich Meinecke and Gerhard Ritter blamed the Third Reich and its excesses simply on the Weimar 'politics of the masses' and on totalitarianism, an explanation that matched the anti-Soviet and anti-Communist line of the day. As late as 1961, according to public opinion polls about election candidates, three-quarters of West German adults thought that having fled abroad and served in foreign armies, as chancellor candidate Willy Brandt had done during the Nazi years, marked a man as unworthy of high political office, perhaps even a traitor to the nation. Underlying the public support for the anti-nationlist Adenauer regime was evidently an unspoken identification with the past of the nation, right or wrong, and a widespread aversion to bringing old Nazis to justice.

In the 1960s, nevertheless, major changes began to occur and a new 'critical generation' of young Germans began to challenge the old shibboleths of the 1950s, including a major assumption of the previous half century, namely that the struggle of the German nation for 'a place in the sun', for European hegemony, or even just for survival took precedence over all other demands for social modernisation: equality for women and youth, democracy at work, at school, and in the family, and true individual freedom for all kinds of dependents and suppressed minorities. Along with the waves of political and student revolt came a new approach to Germany's recent past, comparative approaches to fascist movements which placed national socialism inseparably in the context of bourgeois society and capitalism, and revived the socialist utopias of the immediate post-war years.

Spectacular trials of concentration camp guards, the Eichmann trial, the detente policies with regard to the Soviet Union, and the resurgence of the extreme right and left wing ushered in a new attitude towards the German past which culminated in the idea that the Third Reich was no accident, or the result of a conquest of Germany by a lunatic fringe movement, but simply the upshot of the German *Sonderweg*. Once again, historical analysis and the interpretation of German identity clearly pointed towards concrete policies, namely overcoming the residues of the bourgeois class society, and culminated with a model welfare state (the *Modell Deutschland*), and with the Ostpolitik of reconciliation with Germany's eastern neighbours. As social scientists and historians dealing with the evolution of the welfare state have since pointed out, the demands for an egalitarian and socially well-ordered society have been evolving in almost continuous fashion since the welfare laws of Otto von Bismarck. And even though involvement in the two great wars held back this aspect of social modernisation, it advanced mightily, if contrary to Nazi doctrine, even during the Third Reich, as measures similar to the post–1945 reform programme of the British Labour Party were introduced to meet the most urgent needs of rural and urban society.

## The New Paradigm

From the mid-1970s onwards, however, a new paradigm began to appear in West German politics which once more changed the basic mind set and ushered in a conservative rethinking that eventually brought about the much trumpeted *Wende* (turnabout) in Bonn and has characterised the 1980s. Not only was historical thinking once more *en vogue* among widening circles of people but many West Germans thought this a good time for taking another look at where they had come from, historically speaking, and what it all meant. Such a rediscovery of history from the Hohenstaufen rulers of the distant Middle ages to the Eastern European roots of many ethnic Germans that now live in West Germany is in itself commendable and included also a considerable refinement in the conceptualisation of history, 'historicisation', and 'historism'. The broadly-based historical curiosity could not but challenge the taboos that reportedly had made most history teachers freeze up when going over what Saul Friedländer has called the dutiful *Pflichtlektion* (obligatory lesson) about the years 1933 to 1945 and treat them with a sense of distance and moralising rectitude as if their people, by going twice through a time warp, had dropped back into the moral Stone Age and then come back again in 1945. A healthy attitude towards one's collective history should be no different from misunderstanding oneself as a product of a person's family, childhood and circumstances.

The eagerness to seek one's own past in the everyday life even of the Nazi years, however, gave rise to fears that this might lead to a 'normalisation' or routinisation of the diabolical, since much about this *Alltagsgeschichte* was not all that different from other nations' 'normal' development. Against such a seemingly normal background, critics feared, the criminality of the regime and of such 'incomparable crimes' as deliberate genocide as an official state policy ran the risk of appearing as just another relativised historical crime among many, as mentioned earlier. If people do not learn from their past, are they not in danger of repeating their mistakes?

Such historicisation and relativisation particularly shocked the survivors of the Jewish holocaust who saw little consolation in the fine shadings between active and passive support or various mixtures of conformity and non-conformity with the murderous regime. They were angered by Hillgruber's suggestion that a German soldier and patriot had a moral obligation to defend the German lines against the Russian advance in 1944–5. On the other hand, there were many neo-conservative or nationalist spokesmen not only of German, but even more of other nationalities – Hungarian, Croatian, Polish, Czech and Slovak, and others – who fervently believed that in the great rout before the advancing Red Army, all threatened groups had the right to defend their own people, even if this had the effect of temporarily helping the German armies and not speeding up the liberation of the death camps throughout Eastern Europe. Officers and soldiers in the German occupation army, too, claimed the right to fight against the partisans who attacked them and to punish or threaten an occupied civilian population they believed supported partisan actions against them. It is difficult indeed clearly to separate guilt and system-supporting actions in war-time situations in which betrayal may be no less immoral than obedience to harsh orders, and in which betrayal of one's own unit may result in one's own death either at the hands of the merciless enemy or of one's own comrades. The only real solution to these unanswerable moral dilemmas is not to have wars, military occupations, or civil wars.

What is more relevant to the present politics of West Germany than arcane historical debates, moreover, is the underlying ideological dimension that points into the future. The neo-conservative *Wende* of the 1980s has become a signal for a new historical paradigm which aims at winning cultural hegemony over the earlier liberal and socialist interpretations of German identity. No one has expressed this grasping for the power to impart meaning to German history better than Michael Stürmer who, with the support of Chancellor Kohl, defended the neo-conservative quest for *Sinnstiftung* (creation of historical meaning) in the plans to build two official museums of German history, one in Bonn and one in Berlin.

To Stürmer, a historian and florid speech-writer for the chancellor, reinterpreting German history in the neo-conservative sense is a matter of the nation's 'standing tall' again, or 'walking upright' in the future, phrases as dear to German conservative politicians such as Alfred Dregger or the late Franz Josef Strauss as they were to President Reagan, with reference to post-Vietnam and post-Carter America. Stürmer and his conservative friends evidently feel that a strongly emphasised national heritage and collective identity is an indispensable basis for future national self-esteem and a potent antidote to the alleged corrosion of social solidarity under their socialist-liberal (SPD–FDP) predecessors.

To reinfuse future German politics, of all countries, however, with the spirit of nationalism seems a dubious undertaking in view not only of the German past but even more of the future in which the old nation-state may soon be as outdated as powdered wigs and front-loading muskets. Far from a German nationalist revival, the Federal Republic in the 1990s will more likely be dominated by a resurgence of the spirit of Helsinki and of the accelerated integration of the European Community. As the German historian Jürgen Kocka has pointed out, moreover, such *Sinnstiftung* is also an improper assignment for historians whose job is more often to examine and challenge established stereotypes than to confirm them, and whose findings often produce division and conflicts rather than a unifying vision of a nation's history. In the final analysis, it would appear, the proposed 'creation of meaning' for German history is more likely to lead to an invented past rather than to *Vergangenheitsbewältigung*, the mastering of the past. The neo-conservative *Wende*, for all we can know now, may last no longer than the now-defunct social democratic consensus of the later 1960s and 1970s. Much as it may help to understand the past, a modern society needs to look forward and to shape its future.

# PART ONE

# The Governmental System

# 2

# Structures of Government

**GORDON SMITH**

## The State Without A Centre

Over the past forty years the Federal Republic has come to occupy a leading position in Western Europe, shown by its pre-eminent economic position and by a growing political influence. Yet this strength combines strangely with the apparently 'loose' structure of the West German state and a diffusion of authoritative decision-making. One effect is noticeable in the emergence of a particular policy style which relies on the fashioning of a broad consensus rather than the imposition of majoritarian solutions.

This preference for accommodation could be explained on purely political grounds through the learning of bitter historical lessons: as a reaction against the divisive character of politics in the Weimar Republic on the one hand and against the authoritarian impress of the Nazi dictatorship on the other. Yet political attitudes were also decisively shaped by the terms on which the Federal Republic came into being and – more gradually – by the way in which the institutional structure operates. The idea of 'a state without a centre' has to be understood in several senses and is caused by a number of different factors.

Fundamental to all subsequent development was the division of Germany after 1945. The creation of a separate East German state meant that the Federal Republic was cut off from the leading cities of the former Reich, such as Dresden and Leipzig, as well as from important industrial areas. Above all else, the division robbed Berlin of its position as the German capital. This loss has never been made good in Federal Republic. It is true that Berlin (West) may still be counted as the largest industrial centre but – divorced from its immediate hinterland and separated from West Germany – West Berlin is not economically viable, and it is dependent on subsidies from the Federal Republic for over 50 per cent of the city's annual budget. Nor, because it is not recognised as an integral part of the Federal Republic, would it be possible to give West Berlin the legal status of a capital city.

Shorn from this historical centre, the Federal Republic lacks a single focus of national attraction and influence. No other metropolitan area has arisen to take the place of Berlin. Bonn, as the capital, naturally enjoys a political pre-eminence of sorts, but its original designation was an arbitrary choice favoured by Adenauer, and – within a federal system – Bonn could not become the dominant political forum as it might have been in a unitary state. Nor does Bonn have any pretension to be the hub of economic, social and cultural life. Frankfurt, the seat of the Federal Bank, is the foremost financial and commercial centre of West Germany. The chief industrial centres are also scattered, with the more traditional ones, for instance around Düsseldorf, and the new ones in Baden-Württemberg and Bavaria. It would be wrong, too, to underestimate the significance of the numerous historic cities in the Länder – such as Bremen, Cologne, Hamburg, Munich and Stuttgart – for they have continued to maintain themselves as influential social and cultural centres. Traces of the old, pre-Bismarckian Germany still hold a place in a late twentieth century society. This provincial inheritance lies behind the institutional framework of the Federal Republic.

It may be tempting to treat the absence of a sole 'unifying nexus' as a source of weakness for the West German state. But is this so? As is the case for most countries, the Federal Republic has problems of economic imbalance and disadvantaged regions, but they have not proved to be as acute as for those states which have a single, dominant and prosperous metropolitan region and with most of the rest coming to regard themselves as permanently 'underprivileged'. What is particularly noteworthy in looking at the history of the Federal Republic has been the absence of centre-periphery tensions. It seems that if there is no 'centre', there will be no periphery either.

External influences have also had a bearing on the way the Federal Republic has developed. As a state called into existence by the Western allies, the Federal Republic was from the outset in a position of 'dependent sovereignty'. With the admission of West Germany into NATO in 1955 the overt expression of dependency was removed, but the earlier circumstances have had long-lasting effects. This is true for matters of security as it is in the sphere of economic cooperation and integration. Whilst the growth of supranational organisation limits all states in their freedom to take unilateral action, the Federal Republic began its life and has grown to maturity within a network of interdependence.

Two kinds of effect can be noted. One is the way in which external questions quickly become issues in domestic politics: there is no fixed line between *Innenpolitik* (domestic politics) and *Aussenpolitik* (foreign affairs). The other effect has been the tendency of West Germany governments to follow the lead of others rather than to assert their own priorities. A certain ambivalence is, however, becoming discernible: the Federal Republic is able to take a more relaxed view than others in the face of an eroding national sovereignty within Western Europe, but at the same time suppressed resentments felt against her 'dependency' have undoubted political potential.

## Subordination of the Traditional State

The apparent diffusion of the federal Republic can also be traced to the weakening of the previously influential 'state ideology' that had coloured German thinking since the nineteenth century. This view had promoted the idea that 'the state' was divorced from – and even superior to – civil society. The state was regarded as a unifying bond which served higher national purposes, and its unity counteracted the fragmentation caused by competing social interests. The political parties were one of the expressions of this social diversity, and as far as was practicable they were to be kept well away from the exercise of state power.

Following the destruction of the National Socialist dictatorship and under the influence of allied occupation, the reaction against the old view was complete, and it was given practical expression in the removal of the traditional state elites – the bureaucracy and the armed forces – as representing independent bastions of state power and authority. As a matter of fact, this downgrading had already been largely accomplished as one consequence of the totalitarian 'social revolution'. In the Federal Republic the major task was to ensure that their autonomy and special status would not be restored.

It is in this context that the concept of the *Parteienstaat*, the 'party state', is of leading importance, since it represents the antithesis of the old state ideology. The *Parteienstaat* not only brings the state and civil society together on an entirely new footing, it also implies that the political parties assume a predominant role within the state. Such a superiority is normal for all established liberal democracies, but there has been a further consequence in the Federal Republic: party influence has become paramount in all the higher reaches of government and the public service – in other words, a party-politicisation of the bureaucracy. The all-pervading influence of the parties is apparent throughout the federal system. Party patronage has its shadow-side, since it can result in undesirable political pressure being exerted and in the making of appointments that are not primarily based on merit. However, the benefit has been that with the break-up of the old officialdom, the *Beamtentum*, the primacy of political leadership is assured.

Subordination to the political realm is apparent as well in considering the position of the armed forces in the Federal Republic. Historically they were able to regard themselves as uniquely independent of political control and to constitute 'a state within a state'. But the modern Bundeswehr could have no such ambitions. Partly the subordination of the military came about during the years of the dictatorship, but its subjugation was ensured largely because the build-up of the West German armed forces took place within the Western alliance system, so that from the beginning the Bundeswehr was subject to an overarching international control. The old military elite, along with its values, was thus unable to survive the double defeat inflicted by National Socialism and the Second World War. It is also important to note that by the time the Bundeswehr was formally established in the Federal Republic, in 1956, the parties had been firmly in charge of the new state for several years: they were able to dictate the terms on which the armed forces would function, and one of these conditions – the introduction of national conscription – avoided the danger that a professional and homegeneous military elite would once more emerge.

The cohesion of the West German state has depended critically on the ability of the parties to supply an integration in the absence of the traditional elites and the values they upheld; the decisive breaks in the continuity of the political system prior to the foundation of the Federal Republic necessitated that the parties should act as the ubiquitous linking mechanism. Yet in the special circumstances that have faced West Germany – for instance, in the lack of a secure sense of national identity – the *Parteienstaat* may appear to be an imperfect substitute for the more traditional forms. The loyalties that the parties mediate to the state are essentially political in character, even if they are not necessarily sharply partisan. In some ways the dominance of the *Parteienstaat* may have saddled the parties with too great a responsibility, and this overextension can lead to a negative reaction. In recent years one effect has become noticeable in the fall in public regard for the parties. This feeling of a disenchantment with the parties and a sense of estrangement from them is encapsulated in the term *Parteiverdrossenheit*. This is a negative judgement that belies the high levels of electoral participation, and it is also a rather ironical commentary on the performance of a political system which on almost all standards has proved to be both stable and effective.

## The Basic Law as a Structure

Standing alongside the more recent development of the *Parteienstaat* is the far older doctrine of the *Rechtsstaat* which – in drawing upon German legal and constitutional traditions – complements the political element. Indeed, in some respects it can even be taken as providing an alternative perspective on the nature of the West German state. These traditions find an approximate equivalent in Anglo-American understanding of the 'rule of law', but the concept of the *Rechtsstaat* goes much further – and at first sight dangerously so – in identifying the state itself with law, 'right' and justice. This emphasis is essential for an appreciation of how the Basic Law affects the popular expectation of how governments should function and, more generally, the consequences for political attitudes and behaviour.

What is sometimes surprising is the high regard with which the Basic Law is held in West Germany. At least in comparison with many other constitutions it is of recent origin and it was intended to be only a temporary device pending reunification. It is especially surprising considering that the Basic Law is itself a largely unremarkable document, more concerned with instrumentalities than with high principles, and it is certainly not a radical democratic statement.

Yet the significance of the Basic Law becomes much better explicable once the connection with the *Rechtsstaat* is made: the West German constitution deliberately reinvoked the respected tradition that in previous regimes has been either suppressed or at most only partially realised. What was new in the Federal Republic was that – with the anchoring of the *Parteienstaat* – an essential political support existed that had previously been lacking. None the less, the status of the Basic Law owes as much to its *Rechtsstaat* origins as it does to the favourable political context.

The success of the Basic Law in attracting a strong popular attachment is evident in its normative power. It is not too much to say that the Basic Law established the framework within which political debate is conducted; it is the essential point of reference. It is the constitutional norms – that is, legal rather than political – which condition the expectations and attitudes of the participants. The Basic Law thus both presupposes and encourages a consensus on the nature of the authority of the state. In these respects the Basic Law goes further than the constitutions in many other countries where the constitution is treated more neutrally in terms of the government and state structure. In the Federal Republic the Basic Law functions as a key part of the structure.

## The 'Cooperative' Constitution

Historical circumstances worked against the emergence of a definitive 'centre' in West Germany, but it is probable that the nature of the constitution would have had a similar effect anyway. Added together, the two sets of influences have made the political system curiously dispersed, but nevertheless there are just as important countervailing tendencies that encourage an articulation of the various working parts.

The deliberate dispersion of state power set out in the Basic Law follows the traditional doctrine of 'constitutionalism', and in institutional terms results in a series of 'checks and balances'. The total effect is complex because the powers and competences of the institutions interlock at several levels. What these arrangements mean in practice is that a number of different sets of actors become involved in the policy-making process, with the result that policies can ultimately be agreed and implemented only if at *some* stage an integrative solution is forthcoming. It is important to appreciate that no consensus needs to be present at the outset – party-positions may be sharply opposed and the interests of the Länder may be quite divergent – but a resolution has to be effected. It is the way in which the structures are designed and operate that brings this about. In other words, the institutional structure represents a consensus-*inducing* mechanism: it is the process that fashions the consensus, rather than the latter necessarily being present beforehand.

It would be unrealistic to suppose that somehow the Basic Law's provisions could alone have produced this integration. If political evolution in the Federal Republic had taken another course – for instance towards a fragmented party system along the lines of the Weimar Republic – then this attempted constitutional reconciliation could easily have failed. That weakness or immobilism was avoided has been largely because the two major parties have been dominant for the whole period and because for most of the time their policies have not been strongly antagonistic. Present trends may indicate that their dominance is waning, and the question arises as to the consequences of a movement towards a more pronounced multi-partism. It might follow that consensus-building would be made more difficult, but the structures have now been so long in place and the pattern of political accommodation is now so firmly set that a radical departure would be difficult. Moreover, the way in which the system has operated over the years has had a deep-seated influence on popular attitudes and expectations as to how it should work: the institutions have formed a particular kind of political culture.

How the Basic Law has fostered an interdependence is most readily apparent in the federal structure. Although the analysis of federal trends is the subject of a separate chapter (Chapter 3), it is worthwhile to emphasise the main attributes, in particular how the Basic Law leans towards the mixing of federal and Land competences rather than their separation – leading towards a 'horizontal' rather than a 'vertical' distribution of power. This kind of spread necessitates careful coordination between the two layers of territorial authority, and it thus requires permanent negotiating structures bringing federal and Land authorities together to secure the implementation of federal policies. The 'horizontal' emphasis of German federalism – federal legislative authority and Land executive responsibility – is made more complex by the specification in the Basic Law of a number of 'mixed' categories all of which effectively involve a degree of coresponsibility between the federation and Länder (see Chapter 3). In addition, the creation of several joint policy-making bodies, such as the Science and Educational Councils, the Financial Planning Council and the Economic Planning Council, underlines the necessity of securing cooperation over diverse fields.

The weight given in the Basic Law to securing cooperation means that in practice German federalism relies on an 'intertwining' of policy formation and implementation, a *Politikverflechtung*, bringing the two sets of authority into a series of close relationships. This form of inter-governmentalism develops into a bargaining relationship which, as economic and social needs have required greater policy unification, have tended to favour the federation over the Länder.

Three factors shore up the position of the Länder, which gears the system to marginal adjustments rather than a sudden lurch towards the centre. One is the principle of tax-revenue sharing (*Gemeinschaftssteuern*) which gives the Länder an assured proportion of the yield from various types of taxation. Alterations in the shares accruing to the federation and the Länder are subject to federal legislation, and it is here that the strategic role of the Bundesrat comes into the reckoning as the second protective factor in giving the Länder an effective voice at the federal level (see 'Parliament and Government', below). The third factor is the power of the Federal Constitutional Court (*Bundesverfassungsgericht*) which, in interpreting the Basic Law, has prevented any overt erosion of the position of the Länder. This contribution can be considered within the wider context of the Court's constitutional jurisdiction.

## Constitutional Jurisdiction

Two aspects of the Basic Law should be emphasised. One is its detailed nature: with some 146 articles, including numerous amendments and amplifications over the years, the Basic Law requires authoritative interpretation. The second aspect, already mentioned, is the normative authority which is invested in the constitution: as the final arbiter between competing claims, the Court reflects this authority in delivering its findings. To these features should be added the guarantees of its independence that the Constitutional Court enjoys. Even though its personnel are subject to quasi-political appointment (by the Bundestag and Bundesrat) in all other respects the Court is free from external influences and pressures.

Much of the work coming before the Court is concerned with the upholding of personal freedoms and civil liberties in accordance with Articles 1–19 of the Basic Law (see Chapter 16), but in the present context the interest centres on the competences of the Constitutional Court in disputes between the major organs of the state, and in particular its controlling function over federal legislation.

Direct references to the Court, that is apart from cases referred to it from Länder courts or from lower federal courts requiring rulings on constitutional points (the so-called 'concrete control of norms'), is restricted – the federal president, the federal government, the individual Länder governments, and one-third of the Bundestag members. Direct disputes over the competences of these major participants are infrequent in comparison with the rulings the Court is required to on the validity of federal legislation. The fact that reference can be made to the Court immediately a law has been enacted, but before it has been implemented, gives rise to the second distinctive category of 'abstract control of norms'. It is in exercising this function that the Court illustrates the intermeshing of powers. In the first place, the close proximity of the legislative process and the reference to the Court that may occur in the 'abstract control of norms' effectively makes the Court a kind of adjunct to the legislative procedure. This effect is compounded if, as has usually been the case, it is the political opposition that appeals to the Court after it has been unsuccessful in the legislature.

The intermeshing is made even more apparent when the Court takes it upon itself to exercise a *de facto* amending power. This it can effectively accomplish in stating why it thinks a particular law is does not fully conform with the relevant part of the Basic Law (which article *is* relevant the Court decides), and – further – it can indicate in what respects the law should be changed to ensure conformity. The stipulation may even go as far as to indicate in quite specific terms what it would find acceptable. One consequence of the Court's involvement is that the federal government in preparing legislation has to think just as much in terms of possible reference to the Constitutional Court as it concerns itself with likely opposition in the Bundestag or Bundesrat.

One assessment of the role of the Court is negative: that the German approach leads to an undesirable 'judicialisation of politics', but it is necessary to take a more sympathetic view. One factor of historical weight is the interdependence of law and politics – they are not completely separate realms. Another – less beneficial – is the proclivity for codifying relationships in legal form, in other words their 'juridification' (*Verrechtlichung*) which inescapably introduces the law into disputes that otherwise, and in other countries, would be essentially political in character and resolved by political means (for an example of this mode, see Chapter 15).

A third factor is functional to the cooperative operation of the political system. If the disputants are unable to resolve their differences, the adjudication by a third party is a way of avoiding an undesirable imposition or an impasse. This aspect applies to the relationship between the federal government and the Länder: reference to the Constitutional Court is an acceptable way of 'externalising' the problem, of particular relevance in matters relating to 'structural aid' subsidies from the federation to the Länder and the basis of apportionment among them. In a ruling of 1986 the Court thus rejected proposals from the federal government on the grounds that the criteria employed were insufficiently objective or realisable – and suggesting others. The doubt here is whether a judicial body has adequate expertise take on tasks so outside its normal province.

## Parliament and Government

In contrast to the diffusing effects apparent in other features of the constitutional system – the federal structure and the consequences of constitutional jurisdiction – parliamentary government requires a close relationship between the legislative and executive branches. For the Federal Republic there is a tight unification maintained between the Bundestag and the federal government, although once the position of the Bundesrat is brought into the reckoning a much more complex picture emerges.

*The Bundestag*

As in all parliamentary systems, the responsibility of government is to a popularly-elected body, the Bundestag, which is elected for a four-year term. The actual election of the chancellor by the Bundestag at the beginning of this term unambiguously locates sovereign power in the Bundestag: parliamentary power cannot be circumvented as it was in the later stages of the Weimar Republic, and the sole power of the Bundestag to dismiss a serving chancellor has the same effect.

These general relationships, however, say little about the kinds of connection that obtain during the life of a government, how effective and powerful the Bundestag is in practice. It has the characteristic of being an *Arbeitsparlament*, a 'working parliament', meaning that its contribution is made chiefly through detailed legislative activity and the scrutiny of government policies. The contrast usually made is with the British House of Commons which conforms more to the alternative model of *Redeparlament*, a debating parliament. The distinction does have important implications, since inevitably the German tradition ties the Bundestag more to the government's legislative programme, although of itself this bias need not detract from the legislature's independent authority. What it does imply is that, in being geared to a legislative throughput, the Bundestag is weighted towards being an 'expert' body. This in turn means that the focus of activity is in the work of the specialised committees which run in parallel to the corresponding federal ministries. The parties, in government or opposition, find that this specialisation requires them to have technical expertise available in their ranks – rather than rely on qualities appropriate to a debating assembly. One result of this skewing is that the Bundestag is not suited to being a political forum or serving as a focus of public attention and communication, even though its detailed control over government is probably as effective as for other parliaments.

In other ways, the Bundestag is relatively divorced from the government and its ministers. The parliamentary groups of the parties, (the *Fraktionen*) have their own identity; government ministers seat separately from their party *Fraktion*, and party speakers in debate have one allocation and ministers another. The sense of distance is increased by the fact that recruitment to ministerial office is not necessarily preceded by experience as a Bundestag member. Indeed, an alternative route may better serve an individual's career ambitions. Achieving office in a Land government is likely to be a better recommendation, and that path has proved to be a rewarding one for chancellor candidates and chancellors – see Chapter 4. Eminence in other walks of life – say, a university professor – provides credentials perhaps superior to many years in the Bundestag, all of which reduces the Bundestag as a primary source of political authority.

Too great a stress should not be put on the separation of Bundestag and government. In particular the chancellor – and through him the government ministers – has to have the support of the majority parties. An all-important link is maintained through the now-accepted practice of the chancellor being able to have his own nominee as the leader of his party's Bundestage *Fraktion*. Helmut Schmidt and before him Willy Brandt relied on the organisational abilities and persuasive powers of Herbert Wehner in mustering support of SPD deputies, and Helmut Kohl depends on Alfred Dregger, former CDU party leader in Hesse. Restiveness within the *Fraktion* is most likely to arise over compromises that have to be made between coalition partners, and they have to be sold to the respective party groups. This is especially the case in the watering-down of party commitments to suit the junior coalition partner – since 1969 the FDP.

The chances of a government being defeated on its legislative programme are small; since party discipline, *Fraktionszwang*, is strict. governments are far more likely to succumb to internal pressures, in which the Bundestag is only one element, and it may not even be the main source of tension. In the early years of the republic, there were frequent defections of junior coalition partners, but only in 1982, when the FDP brought down the Schmidt government, has this been a direct expression of the will of the Bundestag. It is discontent within the majority party that has proved to be the most potent cause of government weakness, but the mood of the majority party in the Bundestag may not be the most significant locus of revolt. In the past, dissatisfaction has become apparent in the higher echelons of the of the national party leadership as well as from the party leadership as well as from the parties in the Länder. Powerful party leaders in the Länder can also make their influence felt within the Bundestag: they can expect to command a following among Bundestag members from the same Land, and this other loyalty may have an erosive effect on a government's standing. The departure of several chancellors – Adenauer, Erhard, Brandt and Schmidt (see Chapter 4) – can be traced to this wider loss of confidence, not to a simple revolt in the Bundestag.

In evaluating the role of the Bundestag, attention has to be paid to the constitutional framework and to established practices, but the nature of the party system is also a determining influence. The three-party system (or four in this context if the CSU is counted separately, although it forms a common group with the CDU in the Bundestag) has led to a highly structured and predictable legislative chamber. In the 1980s the pattern has changed slightly with the representation of the Greens since 1983, but their impact – apart from lending more bite and colour to the proceedings – is limited, since the two major parties dominate and disagree little on fundamentals. Should the balance of party strength alter substantially in the 1990s, or even revert to the multi-partism of the 1950s, then the Bundestag could gain in prominence – even though the consequences could be less satisfactory.

*The Bundesrat*

Quite different considerations affect the federal government in its dealings with the Bundesrat. The special features of its composition and the functions and powers ascribed to it in the Basic Law make the Bundesrat unlike other second chambers, and it underpins the federal structure in ways that are more effective than is the case of a directly-elected senate on the American model. The composition of the Bundesrat, delegates nominated by Land governments and acting on the instructions of those governments, reflects party fortunes in the Länder: the party majority in the Bundesrat need not correspond to that in the Bundestag, and coalitions formed in the Länder may not be the same as the federal coalition in Bonn (see Table 2.1).

Even though the party composition of the Bundesrat is normally decisive in the attitude taken towards federal legislation, the various delegations are there also to look after their particular Land interests. These limitations on the ability of the federal government to influence the decisions of the Bundesrat would not be so serious if the powers of the latter were not so formidable. Besides the necessity of securing a two-thirds majority for constitutional amendments, the Bundesrat has a wide legislative competence, including the approval of the federal budget, and its position is strengthened by the absolute veto it can wield on all legislation that directly affects the Länder. Since it is the Länder that are required to implement the bulk of federal legislation – and therefore legislative measures inevitably have to deal with this aspect – the necessity of securing the cooperation and consent of the Bundesrat is a considerable constraint on the federal government.

Rather than a legislative organ, the Bundesrat is better thought of as a meeting place of governments. This feature is made evident in Article 50 of the Basic Law which stipulates that the Länder shall participate *through* the Bundesrat in the legislation *and* adminis-

TABLE 2.1   *Composition of Bundesrat and Land Governments* [1]

| Land | Bundesrat seats | Government | Head of government |
|---|---|---|---|
| Baden-Württemberg | 5 | CDU | Lothar Späth |
| Bavaria | 5 | CSU | Max Streibl |
| Bremen | 3 | SPD | Klaus Wedemeier |
| Hamburg | 3 | SPD–FDP | Henning Voscherau |
| Hesse | 4 | CDU–FDP | Walter Wallmann |
| Lower Saxony | 5 | CDU–FDP | Ernst Albrecht |
| North Rhine-Westphalia | 5 | SPD | Johannes Rau |
| Rhineland-Palatinate | 4 | CDU–FDP | Karl-Ludwig Wagner |
| Saarland | 3 | SPD | Oskar Lafontaine |
| Schleswig-Holstein | 4 | SPD | Björn Engholm |
|  | 41 |  |  |
| Berlin (West) | (4) | SPD–Greens | Walter Momper (ruling mayor) |

Note:
1 Government composition as in mid-1989. Land elections due in 1990: the
  Saarland, North Rhine-Westphalia, Lower Saxony and Bavaria, in that order.

tration of the federation. This provision is in the German federal tradition: the federal government participates in the work of the Bundesrat, in consultation and in committees.

As much as any other institution, the Bundersrat exemplifies the 'cooperative' character of the West German constitutional system. The lack of any direct elections, the fact that the Länder governments are in the first place responsible to their own electorates, and their natural concern to guard their own status and authority means that the federal government has little choice but to adopt an accommodative stance. For their part, the Länder have been increasingly drawn into a range of cooperative tasks (*Gemeinschaftsaufgaben*) with the federal government, and although this sharing of functions has the effect of giving the Bundesrat a greater say in legislation, the autonomy of the Länder is thereby diminished, especially since the extension of coresponsibility has implications for the basis of revenue-sharing as well as for levels of federal subsidies (see Chapter 3).

In the past the CDU could expect to have a much easier ride than the SPD when in federal office. The SPD–led government in the 1970s faced a hostile majority of CDU–CSU governed Länder which made acceptable compromises difficult to achieve. After 1982, the CDU was again in a favourable position, but in the later 1980s a string of SPD victories in the Länder altered the balance considerably. In 1985 the SPD ousted the CDU in the Saarland, and in 1987 the SPD (in coalition with the FDP) wrested back control of Hamburg; in 1988 it won Schleswig-Holstein from the CDU (see Table 2.1). This trend almost led to a switch in the Bundesrat majority when, late in 1988, the SPD came within an ace of unseating the CDU in Lower Saxony on a motion of censure. But, whatever the formal majority, any Land government will be sure to consider its own interests when these clash with the views of its federal party.

## German Corporatism

Patterns of policy-making in the Federal Republic are usually described in terms of a liberal or societal corporatism in which there is a form of partnership between the state and organised interests. In its West German expression there are some particular features that have to be taken into account: the relative weakness of central direction, the diffusion of policy formation, and the interlocking of numerous decision making arenas. These three aspects are obviously closely related, and they all help to confirm the characterisation of the Federal Republic as 'a state without a centre'.

It would be a mistake to suppose that this style was somehow stamped out of the ground in the era after 1945 and that its establishment wholly depended on the institutional structures that resulted from the Basic Law. Although they have been of leading importance in underpinning German corporatism, its roots can be traced well back into the nineteenth century. Under Bismarck's influence, what initially took shape was a form of state-directed corporatism; even so, the 'incorporation' of social interests at that time was largely possible because the 'free associations' were willing and able to adapt to the new mould. Societal corporatism as it exists at present has relied on the grafting of institutions on to pre-existing traditions of social cooperation and regulation.

Underlying its apparently smooth operation in the Federal Republic have been important ideological factors, both political and economic. These have contributed to the cementing of corporatism because of the willingness of the founding parties – CDU, SPD and FDP – to adopt what amounted to a common ideological front (for the SPD not until the late 1950s). This is epitomised by their shared adherence to the concept of the *soziale Marktwirtschaft* (social market economy). Even though the bracketing together of two inherently opposed principles – that of economic liberalism with social responsibility – appears to be an uneasy juxtaposition, the practical outcome has been to provide the basis for a harmonisation of competing interests.

For this reconciliation to succeed over the longer term the commitment of the parties might by itself have proved insufficient, since the interests in society that they serve are substantially different. Of vital significance has been the ability to secure continuity and consistency over time, and this has come about by the exceptional continuity of party participation in government. Unlike the practice in Britain and the United States, where the parties are attuned to alternating in government, in the Federal Republic there has been no complete change of the parties in office during the whole forty years of its existence. Abrupt and divisive switches in the direction of policy – however much an individual party may wish it – have simply not been feasible.

At the same time, however, other factors make it difficult for the parties in federal government to push through their desired policy objectives without the active cooperation of a range of interests and other political actors. It has already been indicated just how important the institutional structures are in this respect – the federal structure, the Bundesrat, the Federal Constitutional Court – and it is within this framework that economic and other interests organise themselves and act in the policy-formation process to their best advantage.

These structural conditions make it difficult for the federal government to impose central direction, and in German circumstances it would be unrealistic to think of industrial or economic policies finding their place within an ambitious and comprehensive 'national plan'. The difficulty of exercising corporatist management of the economy 'from the top' is illustrated by the failure of 'Concerted Action' (*Konzertierte Aktion*) to find a permanent place in the system. This initiative by the federal government in 1967 as a way of coordinating economic policy by means of a 'summit tripartism' was seen at the time as completing the edifice of German corporatism, but ten years later it was permanently abandoned.

This episode does not point to the fragility of corporatism; on the contrary it draws attention even more to the sources of its strength – that is, within particular economic and industrial sectors and at a host of intermediate levels. This infrastructure of coordination based on decentralisation is embodied in and well illustrated by the principle of *Subsidiarität* (subsidiarity) which can be only partially rendered by the idea of a devolving of responsibility to lower units which, within their area of competence, they exercise on their own initiative.

How the principle is applied in different contexts will be shown elsewhere in this book (see Chapters 3, 8, 9 and 15). The diversity of application – to the working of federalism, in economic spheres, the provision of the social services, the regulation of industrial relations – indicates how entrenched this corporatist style has become.

Partly it is shown by the public-regulatory functions vested in essentially voluntaristic bodies, and partly by the autonomous authority granted to a variety of public institutions. An example of the former are the local associations of industry and trade, and in the latter grouping the Bundesbank, with its independent power over the control of the monetary policy (as shown in Chapter 8), precisely illustrates the powerful constraints that hem in the federal government.

Little of this devolution and self-regulation, it should be added, takes place just because of custom and accepted practice or through the invoking od such formulae as 'social partnership' to bring together disparate interests. Behind German corporatism stands the close regulation provided by the legal framework and the courts. The 'legal ethos' that suffuses German politics is one aspect of a characteristic that underlies public and politcal culture.

In this review of the structures of government in the Fedral Republic, one feature will have atracted notice: the absence of significant 'developments'. What has to be concluded is that – in witnessing the substantial changes that have taken place in recent decades, affecting policy and politics over wide areas – we have to appreciate the stability, even inertia, of the basic institutions. The system is static because it works.

# 3

# Territorial Government

## SIMON BULMER

### The Relevance of Federalism

The Federal Republic of Germany's establishment can be seen as
resting upon three fundamental principles: parliamentary democracy, the rule of law (which also sets down certain social responsibilities in the *sozialer Rechtsstaat*, Social constitutional state) and a federal system of government. The practice of all three principles has
evolved over the period since 1949. In the case of federalism the
changes have been particularly great and have led some observers
to question whether the very principle of federalism has been
undermined.

This questioning of West German federalism has come about
through the gradual transfer of policy responsibilities away from the
states, or Länder, to the federation, or Bund, in one of two forms.
On the one hand, there have been constitutional amendments having
this effect. Between 1949 and 1984 there had been 35 laws amending
the constitution, of which no fewer than 24 have had a direct or
indirect impact on the federal order (Laufer, 1984, p. 12). On the
other hand, there has been a tendency for the Länder to become
increasingly dependent upon the federation in financial terms, thus
giving the latter still further power. As a consequence of this development, it is legitimate to question the relevance of federalism to the
West German political system of today.

However, posing that question requires consideration of the peculiar circumstances that led to the very establishment of federalism in
1949. In this, a comparative perspective is informative. The overwhelming majority of federal systems have come about as the result
of 'forces – economic, social, political, cultural – that have made the

40

outward forms of federalism necessary' (Livingston, 1952, p. 83). In the West German case, federalism was less the result of internal forces of this nature. Rather, it was an attempt to avoid the excessive centralisation of power witnessed under the Nazi regime: a desire both of the Western occupying powers and of the emergent internal political elite. The presumption in favour of a federal system of government during the drafting of the constitution also drew on the history of the federal principle in Germany, dating back to 1871.

Of the territorially concentrated forces which normally lie behind a federal society, religion had been of some importance historically. However, this had been weakened by the division of Germany and has subsequently declined further as a result of the process of secularisation. Moreover, most of the Länder boundaries were artificial creations of the allied powers; in 1945 the Hanseatic cities of Bremen and Hamburg, and the state of Bavaria, were the clearest cases of pre-existing political entities. West German federalism has thus always had a somewhat synthetic character, making it a case which is difficult to accommodate within much of the literature on comparative federalism. The question of its relevance today cannot be detached from these peculiar origins.

## The Institutions of West German Federalism

In institutional terms federalism is usually regarded as a two-tiered system of government that endows each level with independent responsibility for some policy areas, whilst others are shared between the two. In addition, the independence of the two levels must be assured in some form. The latter requirement is fulfilled in the Federal Republic (FRG) in two ways. Firstly, the Basic Law states that any attempts to change the division of the federation into Länder 'shall be inadmissible' (Article 79, §3). Moreover, the catalogue of legislative and administrative responsibilities is set out in the Basic Law. Secondly, the Federal Constitutional Court acts as umpire in disputes relating to the federal system.

The basic value governing the assignment of powers to the Bund (federation) and Länder is that of *subsidiarity*. Under this, state functions should be allocated to the lowest level of government in the first instance. Only if the task proves to be beyond that level's capacity should it be passed up the hierarchy. In the Basic Law subsidiarity is expressed through the Länder being responsible for legislative powers other than those explicitly assigned to the federation. Moreover, the Länder have extensive responsibilities for the administration of both federal and Land law. In fact, some of these tasks are carried out in conjunction with the various local government authorities. The principle of subsidiarity thus extends downwards below the Länder, although the organisation of local government is the constitutional responsibility of the Länder (Article 28, §2).

The evolution of West German federalism over the post-war period has been characterised by the transfer of legislative functions to the federation as questions have been raised concerning the capacity of the Länder to deliver adequate policies. This development may be regarded in terms of the principle of subsidiarity, as outlined above. In other words, there must have been some consensus that exclusive Länder authority has shown weaknesses, for their governments' agreement is required in the Bundesrat for the necessary constitutional changes. A major stimulus for creeping centralisation has been the international interdependence of the FRG. Its centralising impact has found strong normative legitimation in the constitutional principle that the federation may legislate in certain areas for 'the maintenance of legal or economic unity, especially the maintenance of uniformity of living conditions' (Basic Law, Article 72, §3).

There are four ways in which legislative power is assigned under the West German Basic Law. Firstly, there are those policy areas where exclusive responsibility is assigned to the federation (Article 73). Secondly, in matters of concurrent legislative powers, the Länder may legislate as long as the federation has not done so. Article 75 lists the policy areas where the federation sets framework conditions, which the Länder must incorporate in their own legislation. Finally, there are those policy areas where the principle of subsidiarity, embodied in Article 30, continues to apply; in other words the Länder continue to have exclusive authority for them. Examples of the different responsibilities are set out in Table 3.1.

In the administrative arena the Länder are charged, under Article 83 of the Basic Law, with implementing the bulk of federal legislation in addition to their own laws. This extensive administrative role undertaken by the Länder is a distinctive feature of German federalism and comes about because the Federal government has a very limited range of field agencies responsible for implementing its own policies. Most policies are thus implemented by the Länder (following the principle of subsidiarity) and in this task they have a significant degree of discretion. It is in recognition of this administrative role of the Länder that much federal legislation requires the agreement of Bundesrat. Finally, it should be pointed out that Länder courts are responsible for most of the administration of justice.

In brief, the institutions of federalism consist at each level (and in each Land) of a government, which is headed by a chief minister,

TABLE 3.1 *Legislative competences of the Federation and Länder*

| Federation | Länder |
|---|---|
| Exclusive powers | Exclusive powers |
| Foreign affairs | Cultural affairs (including broadcasting) |
| Defence | |
| Citizenship | Education |
| Passports, immigration, etc. | Health Service |
| Currency matters | Police |
| Customs and free movements of goods | |
| Post and telecommunications | |

| Framework conditions |
|---|
| Principles of higher education |
| Hunting and conservation |
| The press and the film industry |
| Land distribution and regional planning |

| Concurrent powers |
|---|
| Civil and criminal law and sentencing |
| Registration of births, deaths and marriages |
| The law of association and assembly |
| Residence and establishment of aliens |
| Production and use of nuclear energy |

and which is accountable to a democratically elected parliamentary body. Each system of government has its own constitution, constitutional court and civil service. The exact details differ from case to case (see the Guide to Further Reading at the end of the book).

The Federal Constitutional Court and the Bundesrat deserve especial mention. The Court's role is to 'act as arbiter of the federal system' (Blair, 1981, p. 9). Constitutional disputes between the Bund and Länder may take one of two forms. One is in the shape of a complaint concerning rights or duties under the Basic Law. The other is by way of a request for a ruling on the constitutionality of a federal or Land law or on the compatibility of Land and federal law. Such rulings may be requested by either the Bund or by a Land or by Länder. The Court's judges are not neutral with regard to the federal structure; half are appointed from the Bundesrat, reflecting Länder interests, while the other half are appointed by the Bundestag, reflecting the interests of the federation. This balance places the Constitutional Court in a unique position.

The Court's importance in influencing federalism has been catalogued in Blair's study. One example was the so-called 'Television Case' of 1961. The Christian Democratic-led federal government of Chancellor Adenauer had sought to establish a second television channel by administrative decree. This was challenged by the SPD–led state governments on two grounds. Firstly, they argued that it was a breach of Länder responsibility for cultural policy; the first channel having been created by treaty between the Länder. Secondly, they argued that the manner in which Adenauer's federal government had sought to obtain Länder agreement was contrary to the principle of federal comity (whereby no federal or Land government may act with disregard for the interests of other component governments of the FRG). On both counts the Court ruled in favour of the SPD–led Länder.

This example illustrates the fact that some constitutional disputes combine federal issues with party political ones, for it was the SPD–led Länder governments which took the case to the Court. This situation also occurs in the other key federal institution, the Bundesrat. This institution brings together members of the Länder governments. The delegation of each Land votes en bloc, with the number of votes depending on the state's population. Like the Bundestag, the Bundesrat has an important committee system, Bundesrat committees normally bringing together Länder civil servants who thus have a different type of expertise from that in the Bundestag. The importance of the Bundesrat lies in its role in the legislative process. This varies according to the nature of legislation. In the case of 'normal' federal legislation the Bundesrat may force a suspensive veto. However, in a wide range of legislation affecting the vital interests (*Zustimmungsbedürftige Gesetze*) of the Länder, the Bundesrat has an absolute veto. In the absence of a clearcut catalogue of what legislation falls into which category, an expanding amount of federal legislation has been assumed to require the consent of the Bundesrat, a practice largely confirmed by the Federal Constitutional Court in 1974. Instead of some 10 per cent of legislation requiring Bundesrat consent, as originally anticipated, the figure has now exceeded 50 per cent. Regardless of whether the Bundesrat's consent is required or not, where it rejects legislation approved in the Bundestag a complex conciliation procedure is introduced with a view to reaching agreement.

The importance of all this for the centralising trend in post-war federalism can be seen in four ways. First, the Constitutional Court can be requested by the Länder to judge whether the trend is legitimate or assisted by unconstitutional actions by the federation. Second, a two-thirds majority in the Bundesrat is required for a constitutional transfer of power to the federation. Thirdly, the Bundesrat has an absolute majority over matters affecting those legislative powers the Länder share with the Bund, those policies they administer and any measures affecting Länder finances. Finally, it should be noted that the extension of the Bundesrat's powers has offered some compensation for the creeping process of centralisation that becomes evident in the post-war evolution of West German federalism.

The institutions of federalism thus act as watchdogs over the balance of power between Bund and Länder. However, federalism is a function of societies, not of constitutions (Livingston, 1952). Hence the institutions of West German federalism cannot be detached from the extent of unity or diversity in society. Faced with an array of new challenges over the post-war period, many resulting from international interdependence, West German society has not served as a strong support for maintenance of the original federal balance of power. Rather, on a range of issues, including higher education provision, environmental policy, macroeconomic management and regional policy, there has been (at least) a readiness to accept the federal government as having an increased role in the maintenance of welfare and of relatively uniform living standards.

## Explaining the Evolution of Federalism

The original intention of the Parliamentary Council, which drafted the Basic Law, was that the Länder should have precedence in the federal system. In fact, there has been a large, albeit gradual, increase in the number of policy areas where the Länder have to work together with the Bund rather than having autonomy.

This situation has arisen from two pronounced periods of centralisation, identified by Klatt (1986). In the 1950s the federation experienced a relative increase in its power. This occurred through three main routes. Firstly, the ending of the allies' occupation statute gave the federal level legislative responsibility for foreign policy and defence. The Länder received no corresponding extra powers. Secondly, a number of new issues came onto the political agenda and the federal level acquired legislative responsibility for them, for example civil aviation (exclusive responsibility), or 'the production and utilisation of nuclear energy' (concurrent powers). These two cases show how policy areas, not important when the Basic Law was drafted, have not gone exclusively to the Länder according to the principle of subsidiarity. Instead, the Bund has identified a federal interest. Thirdly, the system of apportioning tax revenue between the two levels of government was reformed to the benefit of the Bund in 1955.

The second period of centralisation came with the economic and financial reforms of 1967–9. This period coincided with the Grand Coalition in Bonn, composed of both Christian and Social Democrats. With minimal federal opposition and with minimal *party* political conflict between Bund and Länder governments, it was possible to achieve significant changes to the federal order. It was during this period that the federation obtained macroeconomic policy instruments designed to combat the effects of economic recession. However, because the Länder and local authorities are responsible for such a large part of public expenditure, it was again necessary to encroach upon Länder powers. Far-reaching developments also stemmed from financial reform, which led to a number of constitutional amendments designed to ensure a more efficient provision of services. Under these changes several policies were designated cooperative tasks (*Gemeinschaftsaufgaben*). The result was a further weakening of Länder autonomy, whilst increasing the extent of interdependence between the two tiers of government.

The objective of the changes was to introduce 'cooperative federalism' as the leitmotiv of Bund-Länder relations in the 1970s. The changes were an attempt to justify the continuance of federalism at a time of increasing centralisation. In particular, they sought to emphasise the predominance of those policy areas where the Bund and the Länder act in harness over the areas where they act autonomously of each other.

The balance sheet of federalism by the end of the 1970s thus shows the Bund holding a rather dominant position. This was the product not only of it gaining new exclusive powers but also stemmed from its acquisition of shared power through framework or concurrent legislation (see Table 3.1). Where it shares power, the Bund often sets the principles of legislation, giving it a position of some advantage. The predominance of the Länder in the administration of policy scarcely represents compensation. In addition to these changes, the Bund has also strengthened its financial power. Alongside the position of the Bund, the handful of powers remaining under exclusive control of the Länder is negligible. The only indirect compensation comes in the form of the more 'Länder-friendly' interpretation of the Bundesrat's powers.

How, then, can this creeping centralisation be explained?. The argument offered here is that increasing international interdependence has brought a series of challenges to the federal system and especially to the Länder. These have been particularly acute from the 1960s, given the difficulty of satisfying ever-increasing popular expectations regarding the standard of living, social provision and, in the 1980s, regarding quality of life issues such as the environment. Two examples will serve to illustrate this argument.

In the 1960s there was a recognition in the FRG that an insufficient number of young Germans were attending higher education. In order to avoid this crisis – known as the *Bildungskatastrophe* – from translating into scientific backwardness, and hence international economic weakness, new policy initiatives were launched. These involved constitutional changes that introduced the federation, in both planning and financial capacities, into a policy area where the Länder had previously had autonomy (Katzenstein, 1987, Chapter 7).

In the 1980s the environmental policy area has come to play a prominent role in German politics. Increasingly, environmental issues such as air and water pollution have become international issues. In consequence, Länder responsibility has appeared to be anomalous. This became all too clear in 1986 when a series of chemical spillages into the Rhine in Switzerland had environmental repercussions on the Rhine in the FRG. More dramatic in 1986 was the Chernobyl nuclear accident in the Soviet Union. The environmental impact of the accident was serious enough. However, the contradictory and disorganised responses of Länder (and some federal) agencies further called into question the decentralisation of responsibilities. The Kohl government's decision in June 1986 to establish a federal ministry responsible for environmental affairs was a response to popular concern at the lack of a central agency to coordinate environmental catastrophes.

In fact, these examples not only illustrate a centralisation towards the Bund but also, in some cases, relate to the increasing responsibilities of the European Community (EC). The EC has acquired constitutional authority for environmental matters and has also begun to introduce legislation relating to higher education, for example (see below).

These two case studies demonstrate how the internationalisation of policy issues challenges the appropriateness of Länder responsibility. There are three components to this: the external stimuli deriving from international interdependence, societal expectations of a reasonable uniformity in living standards combined with a preparedness to accept some governmental centralisation and, as a counterbalance, the guarantees offered by judicial and legislative constraints. It is against this background that a federal system has emerged, characterised by extensive intergovernmental relations between the two tiers of government but also with links to the European Community.

**The Tensions of Federalism**

Intergovernmental relations within the federal system take several forms. The common thread is the attempt to provide rational policy solutions to contemporary needs. However, given the commitment to a federal system, a number of tensions arise. How far can rational policy solutions emerge where the federal and Länder governments are democratically accountable to different constituencies? How far is the consensus needed in intergovernmental relations compatible with the need for optimal policy solutions? How far are intergovernmental relations compatible with a democratic system? The answers to these and other questions depend on the differing forms of inter- governmental relations.

*Länder-Länder Relations*

This form of coordination at the Land level dates from the very establishment of the FRG. It involves policy coordination by Länder ministers or civil servants on those areas where they have exclusive legislative power. The coordination also relates to the many policy areas where the Länder have responsibility for the execution of policy.

A major explanation for such coordination was an attempt on the part of Länder governments to prevent diversity undermining efficiency. For instance, a diverse educational system could act as a barrier to labour mobility, so, in order to forestall the Bund's inter- vention in the interests of ensuring reasonable uniformity (as pro- vided for in the Basic Law), the Länder governments sought to achieve this amongst themselves (Blair, 1981, pp. 215–20). Already by 1961 there were over 300 agreements or treaties between the Länder. Many of the agreements addressed very mundane issues, such as establishing common principles for bussing children to school or standardising regulations on the administration of paperwork at the offices of the courts or of the public prosecutor: both matters of Länder responsibility. Länder-Länder relations are generally conduc- ted in a cooperative manner, especially where the meetings are held at the civil servant level.

Agreements are usually supervised by standing committees bring- ing together the responsible authorities. These need not comprise all the Länder. For example, the states of Hamburg, Lower Saxony and Schleswig-Holstein are responsible for the regional broadcasting company, Norddeutscher Rundfunk. On the other hand, the creation in 1961 of Zweites Deutsches Fernsehen, the FRG's second tele- vision channel, required the participation and agreement of all the

Länder. Both these arrangements are regulated by treaty (*Staatsvertrag*).

However, the potential for political conflict is present, especially as Länder governments are responsible to different constituencies. This occurred with attempts to reform the West German broadcasting system to cope with the 'new media': cable and satellite television. As one of the few remaining areas where the Länder retain exclusive authority (as part of cultural policy), it was imperative for them to be able to respond to the new challenges. However, CDU– or CSU–led coalitions were, for a variety of political reasons, in favour of opening up to private broadcasters, whereas the SPD–governed states were not (Humphreys, 1988). This resulted in protracted negotiations, somewhat anomalously characterised as Länder politics, given that the new media have not only cross-regional implications but international ones too. Sub-national regulation of international media conglomerates was simply unsustainable, so the Länder governments were ultimately obliged to reach a consensus in order to retain some semblance of authority in the policy area (Berg, 1988).

## Bund-Länder Relations

Just as Länder-Länder relations can be fraught with different regional interests, so also can those which additionally involve the federal government. The main difference is that the tensions, particularly those of a party political nature, are likely to be more transparent by virtue of having the Bundesrat as a forum where they may be vented. Furthermore, disagreement about the constitutional rights and political influence of the two levels of government adds a vertical dimension to any (horizontal) disagreement amongst the Länder of the type illustrated. Again, however, the vast majority of Bund-Länder contacts are maintained at the civil servant level, for example about the administration – by the Länder – of federal legislation and thus are not party political in nature. The number of committees runs into hundreds.

One example of coordination is provided by federal highways (comprising the Autobahn and trunk road network). This is a federal responsibility but is administered by the Länder (Garlichs and Hull, 1978). One would therefore expect a strong federal lead on highway planning. However, despite having full formal authority for the policy area and over where to allocate funding, and despite paying for the entire federal highway programme, evidence revealed a low degree of central control. Foremost among the explanations was the high degree of dependence on the information and expertise of the

Länder (in the Bund-Länder transport ministers' committee). Any attempt to intensify highway planning simply further increased the level of dependence on the Länder ministries.

Without doubt there are other policy areas where the federal government *is* able to operationalise its predominance, but this case illustrates a recurrent problem of intergovernmental relations, namely a tendency towards bureaucratisation and immobilism. This is further reinforced by strong German preferences for consensual Bund-Länder relations even if this clashes with both the provision of an appropriate policy and with the principle of democratic accountability.

*Joint Tasks*

Precisely these criticisms of policy inefficiency were first raised in connection with joint tasks in the studies by Scharpf *et al.* (1976) and Scharpf (1985). The joint tasks were created in 1969 to spearhead the new spirit of cooperative federalism. Recognising the difficulties the Länder had in financing certain policy areas of national import-ance, a constitutional amendment brought the Bund into policy-making in two ways. Firstly, it took on a policy planning function; secondly, it provided much needed financial resources. Three policy areas were assigned to the new joint task arrangements in the Basic Law (Article 91a): expansion and construction of higher education institutions; the improvement of regional economic structures; and the improvement of the agricultural structure and of coastal pres-ervation.

In each of these areas policy-making is conducted according to a specific model of Bund-Länder relations. The federal government has eleven votes, cast *en bloc*, while the Länder have eleven votes, one for each Land (including West Berlin). Despite the provision for qualified majority voting, Scharpf has argued that there is a tendency to vote unanimously because of shared institutional inter-ests. In his view this has led to a 'joint decision trap', where reaching a consensus may prevail over agreeing on the most appropriate policy. In the case of agricultural structures the policy favoured the northern Länder at the expense of the inefficient smallholdings of the southern states: precisely where reform was most needed (Sch-arpf, 1985, pp. 13–14). A reorientation of policy towards the areas of greatest need proved highly problematic.

In the case of the regional policy cooperative task, the share-out of federal funds was highly inflexible. Despite the fact that the Bund's involvement was supposed to give an overall shape and effectiveness to regional aid, the joint task proved unable to adapt to such serious regional problems as the decline of the steel sector in the Saarland, or of shipbuilding in Bremen; *ad hoc* programmes were necessary, undermining rationality (Scharpf, 1985, pp. 14–15).

Clearly the cooperative tasks, hailed as one of the new policy instruments of cooperative federalism, have in fact called into question its viability. The tendency towards sub-optimal policies and bureaucratic procedures was scarcely a great advertisement.

### Bund-Länder-EC Links

The grafting of a supranational level of government, namely the EC, onto some existing Bund-Länder arrangements has rendered intergovernmental relations still more impenetrable. For example, this occurred in both the case of regional policy (from 1975) and of agricultural structures (from 1972). However, in both cases the federal government has in fact been able to play a more dominant role because of its claims to exclusive responsibility for foreign affairs (see p. 56 below).

### Summary

The operation of intergovernmental relations failed to match the aspirations of cooperative federalism. On the one hand, in those areas where the Social-Liberal federal government (1969–82) sought to introduce new legislation for change, it encountered a hostile opposition in the Bundesrat (Paterson and Webber, 1987). During this period the Mediation Committee had to be used much more than in any other (Laufer, 1984, p. 24). Some legislation had to be abandoned or, at least, watered down in order to satisfy the centre-right majority of Länder governments in the Bundesrat. On the other hand, in the existing Bund-Länder frameworks, there was also a negative balance. Policy-making was bureaucratised, the Länder and federal governments were obliged to compromise on their goals, democratic control was seriously weakened – the Länder parliaments losing much of their power – and there were some sub-optimal policy outcomes. Cooperative federalism, introduced as a way of achieving effective policy responses to international interdependence, proved in fact to fall short of its high aspirations.

## The Finances of Federalism

In addition to the four forms of intergovernmental relations discussed above, there are also those relating to financial matters, as governed by the 1969 Finance Reform. Just as policy responsibilities have tended to move towards the centre, so there has been a pattern of the Bund increasing its influence over the funding of policies. The Länder (and local government), have been left with the responsibility for carrying out the actual expenditure. Once again interdependence has played a role. The international recession induced by two oil shocks has had an impact on both the vertical relationship between Bund and Länder as well as on the relative affluence of individual Länder.

The taxation system of the FRG finds its basis in Articles 104a – 115 of the Basic Law. These articles set out the areas of expenditure for which the Bund, Länder and local government are responsible; the level of government receiving the different types of taxation and other revenue is also set down. In both cases, there are some areas of exclusive responsibility (to either the Länder, the Bund or to local government) and important ones of shared responsibility. In order to ensure that revenue and expenditure commitments approximate at each level of government, there is a complex system of financial equalisation (*Finanzausgleich*). This takes three forms. First, there is a vertical system enabling the Bund to make various types of payment to the Länder. Second, there is horizontal equalisation between the Länder; rich states must make payments to the poorer ones. Thirdly, there is a system of equalisation between the local authorities in a particular Land. Several issues arise from all this.

Perhaps the biggest of these has been the wrangling between the Länder about how fair the horizontal equalisation system is. Under the system North Rhine-Westphalia, Baden-Württemberg, Hesse and Hamburg have been contributors, while Bavaria, Lower Saxony, Rhineland-Palatinate, Saarland and Bremen have been beneficiaries. The dispute over financing led the five SPD–ruled Länder, along with Baden-Württemberg, to challenge the system before the Constitutional Court. This group thus comprised states with differing interests; some thought they were receiving too little, others that they were paying too much. The Court's decision in June 1986 did not result in a clear picture of who had 'won' because much of the system was declared to be contrary to the constitution (Geske, 1986)! In addition, the Court ruled that there should be changes to the vertical equalisation system as well. As a result the system needed an overhaul, for completion by 1988.

The question of distributive politics, illustrated by equalisation, is to be found in many aspects of the FRG's intergovernmental relations and occurs in all four forms discussed in the previous section. The finances of broadcasting, for example, involve horizontal equalisation amongst the Länder. Agreeing an increase in the licence fee can be highly politicised, for it requires unanimous agreement by the ten Länder and West Berlin (eleven electoral cycles!). The three other forms of intergovernmental relations also apply. There are Bund-Länder negotiations on the size of federal grants for delegated functions – i.e., where the Länder administer federal expenditure programmes. In the case of the joint tasks, there are both horizontal and vertical issues of financing. The horizontal level is concerned with ensuring a fair allocation of project expenditure for each state. However, since all projects are funded equally between Bund and the relevant Land, the total size of the federal government's budget is critical. The ECs own regional and agricultural structural funds add further complications to these two joint tasks. The EC is also involved on the revenue side. As one of its major revenue sources is Value Added Tax, which in the FRG is a revenue shared between Bund and Länder, all three tiers of intergovernmental relations are involved.

Another issue concerns the curious form of interdependence that exists in the federal system. The Länder are financially dependent upon the Bund in the sense that they have more expenditure commitments (including those on behalf of the Bund) than they receive in revenue. This dependence is greater for those Länder reliant on horizontal equalisation receipts. However, for the local authorities the situation is even worse because they have important expenditure commitments but their independent income sources are very small.

This is not to say that the federal government does not depend on the Länder in some respects. Following the economic reforms of the late 1960s the Bonn government has certain powers to influence the level of activity in the economy, for instance during an economic recession. However, the Länder and local government are responsible for their own (autonomous) expenditure plans, and for implementing those of the federal government; nearly two-thirds of public expenditure is actually carried out by the Länder and local government and, in the case of public investment, the figure rises to some 80 per cent. Operation of the macroeconomic policy instruments is thus dependent on achieving a consensus in the two Bund-Länder policy-making committees, the Business Cycle Council and the Finance Planning Council. Whilst a consensus may have been achieved, the resultant policy has been less than successful (Knott, 1981).

The pattern and nature of intergovernmental relations can thus be seen to extend to the financial aspect of federalism, too. Once again there is a dense network of intergovernmental contacts which tend to weaken policy responsiveness to the challenges from the international economy.

**North–South Problems**

Just as the international recession had a deep impact on the West German macroeconomy, so new technologies and the newly industrialising countries have created serious challenges for older industries, such as steel and shipbuilding. The concentration of these industries in a few Länder has a resultant impact upon regional balance and thus on territorial government. The impact upon the Länder has been exacerbated by the structure of the federal system. The most dramatic example has been the city state of Bremen. The industrial importance to it of both steel and shipbuilding means that their decline not only weakens the local economy but, by leading to mounting deficits, affects the state's ability to provide effective government.

Developments from the mid-1970s have suggested the emergence of a North-South divide in the FRG. Caution has to be exercised in this connection because a general trend can be supported only by certain data. There have always been some Länder with more productive economies than those of others (as measured by gross domestic product (GDP) *per capita*). It is in most cases the more productive states, with their economies based upon heavy industry, that are now experiencing decline. These Länder are in the North and, despite their relative decline, they remain more productive than most of the Länder in the South.

One study has given particular attention to this issue and divides the Länder into four groups (Körber-Weik and Wied-Nebbeling, 1987):

(a) Lower Saxony, Rhineland-Palatinate, Saarland and Bavaria are experiencing high growth rates in economic activity and affluence but from a relatively disadvantaged starting point.
(b) Hamburg, Bremen, West Berlin and North Rhine-Westphalia are experiencing slow growth rates but from a relatively strong initial position.
(c) Hesse and Baden-Württemberg are experiencing high growth rates from a relatively favourable starting point.
(d) Schleswig-Holstein has a relatively weak economy and low growth.

The simple formulation of a North-South divide is thus shown to be more complex. The only set of figures supporting such a divide are those on unemployment growth rates. On this yardstick all the northern Länder plus the Saarland have rates above the German average, while the southern states fall below the average (West Berlin is near the average).

Not surprisingly, the tendency towards a North–South divide has sparked two policy debates: firstly, on how best to ensure balanced economic growth in the FRG and, secondly, on how best to attract industrial investment. In practice, it has been the competition between the Länder for attracting new investment that has predominated. Länder governments, regardless of party political complexion, have preferred to pursue fairly interventionist policies for the benefit of their own state. Much less attention has been given to the question of whether there is sufficient new investment and enterprise to justify Länder expenditure on infrastructure projects and technology parks (Sturm, 1989).

The CDU–governed state of Baden-Württemberg serves as an example of interventionist policies coupled with a positive image of economic dynamism. Under the influence of its minister-president, Lothar Späth, an extensive array of policy instruments has been used: training policy, financial aid to facilitate the development plans of small- and medium-sized enterprises, an extensive programme of promoting high technology, and a system of export guarantee credits (Schoeck, 1987). This extensive policy has been dubbed 'Späth-Kapitalismus' (Späth-capitalism) and has led to criticism of its interventionist nature by former FDP federal economics minister Count Lambsdorff (Kloten, 1987, p. 850). Baden-Württemberg, and similarly Bavaria, have used these policy instruments to try and attract the new technologies to the areas around Stuttgart and Munich respectively.

In North Germany, similar policies have come to be developed but only as a response as the crises in shipbuilding, steel, shipping and fisheries have developed. These crises have tended to give the states something of a negative image: the dynamics of growth in the South seem to overshadow continuing strengths in the North. For the northern states, especially Bremen, attempts to facilitate restructuring of declining industries reduce the funds available for promoting new technology. In addition, the four states of Bremen, Hamburg, Lower Saxony and Schleswig-Holstein have proved unable to work together in an effective manner to tackle some of their common problems, for instance in shipbuilding. Instead there has even been a kind of competition among these Länder for inward investment. For example, grants have been available to enable industrial relocation in Schleswig-Holstein, which skirts the northern side of Hamburg. Firms have opted to take these grants and locate just outside the city state. This then represent a loss of business tax revenue to Hamburg. The nature of the federal system thus introduces distortions, underpinned by party-political differences between the four Länder on the nature of policy. It also raises questions about the viability of the city states.

## Länder, Bund and the EC

Ever since the European Coal and Steel Community came into being in 1952 the Länder have been affected by European integration (Bulmer, 1986, Chapters 5 and 6; Bulmer and Paterson, 1987, Chapter 8). Initially the impact was restricted but it was already recognised that European integration would increasingly affect Länder interests. This concern was never a matter of objection, for European integration received wide support in the FRG as the means to international rehabilitation (see Chapter 11). The Länder also proved to be strong supporters and found the aspirations to European federalism attractive. With the 1957 Treaties of Rome establishing wider objectives, more numerous Länder responsibilities were potentially affected: educational and vocational training, transport policy and taxation, for example. Nevertheless, the Länder remained supporters of integration. In fact, the stagnation of the EC in the 1960s meant the actual – as opposed to the potential – clash of interests was contained. Moreover, the Länder governments had ensured the existence of a consultation procedure via the Bundesrat when they ratified the Rome treaties. In addition, they had created, in 1959, the post of Länder Observer, whose task was to keep them informed of important EC developments.

This system functioned fairly satisfactorily until the 1970s. By this time the Länder had become more sensitive to intrusions upon their competences. Not only had they developed vested interests over the post-war period but they had become concerned about the loss of powers more generally to the Bund. In consequence, there was a less positive response to the expansion of EC activities in the 1970s, such as into regional policy. In the case of the EC's developing environmental legislation, the Länder even questioned its constitutional authority.

The problem at this time centred on the fact that the Länder were dependent upon the Bund's goodwill if they were to be able to influence EC legislation. The Bund made full use of the Basic Law, Article 73, assigning it exclusive responsibility for foreign relations. Nevertheless, the federal government was heavily dependent on the Länder in two ways. It often lacked the necessary expertise on draft EC legislation. It also was dependent on the Länder to implement EC policy. Hence, in practice there was a need to develop Bund-

Länder intergovernmental relations, of the type discussed above, to facilitate smooth running. From the mid-1970s the Länder sought a more formalised system of coordination with the federal government. This led to the creation of a new Bund-Länder procedure in 1980, alongside the existing use of the Bundesrat. The new channel of policy-making proved, however, to be unsatisfactory to the Länder because it came into play only on the rare occasions when their (very few) *exclusive* legislative powers were affected by EC proposals.

Matters came to a head during the 1980s. The catalytic factor was the Single European Act (SEA), signed by EC foreign ministers in February 1986. It represented the first comprehensive revision of the EC treaties, and the formal transfer to the EC of areas of their authority caused great resentment to the Länder, particularly as the package had been negotiated by the Bonn Foreign Office. The SPD–governed states and CSU–governed Bavaria raised consider-able opposition to the constitutional impact of the SEA, with some support from the other states as well. The ultimate sanction available would have been to refuse ratification in the Bundesrat, an act which would have been very dramatic because it would have torpedoed the SEA completely. In the event the Länder won the right to a more secure and wide-ranging form of Bund-Länder coordination on Euro-pean policy. This was finally agreed in December 1987.

What was the substance of Länder concern? The EC was regarded as undermining the subsidiarity principle of the Basic Law; the EC was thus increasing the centralisation of power onto the Bund. The policy areas potentially most affected were education and culture, broadcasting, agriculture, regional policy, consumer protection and research policy. From this catalogue it can be seen that the EC is increasingly intruding upon Länder competences and, in doing so, causing the federal government's involvement as an intermediary and upsetting the Bund-Länder balance into the bargain.

For its part, the Bund has been concerned at the increasing number of Länder offices being set up in Brussels. Although these are part of the (competing) policies for inward investment, there is concern that they – along with the above new consultation procedure – may weaken the federal government's efforts to have a coherent European policy (see Chapter 11).

In the case of Länder links with the EC, further effects of inter-national interdependence may be observed. The EC's widening areas of responsibility have come about largely as a response to inter-national events. Its involvement in broadcasting and research policy are a reflection of the inadequacy of *national* policies. Efforts to create a single EC market able to compete with the United States and Japan will have an effect on other areas, such as consumer protection or public procurement.

## The Future of German Federalism

The idea of a federal system is to keep government at the closest level to the population, while assuring an efficient allocation of resources. The tension between decentralisation and efficiency has been seen as a critical one in the evolution of West German federalism. The cyclical development of the international economy, technological change, the new international division of labour, regional export dependence, protectionism and subsidies: all these issues appear beyond the control of nation states. It is therefore small wonder if serious challenges are presented for the Länder.

The 1950s and 1960s witnessed a clear centralisation of powers in the West German federal system. The introduction of 'cooperative federalism' from the end of the 1960s provided a new framework of Bund-Länder interdependence to cope with international developments. It slowed down the process of centralisation but regional and local democratic accountability was not promoted. Indeed, the dense network of intergovernmental relations reduced democratic control at both levels of government. The use of the Bundesrat, during the period 1969–82, as an instrument of party-political conflict (in addition to its other functions) may have given vent to the suppressed democracy of cooperative federalism but, in some ways, the end-result was the same. Just as intergovernmental relations tended to obstruct policy innovation, so party politics did via the Bundesrat.

When Chancellor Kohl came to power in 1982, he brought into his coalition some of the politicians who had been important actors in the Bundesrat, for example Herr Stoltenberg, the former minister-president of Schleswig-Holstein, who became finance minister in Bonn. It is not surprising, therefore, that an improvement of Bund-Länder relations was on Kohl's agenda (Klatt, 1986). This was to occur not only through closer political relations but also by a reduced federal role in intergovernmental relations. The federal government even disengaged from some policy areas, for example certain educational grants. Another measure of goodwill was the creation of a minister of state responsible for federal issues, located in the Chancellor's Office.

However, the aspirations of the Kohl government have not been fulfilled. There has been discontent among the Länder about financial issues resulting from the federal government's wish to cut its expenditure. These tensions have been quite pronounced even with the CDU–governed Länder, especially Lower Saxony. There have been problems over agricultural structural policy (an effect of EC policy changes) and tax reform (designed to increase national economic efficiency). Further, the decline of the German steel sector, itself the result of international developments (and with the EC involved), has led to North Rhine-Westphalia seeking federal aid. On matters such as these, the Länder governments act as powerful regional lobby groups. On top of this, the SEA heightened tensions still further.

A common feature, therefore, of much of the shift in federal policy responsibilities has been the driving force of internationalisation. For a state such as the FRG, with its commitment to liberal trade and European integration, its interest in special relations with the Eastern bloc and a security dependence on the United States, it is simply not an option to resist this development. And West German society is prepared to accept this situation, because of its homogeneous and relatively centralised nature. Since federalism is constitutionally non-negotiable (and underpinned by the vested interests of political elites), it has thus to be seen to deliver satisfactory solutions to the (predominantly international) problems of the day. It is the search for a balance between these conflicting circumstances that is the essence of territorial government in contemporary West Germany.

# 4

# Political Leadership

**GORDON SMITH**

Throughout the life of the Federal Republic the ability of the political system to produce competent leaders has been of critical importance. For a people initially so uncertain about themselves and their future, it is doubtful whether a stable democratic system could have evolved without adequate leadership; nor over the years would the present high level of popular attachment to the parliamentary republic have been built up. We need only to make the contrast with the Weimar Republic: its instability and the low esteem accorded to the parliamentary regime were both associated with mediocre political leadership. Earlier, Max Weber, in analysing the defects of Imperial Germany, saw its principal weakness in the failure to provide for adequate political recruitment and the means by which effective political direction could be ensured (Beetham, 1974).

How has this 'historical problem' been overcome in the Federal Republic? To answer this question we have to examine the structural conditions – the opportunities and constraints – that are particularly important in the West German case. It is also necessary to look at the various 'dimensions' along which leadership can be assessed. Neither of these aspects, however, can properly be assessed without at the same time paying attention to the contributions of the prominent leaders – the capabilities and styles of successive federal chancellors. First, what helps decide which politicians emerge as leaders within the major parties?

## Leadership Selection

Particularly in West Germany the federal structure of the state has had a pervasive influence on the process of political recruitment, and it also sets the terms on which political leadership is exercised. The federal system both shapes the organisation of the parties and affects the distribution of power and loyalties within them. Thus in addition to the party as a national organisation and its parliamentary grouping, the *Fraktion*, there is a third element: the party organisation within each of the Länder. With the parties in the Länder responsible for a wide range of government functions, and their governments powerfully represented in the Bundesrat, the Länder parties are far from being subordinate offshoots of the national party. This territorial infrastructure makes political careers heavily dependent on securing a stronghold in one or other of the Länder.

Those who choose to make their career solely in Land politics – as party leader and possibly as minister-president – can become important national figures and will anyway be influential within the party's national organisation. A contemporary example is Lothar Späth, the popular minister-president and CDU party leader in Baden-Württemberg; he has in fact been widely mentioned as a possible successor to Helmut Kohl as chancellor, even though he has had no federal ministerial experience. Similarly, Oskar Lafontaine, having won power for the SPD in the Saarland, has emerged as a likely chancellor candidate for the party. By itself, service in the Bundestag is no special recommendation, whereas in Britain several years as an MP is normally a precondition for further advancement.

The career patterns of most chancellors and chancellor candidates confirms this view. Adenauer belongs in a category of his own, since he was a product of Imperial Germany and the Weimar Republic. Ludwig Erhard was also an exception, but the fact that he achieved his rise to success as an economic technocrat meant that he did not move up through the ranks in Land politics, and this lack of a secure party base helps to explain the suddenness of his downfall. Others such as Kiesinger (chancellor during the Grand Coalition and previously minister-president of Baden-Württemberg), Brandt (who made his name as ruling mayor of West Berlin), and Schmidt (who first served in the Bundestag, but subsequently achieved fame in Hamburg) all show a typical progression for the principal leaders. Kohl also exemplifies the pattern. Despite his chequered progress to the top, Kohl was able to combine his hold over the Rhineland-Palatinate (he had become minister-president in 1969) with a secure place in the CDU's national organisation (see 'Party Management' below). The same applies to chancellor candidates: Strauss in 1980

(CSU leader and minister-president of Bavaria); Hans-Jochen Vogel in 1983 (former mayor of Munich and later SPD leader in Berlin); Johannes Rau in 1987 (SPD minister-president of North Rhine-Westphalia). Rainer Barzel, the CDU chancellor candidate in 1972 was exceptional in having come up through the parliamentary ranks. Significantly, however, he was quickly thrust aside as party leader when he failed to oust Chancellor Brandt.

Success in Land politics has two aspects. One is that the ability to manage the Land party and to win elections is an important qualification for national leadership. Prominence in the Bundestag is not a guide. The Bundestag is anyway not the sole focus of political life, and a member may be there thanks to having a sufficiently high place on the party list rather than through enjoying popular support. Nor are federal ministers necessarily any better placed, especially if they are appointed because of their expertise in a particular field and also lack significant territorial following. The present minister for the environment (appointed in 1987), Klaus Töpfer, is a case in point. He was previously a university professor in environmental science before becoming environment minister in the Rhineland-Palatinate. It is noteworthy that he has sought to strengthen his position by being adopted by the Saarland CDU to contest the next Land election against the serving minister-president, Lafontaine. The second aspect of success in Land politics is that a party leader can deal on equal terms with powerful leaders in the other Länder. These relationships and alliances are important in determining the direction the party takes, and chancellors have to be wary of antagonising the 'party barons' in the Länder.

## The Adenauer Model

A complicating factor in comparing West German chancellors is that they appear to have had very little in common. The starkest contrast is between the 'visionary' Willy Brandt and the present incumbent, the 'pedestrian' Helmut Kohl. Again, the forceful managerial style of Helmut Schmidt can be set against the uncertain hold of Ludwig Erhard – their only shared characteristic perhaps was that of being 'charismatic losers' (Wildenmann, 1986). A unifying link is that they all stand in the long shadow of Konrad Adenauer. He continues to provide a yardstick of comparison, but how relevant is the early development of the Federal Republic to the present time?

Adenauer's exceptional tenure of office, from 1949 until 1963, is indelibly stamped as the era of so-called 'chancellor democracy' (Ridley, 1966), a term used more in criticism than in approval.

Literally, it stands opposed to the ideals of parliamentary democracy, but the opposition should not be exaggerated, since at no stage under Adenauer were parliamentary powers subverted. Instead, his dominance was expressed in three main ways: his control over the governing CDU, his overtowering presence as head of government, and his relative freedom from pressures exerted by coalition partners. This dominance, together with the sustained economic recovery and a largely successful foreign policy, added a further ingredient to chancellor democracy: elections were contested in terms of support for Adenauer, a form of plebiscitary approval, with the CDU the way for voters to express their support.

To treat this version of chancellor democracy as a relevant model for others to follow would be in wrong several ways. Both the conditions in which political leadership is exercised and the standards of judgement that are applied to it are now substantially different. Adenauer profited from the fact that in its formative period the CDU was hardly a cohesive party; to a large extent the CDU depended on Adenauer's successes for it to become welded into a permanent national force. The party system has also changed fundamentally since the 1950s in making coalition government inescapable, a dependence that has increased during the 1980s as the two major parties have lost electoral support. Finally, we have to question whether Adenauer's single-minded pursuit of his objectives and his domineering style would still be acceptable to the parties as well as to the electorate; in contemporary Germany there is a different understanding of democracy in contrast to the passivity that marked political culture during the Adenauer years.

On all these grounds it seems that continuing reference to the outworn model of chancellor democracy only clouds the issues that affect present-day leaders; its use misleadingly makes them appear deficient in one way or another. Yet there are also some good reasons for not abandoning the 'model' entirely. Thus, whatever else may have changed in the succeeding years, the constitutional structure of the republic has remained identical to its initial form – and precisely this form was thought to provide a chancellor with ample opportunity to exercise strong and decisive leadership. Another reason for not discarding the precedents set by Adenauer is that they help to establish a number of dimensions within each of which the performance of government leaders can be judged, and that is true whether or not Adenauer is regarded as having operated in special circumstances. What 'chancellor democracy' does give, therefore, is a useful framework for contemporary analysis besides also a guide to how leadership in the Federal Republic is developing.

## Constitutional Factors

A major concern of the Basic Law was to stabilise and strengthen the position of the chancellor in relation both to the parties and to the president. The downgrading of the presidency to a virtually titular head of state secured one objective, whilst there are a number of provisions that enhance the chancellor's position *vis-a-vis* the parties. The requirement for the formal election of the chancellor by the Bundestag for a four-year term (Article 63) and his premature dismissal only by means of the vote of constructive no-confidence (Article 67) – that is, by electing a new chancellor – has been a stabilising influence, even though the underlying reason for the long tenure of chancellors is to be found in the nature of the party system. Both Helmut Schmidt, 1974 until 1982, and Helmut Kohl, from 1982 and in all probability at least until the early 1990s, share with Adenauer the attributes of chancellor-longevity.

TABLE 4.1   *Chancellors and coalitions*

| Chancellor | Period | Years | Coalitions | Departure |
|---|---|---|---|---|
| Adenauer | 1949–1963 | 14 | CDU–CSU, FDP (and smaller parties)[1] | Resignation |
| Erhard | 1963–1966 | 3 | CDU–CSU, FDP | Resignation |
| Kiesinger | 1966–1969 | 3 | CDU–CSU, SPD | Election Defeat |
| Brandt | 1969–1974 | 5 | SPD, FDP | Resignation |
| Schmidt | 1974–1982 | 8 | SPD, FDP | Bundestag defeat |
| Kohl | 1982– | (7) | CDU–CSU, FDP | |

Note:
1 The CDU–CSU had an absolute majority from 1957–1961.

Chancellors also enjoy constitutional backing in running the government; they have the sole right to appoint and dismiss ministers and are alone responsible to the Bundestag. Their authority is also enhanced by the power to determine the general guidelines of government policy, the *Richtlinienkompetenz*, although in fact this clause of the Basic Law (Article 65) was resurrected from the Weimar Constitution where it proved of little help to government leaders, and it is also qualified by the *Ressortprinzip* which gives individual ministers the power to run their own departments 'autonomously'. In this context the chief limitations a chancellor faces are political: his constitutional powers are weakened to the extent that a coalition party is able to exert pressure – by being able to modify or veto particular measures, by insisting on nominating its own ministers for specific posts, and ultimately by threatening to or actually withdrawing from the government. Against the backcloth of constitutional authority, the coalition constraint acts as a disturbing factor of varying intensity.

An important constitutional restriction on the chancellor is the barrier placed in the way of calling an early election; there is no equivalent of a British prime minister's ability to hold a 'snap' election. In the context of West German coalition politics the absence of the power of dissolution means that chancellors are denied a useful weapon to control a fractious coalition partner – as the FDP has often proved to be. The Basic Law (Article 68) stipulates that only when a government has been defeated on its own motion of confidence can the chancellor request the Federal President for a dissolution of the Bundestag. On the two occasions when this procedure has been used (Brandt in 1972 and Kohl in 1982) the government had first to engineer its own defeat, a cumbersome process, and one which also required the cooperation of the FDP (Irving and Paterson, 1983).

There are two other constitutional elements that have a potentially limiting effect on political leadership, at least in the sense of promoting a diffusion of authority. One is the power wielded by the Federal Constitutional Court which, through its right of interpreting the Basic Law, not only narrows the scope of government legislative competence but also serves as an alternative 'state symbol' divorced from the political realm. The other diffusing force relates to the federal structure of the state; quite apart from the competences of the individual Länder which restrict the power of the federal government, their direct representation in the Bundesrat gives them a special place in the legislative process, and unlike the position in the Bundestag where a chancellor can rely on majority support, the interests of the Länder do not necessarily coincide with those of the federal government even when the party composition of the Bundesrat is nominally similar to the line-up in the Bundestag.

This summary of the constitutional factors that in one way or another affect the position of the chancellor should make it evident that the Basic law does not at all guarantee the incumbent an easy exercise of power, and in many respects the constraints inherent in the various checks and balances outweigh the greater stability given to the chancellor in respect of the parties in the Bundestag. A conclusion might be that there never was much in the way of constitutional impetus behind the concept of chancellor democracy, but it would neglect the added status given to the chancellor in eliminating the president as a rival source of authority – particularly in the early years of the republic, this new concentration of authority benefited Adenauer.

## Dimensions of Political Leadership

There are four distinctive areas in which the success of chancellor can be evaluated, and together they supply the necessary *political* ingredients for a version of chancellor democracy to be practised:

- The chancellor and the electorate.
- Party management.
- Government and coalition coordination.
- Foreign policy.

None of these dimensions by itself constitutes a necessary condition for the success of a chancellor; nor is any one of them likely to prove a sufficient condition either. In other words, some kind of aggregation will make for a winning (or losing) combination. For Adenauer, the question of 'party management' scarcely arose in its modern form, since his early ascendancy in the newly-formed CDU – effectively before the Federal Republic came into being – and his domination over the party in the 1950s (Heidenheimer, 1960) ensured that the CDU became a kind of chancellor-election association, a *Kanzlerwahlverein*. This advantage, together with Adenauer's successes in the other directions, has to be contrasted with the much patchier record of his successors.

## The Chancellor and the Electorate

Electoral popularity, unless it can be consistently translated into votes for the chancellor's own party, is a dubious pointer to the long-term standing of a leader. By the same token, however, unpopularity with the electorate is not a decisive handicap as long as the party can retain governing power. Both propositions can be illustrated by the contrasting fortunes of Erhard, Schmidt and Kohl. For Erhard, the architect of Germany's 'economic miracle', the popular acclaim and his personal leaning to be a *Volkskanzler*, a people's chancellor, was amply confirmed by the CDU's advances in the 1965 election. Yet in the following year he was bundled out of office, partly at least because of a sudden loss of support shown by a single land election and worries about an economic recession. His supposed rapport with the electorate did not save him from the unrest within the CDU.

In the case of Chancellor Schmidt it is relevant to draw attention to the so-called 'chancellor-effect' – that is, the electoral bonus which a widely popular chancellor was thought to bring to the major governing party, as of course was the case for Adenauer in the 1950s, Erhard in 1965, and Brandt in 1972. But from the 1970s onwards this 'bonus' has disappeared. Helmut Schmidt was consistently favourably regarded by public opinion well outside of the ranks of SPD party supporters, and yet the party's share of the vote fell in 1976 and stagnated in 1980. There are three – compatible – explanations for this rather strange outcome. One is that voters make a distinction between the chancellor and his party; supporting one does not automatically imply supporting the other. A second reason is the wish not to see the FDP, the junior coalition partner, eliminated by falling foul of the '5 per cent clause'. A third reason, facilitated by the first two, is the increasing tendency for voters to think in terms of supporting a particular coalition – the social-liberal one in the case of Schmidt, rather than the SPD. This 'coalition mentality' also has a rational basis: voting for the FDP (aided by the device of ticket-splitting) signalled unease with tendencies within the SPD – for instance over defence issues – and voters thus saw the FDP as a desirable 'corrective'.

These various motivations leading to tactical voting are reinforced by a declining sense of party-identification which makes the popularity of a chancellor of uncertain value to his party. Both Erhard and Schmidt lost office in mid-term despite their previous success at an election. For Helmut Kohl the considerations are entirely different, since he has never had the pretensions to be a *Volkskanzler*, and he is regularly well down on popularity ratings. In some respects, too, he could in the past have been treated as a typical 'loser': as the CDU–CSU chancellor candidate in 1976, Kohl failed to dislodge the SPD–FDP coalition, and for the 1980 election he was replaced as chancellor candidate by Franz Josef Strauss. He was able to come to office in 1982 only because of the defection of the FDP from Schmidt's government, not by virtue of electoral choice. This catalogue was interrupted when Kohl succeeded in calling an early election in 1983 – precisely in order to win electoral backing and legitimacy for the new coalition. Yet although the CDU vote rose, the favourable result can be interpreted as just as much due to the disarray of the SPD and discontent among FDP supporters following their party's change of course as it was through any attraction exercised by Kohl. It may even be tempting to regard the CDU's confirmation in office in the 1987 election as happening *despite* the chancellor: his public image was poor, his leadership was uncertain, and he was not helped by some notable diplomatic gaffes – the likening of Gorbachev to Goebbels and the reference to the GDR as a 'concentration camp'. The CDU vote fell substantially, and again the switching of votes within the coalition parties was in evidence: the rise in support for the FDP can be seen as a corrective – this time as a reaction against right-wing tendencies within the CDU–CSU (Irving and Paterson, 1987; Smith, 1987).

From the rather disparate cases of Erhard, Schmidt and Kohl, it becomes apparent that the electoral component of a chancellor's leadership has been of declining significance. Although the appeal of a strong personality may upset the trend, with – say – a figure such as Oskar Lafontaine rallying wide support for the SPD, for the present it is more productive to concentrate on the other dimensions of political leadership, especially with the example of Kohl's chancellorship in mind.


## Party Management

A feature of the major West German parties is the dualistic structure of leadership that can be maintained: a party's serving chancellor or chancellor candidate is not also necessarily the party's leader. The practice has, however, varied considerably. Adenauer combined both roles. Moreover, he held on to the party leadership after ceasing to be chancellor in 1963. From the beginning of Erhard's term of office his authority was undermined within the party by Adenauer's hostility and machinations. By the time – early in 1966 – that Erhard did eventually succeed Adenauer as party leader it was too late for him to stamp his authority on the party, even if he had possessed the ability to do so.

The obvious inference is that it is preferable for a chancellor to combine both roles. Brandt, when he became chancellor in 1969, had already led the SPD for several years, but after he resigned as chancellor in 1974 in favour of Schmidt, Brandt retained the party leadership – in fact holding the post right up to 1987. It might be thought that Schmidt was from the beginning placed in a disadvantageous position, but it is arguable that as party leader he would have experienced far greater opposition from within the party at an early stage, and the functional division of authority between Brandt and Schmidt worked harmoniously enough until the early 1980s. Nevertheless, the effect of the division was to divorce Schmidt from the party and the sentiments within it, especially those that were strongly opposed to his defence policies (Paterson, 1981). His prized autonomy as chancellor ultimately led him to become increasingly isolated in the party, and that became quite evident once he lost the chancellorship.

In contrast to Schmidt, Helmut Kohl displays most qualities of capable party management. Unlike Brandt or Schmidt, he had held no federal ministerial post before becoming chancellor in 1982, but he had for many years worked assiduously within the CDU, first as leader of the party's youth-wing, later as minister-president of the Rhineland-Palatinate, and as long ago as 1970 he had contended for the CDU's chancellor candidature. His failure to win the 1976 election for the CDU did not lead to his political demise, since he still had a firm hold as party leader (since 1973) and from 1976 onwards combined this post with that of *Fraktionsvorsitzender* (leader of the parliamentary party) (Pridham, 1977). Once Kohl finally became chancellor, he had secured the important bases of power within the CDU, and his lack of federal ministerial experience was not a real handicap; moreover, his entrenched party position more than compensated for his lacklustre electoral attraction.

Kohl's steady way up through the CDU, securing alliances and points of power, is reflected in the importance he attaches to party management; above all it is seen in his assumed role of acting as an integrator of different viewpoints rather than a leader who pushes his preferred policy options. This style is possibly a prerequisite for a CDU leader (to a more limited extent it applies to the SPD as well), since he has to operate within the constraints that are inherent in the conception of a *Volkspartei* (people's party) (Smith, 1982). The diffused appeal of the *Volkspartei* requires the chancellor to settle on a policy-mix to satisfy disparate strands in his own party and the electorate at large. Kohl's self-confessed 'inductive' approach shows no particular orientation (Zundel, 1989): whether in the commitment to nuclear energy, reform of the Bundespost, extension of conscription, the resettling of ethnic Germans in the Federal Republic, limitations on the ability of unions to call selective strikes, pushing for the creation of an EC internal market. These were all measures that appealed selectively within the CDU.

Kohl has also proved adept at balancing the claims of the CDU in the Länder and those of the Bundestag *Fraktion* of the CDU. Nonetheless, he has perhaps been more successful in disposing of potential rivals than in arousing enthusiasm for his leadership in the party. As chancellor for several years, Kohl has come to rely on the advice of his numerous experts, and that is a potential cause of tension with the parliamentary party. Thus in 1988 his appointment of two technocratic 'outsiders' as ministers (Rupert Scholz, a legal expert, to the defence ministry and Ursula-Maria Lehr (a university professor) to the ministry for family affairs) led to rumblings of discontent in the *Fraktion*. Yet a West German head of government is also expected to maintain a certain distance from his own party, an aloofness that would not work in the British parliamentary system.

## Government and Coalition Coordination

That security of being party leader does not automatically lead to security for the chancellor is amply demonstrated in Brandt's case. So long as the momentum of his Ostpolitik lasted (from 1969 until after the 1972 election), the defects of his governing style were not apparent. That momentum was also reinforced by the perilously small Bundestag majority of the SPD–FDP coalition and by the sustained onslaught mounted by the CDU–CSU in opposition: the SPD and the FDP had to rally round the chancellor. Although the immediate cause of Brandt's resignation in 1974 was the unearthing of an East German spy on his personal staff, the scandal was in itself hardly a justification for Brandt to go. More to the point was the mounting dissatisfaction felt by leading people within the SPD: he had lost his grip on government and the direction of coalition cabinet. For Brandt, it was not the case that he lacked coordinative skills, but rather that the piecemeal process of domestic reforms and coalition haggling palled for him in comparison with the stimulation of pursuing the Ostpolitik.

Schmidt's pragmatic managerial style of governing provided a sharp antithesis, and his expertise in defence matters and in economic policy enabled him to keep a watchful eye on several departments. The onset, too, of the economic crises in the 1970s also involved Schmidt heavily in detailed decision-making. Schmidt dominated his cabinet in ways somewhat reminiscent of Adenauer, but the parallel is inexact, since Schmidt principally immersed himself in intermediate and short-range policies and decisions, coping with crises, whereas Adenauer's concerns were linked to his grander strategic objectives. For Adenauer, economic policy, safely left to Erhard, had little intrinsic interest, only – instrumentally – in strengthening the position of the Federal Republic.

Kohl falls into a different category, since his style is more collegial than managerial. He can claim no special expertise and has described himself as a 'generalist' – an unusual recommendation for a German politician – but he relies on numerous experts. Moreover, as with his predecessors, Kohl has at his disposal the considerable resources of the Chancellor's Office the *Kanzleramt*, as well as the *Presseamt* (Press Office), the former not only providing information and policy analysis but also serving as a means of coordination with the permanent heads of the various departments, whilst the latter is chiefly concerned with dissemination of the government's plans and achievements to a wider public. This apparatus at the service of the chancellor is ideally suited to Kohl's version of leadership which is consolidative rather than innovative.

Chancellors have to come to terms with the relative degree of autonomy ministers have in running their own departments. The constitutional support they have is reinforced by the presumption that they should have a special expertise relating to their ministerial responsibilities. This expectation narrows the field of choice in appointments made by the chancellor, and it also prevents him making extensive reshuffles in the cabinet: ministers tend to stay put. This immobility may make it difficult for a chancellor such as Kohl to stamp his authority on many aspects of government, and limits his ability to promote younger party loyalists.

A further complicating factor for all chancellors since 1961 has been the necessity to govern through a coalition, and for the CDU there is the additional problem of having to deal with the quasi-independent CSU. The strategic position in the party system occupied by the FDP in its ability to effect an alternation in government by switching between the CDU and the SPD gives the party a weight quite out of proportion to its parliamentary representation, and it means that the FDP has to be placated much more than would be the case if there were a wide range of coalition possibilities. The FDP is effectively able to nominate its own ministers and given the principle of 'autonomy', there is a sharp restriction on the chancellor's power. It also means that a second level of coordination is needed: regular meetings of the leading figures in the coalition to settle priorities and hammer out policy differences.

Essentially this format has remained unchanged since the FDP first went into coalition with the SPD in 1969, and when the FDP sided with the CDU in 1982 three of its four ministers retained precisely the same posts they had held in the Schmidt government, but the fourth did not because of objections from the CSU. Significantly, it was the ministry of justice that was in contention, highlighting the differences between the FDP and the CSU on the broad issue of civil rights. The animosity between the two parties has been a major cause of tension within Kohl's government, although it has not materially affected the chancellor himself, and possibly he has also been able to play off one against the other. At all events, with the death of the CSU leader, Strauss, in 1988 a disruptive force for Kohl has been removed, so that the relationship between CDU and CSU is less problematic than at any time since the late 1960s.

As well as the particular issues that weaken coalition cohesion, there is the constant need of the FDP to maintain its own profile to the electorate; it makes demonstrative policy gestures that may weaken a chancellor's authority. The FDP thus feels no compunction in airing cabinet disagreements or trumpeting concessions that it has been able to win. Yet the present distribution of party strength means that the FDP has 'nowhere else to go', unlike the situation in 1982; in consequence, Kohl is in a far stronger position than Schmidt was: the FDP cannot press its demands too far, unless (at the next federal election due at the end of 1990) the SPD recovers sufficiently to make a coalition with it feasible. If it does not, then Kohl could eventually match Adenauer's long reign.

## Foreign Policy

There are two reasons for treating the broad area of foreign policy as of special importance in evaluating the role of West German chancellors (see Chapter 10). (Why domestic policies are less suitable for this purpose will be discussed subsequently.) Firstly, it is a field that has been of special concern to successive chancellors. In the present context 'foreign policy' has to be understood in its wider sense, that is, also to include relations with the European Community, inner-German relations – the *Deutschlandpolitik* – as well as aspects of defence policy, since particularly for the Federal Republic these matters closely relate to foreign policy questions. The second reason is bound up with the whole historical development of the republic since its foundation: the search for security, the need for international rehabilitation, and the problem of the division of Germany have all in one way or another been dominant themes over the past forty years.

A primary distinction needs to be made between those chancellors who have strong foreign policy objectives and have pursued them in an imperative manner, and those who have been content to maintain the status quo or take limited initiatives. Adenauer and Brandt belong in the first group and Erhard, Schmidt and Kohl in the second. This may seem a somewhat unfair allocation, since much depends on the international situation at the time. Nonetheless, there is a sense in which both Adenauer and Brandt thought in terms of a 'grand design' whereas the others emerge as 'managers'. Helmut Schmidt is a partial exception: he has, after all, been credited as the originator of NATO's momentous 'twin-track' decision which ultimately led to the agreement on nuclear weapons reduction, and he was also the moving spirit in the creation of the European Monetary System (EMS). Both were to prove substantial contributions, and Schmidt also promoted the international status of the Federal Republic.

A major variable in the foreign policy dimension is the extent to which a chancellor is free to determine for himself what initiatives should be taken. Adenauer was exceptionally fortunate in this respect, since at least until 1961 he was virtually able to decide the lines of foreign policy without constraints from a coalition partner or from his own party.

However, since the beginning of Brandt's term of office, the FDP has permanently occupied the foreign ministry. In fact, this limitation did not restrict Brandt, since the mainstay of the SPD–FDP coalition formed in 1969 was the agreement on the broad thrust of the Ostpolitik initiative, and in its successful conclusion Brandt emerged as a European statesman on a par with Adenauer.

Subsequently, a different pattern has been evident. The FDP has come to believe that it has the freehold of the foreign ministry, and the present incumbent, Hans-Dietrich Genscher, has held the position continuously since 1974. Significantly, Schmidt made his mark in areas where he had special qualifications (defence, economics) and which concerned matters not the preserve of the foreign ministry.

Helmut Kohl has a double handicap: his lack of any special expertise has already been mentioned, and additionally he 'inherited' the long-serving Genscher from Schmidt's government. Whilst it would be incorrect to see the FDP as following an independent foreign policy line, the term 'Genscherism' has been coined to indicate a particular slant: an emphasis on an understanding with the Soviet Union and a rediscovery of *Mitteleuropa* (central Europe). In these circumstances Kohl appears to have taken a secondary role. Genscher has been in the driving-seat as far as the Ostpolitik was concerned (not least because of Kohl's ill-advised comment about Gorbachev), and Strauss busied himself in acting as a kind of unofficial foreign minister for the CSU. Kohl has, however, had bouts of activism in EC matters and in relationships with the GDR, but the normalisation that has taken place between the two states reflects more the basic changes that have occurred in the attitudes of the CDU and does not permit Kohl to take the credit for taking the Federal Republic on some new course.

## Evaluating Chancellors

This review of the separate dimensions in which the performance of the different chancellors can be assessed will have made it clear that direct comparison of their overall stature is difficult. Certainly, on most counts Adenauer stands out, although this judgement applies only at the latest until 1961; by then the CDU was becoming increasingly assertive, the election of that year was a severe reverse for the party, in 1961, too, the erection of the Berlin Wall revealed the failure of Adenauer's 'policy of strength'.

For all of Adenauer's successors the picture is much more mixed, with some interesting contrasts, and there is a marked correlation between performance and personal characteristics: individual personality relates to electoral attractiveness; organisational skills lead to successful party management and government coordination; a strong vision equates with a 'grand design' in foreign policy. What Kohl may lack in 'personality' and 'vision' is thus counterbalanced by his considerable organisational skills. Whether that is a recommendation for political leadership or should rather be treated as a guide to a chancellor's powers of survival is another matter. In the final analysis Kohl's survival depends on his ability to hold the CDU *electorate* together; success in party organisation is not enough.

Events in the early part of 1989 indicated that Kohl could not staunch the losses in support. Defeat for the ruling CDU in Berlin (January) and in the March local elections in Hesse, entailing the loss of Frankfurt, set the CDU in disarray. The results were seen within the party to be caused by Kohl's lack of firm direction, and the general regard for the chancellor sank to new low levels.

In a desperate attempt to restore his and the CDU's fortunes in advance of the federal election due in 1990, Kohl took a number of radical steps: a cabinet shake-up (including the dismissal of the defence minister, Scholz), abandonment of the unpopular withholding tax on interest payments, and cancelling the planned increase in length of military-service conscription (15 to 18 months). Most significant was the attempt by Kohl to secure a reversal of NATO policy on the modernisation of tactical nuclear weapons, despite the Federal Republic being a party to the decision. These changes in policy – although they accurately reflected the trend of public opinion – were widely regarded as electioneering, rather than showing Kohl's power of political leadership.

A further complication is evident in comparing the performance of chancellors in the realm of domestic politics. One criterion is that of policy innovation, the setting of new objectives for society or seeking its restructuring. Yet it is difficult to point to examples of such innovatory leadership in the Federal Republic. One obvious exception was adoption of the philosophy of the 'social market economy' by the CDU under Adenauer, although the main outlines were already evident before 1949 with the implementation of Erhard's currency reform in 1948. For its part, the SPD set its face against radical change with the adoption of the Godesberg Programme in 1959, and later when the party was in power under Brandt and Schmidt the party's programme gave no real basis for new departures.

Leaders have supplied the rhetoric. Brandt spoke of 'daring more democracy' in the Federal Republic, and Kohl promised that the return of the CDU to office in 1982 signalled the beginning of '*die Wende*' a fundamental change of course affecting both society and the economy. Yet neither chancellor was able to deliver on these promises. Two kinds of explanation can be offered. One refers to the constitutional and political constraints that a 'reforming' chancellor encounters. In practice, reforms have to be made by securing a wide consensus, since social interests are expressed through a variety of institutions, and changes have to be made incrementally.

The second kind of explanation points to the terms on which the Federal Republic has developed. Dahrendorf has applied the concept of 'strategic change', arguing that such change occurred in the formative period under Adenauer, both in foreign policy (alignment with the West) and domestically (the social market economy). Since then the institutional structures have become increasingly rigid, with the result that the scope for political leaders to initiate radical change is more restricted. The second explanation dovetails with the first.

An open question is whether – and if so in what respects – basic innovations are desirable in the Federal Republic. Even if innovatory leadership is difficult, it can be argued that this need not prevent the exercise of a decisive *reactive* leadership, as for instance was shown by Schmidt in his response to the upsurge of terrorism in the late 1970s. In a similar vein, it can be argued that Chancellor Kohl, in effectively changing West Germany's security orientations away from NATO's established position in a quite fundamental sense, was precisely taking a reactive course: the fear of losing office was the trigger, not the implementation of a guiding idea. Nevertheless, whatever the motives, Kohl's reaction was innovative.

Innovatory policies can be fashioned on a piecemeal basis, and an incremental process can help to foster a wide consensus, as the growing awareness of the ecological crisis within the parties and the general public illustrates. In this form of innovation it seems sufficient if the parties are responsive to wider opinion and if the chancellor is decisive enough to establish firm priorities.

This kind of leadership may call for the capabilities of a chancellor such as Kohl rather than those of an Adenauer-like figure. Unlike any of his predecessors, Kohl is a typical product of the form of party democracy and the *Parteienstaat* (Dyson, 1982c) that has evolved in the Federal Republic and knows how to work within the constraints it imposes. Yet there is also room for doubt as to whether the fixed pattern of bargaining and decision-making relationships – strongly institutionalised as well as being diffused throughout the federal system – is not in danger of weakening political leadership. Up to the present the Federal Republic has been well served by these structures and a supportive political culture. It remains to be seen if in the future chancellors will find them too inflexible.

# PART TWO

# Politics and Society

# 5

# Political Ideology

**PETER PULZER**

## The Revival of Ideological Conflict

Writing an introduction to Walter Laqueur's history of the German Youth Movement in 1962, Richard Crossman, future Labour cabinet minister and himself no mean ideologue, observed:

> There are many complaints that youth in the Federal Republic is material-istic, egotistical and unwilling to accept any civic or political responsibilit-ies. In themselves these characteristics are unattractive. But in the case of Germany they may well be a stage on the road to normality. A healthy democracy is impossible without a healthy scepticism, constantly corroding the adulation of leaders and uncritical acceptance of ideology on which totalitarian rule depends (Laqueur, 1962, p. xxii).

It reminded one of the mythical German student of the reconstruc-tion period who, asked which two books had influenced him most, replied: his father's cheque book and his mother's cookery book. Three years later a seminal book, Ralf Dahrendorf's *Society and Democracy in Germany*, argued that the road to normality had been largely completed. Thanks to the pattern of post-war economic development, thanks also to Hitler's destruction of many of the traditional elites, Germans had abandoned their 'special path', the *Sonderweg* that had diverted them from evolving as a normal liberal society. They had for the first time become a 'modern' polity in which free, politically mature individuals acted confidently and rationally:

> The chances of liberal democracy in a German society have never been as great as they are in the German Federal Republic . . . authoritarianism of the traditional kind has become impossible in German society (Dahren-dorf, 1968, pp. 442, 438).

Scarcely was the ink dry on this verdict than its opposite was forcibly asserted. Ideological offensives generally arise out of a combination of causes. They need a favourable intellectual conjuncture: the exhaustion of an older set of ideas, the retirement of a generation of opinion-leaders, perhaps an external impulse. They also need spectacular events to detonate public receptivity to what would otherwise remain obscure pamphlets or esoteric café debates. Only then can we speak of ideas whose time has come. The reply to Dahrendorf, in effect if not in intention, came in 1966 from Karl Jaspers, a distinguished philosopher and veteran nonconformist. The occasion was the prospect of a Great Coalition between Social and Christian Democrats and speculation that this, or another, government would pass emergency legislation to acquire special powers in the event of war or an international crisis. But this challenge to the complacency of his fellow-citizens, *Wohin treibt die Bundesrepublik? (Where is the Federal Republic drifting?)* was clearly the outcome of long reflection. For Jaspers, who remembered the Weimar Republic and the Empire, nothing of substance had changed since 1945. The Federal Republic's rulers, like their predecessors, wanted to exclude the citizen from the political process. An all-party government and the emergency laws would complete this exclusion:

> We see the possible path: from the party oligarchy to the authoritarian state; from the authoritarian state to dictatorship; from dictatorship to war (Jaspers, 1966, p. 174).

Jasper's denunciation of West German politics was not an expression of specific discontents. He did not simply complain that institutions failed to live up to the expectations placed in them, or that otherwise honourable politicians had pursued mistaken policies. On the contrary, though West Germany had a parliamentary form of government,

> The structure of our state rests on fear of the people, of distrust of the people. The distrust to which the people would in turn be obligated towards parties, government and politicians, does not manifest itself sufficiently or effectively (Jaspers, 1966, p. 167).

The critique is unqualified and unconditional. It was the first example of a new genre that was to become commonplace in the following twenty years, the *Totalkritik*, the fundamental rejection of everything the Federal Republic stands for:

> The Federal Republic has lost its way in a world of fantastic misconception . . . It has reached an impasse without exit. It can escape from it only if it turns round, comes to terms with its real position and bases its politics on foundations that are firm and not fictitious . . .

All politicians in the Federal Republic seem to be engaged in reciprocal deception. Of those who are aware of it, none dares to say so. They want to be collectively blind . . .

The turn-around of the Federal Republic's policies, whether in foreign or domestic policy, cannot come about on this or that special issue. If it is to be successful it must happen in its entirety (Jaspers, 1966, pp. 257–8).

In other words: Everything must change before anything can change.

*Totalkritik* is distinguished by style as well as substance. It is by definition ideological, since it presupposes an all-explanatory model of what is wrong and an all-encompassing model of what ought to be. Beyond that, it can cover an almost infinite range of utopias. Jasper's own was that of an idealised liberal democracy. But the apocalyptic tone and the all-or-nothing prescription were a common feature of the re-ideologisation of West German politics in the late 1960s.

The Great Coalition of 1966–69, which seemed to symbolise the ultimate stage in the post-war West German consensus, and the emergency legislation duly passed in 1968 (which did no more than transfer to the Federal government powers hitherto exercised by the allied military authorities) were not the only factors causing many to question the achievements of the post-war period. Some of these were peculiar to Germany, others world-wide. Some were directly political, others social. There were, for instance, the large-scale trials of concentration camp guards in Frankfurt in 1965, which publicised in detail what many had only vaguely known, and which added to the distrust and suspicions that the post-war generation had of their parents. Simultaneously there was a debate on suspending the statute of limitations as it applied to war crimes. There was the war in Vietnam, tacitly supported by the West German government, which changed the image of America for many: the great protector, the home of the New Deal and author of the Marshall Plan, became the great oppressor. There was the wave of the New Politics, the campus revolt that spread across the United States from Berkeley to Harvard, in response not only to the Vietnam war but to the sudden expansion of higher education. Universities doubled and tripled in size, without changing their structures or adapting to the needs of first-generation students who had not, like their predecessors, imbibed the traditional academic ethos from their families. This explosion was common to America and France, to Britain and Germany. But it was more intense in Germany, and the fall-out more extensive, because the inter-generational divide was deeper and post-war ideological vacuum was more in evidence.

## The Quality of Political Life

One did not have to accept Jasper's *Totalkritik* to appreciate that post-war Germany was somewhat defective in the quality of its political life. To be sure, Bonn was not Weimar, in the words of Fritz René Allemann's analysis (Allemann, 1956). Government was stable, cabinets did not collapse in crisis, there were no major parties determined to overthrow the system, no generals, judges or civil servants who were secretly – or openly – disloyal. Political violence was virtually unknown. But there were negative virtues. The men who had led Germans out of the rubble and ashes of Year Zero (1945) were foxes, not lions. Konrad Adenauer and Kurt Schumacher, Jakob Kaiser and Theodor Heuss were the generation that had failed to stop Hitler. Some of them resisted after 1933, some withdrew, some colluded. All were burnt children who knew what the fire was like. Their vision after 1945 was one of disaster-avoidance, not a new heaven and a new earth. Their task was to enable Germans to rejoin, step-by-step, the rest of the human race, above all to anchor as much of Germany as possible – and that in the end meant the British, American and French zones of occupation – in the West: by founding the Federal Republic in 1948–9, by joining first the European Coal and Steel Community (ECSC) in 1950, then NATO in 1955 and finally the Common Market in 1958.

The political consensus that emerged in these years was liberal-conservative: capitalist with a social conscience. Above all, it was anti-Communist. With the collapse of the Third Reich and the arrival of the Red Army on the Elbe, it was the present, not the past tyranny that posed the threat. It did so especially for the Churches which were, however undeservedly, the chief repositories of moral authority after 1945. They saw National Socialism not as a counter-revolutionary movement or a capitalist conspiracy, but as the perversion of secular and materialist ideas, a bastard child of the French Revolution. For Cardinal Frings, Archbishop of Cologne and one of the main patrons of a new, inter-confessional Christian Democratic Union, 'The enemy stands on the left, that is in the camp of the materialist *Weltanschauung* [World philosophy]' (Schmidt, 1987, p. 240).

Such a development was a grave disappointment to re-emergent forces of the left, who had assumed that they would be the heirs of any revulsion against the Third Reich and the beneficiaries of the proletarianisation of the German people after the collapse. Yet the left, too, were burnt children; they shared the new-born right's suspicion of popular sovereignty, or at least of their fellow-citizens' ability to exercise it. They, too, saw political life as St Augustine had done, in terms of the burden of Original Sin. It was not some sceptical Catholic conservative but Georg-August Zinn, Social Democratic Minister-President of Hesse, who told the Parliamentary Council in the debates on the Basic Law: 'We cannot afford to rely on the masses' (Merkl, 1963, p. 81). In any case, any Social Democrat hopes of a fruitful anti-Fascist alliance with the Communists were soon dashed by the forcible amalgamation of the two workers' parties in the Soviet zone and the rapid establishment of a single-party dictatorship there. They also, therefore, in the end committed themselves to a pro-Western orientation, even if not at first to its military implications. The ideological spectrum in the infant Federal Republic was thus further narrowed.

The early years of West German politics, both before and after the formation of the Federal Republic, were not free from political polarisation, whether on economic policy, church-state relations or foreign policy. Industrial relations were far from peaceful and in the mid-1950s there was a major confrontation on the question of German rearmament within the framework of Western integration. Petitions and mass demonstrations, supported by the trade unions and parts of the Evangelical Church under the slogan *Kampf gegen den Atomtod* (struggle against nuclear death) were the last great challenge to the consensus that Adenauer had set out to create. That consensus became complete in 1959 at the SPD's Bad Godesberg conference, at which the Social Democrats finally accepted the mixed economy, and, in 1960, military integration with the West. They abandoned Marxism as the sole inspiration of their programme, claiming to be rooted instead in Christian ethics, humanism and classical philosophy. Practice had in any case preceded proclaimed principle for some years. In economic matters, consensus had, if anything, arrived earlier and gone further still. The unified post-war trade union federation, the DGB, supra-partisan but *de facto* closer to the Social Democrats than any other party, accepted, from the early 1950s onwards, a role of maximising its benefits from the re-established market economy. It fought for, and got, codetermination in heavy industry. But codetermination entailed the abandonment not only of nationalisation but of the class struggle. Indeed labour law imposes on works councils the obligation to maintain industrial peace (*Friedenspflicht*) (Markovits, 1986, pp. 40, 44).

## The Demand for Democratisation

It was this farewell to conflict, which in any case corresponded with deep-seated German desires for harmony in state and society, that most disturbed the new generation of critics. They saw a Germany that continued to be divided between rulers and ruled, between the few who decided and the many who accepted. Little seemed to have changed since Kurt Tucholsky had asserted in the 1920s that it was the ambition of every German to sit behind a counter and the fate of every German to stand in front of one. The watchword of all critics, whether radical or reformist, was therefore 'democratisation'. For Willy Brandt, leader of the SPD, democracy needed 'to embrace the whole of social life' (Brandt, 1969). The social philosopher Jürgen Habermas, chief mentor but also critic of the new radical generation, defined 'the democratic form of will-formation' even more explicitly: it would enable decisions 'to derive from a consensus achieved in a discussion without domination' (Habermas, 1969, p. 127). When Brandt became Chancellor in September 1969 he announced that, 'We are not at the end of our democracy, we are only just beginning' (von Beyme, 1979, p. 281). What all the critics had in common was the feeling that even if German constitutional life had now been democratised, German society had not been. What such democratisation should consist of, and what it would look like when the process was complete, was a matter on which there was a wide range of views. And even where there was agreement on ends, there was disagreement, and often conflict, on means.

The demand for democratisation had three basic components. Firstly, the creation of the 'mature citizen' (*mündiger Bürger*), aware of rights and no longer deferential towards authority. Secondly, the creation of equality of opportunity, especially through educational reforms. Thirdly, the creation of greater tolerance for nonconformity and of a greater variety of 'social spaces', in which different life-styles could flourish. All of these any conscientious, liberal-minded person could agree with; all of it was consistent with the existing political order, as defined by the Basic Law. It was the realisation of at least some of these objectives that the Brandt government had in mind when the new Chancellor told his fellow-citizens to lose their fear of experimentation – a universally understood allusion to the CDU's 1950s election slogan: 'No experiments'.

Some democratisers, however, wanted to go a great deal further. For them, the personal and collective freedoms that went with man's self-determination could not be realised within the existing economic order: there could be no emancipation without the transformation, or indeed destruction, of the existing distribution of wealth and power. This presupposed both a radical critique of the existing state of affairs and a blueprint for the post-revolutionary order: in other words, a re-ideologisation of politics, for without the ideological gospel there was no chance of raising the consciousness of those who were to carry out the transformation. Democratisation meant *knowing why* one needed to democratise. This call adopted the tone, if not the content, of Jasper's *Totalkritik*.

In one form or another, the radical democratisers were Marxists. The revival of Marxism was the most important event in the ideological history of the Federal Republic in the late 1960s. Few of the Marxists of this period were orthodox. They disliked, and in many cases strongly opposed, the Communist regimes of Eastern Europe; indeed, one of the main figures of the Marxist revival, Rudi Dutschke, had grown up and studied in the German Democratic Republic and had left for West Berlin to escape the stifling orthodoxy east of the Iron Curtain. In part they were inspired by the Italian heterodox Marxist Antonio Gramsci. In part they derived their ideas from the Frankfurt School, founded before the war by Theodor Adorno and Max Horkheimer and whose leading post-war German representative is Jürgen Habermas. Many of them were influenced by Herbert Marcuse, a member of the Frankfurt School who had stayed in America and who argued that under modern capitalism the proletariat could no longer be expected to initiate a revolution; that task now fell to intellectuals, in particular to intellectual youth – i.e., students (Marcuse, 1969). This idea was very attractive to students. *Totalkritik* and total protest, in so far as it came from the left, was largely the property of students broadly defined, ranging from the senior classes of *Gymnasien* (academically-orientated secondary schools) to the younger generation of graduates, mostly in the arts and the social sciences and concentrated in teaching, the media and the social service professions.

The incubation period of this protest was quite long; its eruption sudden. Marxism had never quite disappeared from the West German ideological map. The SPD's student wing SDS (Sozialistischer Deutscher Studentenbund, Socialist Students Federation) did not accept the parent body's disavowal of the ancestral creed and was suspended from the party in 1961. A handful of academics, of whom the most prominent was Wolfgang Abendroth of Marburg University, continued to proclaim themselves Marxists. But until the late 1960s they were a sect on the margin of public consciousness. What mobilised them was the coincidence of the Great Coalition, the emergency legislation and the war in Vietnam. What served as a flare to rally mass support was the killing of a student by the West Berlin police in 1967 in the wake of a demonstration against a visit by the Shah of Iran. Here was proof, for anyone that needed it, of the essential oppressiveness of the state, of the kid-glove fascism inherent in the existing order. As the scope of protest broadened and the causes of discontent multiplied, the bearers of the counter-politics became a movement, the extra-parliamentary opposition (*Ausserparlamentarische Opposition* – APO). In form and message it was the ancestor of all later protest movements in the Federal Republic. If many of its followers had no clear ideological motivation, its leaders, inspirers and – as time went on, its cadres – undoubtedly had one. This was especially true of one of the movement's main journals, *konkret*, edited for a time by Ulrike Meinhof. All subsequent ideological developments in the Federal Republic are either an extension of the APO or a reaction to it.

The APO was the extreme, on occasion violent, expression of a much wider desire for change and reform in the Federal Republic which is to be explained as much by the passage of time and of generations as by specific events. The change was to take the form of the liberalisation of many public institutions and social processes, but also of a revised attitude to the partition of Germany and the acceptance that the German Democratic Republic had come to stay. Symbolic of the shift in the climate of opinion was the changing of the guard in the Free Democratic Party (FDP), which had been excluded from power by the formation of the Great Coalition. Under the leadership of Walter Scheel it transformed itself from a socially conservative, rather nationalistic party of nineteenth century free enterprise and anti-clericalism into a vehicle for legal reform and non-collectivist middle-class social concern. The new programme was codified in the Freiburg Theses of 1971, which also talked of 'democratisation' (Flach *et al*, 1972, pp. 62–4); the FDP showed its inclination early by contributing to the election of the Social Democrat Gustav Heinemann to the Federal Presidency in the spring of 1969, and by the speed with which Free Democrats and Social Democrats formed a government when their parties gained a narrow majority in the Bundestag election of September 1969. This alternation, the first transfer of power in the history of the Federal Republic, was in itself symbolic. The reconstruction generation handed over to those who had been liberated by the successes of the early years.

Unlike many of the APO, the new Brandt government believed that change could and should take place within the framework of the existing order. What they shared with the APO, indeed what held together the whole spectrum of reformers and radicals, was a revived political optimism: a recovery of the belief that progress was possible, that happiness could be enhanced and evil diminished by rational human beings acting in concert. The most clearcut success of the Brandt government lay in foreign policy, with the revision and stabilisation of relations with Eastern Europe under the general cover of detente and known as Ostpolitik. Its domestic programme, like many schemes of reform, caused more frustration than satisfaction. Were the new freedoms to be for individuals or for groups? If only for individuals, as for instance in the liberalisation of the abortion laws, would this not leave the basis of society untouched? If for groups, especially those that determine how economic benefits are to be shared, as in the extension of industrial codetermination, is this any more than a redistribution of privileges, in this case in the direction of trade unions? Above all, what *is* the democratisation of society and how can it be implemented? Ambitious schemes to let everyone have a say in large educational institutions could – and did – lead either to chaos, or the domination of the participatory process by hard-line cliques. By the time Brandt was forced to resign in 1974 over an espionage scandal in his private office, the climate had once more begun to change, and faith in progress shaken.

## Doubt and Disillusionment

As before, the impulses were external as much as domestic. The oil shock of 1973 put an end to the assumption that continuing growth could supply a continuing expansion of social benefits. But even before that doubts had begun to arise about the wisdom of giving priority to economic growth, without regard to the social, cultural and environmental consequences of this. The Club of Rome's report, *Limits of Growth* (1972) had a more profound effect in Germany in this respect than in many other developed countries. Brandt's successor, Helmut Schmidt, with his emphasis on managerial competence, signalled not only a response to the harsher international economic climate but a changed style in political expectations and solutions. As the era of reform came to a close, new ideological alignments emerged in the Federal Republic. These can be divided into three broad categories. The first may be called limited liberal disillusionment, the second augmented radicalism, the third revived conservatism. None of these has one recognised spokesman or a distinctively coherent programme. They are, rather, clusters along a continuum. But most of those who have sought to influence West German opinion since the mid-1970s fit into one or other of these categories.

That the enthusiastically-launched reform programme of the Brandt government achieved less than it promised, or even than its most moderate adherents expected, was widely acknowledged. Typical of the disappointed utopian is Winfried Vogt who confessed:

The abolition of the domination of man over man has not advanced one step . . . indeed the demand itself nowadays has an almost embarrassing, romantic-pathetic sound (Habermas, 1979, pp. 381ff).

Perhaps more significant is the verdict of an eminent non-utopian, Ralf Dahrendorf, who saw a more profound ideological revolution at work than the rude awakening of a naive dreamer. What the oil shock, the declining growth rate in the capitalist world and the escalating costs of Brandt's reforms signified was the 'end of the Social Democratic century'. Social Democracy was, for him, not the programme of a party, but the theme of an epoch. Its components were growth, equality, work, rationality, state and internationalism. But what happens, he asked:

> when, for whatever reason, growth can, over a longer period, not be achieved at an adequate rate . . .

> when the maintenance of this level [of welfare] can no longer be maintained . . .

> when – to use Hannah Arendt's vocabulary – a society based on work runs out of work . . .

> when entirely new attitudes gain ground, the return of the sacred, perhaps, or a new social ethic, let alone fear . . .

> when people's hopes turn away from the state, because it is no longer seen as benevolent but as an expensive failure . . .

> . . . when, in place of hopes in international co-operation, a reversed view in the direction of smaller units predominates? (Dahrendorf, 1983, pp. 16–24).

All of Dahrendorf's questions have proved timely, though the answers to them have not necessarily been: 'social democracy comes to an end'. The policies and priorities of Helmut Schmidt showed the limits that social democracy had reached, but also how firmly it remained entrenched. True, beating inflation took priority over maintaining full employment and the expansion of the welfare state came to a halt. But the role of the state as adjudicator of social claims and provider of safety nets has remained in West Germany, even with the departure of the SPD from office – certainly in comparison with some other Western countries. Nevertheless, even if there was not a reversal of policy, a *Wende*, as Germans like to call it, there was a change of emphasis; an end, if not of the social democratic century, then of progressivist euphoria, of that faith in the ability of politicians to increase human happiness that marked the year 1969.

## The Environment, Terror and Peace

Beside this liberal disillusionment there arose an augmented radical-ism. Some of the protest of the late 1960s had been absorbed by the SPD and the FDP and this had been one of Brandt's main aims. But the potential remained, as did the habit and style of *Totalkritik*. What disappeared was the faith in progress. As the theme of protest moved from the emergency legislation and the Vietnam war to the environment and the arms race, as the student-dominated Marxist wave of protest ebbed, a mood of despair and the language of the apocalypse took over. The temporal coincidence of the Club of Rome's report and the oil shock reinforced the anti-capitalist sus-picions of the protesters. Not only was capitalism threatening the very future of the universe, it was not even any longer capable of delivering on its own terms. As early as 1972 the growing number of local, *ad hoc* environmental citizens' groups formed themselves into a national federation, the BBU (*Bundesverband Bürgerinitia-tiven Umweltschutz*, Association of Citizens' Groups for Environ-mental Protection). Some of its leaders were, or became, prominent in the SPD, though in the main the new body was the ancestor of the Green Party. Its ideologues, whether they leaned to the left or the right, shared a sense of imminent doom. For the ecologist Her-bert Gruhl, who came from the CDU:

> The total war of man against the earth is in its last phase . . . at the end there will be the fastest possible nothing for the greatest possible number (Gruhl, 1975, p. 219).

Erhard Eppler, the former acting president of the lay assembly of the German Evangelical Church and for many years chairman of the SPD in Baden-Württemberg, saw a 'historical caesura in the second half of the 1970's':

> Mankind has arrived at frontiers of which it either knew nothing, or did not want to know anything in the two preceding centuries (Eppler, 1979, p. 9).

It was a long way from Rudi Dutschke's conviction of 1967 that mankind had never been closer to fulfilling the dream of the Garden of Eden. (Dutschke, 1980, p. 13).

Though the mood of the *Totalkritiker* had changed, their prescrip-tion did not. They were guided, then as earlier, by Hegel's obser-vation that once the realm of the imagination was revolutionised, the real world would not be able to resist for long. What was needed was a *Bewusstseinswandel*, a transformation of the imagination, and only those who were free from the false consciousness that informed all defenders of the existing order could show a misled public the way. Just as Rudi Dutschke claimed to have begun 'breaking through his false consciousness . . . by our enlightenment, by our provocations and mass actions' (Bergmann *et al.*, 1968, p. 89), so the celebrated fantasy fiction writer Michael Ende – a German Tolkien – insisted that reacting to catastrophe required:

> . . . an entirely new form of consciousness, that is something we must all begin to learn . . . We must all, whether we want to or not, learn to think prophetically (Eppler, *et al.*, 1982, p.70)

and Eppler echoed, 'I get the impression that many politicians live in a world that no longer exists' (Eppler, *et al.*, 1982, p. 84).

While many graduates of the protest generation turned to apocalyptic words, some turned to apocalyptic deeds. One of the children of the age of political re-awakening and its disappointments was terrorism. There were never more than a handful of terrorists – known to themselves as the *Rote Armee Fraktion* (RAF, Red Army Column) and to their enemies as the Baader-Meinhof gang – or more than a few thousand active supporters. However, they also enjoyed the logistical and financial backing of similar ultra-left groups elsewhere in Europe, especially France and Italy. The ideological justification for terrorism, the 'propaganda of the deed', has not changed in a hundred years. It is the extreme means to the transformation of consciousness. It aims to stir the masses out of their apathy by demonstrating how vulnerable the existing order is, and how repressive when it responds. In West Germany the intensity of both the challenge and the response has to be seen in the light of the post-war history of the Republic. By the early 1970s it had been in existence for a mere quarter of a century. It was, according to the Basic Law, a provisional structure pending a peace treaty with a re-united Germany. Its relatively weak legitimacy, its heavy dependence on the existing geo-political alignment, the uncertainty surrounding the future of Germans as a nation, all helped to make it an easy target. This weak legitimacy also explained the *grande peur* (great fear) that gripped many West Germans as a small group of *kamikaze* activists succeeded in spectacularly kidnapping or murdering a series of highly-placed public figures with apparent impunity: first Jürgen Ponto of the Dresdner Bank, then Siegfried Buback, the chief Public Prosecutor and finally Hanns-Martin Schleyer, president of the West German employers' federation. The climax of their activities came in 1977, with the kidnapping and murder of Schleyer and the hijacking of a Lufthansa airliner with the aim of securing the release of imprisoned RAF members. With the storming of the airliner, the capture of Schleyer's murderers and the collective suicide of the imprisoned RAF leadership, the effectiveness of terrorism was at an end. Sporadic terrorism has continued and new recruits lay claim to the RAF mantle. But they lack the theoretical grounding that the first generation gained from their Marxist apprenticeship in the 1960s: they are a shadow of the original RAF.

Violence of another sort has characterised one of the other developments of the protest movement. From within the largely pacifist-anarchist consensus of the alternative politics there emerged a hard core of Marxist-Leninist fanatics of various leanings – Stalinist, Maoist, pro-Albanian – known collectively as the K-groups. Their numbers were negligible, but their tight and dedicated cadre organis-ation enabled them to infiltrate the loose and more broadly-based coalitions that existed on many campuses, and that organised large-scale demonstrations against nuclear power installations, urban redevelopment schemes (often involving mass squats) and environ-mentally insensitive construction projects like the new runway at Frankfurt airport. The premeditated violence that occurs at the margin of most of these, culminating in the shooting of a policeman in 1987, results, as is no doubt intended, in governmental curtail-ments of the right to demonstrate.

The final great wave of protest was that of the 'peace movement'. Here, too, the conjuncture of intellectual antecedents and external political impulses was crucial. Anti-militarism was a natural reaction to the experience of the Third Reich and had already surfaced in the 1950s when a German contribution to NATO was first instituted. To it was added the fear that in the event of a war between the superpowers Germany, East and West, would be the main battle-field. The more weapons were stationed in West Germany, the more vulnerable it seemed. In a more direct political sense the peace movement reflected disillusionment with the outcome of detente. Detente did not, as many had hoped, lead to a permanent atmos-phere of cooperation between the superpowers. On the contrary, from the mid-1970s on, relations again deteriorated: the Soviet invasion of Afghanistan in 1979 and the election of President Reagan in 1980 seemed to confirm that. But the biggest single stimulant was the 'twin-track' policy launched by Helmut Schmidt in 1979: NATO would install medium-range Cruise and Pershing II missiles in West-ern Europe, including West Germany, unless the Soviet Union with-drew the SS–20 missiles that had recently been added to its arsenal.

The peace movement appealed to all those whose guiding principle since the 1960s had been distrust of established power-holders and official politics, enhanced by a dislike, amounting at times to a hatred, of America. It also appealed to those who were convinced that unless their prescription was accepted, imminent disaster would follow: 'The destruction of mankind has begun', Günter Grass wrote at the height of the anti-missile campaign (Grass, 1982). But it did not appeal to those alone. As in the 1950s the hundreds of thousands who converged on Bonn in 1981 and 1983 were united by a fear that they were witnessing a mindless arms race in which neither of the antagonists was interested in dialogue. Like all the waves of protest this one subsided, too. The missiles were installed and the world did not come to an end. Indeed in 1987 they were dismantled by the mutual agreement of the Great Powers. Of all the legacies of twenty years of protest only one has maintained staying power: concern over the environment.

The ideologues of reform and *Totalkritik* have undoubtedly affected the political agenda of the Federal Republic. But the polarisations of opinion that they have introduced have not corresponded neatly with party lines. The reform euphoria in both domestic and foreign policy encompassed more than just the Social and Free Democrats and cut deep into the normal support of the Christian Democrats. So, too, the reactions against the protest movements divided party loyalties. In particular, after 1974 the battle over conventional *versus* alternative politics, whether on nuclear power or defence policy, was carried on within the SPD and eventually led to the fall of the Schmidt government, as the Chancellor lost the confidence first of some of his own party and then his coalition partner. But the long-term stabilisation of a protest movement has also institutionalised it. There is now an established counter-culture, consisting largely of students, young graduates and the artistic-literary intelligentsia in all the larger urban centres. They are united by a rejection of the dominant social conformity of the Federal Republic, its hierarchical organisations and the policies it has pursued since 1945; they are divided by whether to participate at all in conventional politics and on the question of violence. In the end, having begun to contest local elections with 'alternative lists' they formed themselves into a political party, the Greens. They entered the Bundestag in 1983, having previously succeeded in entering the majority of Landtage. Since then they have maintained themselves at a steady 6 to 8 per cent of electoral support, despite much-publicised internal conflicts and generally unfavourable media coverage. Though their name and much of their iconography implies an emphasis on ecology, they are best understood as a coalition of the radical urban left. Their supporters are overwhelmingly young (under 35), highly educated (having an *Abitur*, or a university degree), employed in the public-sector social services or media and living in university towns and major metropolitan areas. Their status is thus paradoxical: the occupational groups from which they recruit are relatively privileged economically, but the typical Green regards himself as politically marginalised or excluded. They specifically address opponents of nuclear energy, neutralists, feminists and gay liberation groups and claim to speak for the unrepresented, such as immigrant workers and asylum-seekers.

The radical wing ('fundamentalists') continue the *Totalkritik* tradition. They see opposition as a permanent mission against the 'all-party coalition against the environment and peace' (Bock, 1982, p. 156), their role as that of an 'anti-party party' against 'the many incompetent men in power' (Kelly, 1984, pp. 17, 37). Hence the emphasis on rank-and-file participation (*Basisdemokratie*) and the biennial rotation of elected parliamentarians which had, however, to be abandoned as both impracticable and unconstitutional. Once elected, many Green parliamentarians, with growing support from rank and file, saw opportunities for practical cooperation at least at the local or Land level. This more moderate wing ('realists') was prepared to accept political responsibility, a course that led to the short-lived SPD–Green Land coalition in Hesse, in which the 'realist' Green Joschka Fischer was environment minister. The logic of this course, which got the upper hand within the party as a whole in 1988 and 1989, was to downgrade the Greens as a movement of the streets and make them a parliamentary party 'attractive to the socially concerned and ecologically oriented new middle class' (Fischer, 1988, 34).

## Conservative Counter-attacks

Protest creates counter-protest; change gives birth to reaction. It would be surprising if the rise of an ideological left had not met with a response on the right. For the first twenty years of its existence the Federal Republic was a conservative state, but the conservatism was implied, not explicit. It was a conservatism of social and moral values, not of the legitimacy of inherited structures. It could hardly have been otherwise: the traditional components of German conservatism – nationalist rhetoric and authoritarian government – were too discredited. Whatever the long-term hopes of German re-unification, the basis of the Federal Republic's foundation was the separation of state and nation. This, too, affected the kind of conservatism that dominated the early Republic. Until 1945 Germany's foreign policy and Germany's sense of national mission had been related to the centre of Europe: Germany was not part of the barbaric East, but neither was it part of Western civilisation. After 1949 such an option was not available. The Federal Republic belonged to the

West: economically, strategically, politically, intellectually. That was part of its definition. On the one hand that implied an instinctive anti-Communist consensus and nothing could be more welcome to conservatives. But it also meant a farewell to traditional German conservative suspicions of rationalism, industrial society and parliamentary government – all the things that went with Western civilisation. Slowly, but from the 1950s onwards irrevocably, West Germany became conservative in a Western way: it became a stable, capitalist parliamentary republic.

This did not mean there was no nostalgia for other pasts, whether monarchical or totalitarian, or that there was no neo-Nazism, open or covert. There was a sizeable neo-Nazi wave in the early 1950s, associated with the Socialist Reich Party of Major Remer, who had personally helped to foil the plot against Hitler in 1944. There was another in the mid-1960s, associated with the National Democratic Party, at the time of the first serious post-war economic turn-down and the Great Coalition – i.e., in the absence of a legitimate opposition party. But none of these reappearances had any staying power and none had a political message that had not been heard before. The one item of continuity on the radical right is a newspaper, the *Deutsche National- und Soldatenzeitung (German Nationalist and Soldier's Paper)*, whose circulation of between 100,000 and 150,000 indicates the size of the hard core of this constituency. Full-blown Nazism is too discredited a creed to serve as a receptacle for anti-progressive sentiment, even at a time when the violent left is on the offensive. And the politicisation of personal and social life that characterised National Socialism makes it an unsuitable refuge for those fleeing from similar ambitions proclaimed by the left.

The first reaction to the reform wave was a response to its democratisation programme. In part, this simply expressed the outrage of a number of academics, many of them formerly on the Left, at the chaos caused by student revolutionaries and their allies in various universities. The *Bund Freiheit der Wissenschaft* (League for the Freedom of Scholarship), though predominantly conservative in composition, also included Socialists, some of whom in the course of time drifted to the Right, like Hermann Lübbe and Wilhelm Hennis, while others, like Richard Löwenthal or Kurt Sontheimer, remained with the SPD. They were appalled by the assault on rationality in much of the revolutionary sloganising and by what Löwenthal called the 'romantic relapse' inherent in the student movement (Löwenthal, 1970). It was also a response to the claims that the democratisers – or at least some of them – made to a monopoly of enlightenment. For the sociologist Helmut Schelsky they were like a priestly caste:

a new intellectual 'clergy' [that] tried to secure domination over 'secular' events and political and economic action for its own benefit and in accordance with its set of aims (Schelsky, 1975, pp. 15–16).

But above all it sought to deny that the demands for democratisation were theoretically valid or socially beneficial. The political scientist Wilhelm Hennis argued that the 'democratisation' of the social sphere would merely result in its total politicisation. It ignored the distinction between the public and the private sphere, between the state and civil society (Hennis, 1970, pp. 24, 27). Democracy relates to the choice of government, not to the running of a factory or a school. At the very moment that Habermas was complaining about the so-called objective constraints which monetarise and bureaucratise more and more areas of human life and transform more and more relationships into commodities and objects (Habermas, 1982), conservatives like Arnold Gehlen and Eugen Forsthoff were defending the manager, the expert and the wealth-creator against 'moralising intellectuals', (Gehlen, 1974, p. 9) egalitarians and those 'value-creators [who] represent the unproductive class that exploits the wealth-creators' (Schelsky, 1975, p. 180). Those who elevated 'quality of life' over the 'achievement ethic' (*Leistungsprinzip*) were reminded that 'justified pride in one's own achievement is certainly also part of the quality of life' (Gehlen, 1974, p. 30). The distinction between the political and economic spheres was necessary if management was to be able to manage. What present-day conservatives admire about technocracy is the authority that it gives to the expert. As for the party cartel that Jaspers had complained of, this was exactly what industry needed:

> An institutionalised party system corresponds to a high degree with the requirements of industrial society, which is dependent on a rationally functioning state (Forsthoff, 1971, p. 93).

These critics of the gospel of progress were the prophets of the partial policy revision that took place at the handover from Brandt to Schmidt: the return to sobriety and limited objectives, the emphasis on the possible rather than the desirable. But for most spokesmen of conservatism that was only the beginning. What was needed was a recovery of faith in capitalism, a renewed recognition that it was capitalism that was truly progressive. At the very moment that the left, disillusioned by the Brandt years, overwhelmed by environmental concerns and the arms race, began to sense disaster in its nostrils, the right re-occupied the ground of confidence and optimism. What inspired the right was West German economic achievement and, even more, West German economic potential. It is therefore not surprising that the slogan of the Bavarian Christian Social Union, in many respects the most conservative of West Germany's major parties, is *'Der Fortschritt spricht bayrisch'* ('Progress speaks Bavarian'). The achievements of Bavaria's high-technology industry and export leaders, like Siemens, Audi and BMW, were eminently compatible with law and order, Church and family, anti-communism and compulsory Aids-testing. Nor is it surprising the campaign slogan of the CDU in the 1983 election, following the fall of the Schmidt government, was *'den Aufschwung wählen'* ('vote for recovery'). Conservative confidence was to replace the doubts and pessimism of the final Schmidt years. This was to be the *Wende*, the great turn-around.

The break with traditional conservative thinking that this attitude implied was not complete, however. The conservatives of the 1970s accepted industrial society, as those of the 1920s and 1870s had not. But they were traditional in insisting on a clear distinction between the right to choose one's government and the right to a say in every economic and social process. They admired and defended the hierarchical structure of modern industry. As early as 1961 Schelsky had maintained that 'nowadays it is often not the politicians who represent the public interest, but the experts of the scientific-technical state' (Schelsky, 1961, p. 29).

## National Identity

They were traditional also in the rediscovery of the nation. Not that the idea of German national aspirations had ever gone away entirely. In its extreme restorationist form it was largely an underground phenomenon, associated with neo-Nazism. Just as in the 1970s the homeless electorate of the NPD was for the most part absorbed by the mainstream parties, so small ultra-nationalist terrorist groups emerged to parallel those on the left – *Wehrsportgruppen* (military sporting groups), rather on the lines of 'survivalist' groups in other Western countries. Though they engaged in much rhetoric about national revival and reversing moral decay, their main recruiting agent was xenophobia. Their hatred and resentment was directed at immigrant workers, asylum seekers and the increasingly cosmopolitan appearance of West Germany's cities, a new and disorientating development in a country that, unlike America, France or Britain, had no experience of acting as a melting-pot.

However, the mere existence of these groups, the fact that minor ultra-right parties began fighting elections again and the pan-German tones of some neutralists on the left – Günter Grass, for instance, talked of the anti-missile movement as an 'all-German responsibility'

(Bracher, 1986, p. 399) – caused some concern to conservatively-inclined politicians, historians and publicists. For some decades the Federal Republic's integration with the West, and in particular its leading role in pushing for European unification, seemed to provide a satisfactory alternative to nationalist sentiment. As disillusionment set in with the way the European Community was developing, as national sentiment survived or revived in Europe to an extent that many, especially Germans, had not anticipated in 1945, the question of a West German political identity once more became salient. There was a risk that a new generation might grow up that felt neither European nor German, or whose only knowledge of the German past was, in Ernst Nolte's phrase, a 'negative myth', with an emphasis on the origins and crimes of the Third Reich. Such a state of affairs could easily lead to anarchy and disintegration: 'In a country without memory, everything is possible', the conservative historian Michael Stürmer warned (Stürmer, 1986). It is this concern that gave rise to the so-called '*Historikerstreit*' – the historians' dispute which burst upon the public in 1986 but which had been bubbling within the historical profession for some time before. At the core of this dispute was the question whether German history was to be 'normalised' or not: Was it the story of a thousand years, interrupted by a thirteen-year horror alien to its tradition, or was the Third Reich the central, traumatic experience of the German past that made the history of Germany different from anybody else's? ('*Historikerstreit*', 1987).

What the historians' dispute has once more emphasised is the extent to which the Federal Republic is a child of the German past. Both in its institutions and in its thinking it defines itself negatively in terms of the Third Reich, the Weimar Republic and even the Empire of 1871. For the Founding Fathers of the Parliamentary Council and for the reconstruction generation the Federal Republic was to be what the Third Reich and Weimar had not been. The first nineteen articles of the Basic Law, with their guarantee of civil rights, and the creation of a Constitutional Court (Articles 93, 94) to guard these rights, were designed to shut the stable door on the democratic horse. So was the legal prohibition of political parties that threatened the liberal-democratic order (Article 21). But if Bonn was not to be the Third Reich, it was not to be Weimar either. The Articles of the Basic Law that regulated the appointment of the chancellor, votes of confidence and the dissolution of the Bundestag as well as the various versions of the electoral law, with their increasingly severe discrimination against splinter parties, were all meant to ensure that the new republic should not suffer from the instability of its predecessor.

## Sober Rationality and Pragmatic Reflection

What no constitution and no act of parliament could ensure, however, was an end to the ideological polarisation of the earlier years of the twentieth century. Yet that is precisely what did happen: sober rationality and pragmatic reflection replaced the pursuit of fanciful, naive and, in the end, murderous ideals. And it is that that made an increasing number of the second generation of West Germans dissatisfied with their republic, a discontent that flourished particularly in the vacuum between the Adenauer and the Brandt eras. It found expression on the right in the comet-like rise and fall of the NPD, which appealed to those who felt that too much had been abandoned in the drive for modernisation and in the growing acceptance of permanent national division. It found much stronger expression on the left, among those who felt that not nearly enough had changed, that the democratic provisions of the constitution had in too many cases remained hollow formalities. Having failed to run a democracy once, Germans were understandably sensitive to the fear that they might fail again – not, this time round, through physical disintegration, but through the incapacity to breathe the spirit of democracy into authoritarian institutions. Just what *had* changed since 1945 in the bureacracy, the judiciary, in schools and universities, in the ownership and management of property, they asked? The Federal Republic was not only the self-conscious negation of the recent past, it was also its heir and successor: whatever else 1945 had been, it was not Year Zero. This German sensitivity to the imperfections of their democracy is understandable: the new democratic consensus 'was the product not of a long history, but the experience of *one* formative succession of catastrophes and resurgence' (Löwenthal, 1970).

In its critique of the established order the student revolt was effective: it set out to 'unmask', and succeeded. In its attempt to formulate a new order, it did not. Indeed, the coincidence between the incipient failure of the reform programme, the oil shock and growing concern about the environment created nothing less than a crisis of the idea of progress. Where *Totalkritik* had originally been based on limitless faith in man's capacity for self-improvement, it was now obsessed with the imminence of global disaster. The counter-trends to this have necessarily been less uniform and cohesive. There has not been one single *Wende*. The revolution of declining expectations came with Helmut Schmidt's assumption office. Along with it came a growing scepticism towards world-reforming gospels and indeed of the capacity of the state or society to implement them. A loose party of alternative politics continued to exist. Its style remained constant, though the subject of its protest changed: emergency legislation, anti-terrorist measures, nuclear power, airport runways, acid rain, NATO missiles. But there is not a single 'other side'. There are those who preach a recovery of traditional morality and patriotic virtue, and those who believe in technocratic-capitalist progress.

The majority of West Germans favour neither revolution nor restoration. The 1983 election, which confirmed Chancellor Kohl in power, showed that there is no majority for alternative politics. But, by also bringing the Greens into the Bundestag, it showed that alternative politics has an established niche. There is a broad spectrum from the moderate left to the moderate right, with many intermediate positions, which yet accepts that the Federal Republic is a modern, industrial state firmly anchored in the West. The Socialist Jürgen Habermas speaks for it when he asserts, 'The unconditional opening of the Federal Republic to the political culture of the West is the great intellectual achievement of our post-war epoch' (Habermas, 1987, p. 135); the Liberal Ralf Dahrendorf, in his confidence that 'in the end modernity is useful to man and will appeal to him' (Sontheimer, 1983, p. 120); and the more conservative Karl-Dietrich Bracher when he concludes that though most of his fellow-citizens identify with both the German nation and the Federal Republic, they live in a 'post-national democracy' (Bracher, 1986, p. 406). In the space of forty years West Germans have passed from quiescence through turbulence to quiescence. What will be the next phase? To quote Dahrendorf again, 'a little "ungovernability" won't kill German democracy' (Dahrendorf, 1983, p. 235).

# 6

# The German Voter

RUSSELL J. DALTON

## From Stabilisation to Volatility

For the first three decades of its existence, the West German party system was noted for its growing stability and cohesion (Loewenberg, 1979; Smith, 1986). Fourteen parties competed in the first national elections in 1949, and eleven won seats in the Bundestag. In just a few short years, however, German voters rejected the appeals of narrow special interest parties and radical parties on the extreme left and right, and most citizens concentrated their support behind one of the two largest parties. On the right, the CDU–CSU consolidated the support of several smaller parties and became the major conservative force in electoral politics. The SPD similarly dominated the left end of the political spectrum. The small FDP continued the liberal tradition from the pre-war party system. After the 1961 election only these three parties were represented in parliament, and the structure of a stable 'two-and-a-half' party system was established.

These long-term trends of electoral stabilisation and ideological convergence have been reversed for the party system of the 1980s. The two major parties still dominate the partisan landscape, but their share of the crucial party-list votes (*Zweitstimmen*) has decreased since 1979. More people now shift their party voting patterns between elections, and split-ticket voting between candidate and party-list votes has similarly increased. Turnout in the 1987 Bundestag election dropped off significantly, though remaining high (84 per cent) by British and American standards. Voting differences between class and religious strata have narrowed. In addition, new political parties – especially the anti-establishment Green party – are challenging the prevailing partisan order. The Greens initial entry into parliament in 1983 marked the first time a new party had won Bundestag representation since the 1950s. In short, West Germany has seemingly begun to experience some of the same trends of increasing partisan volatility and fragmentation that have recently appeared in Britain, the United States, and several other advanced industrial democracies (Dalton *et al.*, 1984; Crewe and Denver, 1985).

This chapter describes and explains these new developments in West German electoral politics, and considers the implications of these trends for the party system. We first discuss the erosion of the social bases of partisan alignments. Then, we document the growing volatility and fluidity in West German voting behaviour. Finally, we appraise two alternative models – realignment versus dealignment – as possible explanations for these trends and consider what the future may hold for West German voting behaviour.

## Social Cleavages and Political Change

The strength and stability of West German party alignments during the 1950s and 1960s were partially drawn from the underlying structure that class, religion, and other social cleavages gave to the party system. Attachments to social groups were strongly felt; many voters closely identified with their social class, religious group, community, or region. Social networks within these groups were tightly drawn and individuals listened to the advice of the unions or church leaders in making decisions. Moreover, the political parties developed strong political ties with their respective clientele groups. The CDU–CSU was the party of business, the middle class, and Catholics; their 'Christian' label openly proclaimed their religious orientations. Throughout most of the 1950s, the SPD promoted its Marxist ideology in support of the working class and harshly criticised the capitalist and religious values of the Union parties. Even after the party reformed its programme at the 1959 Godesberg conference, the working class and secular orientations of the SPD persisted in these criticisms, albeit in more moderate tones. This produced a clear pattern of partisan alignment; each party bloc was embedded in its own network of support groups and offered voters a distinct political programme catering to these group interests.

In an environment where voters were still hesitant to become engaged in politics and where social cues furnished clear guidance on which party best represented people like oneself, many voters could make their voting decision based on their position in the social structure. Members of the working class disproportionately supported the SPD, whilst a majority of Catholics and middle class voters endorsed the CDU–CSU. The lines of social cleavage were clearly drawn, and voting patterns reflected this clear and stable social base.

The transformation of post-war West Germany has, however, gradually eroded these social cleavages and thus created the potential for partisan change (Baker *et al.*, 1981). Increasing social and geographic mobility weakened the bonds that linked individuals to group and community networks. Government policies and social forces developed an advanced industrial society in the Federal Republic which altered the social composition of the electorate. Other trends generally increased the social and political diversity of West German society, eroding the closed structure of traditional social networks and attenuating the impact of social cues on partisan behaviour.

Figure 6.1 portrays several broad indicators of this general weakening of the traditional group bases of West German society. The class cleavage is one of the most widely noted examples of the changing composition of the West German electorate. Class politics is normally equated with the conflict between the proletariat and the bourgeoisie, with farmers providing a secondary source of social cleavage. Partisan politics in the Federal Republic generally pits the working class movement and the SPD against the conservative-led forces of the old middle class (business owners and the self-employed). Yet the size of the three traditional class strata – blue-collar workers, the old middle class, and farmers – and thus their relative impact on electoral outcomes have steadily declined over the past three decades (solid line in Figure 6.1). In the 1950s, these three groups accounted for about 75 per cent of all heads of household; by the 1980s, less than 50 per cent of all households are headed by an individual from one of the three traditional class groupings.

A long-term decrease in the number of farmers and blue-collar workers has been compensated by the rapid growth of a 'new' middle class (Baker *et al.*, 1981, Chapter 7; Pappi, 1973). The largest occupational category now is composed of salaried white-collar workers (*Angestellte*) and civil servants (*Beamte*). This group is called the new middle class because it is not integrated into either the unionised working class network or the old middle class milieu. Members of the new middle class tend to be political moderates, adhering to a mix of economic centrism and social liberalism. Without sharp class cues to guide their behaviour (or a group infrastructure to develop such cues), the voting patterns of the new middle class are more fluid and subject to greater inter-election change, contributing to the processes of electoral change we are studying.

A related dimension of socio-cultural differentiation is the rural-

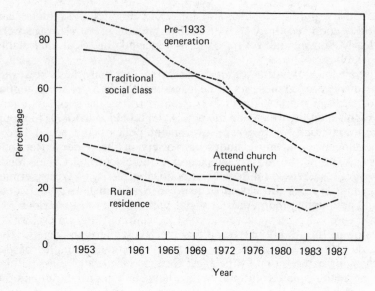

FIGURE 6.1   *The decline of tradition*

Note: Data German Elections Studies, See Appendix.

urban cleavage. Social change and modernisation diminished the traditional rural sector as the number employed in farming rapidly dwindled and the Federal Republic became a more urbanised nation. In the 1950s, about a third of the electorate lived in villages of fewer than five thousand people (see Figure 6.1); now only about a tenth of the electorate lives in a small village. Part of this trend is due to administrative reforms which decreased the number of small communities, but a steady urbanisation process was also at work. Moreover, even among the remaining rural population, the geographic and social distance to urban centres and urban lifestyles has decreased.

This migration to the cities involves more than just a change in residence. The closed social networks, homogeneity of opinion, and conservative values of rural societies epitomise the type of social organisation in which group-based cues heavily influence individual choices. In contrast, urban life includes a more fluid style of social relations and exposes individuals to a greater diversity of political experience. Community influences and other compulsory associational networks tend to weaken in urban settings, which enables individuals to exercise greater freedom of choice in politics and other aspects of their lives.

The erosion of traditional social divisions is also evident in the religious cleavage. A generation ago, conservative German politicians characterised elections as a competition between Christian good and atheist evil; such rhetoric succeeded in polarising the electorate along religious lines. But the social transformation of the Federal Republic includes a strong secular trend (Figure 6.1). In the 1950s, over 40 per cent of the electorate attended church on a weekly basis; by the 1987 election barely 25 per cent attended church as regularly. Regular church attendance among West German Catholics declined from over 50 per cent in 1953 to barely 30 per cent in 1987. A significant number of people – about a third of the populace – remains integrated into a religious network and thus are potentially influenced by the moral and cultural norms of the churches. But the general secularisation of West Germany society has steadily reduced the size of the religious sector, and therefore the overall role of religion in electoral politics.

Generational change constitutes, albeit in a somewhat different manner, another source of the decline in traditional social divisions. Older Germans raised under pre-war regimes developed their political identities in an environment in which class, religious, and other social divisions were highly polarised. This *Weltanschauung* carried over to shape how these individuals viewed society and politics in the post-war Federal Republic; class and religious characteristics are often important sources of political cues for older citizens. Conversely, younger generations were reared in an environment in which these social cleavages were moderating; social divisions are thus less central in structuring their political beliefs.

It is sometimes easy to forget how rapidly the generational composition of a nation can change. In the early 1950s about three-quarters of the electorate had been socialised under either the Weimar Republic or Second Empire and carried these experiences with them as they made political decisions. This older age group accounts for less than 20 per cent of the electorate in the 1980s. The majority of the public now consists of citizens raised under the regime of the Federal Republic: voters accustomed to the pluralism, individuality, and changeability of contemporary society.

These social trends have lessened the number of citizens who can depend upon their social location to provide them with clear and consistent political cues. More and more voters find themselves in social positions that do not fit the traditional cleavage structure or in positions that expose them to conflicting social cues. In other words, fewer voters now enter each election with fixed partisan predispositions based on their social location. The actions of the political parties further contributed to these developments, as both the CDU–CSU and SPD moderated their traditional group-based appeals in the 1960s and early 1970s to attract support from the new middle class and other uncommitted voters. Without social cues to guide their behaviour, voters became more open to new political appeals from the political parties or other interest groups. Moreover, as the public increases its interest in politics and the availability of political information expands, more citizens are able to reach their own voting decisions without relying on external cues such as the advice of a union leader or their pastor (Dalton, 1988, Chapters 2–4). The potential for substantial political change thus exists, waiting only for political forces to realise this potential.

## Electoral Politics in Flux

Indications of increasing partisan volatility and fragmentation began to appear during the late 1970s. At first, the signs were difficult to detect against the normal background of inter-election shifts in voting patterns. Democratic party systems are never static and the electoral fortunes of parties inevitably ebb and flow. The SPD had, in fact, steadily broadened its electoral base, beginning with the 1957 election and levelling off after 1972; the FDP's electoral results were always uncertain. Still, a number of indicators suggested that the basic stabilising forces of the West German party system were weakening.

One measure of partisan change is the volatility of the party system, that is, the absolute fluctuation in party vote shares between elections. Mogens Pedersen (1979) documented the growth of aggregate party volatility for most Western industrial democracies from the 1950s to the 1970s, but the Federal Republic was initially a deviant case. The West German party system was fairly volatile during its first decade, as the new system took root and party consolidation occurred. In the Bundestag elections between 1949 and 1960, the swing in party vote shares averaged 15.2 per cent from one campaign to the next (that is, the parties that increased their vote share between elections collectively raised their vote total by 15.2 per cent). As party alignments stabilised, volatility decreased during the 1960s (average volatility of 9.5 per cent) and the 1970s (4.8 per cent). This stabilisation occurred as minor parties were absorbed into the larger CDU–CSU and SPD, and as the party system developed an institutional and psychological base within society.

The trend toward electoral stability reverses in the 1980s. Renewed economic problems and new political issues, such as environmentalism and the INF treaty decision, injected new political controversies into the electoral process. Elections in the 1980s are characterised by more intense political and personal rivalry between the parties, especially with the emergence of the anti-establishment Green party. In the last two Bundestag elections, aggregate partisan volatility rises to an average inter-election shift of 7.1 per cent. A similar trend toward party volatility seems apparent at state level elections, as party fortunes have often shifted dramatically throughout the 1980s.

A more direct measure of electoral volatility examines the actual voting patterns of individuals rather than aggregate electoral results. The largest amount of voting change involves exchanges between parties – former CDU voters shifting to the SPD and vice-versa – that counterbalance one another and thus are not captured by Pedersen-type measures of the aggregate change in party fortunes. The amount of individual vote change can be estimated by using public opinion polls to compare present voting preferences to the recall of past votes.

David Conradt (1986, p. 133) has presented evidence of a long-term increase in individual vote shifts between elections (though for contradictory evidence see Klingemann, 1985). Between the 1957 and 1961 elections, for example, barely 10 per cent of the active electorate changed their voting preferences between elections (Figure 6.2). The percentage of vote switchers nearly doubled for Bundestag elections in the 1980s. Furthermore, these analyses probably *underestimate* the true degree of partisan change, because respondents in opinion polls tend to bring their recollections of past vote into line with their current preferences. Thus an even larger number of voters – perhaps as high as a third of the electorate – are shifting their party support from election to election.

Split-ticket voting is another possible indicator of the rigidity of party commitments. When West Germans go to the polls in federal elections they cast two votes. The first vote (*Erststimme*) is for a candidate to represent their electoral district; the second vote (*Zweitstimme*) is for a party list that provides the basis for a proportional allocation of parliamentary seats. A voter may therefore split his or her ballot by selecting a district candidate of one party with the first vote and another party with the party-list vote.

The amount of split-ticket voting has also inched upward in recent elections (Figure 6.2). Up until the late 1960s, less than 10 per cent of all voters split their ballots. The proportion of splitters has increased in the 1980s; about 14 per cent of the electorate in 1987, or one in every seven voters, split their ballots between two different parties. The growth of split-ticket voting partially reflects the increased strength of minor parties that siphon off second votes from

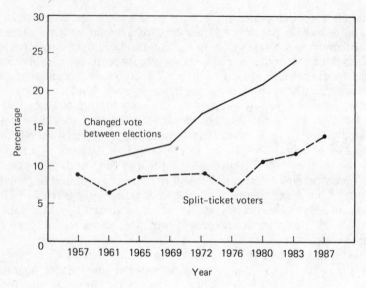

FIGURE 6.2   *Indicators of partisan change*

Note: Inter-election vote change figures from Conradt (1986) p. 133; split-ticket voting figures from Statistiches Bundesamt.
Source: Conradt (1986); Statistiches Bundesamt (various years).

the major parties. But in addition, split-ticket voting exemplifies the increasing fluidity of contemporary party preferences.

Other items from public opinion surveys illustrate the growing partisan fluidity of the West German public. Although the question wording changes over time, the available evidence suggests that voters are becoming less certain in their electoral decisions. In the 1960s less than a tenth of the electorate finally decided how to vote during the campaign; this proportion increased to a quarter of the electorate in the 1980s. Panel studies find that partisan preferences are becoming slightly more changeable even across the few months surrounding an election (Klingemann, 1985, p. 279).

Another sign of the erosion of traditional party alignments is the growing fragmentation of the West German party system. Until recently, most researchers argued that the party system was gradually evolving toward large 'catch-all' parties that would unify voters into competing party blocs and thus stabilise partisan alignments. In fact, the percentage of the vote going to the two large catch-all parties, CDU–CSU and SPD, increased fairly steadily from 60.2 per cent in the first federal elections to a high point of 91.2 per cent in 1976. Since then, the dominance of the two major parties has slowly eroded. In 1987 the CDU–CSU and SPD accounted for a smaller share of the vote (81.3 per cent) than in any election since 1953.

The increase in partisan fragmentation is, of course, closely linked to the emergence of the Green party (*Die Grünen*) as a significant electoral force (Bürklin, 1985; Papadakis, 1984). The Greens do not just represent a new political party, they loudly proclaim that they are a 'party of a new type' and an 'anti-party party'. Drawing upon a base in the new social movements of the 1980s – environmentalism, women's groups, and the peace lobby – they challenge the conventional values of the established parties and campaign for an alternative, New Left ideology. In 1983 the Greens won Bundestag representation and a public forum for espousing their viewpoints, and their improved showing in 1987 heightened the fragmentation in the party system.

In sum, the West German party system still retains a stable base – most voters have enduring partisan preferences and continue to support the same party from election to election – but a growing minority of voters are shifting their partisan allegiances and injecting more fluidity into partisan politics. Our task is to explain this state of electoral flux.

## Models of Electoral Change

While the evidence of increasing fluidity in voting patterns is clear cut, there is more uncertainty concerning the cause of these patterns. Most analysts resort to either a *realignment* or *dealignment* model to explain this ongoing process of partisan change. The two models provide different explanations of the causes underlying recent partisan trends, and thus hold different implications for the future of West German electoral politics.

The realignment approach analyses electoral history in terms of the stable group basis of party support. Most political parties represent a distinct social clientèle and institutionalise this support through a variety of formal and informal mechanisms. With the passage of time, however, group alignments are often strained by the failures of a party to deliver on its promises or by a changing political agenda that obviates the issues that initially determined the lines of political conflict. When this occurs, the electoral system may experience a *partisan realignment*. A realignment is defined as a significant shift in the group bases of party coalitions, and usually in the distribution of popular support among the parties as a result (Dalton *et al.*, 1984, Chapter 1). The patterns of group support may shift abruptly (a critical realignment) or may follow a slower evolutionary change (a secular realignment). Realignments have been a regular feature of American electoral politics for well over a century and probably since the emergence of the first mass-party coalitions around 1900. Similar historical realignments have occurred in European party systems, such as the rise of the British Labour party in the early 1900s or the Gaullist realignment in the French party system of the late 1950s.

The realignment model would explain the heightened partisan volatility of the 1980s as an indicator of the realigning forces existing within the West German party system. As old political cleavages weaken and new cleavages gain force, partisan volatility and fragmentation often accompany this transition period. Indeed, discussions of contemporary partisan politics often claim that the traditional economic and religious cleavages of West German society are being superseded by the new political conflicts of an advanced industrial society. After the bases of partisan support eventually realign to represent the new constellation of political forces, the realignment model predicts that voting patterns should restabilise around the new base of political cleavage.

The dealignment model presents a different view of the processes of partisan change. While the realignment model focuses on the group-based patterns of partisan support, the dealignment model emphasises the electorate's psychological attachment to parties. The term 'dealignment' initially referred to a preliminary step in a realigning process during which the party-affiliated portion of the electorate shrinks as traditional party coalitions dissolve to be reformed in a new shape. Analysts now realise that dealignment, like realignment, can also occur as a distinct electoral period (Inglehart and Hochstein, 1972; Beck, 1984). A dealignment period exists when a large number of voters lack firm affiliations with any political party.

From the dealignment perspective, the growing volatility of the West German party system during the 1980s is not primarily the result of a realignment in partisan loyalties, but reflects a general erosion in the strength of partisan attachments. Dealignment in contemporary party systems is explained either as a consequence of the public's growing political sophistication, which decreases the need for habitual party loyalties (Dalton, 1988, Chapter 9), or as a consequence of the electorate's growing alienation and scepticism of partisan politics (Burnham, 1970, 1978). In either case, with many voters lacking firm ties to a preferred party, voting behaviour becomes more fluid and unpredictable. Dealignment is thus seen as an end-state in itself, and not just a transitory phase on the way to a new stable alignment.

Although both models offer distinct views on the sources of partisan change and their ultimate resolution, it is difficult to separate their effects in the short term. Increased volatility and fragmentation in the West German party system is consistent with both models; partisan decay is an initial step in the realignment model and an end-state in the dealignment model. Moreover, realignments are most easily identified after they are completed and a new partisan order has taken root. While the process of partisan change is working, it is difficult to differentiate a fundamental partisan realignment from transitory inter-election fluctuations. The test of a realignment is its endurance, and this test requires the passage of time. In the short term, any test of these models may be inconclusive. Still, both models offer a valuable framework for analysing electoral change – and the expectations that follow from each model can be judged against the evidence available.

## The Evidence of Realignment

The realignment model suggests that the present fluidity in the West German party system is due to shifts in the group bases of party support. As social forces disrupt long-standing partisan loyalties and stimulate the formation of new party allegiances the party system experiences heightened volatility and fragmentation during the transition period. If a realignment is occurring, it should be visible as social groups shift their traditional patterns of party support to a new pattern of party alignment.

One potential locus for a realignment in voting patterns is the class cleavage. The West German party system is partially built upon the traditional conflict between the bourgeoisie and proletariat, and more broadly the problems of providing economic well-being and security to all members of society. These economic conflicts provided a major source of electoral competition pitting the SPD and its working class constituency against the CDU–CSU and its business and middle-class supporters. And yet, as was discussed in an earlier section, structural changes in West German society are altering the composition and political force of the traditional class cleavage.

Three decades of electoral results point to an unmistakable decline in class voting differences within the West German party system (Figure 6.3). At the height of class-based voting in 1957, the SPD received a majority of working class votes (61 per cent) but only a small share (24 per cent) of middle class votes. In overall terms, this represented nearly a 40 percentage point gap (37 points) in the class bases of party support, rivalling the level of class voting found in Britain and other class-polarised party systems. Over the next

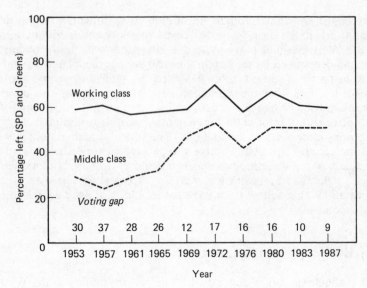

FIGURE 6.3   *The trend in class voting, 1953–1987*

*Note: Data from West German Elections Studies, see Appendix.*

decade, the success of the *Wirtschaftswunder* (economic 'miracle') and moderating party differences (such as the SPD's embrace of centrist policies in the 1959 Godesberg Programme) decreased the level of class voting. The conciliatory climate of the Grand Coalition (1966–9), during which the CDU–CSU and SPD shared control of the federal government, pushed class voting levels even lower in the 1969 election. By the 1980s, class voting differences became nearly non-existent, averaging less than 10 per cent in the last two federal elections. Voting differences based on union membership, income, and other class characteristics also display a similar downward trend in their influence on voting choice (Baker *et al.*, 1981, Chapter 7).

In one sense this shift in class voting patterns fulfils the basic definition of a realignment: increasing SPD support among middle class voters improved the party's electoral showing andenabled it to control the federal government from 1969 until 1982. And yet, if we probe these data more deeply, the evidence becomes more complex. If the two components of the middle class are separated – the old middle class and the new middle class – one finds that two separate electoral patterns are intermixed (Dalton, 1984; Pappi and Terwey, 1982). First, voting differences between the two traditional class antagonists – the working class and the old middle class – have moderated only slightly over time. Franz Pappi cites this evidence to argue that the fundamental basis of the class cleavage has not changed. And yet this interpretation overlooks the fact that the declining number of voters who belong to these two class strata *is* weakening the electoral importance of the traditional class cleavage. Second, the new middle class has been a source of partisan change. As the two traditional class strata decreased in size, the new middle class expanded its share of the total electorate and its share of the combined middle class vote (old and new) as shown in Figure 6.1. This change in the composition of the middle class is electorally important because the new middle class has steadily deviated from the voting tendencies of the traditional bourgeoisie. In the 1950s the new middle class shared the old middle class preference for the CDU–CSU; this produced a large gap in overall middle class-working class voting patterns. As the new middle class gradually moderated its partisan preferences (it now splits its votes about equally between the CDU–CSU and SPD) the overall impact of social class on voting behaviour has weakened. The new middle class has also stimulated electoral change by giving disproportionate support to the new Green party.

The changing voting behaviour of the new middle class has produced a secular realignment over the past three decades; but this realignment also contains elements of a dealignment. The shift in voting patterns is located among a social group – the new middle class – that holds an ambiguous position in the political structure of the Federal Republic and other advanced industrial societies (Kerr, forthcoming). The long-run political orientations of the new middle class therefore remain uncertain. Furthermore, new middle class voters changed their party support from heavily favouring one party to dividing their votes about equally between the two major parties. The overall result has thus not been an exchange of the traditional bourgeoisie – proletariat cleavage for another clear basis of social alignment, but the erosion of the traditional class cleavage without a new class cleavage (as yet) emerging in its place.

A similar pattern of development exists for the religious cleavage. The historical conflict between the Catholic church and Liberal-Socialist parties still clearly appears in voting alignments (Figure 6.4). The gap in SPD voting support between Catholics and Protestants has remained within a 20–25 point range for most of the past three decades; Catholics disproportionately support the Union parties, while a majority of Protestants vote for the SPD. Only for the two most recent elections have these religious voting patterns narrowed significantly. Similarly, the voting gap between religious

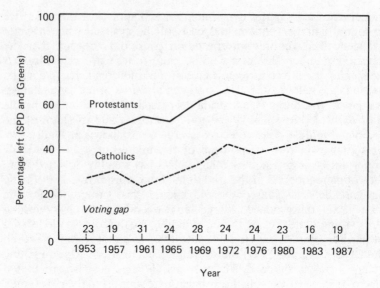

*FIGURE 6.4   The trend in religious voting, 1953–1987*

Note: Data from West German Elections Studies, see Appendix.

and non-religious individuals displays the same marked persistence (Dalton, 1988, Chapter 8).

Despite the apparent endurance of the traditional religious cleavage, the importance of religion as a basis of voting behaviour is also declining – although the pattern of decline is less obvious than in the case of the class cleavage. Even though voting differences between denominations and between religious and non-religious voters have held fairly constant for the past generation, the secularisation of West German society is steadily increasing the absolute number of non-religious individuals. People who attend church regularly are still well integrated into a religious network and maintain distinct voting patterns, but there are fewer of these individuals today. By definition the growing number of secular voters are not basing their party preferences on religious cues. We again thus find that the changing composition of the electorate is lessening the partisan significance of traditional social cues by decreasing the number of individuals to whom these cues are relevant.

As old social cleavages fade, the realignment approach leads us to search for potential new sources of group competition that can replace the weakening ties of class, religion and other traditional social cleavages. Attempts to identify such cleavages have so far returned modest yields. For instance, scholars have discussed the potential emergence of an educational cleavage in advanced industrial societies – between the information-rich and the information-poor (Bell, 1973; Huntington, 1974). And yet educational differences in voting behaviour have declined along with other social status measures (Dalton, 1984, p. 127). Others have searched for an emerging new cleavage based on public-private sector employment, employment in a high technology firm, or consumption patterns (e.g. Gluchowski, 1987; Feist and Krieger, 1987); the impact of these social characteristics on voting behaviour is still weak or non-existent. Marked age differences have recently appeared in voting support for the Green party – over 80 per cent of the green voters in 1987 were aged under 40 – but youth is a transitory life stage without the group infrastructure that could institutionalise a generational cleavage. If new political cleavages are emerging, there is not yet clear evidence that these cleavages will be based on socially-defined groups linked to the structural features of West German society.

More substantial evidence of a newly emerging political cleavage comes from Ronald Inglehart's research on the value changes occurring in advanced industrial societies (Inglehart, 1984; 1989). Inglehart maintains that as a society makes substantial progress in addressing traditional economic and security needs, a growing share of the public shifts their attention to *post-material* goals that are still in short supply, such as the quality of life, self-expression, and personal freedom. These changing value priorities add issues such as environmental protection, nuclear energy, expanding citizen participation, sexual equality, consumer advocacy, disarmament, and human rights to the political agenda. These post-material or 'New Politics' issues, it is argued, may provide the necessary catalyst for a new basis of political cleavage (Baker *et al.*, 1981; Inglehart, 1984; Dalton, 1986).

Partisan polarisation along the New Politics cleavage has grown over the past two decades (Figure 6.5). During the 1970s, voters interested in New Politics goals gave disproportionate support to the SPD, even though the party was only partially responsive to these new issue demands. The formation of the Green party prior to the 1980 election created a focal point for the post-materialist agenda and brought value politics into the electoral arena. About a third of post-materialists voted for the Greens in the last two federal elections, far beyond the party's total electoral returns (5.6 in 1983 and 8.3 in 1987). In overall terms, Figure 6.5 indicates that the gap in the party preferences of materialist and post-materialist voters roughly doubled between 1973 and the last two federal elections as this new basis of party support has become integrated into the West German party system.

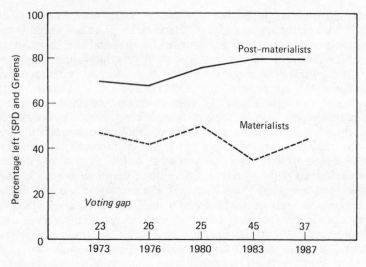

FIGURE 6.5   *The trend in values voting, 1973–1987*

Source: Eurobarometer surveys of the EC.

Despite the growing relationship between value priorities and voting behaviour, the realignment potential of the New Politics cleavage is still limited by several factors (see Dalton *et al.*, 1984, Chapter 15). The process of partisan realignment is normally based on clearly defined and highly cohesive social groups that can develop institutional ties to the parties and provide clear voting cues to their members. A realignment in a group's partisan orientations yields a new, stable party alignment, formalised by the group's institutional representatives who mobilise the votes of their members for the chosen party. In contrast, post-material values are antithetical to massive disciplined organisations such as unions and churches. The New Politics cleavage is thus unlikely to unite voters into exclusive associational groups that can be easily and predictably mobilised in behalf of a specific party. Rather than a cleavage defined by social groups, the New Politics represents an issue cleavage that identifies only a community of like-minded individuals. Without a firm social base, an issue-based cleavage is likely to be more fluid and unpredictable than social-group cleavages such as class and religion.

Another factor limiting the realignment potential of the New Politics is the response of the major established parties. The SPD depends upon the support of labour and the CDU–CSU on their religious supporters, even if these groups are in decline. Party leaders are not likely to turn away from their traditional support networks until the electoral potential of the New Politics is more clearly determined, especially since issues such as nuclear power or nuclear weapons often cause internal divisions within the clientèles of the established parties. The established parties are thus understandably hesitant in adopting clear policy positions on New Politics issues. This lack of representation led to the creation of the Greens, which is itself a sign of realignment in the party system; but the Greens remain a minor party unable to translate the New Politics agenda into policy. Drawing upon the American experience with minor parties, the realignment potential of the New Politics might be maximised if the Greens were able to force one of the major parties – presumably the SPD – into incorporating some Green policies into their own programme. The SPD has taken the first tentative steps in this direction since it moved to the opposition benches in 1982, but the transformation is incomplete. Until the major parties offer unambiguous policy choices, the realigning potential of the New Politics cleavage remains limited.

In sum, the social cleavages that have traditionally structured West German voting patterns are decreasing in importance. The declining impact of these cleavages arises from compositional changes in the number of voters integrated into traditional social groups, as well as a gradual narrowing of inter-group differences. New issue controversies are motivating voters to change their partisan preferences, and this may be the first step in a gradual realignment process (Dalton, 1986). But the realigning process is still incomplete because the erosion of traditional party alignments has not yet produced a new group-based cleavage alignment that has restabilised the party system.

## The Evidence of Dealignment

The stabilisation and consolidation of the party system during the 1950s and 1960s created an environment in which popular attachments to the political parties could strengthen, even though group attachments were being eroded. Public opinion polls found that citizens were developing affective, *psychological attachments* to their preferred party during the 1960s and 1970s (Baker *et al.*, 1981; Norpoth, 1983). These developing party ties structured the voter's view of the political world, provided a new source of cues for judging political phenomena, and promoted stability in individual voting behaviour. By the mid-1970s about half the electorate expressed a strong identification with their preferred party. If any further trend was foreseen, most researchers predicted a further strengthening of these partisan ties.

During the 1980s, however, a number of developments have slowed, or perhaps reversed, this trend towards partisanship. When the parties were unresponsive to the new political issues of the 1970s, many individuals saw this as a failing of the West Germany system of strong party government. Large, mass-based parties appeared unable to respond to the public's rapidly changing issue-interests and the concerns of local citizen groups. New institutional forms – such as citizen-action groups or public interest lobbies – emerged to represent these new political interests. Many party leaders perceived these new political groups as a turning away from political parties as institutions of interest representation (Raschke, 1982; Guggenberger and Kempf, 1984). The stature of the established parties further suffered with the renewal of economic difficulties in the late 1970s and early 1980s. The aura of policy success that the parties had developed during the growth decades of the 1950s and 1960s began to vanish.

Party images were further tarnished by a series of political scandals. In 1982, citizens learned that the Flick corporation had given top party leaders illegal party contributions in return for a multi-million DM tax exemption for the firm. A flood of minor party scandals at Land and local levels further focused attention on the failures of the parties. In 1987, an election 'dirty tricks' scandal in Schleswig-Holstein led to the resignation and eventual suicide of the CDU state party leader. The parties appeared to be self-interested and self-centred organisations, which created feelings of partisan antipathy on the part of the public. During the Flick affair, moreover, the Greens repeatedly emphasised that *all* of the established parties had accepted illegal donations from the Flick corporation.

These events evoked widespread discussions of a crisis of party government (*Parteienverdrossenheit*), as citizens and political commentators debated the failures of specific parties and partisan politics in general (Raschke, 1982; Scheer, 1979; Döring and Smith, 1982). There was also evidence of an erosion in popular support for the party system in general. For instance, a 1983 national poll of better-educated West Germans found that the party system evoked the least faith of any of the dozen social and political institutions included in the survey (US Information Agency, 1984). In short, these developments were creating an environment in which citizens might turn away from partisan politics in general, creating a partisan dealignment.

The dealignment model suggests that the increasing fluidity of West German electoral politics is due to a general weakening of the electorate's psychological commitment to *any* political party. Without stable party attachments – and without clear social group cues – voters are more likely to switch parties between elections, split their ballots, or engage in the other activities that create change in the electoral process.

Although scholars still debate the meaningfulness of psychological party attachment expressed in West German public opinion surveys – Baker *et al.* (1981, Chapter 9); Gluchowski (1986) – Rainer-Olaf Schultze's (1987) preliminary analysis of the 1987 election polls claim that the number of partisan identifiers has decreased during the 1980s. Moreover, Schultze notes that strength of the relationship between partisanship and voting behaviour has dropped off significantly across the last three elections.

Table 6.1 indicates a slight erosion in the strength of party attachments during the 1980s. The full series of available data indicates a more modest trend than Schultze's preliminary analysis, but party ties are apparently weakening. In the 1972 election, for instance, 55 per cent of the electorate felt 'strong' or 'very strong' party ties; by 1987 this group of strong partisans has declined to 41 per cent of the electorate. Similarly, the percentage of non-partisans increases from a low point of 16 per cent in 1976 to 25 per cent of the 1987 electorate. These trends are significant because the strength of partisanship is directly related to the stability of voting preferences, split-ticket voting and the other indicators of electoral volatility that we have observed (Baker *et al.*, 1981, pp. 204–21).

TABLE 6.1   *The strength of partisanship, 1972–1987*

|  | 1972 | 1976 | 1980 | 1983 | 1987 |
|---|---|---|---|---|---|
| Very strong | 17% | 12% | 13% | 10% | 10% |
| Strong | 38 | 35 | 33 | 29 | 31 |
| Weak | 20 | 35 | 29 | 35 | 31 |
| No party, don't know | 20 | 16 | 19 | 22 | 25 |
| Refused, no answer | 5 | 3 | 6 | 4 | 3 |
| Total | 100 | 100% | 100% | 100% | 100% |

Note:
Data from West German Election Studies, see Appendix. Each time-point combines the results of two pre-election surveys and one post-election survey.

There are, admittedly, very modest changes in the partisan orientations of the West German electorate. But the magnitude of these changes is not far different from the widely heralded partisan dealignments in Britain and the United States (Särlvik and Crewe, 1980; Beck, 1984). In Britain, the proportion of the electorate that identified with a major party fell only 6 per cent between 1964 and 1979; the number of partisan identifiers in the United States decreased by approximately 10 per cent between 1964 and 1980. Yet in both countries these incremental shifts substantially affected the nature of electoral politics.

It is premature to conclude that dealignment is a major source of the increasing volatility and fragmentation of partisan politics. In comparison with the long-term evidence of a secular realignment in group voting patterns, we have only a brief time-series from which to judge whether weakening partisan ties are an enduring feature of West German politics, or merely a transitory reaction to the political scandals and the exceptional policy strains of the past decade. Furthermore, more detailed analyses of the sources and correlates of these new non-partisan voters are necessary. Still, survey findings from the 1987 Bundestag election strengthen the evidence that dealignment trends are developing within the West German electorate.

## Consequences of Electoral Change

In the Federal Republic, as in other advanced industrial societies, ongoing changes in the social structure, citizens' values and issue-interests have promoted extensive debate and research into the dynamics of electoral change. The famous observation of Lipset and Rokkan (1967, p. 54) over two decades ago that 'the party systems of the 1960s reflect with but few significant exceptions the social structure of the 1920s' is much less valid for the Federal Republic in the 1980s. The expansion of the new middle class, rising educational levels, and the infusion of post-war generations into the electorate have produced significant changes in the social cleavage structure and its relationship to the party system. As a result, fragmentation of the party system and volatility in partisan choices are both increasing.

We discussed these electoral trends above in terms of realignment and dealignment models of electoral change. On the one hand, the changing patterns of class and religious voting provide some evidence of a gradual realignment in the group bases of party support. On the other hand, the weakening of party attachments during the 1980s points towards a dealignment of the West German electorate.

A longer time scale will be required before we can establish which model is more accurate in describing the course of the West German party system, but for the present, both models point in the same direction: The long-term determinants of voting choice that stabilise

West German voting patterns have generally decreased in import-ance. The influence of social class on voting preferences has substan-tially weakened, as has the impact of religion, residence, and other social characteristics. Similarly, the recent dealignment trend signals a decrease in the impact of enduring partisan loyalties on voting decisions. Fewer voters now approach elections with fixed party predispositions based either on social characteristics or early-learned partisan ties.

We see two general consequences that flow from these develop-ments. First, the decreased impact of long-term determinants of party choice is counterbalanced by a growth in the importance of issues and other short-term influences on voting preferences. Most voters will still habitually support a preferred party, but the tentative-ness of these bonds will increase the potential that a particular issue or election campaign may sway their voting choice, at least temporarily. More and more, party issue positions and political images will determine electoral outcomes, as a substantial group of floating voters react to the immediate political stimuli of the election campaign. There is even some evidence that the images of candidates are playing a growing role in voters' decision-making. This continu-ing shift towards issue-based voting behaviour is likely to continue to inject considerable fluidity into West German electoral politics – at least until (if ever) a new stable group basis of party support forms. This development will affect all parties, creating greater uncertainty over electoral outcomes (and perhaps encouraging the parties to become more responsive to the policy preferences of their electorates).

A second consequence of the trends we have discussed is a change in the political agenda. The traditional economic and security needs of the past are now sharing the political stage with a range of New Politics issues that attract the attention of younger, better-educated, and new middle class voters. These new political interest are, in part, an indirect consequence of the weakening of traditional social cleavages. The erosion of traditional social alignments has opened up a significant portion of the public to these new cultural appeals (Bürklin, 1987).

This New Politics agenda has had a differential impact on the political parties. The political fortunes of the Greens are directly tied to environmental quality, alternative lifestyles, women's rights, disarmament, and other New Politics issues (Klingemann, 1986). But one should not equate the importance of the New Politics dimension solely with voting support for the Greens. The anti-establishment nature of the Greens limits their ability to attract widespread elec-toral support and affect policy change on New Politics issues

(Küchler, 1986). Their presence has, however, forced the established parties to respond to these same issues.

The New Politics places the SPD in a quandary. Although the Social Democrats are a likely partisan outlet for the reformist goals of the alternative movement, many of the issues advocated by the New Left (ranging from the development of nuclear power to the modernisation of NATO nuclear defences) were initially opposed by the party's traditional Old Left working class constituency. The SPD's move to the opposition benches in 1982 eased the party's ability to accommodate the conflicting goals of the Old Left and New Left. In response to the Greens' inroads into the SPD's young leftist constituency, the Social Democrats are now responding to some of the Greens' issues. At a November 1983 party congress the SPD rejected its previous position and publicly opposed the stationing of new NATO missiles in West Germany. The Social Democrats are also developing a new concern for environmental quality and other post-material issues (Bürklin and Kaltefleiter, 1987). The Old Left still dominates the party, but new political forces – such as Lafontaine's Saarland government – are giving the party a two-dimensional image. The SPD now faces the question of whether these two diverse constituencies can be integrated into an electoral force that will return the SPD to government, or whether persisting intraparty squabbles continue to drain the party's energy.

The CDU–CSU is also jumping on the environmental bandwagon for issues such as acid rain, protection of the forests, and exhaust emissions. However, governing responsibility has led the CDU–CSU to pursue conservative policies on other New Politics issues such as citizen participation, women's issues, foreign policy, and minority rights. As result, the CDU–CSU is now more clearly aligned with those who oppose New Politics goals. Thus partisan change extends beyond the Greens, as both large established parties respond (in both directions) to New Politics concerns.

In sum, the trends discussed here do not lend themselves to a simple prediction of the future of the West German party system. It does appear that electoral politics will be characterised by a greater diversity of voting. A system of frozen social cleavages and stable party alignments is less likely to develop in a society where voters are sophisticated, political interests are diverse, and individual choice is given greater latitude. Even the new political conflicts that are competing for the public's attention seem destined to create additional partisan change rather than recreate the stable electoral structure of the past. This diversity, individualism, and fluidity may, in fact, constitute the major new development for West German electoral politics.

**Appendix: Survey Data**

The survey data utilised in this chapter were made available by the Inter-University Consortium for Political and Social Research (ICPSR) in Ann Arbor and the Zentralarchiv für empirische Sozialforschung (Central Archive for Empirical Social Research) in Cologne. Neither the archives nor the original collectors of the data bear responsibility for the analyses presented here.

1953   The Social Bases of West German Politics ($N$ = 3246). UNESCO Institute.

1961   West German Election Study ($N$ = 1679, 1633, 1715). Gerhart Baumert, Erwin Scheuch, and Rudolf Wildenmann.

1965   West German Election Study, October ($N$ = 1305). DIVO Institut.

1965   West German Election Study, September ($N$ = 1411). Rudolf Wildenmann and Max Kaase.

1969   West German Election Study ($N$ = 1158). Hans-Dieter Klingemann and Franz Urban Pappi.

1972   West German Election Study ($N$ = 2052). Manfred Berger, Wolfgang Gibowski, Max Kaase, Dieter Roth, Uwe Schleth, and Rudolf Wildenmann.

1976   West German Election Study ($N$ = 2076). Forschungsgruppe Wahlen.

1980   West German Election Study ($N$ = 1620). Forschungsgruppe Wahlen.

1983   West German Election Study ($N$ = 1622). Forschungsgruppe Wahlen.

1987   West German Election Study ($N$ = 1954). Forschungsgruppe Wahlen.

# 7

# The Party System

## STEPHEN PADGETT

### Aspects of System Change

In the 1980s, the party system, which for a decade or more had exhibited a very high degree of stability, appeared to be changing so much as to suggest a complete breakdown of the existing model. A number of developments combined to cause an upheaval in the party landscape. Firstly, a realignment of the established parties saw the FDP defecting from the thirteen-year-old Social-Liberal coalition with the SPD in 1982 to form a centre-right government under Helmut Kohl. A *Machtwechsel* (change of power) was not unprecedented in the history of the Federal Republic, and the alternation of government on these lines did not in itself mean the break-up of the old party system. However the ensuing polarisation appeared to signal the end of the central orientation of West Germany politics (Smith, 1982). In particular it became doubtful whether the FDP could continue to play its customary role as balancing flywheel and pivot of the party system. Secondly, the breakthrough of the Greens in the election of 1983 marked the entry of a fourth party into a system which had been 'frozen' in a 'two-and-a-half' party mould. The emergence of a two-bloc party system was forseeable, with the CDU–CSU and the FDP on the right and the SPD and the Greens on the left. The electoral dominance of the right combined with the low potential for coalition on the left meant that the balance of party strength became heavily one-sided and the scope for *alternating* coalitions severly curtailed.

Movement in relations between parties bred a sense of flux in internal party life, introducing a third party dimension of party system change. Reviewing their identity and their place in the political landscape, the parties experienced disorientation and uncertainty. The syndrome was most pronounced in the SPD, but the coalition parties were not immune, especially after the poor performance of the CDU–CSU in the election of 1987. For their part the Greens still had to establish their role in the party system, and the unpredictability of the new party acted as a catalyst to further instability. Fourthly, the system was subjected to a process of fragmentation as the giant *Volksparteien* (people's parties), the CDU–CSU and the SPD, suffered a significant weakening of their hold over the electorate, symptomatic of an erosion of their popular legitimacy. Negative sentiment had been generated by a series of political scandals but at its root was a more deep-seated alienation of voters from these juggernaut parties.

In short, the equilibrium of the party system was thrown out of balance, its dynamic distorted and its foundations undermined. It is not clear, however, whether the threatened breakdown is temporary or terminal. Is it possible to envisage a restoration of the old system or has the Federal Republic embarked on a new era of party politics? If the party system has entered a new age, what form will the new system take and how will the dynamic unfold? This chapter examines the nature of party system change in an attempt to answer these questions.

## The Party System Before 1982

The most striking development in the early post-war years was the concentration of the party system. Eleven parties were represented in the first Bundestag (1949–53) reminiscent of the fragmentation of party politics in the Weimar Republic. By 1957 there were four, most of the smaller parties having been absorbed by the CDU or eliminated by the 5 per cent barrier to Bundestag representation. A process of bipolarisation was at work, with the two largest parties, the Christian Union parties and the Social Democrats increasing their combined share of the vote from 60.2 per cent in 1949 to 82.0 per cent in 1957. By 1961 the party system assumed the two-and-a-half party form which was to remain for the next twenty-two years. The pillars of that system were the two dominant *Volksparteien* (people's parties).

This new type of party emerged in response to the increasing affluence and social homogeneity of the post-war era. In this new environment, the class-based ideologies of conservatism and socialism appeared outdated and irrelevant. Class ideologies had tended to identify parties with clearly defined social groups, so restricting their electoral potential. Parties began to steer away from hard-and-fast ideologies and class images, projecting themselves instead as tribunes of the people and reaching out to a broad and diverse electoral catchment. Their attempts to embrace as many different groups and interests as possible led Otto Kirchheimer to coin the term 'catch-all party' (Kirchheimer, 1969).

Parties similar to the *Volkspartei* emerged in many Western European countries, but the West German parties led the way. The experience of National Socialism on the one hand and the proximity of the Communist regime in East Germany on the other means that there was a strong aversion to the ideologies of both right and left. The prototype of the people's party was the Christian Democratic Union (CDU) and its sister party the Christian-Social Union (CSU). Although, broadly speaking, the union parties were conservative, bourgeois, business-oriented and church-aligned, they avoided the overt expression of ideology and class. As voters' parties rather than mass membership parties, they revolved around the personality of the Chancellor and undisputed party chief, Konrad Adenauer. Their success was due to their identification with political reconstruction and economic success rather than to class loyalties.

The dynamic of the *Volkspartei*-system was supplied by electoral competition. Restricted by the Union parties' success to an electoral ghetto, the SPD responded by moving in stages towards a similar style of politics. A milestone on this road was the 1959 Bad Godesberg Congress where the SPD finally divested itself of its working class, socialist identity, in adopting a more humanist outlook and opening itself up to sympathisers who did not share the total socialist faith of party members. The party thus became the model of the social democratic people's party.

The *Volkspartei* system naturally gravitated towards the centre of the political spectrum, and this tendency was reinforced by the logic of coalition politics. The balance of strength, combined with the aversion to single-party government, meant that only one Bundestag election (that of 1957) resulted in a single-party majority. With this exception, elections have left the parties no option but to negotiate coalition agreements usually made and announced prior to the election. In the two-and-a-half party system three coalition pairings were possible, all of which have at some time come about. Pappi's (1984) model of inter-party relations (see Figure 7.1) shows the underlying affinities between the three established parties which served as the foundations for coalition building in the old party system.

Each of the parties represented its own tendency – socialism (SPD), Christian conservatism (CDU), and liberalism (FDP) – but there were important joint interests which bridged the tendencies

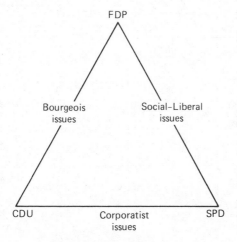

FIGURE 7.1   *The triangular party system*

Source: Pappi (1984), page 12.

(see Figure 7.1). A condition of coalition politics was that in order to be successful each party had to be compatible with one of its competitors, which meant emphasising joint interests and playing down the party's own distinctive tendency. This constraint exerted a moderating and centralising effect upon the party system.

The linchpin of coalition politics (see Table 7.1) was the FDP (Padgett and Burkett, 1986, pp. 164–71). Affinities between the CDU–CSU and the SPD were tenuous, and usually outweighed by the differences arising out of the competing ideological traditions from which the parties originated. Moreover, the parties normally regarded themselves as competitors rather than potential coalition partners. The Grand Coalition was the product of exceptional circumstances. The FDP's ideological dualism (Søe, 1985, pp. 125–6), on the other hand, enabled it to form a strong axis with either of the major parties.

A bourgeois tendency towards economic liberalism coexisted with a social liberal tradition in which civil liberties and social justice were uppermost. From 1949 to 1966 the emphasis of the Free Democrats on economic liberalism gave the party a natural affinity to the CDU, but after the Grand Coalition (from which they were excluded) they made themselves available in 1969 to the SPD. The foundation for the Social-Liberal coalition was the joint interest of the two parties in social reform (initially) and in an open-minded approach to Ostpolitik and international detente. By the early 1980s, however,

TABLE 7.1  *Results of Bundestag elections, 1949–1987*

| | | 1949 | 1955 | 1957 | 1961 | 1965 | 1969 | 1972 | 1976 | 1980 | 1983 | 1987 |
|---|---|---|---|---|---|---|---|---|---|---|---|---|
| CDU–CSU | % vote | 31.0 | 45.2 | 50.2 | 45.3 | 47.6 | 46.1 | 44.9 | 48.6 | 44.5 | 48.8 | 44.3 |
| | ± | | +14.2 | +5.0 | −4.9 | +2.3 | −1.5 | −1.2 | +3.7 | −4.1 | +4.3 | −4.5 |
| | Seats | 139 | 243 | 270 | 242 | 245 | 242 | 225 | 243 | 226 | 244 | 223 |
| SPD | % vote | 29.2 | 28.8 | 31.8 | 36.2 | 39.3 | 42.7 | 45.8 | 42.6 | 42.9 | 38.2 | 37.0 |
| | ± | | −0.4 | +3.0 | +4.4 | +3.1 | +3.4 | +3.1 | −3.2 | +0.3 | −4.7 | −1.2 |
| | Seats | 131 | 151 | 169 | 190 | 202 | 224 | 230 | 214 | 218 | 193 | 186 |
| FDP | % vote | 11.9 | 9.5 | 7.7 | 12.8 | 9.5 | 5.8 | 8.4 | 7.9 | 10.6 | 6.9 | 9.1 |
| | ± | | −2.4 | −1.8 | +5.1 | −3.3 | −3.7 | +2.6 | −0.5 | +2.7 | −3.7 | −2.2 |
| | Seats | 52 | 48 | 41 | 67 | 49 | 30 | 41 | 39 | 53 | 34 | 46 |
| Others | % vote | 27.8 | 16.5 | 10.3 | 5.7 | 3.5 | 5.5 | 0.9 | 0.9 | 0.5 | 0.5 | 1.2 |
| | ± | | −11.3 | −6.2 | −4.6 | −2.2 | +2.0 | −4.6 | +/−0.0 | −0.4 | +/−0.0 | +0.7 |
| | Seats | 80 | 45 | 17 | – | – | – | – | – | – | – | – |
| Greens | % vote | | | | | | | | | 1.5 | 5.6 | 8.3 |
| | ± | | | | | | | | | | +4.1 | +2.7 |
| | Seats | | | | | | | | | | 27 | 42 |
| Turnout | % | 78.5 | 83.2 | 84.5 | 87.7 | 86.8 | 86.7 | 91.2 | 90.7 | 88.6 | 89.1 | 84.4 |

the similarities in perspective between the SPD and FDP were eclipsed by unbridgeable differences over economic policy and it was the Liberals who precipitated the coalition's demise. The renewed ascendancy of economic liberalism in the FDP meant that the party was now much closer to the CDU–CSU and the *Machtwechsel* was the logical outcome. In spite of its small size, the FDP played an integral part in the two-and-a-half party system. Firstly, its pivotal role in coalition building imparted a centripetal force on the system. Secondly, its flexibility in remaining open, in the longer term at least, to either of the major parties was an important condition for coalition alternation.

## The Party Landscape after the Wende

The restoration of the pre–1966 centre-right coalition axis and the breakthrough of the Greens meant a very significant change in party system dynamics. Pappi's triangular model of inter-party relations was replaced by a two-bloc party system based on families of parties – the CDU–CSU and FDP on the right and (more tenuously) the SPD and the Greens on the left. This new formation took shape as the parties shifted ground in the course of the *Wende* and in its aftermath. Inter-party relations were now characterised by assimilation between the parties of the new coalition, polarisation between the CDU and SPD, and divergence between the SPD and FDP. The new party system severely restricted the range of coalition permutations among the established parties, isolating the SPD. On the left, the potential for coalition was low. The SPD and the Greens were incompatible, in spite of a 'greening' of the former on certain issues. The unpredictability of the Greens made them, a 'wild card' in the party system. Political logic suggested that there was no realistic alternative to the centre-right coalition, a conclusion which was confirmed by electoral arithmetic. An asymmetrical electoral landscape heavily dominated by the CDU meant that neither an SPD–FDP nor a SPD–Green coalition could have commanded a majority after the election of 1983. It should be emphasised, however, that the two-bloc party system is still in its embryonic stages. To assess whether it is emerging as a fully functioning model we need to take stock of developments in inter-party relations after the *Wende*.

The coalition bloc effectively consists of three parties, since although the CDU–CSU presents a single *Fraktion* in the Bundestag, the constituent parties are fully independent in terms of organisation and identity. The CDU is a pragmatic *Volkspartei* which plays down its basically conservative outlook, whereas the CSU is much more forthright about its conservatism. Although the CSU is a Bavarian party, its organisation restricted to this Land, it plays a secondary role as the vanguard of conservatism on the national stage. Its late leader, Franz Josef Strauss, was a politician of national standing who personified the party's distinctive identity. Between the CSU and the FDP, political conflict and personal rivalry is endemic. The Bavarians' Catholic conservatism inevitably clashes with the secular liberalism of the FDP, and the two parties compete for a limited number of cabinet posts. In 1982–3 the CSU declared open war on the FDP in an (unsuccessful) attempt to force it below the 5 per cent electoral hurdle to Bundestag representation, an eventuality which would have greatly strengthened CSU influence in the government.

Friction between the CSU and FDP was never far beneath the surface in the coalition's first term, and after the election of 1987 it reached a peak, with frequent talk of a 'coalition crisis'. The sense of crisis was largely manufactured to give added profile to the junior parties in the government. Indeed, for the FDP it was part of a strategy designed to keep alive their traditional role of central axis and pivot of the party system. It enabled them to assert their independence by maintaining the long-term prospects of an opening to the left, a scenario which had lost credibility in the party landscape after the *Wende*. In a two-bloc party system the FDP would be effectively a 'captive' in the centre-right coalition, its previous flexibility curtailed. In as much as the Liberals feel the need to sustain the prospect of an opening to the left, and are able to do so, an important element of the old party system remains intact. Tactics and rhetoric, however, are ultimately no substitute for electoral strength. Both before and after the election of 1987 the combined poll of the FDP and SPD fell some way short of the electoral majority necessary to form a government (see Figure 7.2). A Social-Liberal coalition was simply out of the question in the short term.

The crystallisation of a new formation on the right was not matched by a similar process on the left. Sharp differences of outlook between the Old and the New Left prevented the emergence of a common front. Whilst the Greens belong unequivocably to the New Left there was a 'dualism' within the SPD between Old and New Left. When the SPD was in government, the latter had been suppressed, but with the end of the Schmidt era it took a seemingly inexorable hold on the party. Effectively, it has been argued, the SPD contains two parties in one (Gibowski and Kaase, 1986, p. 5). Disorientation and a crisis of identity inevitably followed, intensified by the electoral challenge posed by the Greens, and its attendant dilemmas. Should the SPD reaffirm its character as a centre-left *Volkspartei*, or incorporate the values of post-materialism in a bid

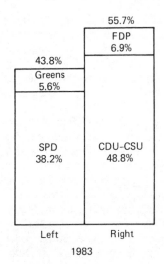 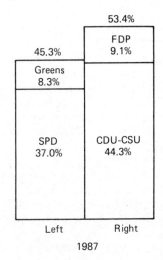

FIGURE 7.2   *Electoral arithmetic of a two-bloc party system*
(*percentage of vote*)

for a new majority of the left? The first path offers the possibility
(albeit at some indefinite stage in the future) of reviving the alignment with the Liberals: the second led towards a red-green alliance.

Both strategies carry perils for the SPD. Reaffirming the party's
*Volkspartei* character means conceding the electoral ground now
occupied by the Greens. On the other hand, a left majority strategy
envisaging coexistence with the Greens is bound to be problematical.
The dilemma is acute, and with neither alternative offering to pay
immediate dividends the SPD's response was to sit on the fence
(Smith, 1987, pp 135–9).

The notion of the two-bloc party system presupposes conciliation
between Old and New Left. However, very little progress has been
made in this direction. Diehards in the SPD – including some of the
party's powerful trade union allies – and fundamentalist Greens are
implacably opposed to such a course. The unpredictability of the
Greens, standing between a parliamentary party and an extra-parliamentary movement, makes them an unpredictable partner for the
SPD. Moreover, on some policy issues, notably defence and security,
the two parties are far apart. To be sure, the SPD has undergone a
certain 'greening'. At the 1986 congress it made the commitment to
'phase out' nuclear energy. However, such moves were motivated
as much by a spirit of competition with the Greens as by a desire
for *rapprochement*. Another factor in the equation is the likelihood
of a left majority (Smith, 1987, pp 139–43). The opposition parties

were eight percentage points behind the coalition in the election of
1987. It is unlikely that either party will take seriously the possibility
of alliance until the left is within striking distance of a majority.
Electoral trends are not propitious. The movement of voters in 1987
tended to be *within* rather than *between* blocs. Not only is the potential for a common front on the left rather limited, but electoral
arithmetic is still loaded against it.

The FDP's concern to preserve at least an illusion of independence, and the SPD's unwillingness seriously to contemplate a red–
green alliance, suggests that the realisation of a two-bloc party system
is not certain. Clearly the equilibrum of the old party system has
been disturbed, but its successor is not yet apparent. The party
system appears to be caught between two ages. Two features of
the 1987 election pointed to a process of continuing, unpredictable
change. Firstly the dominance of the CDU–CSU over the SPD was
no longer so marked. Secondly, both the minor parties gained at the
expense of the *Volksparteien*. Moreover, an inventory of development in the parties since 1983 suggested a certain fluidity in inner-
party relations confirming the impression of *Wende ohne Ende*
(change without end).

## Parties in Flux

### The SPD

The *Wende* of 1982–3 was a watershed for the SPD. Firstly, its
leadership corps was severly depleted by the departure of the outgo-
ing chancellor and his closest associates from front-rank party life.
Secondly, the last years of the Schmidt government had exposed the
party's exhaustion in terms of ideas. Thirdly the 1983 election had
revealed the extent of the SPD's electoral decomposition. Inevitably,
the issues raised in the process of elite renewal, programme review
and electoral consolidation, became entwined with the intractable
question of the SPD's future direction between the Old and the New
Left (see Chapter 6). However, it was indicative of the resilience of
the SPD that the social-democratic policy changes were not
accompanied by acute factional convulsions or the sudden switch in
course experienced by other parties of the European left under
similar circumstances.

In the SPD's top leadership triangle only Willy Brandt remained
after 1982. Alongside him, however, Hans-Jochen Vogel and
Johannes Rau represented the 'old guard', and their succession was
in no way a break with the past. Vogel was a reconciler of the

competing tendencies, whilst Rau, on the centre-right, epitomised the traditional 'labourist' face of the SPD. Although the old guard remained in control in Bonn, however, a new generation of leaders was emerging in the Länder. Oskar Lafontaine and Björn Engholm (minister-president of the Saarland and Schleswig-Holstein) and Gerhard Schröder (top candidate in Lower Saxony) were more representative of the New Left. Elections to the Party Executive at the 1986 conference, moreover, revealed that in the party at large and in the middle levels of its hierarchy, the New Left was gaining ground. Nevertheless, and in spite of some factional mobilisation following the 1987 election defeat, a reshuffle of top party posts later that year showed that the tendencies were still capable of compromise. The accession of Vogel (taking Brandt's mantle as Party Chairman) and Anke Fuchs as Business Manager buttressed the right, but they were balanced by the election of Lafontaine as Vice-Chairman and his emergence as prospective (thought not as yet designated) chancellor candidate.

Programme review was more difficult to accomplish in the same spirit of non-committal compromise. A new basic programme was issued in draft form in 1986, to replace the out-of-date Godesberg Programme of 1959. It was intended to redefine social democracy, making it more relevant to the issues of the 1980s and 1990s. However, the attempt to satisfy both the traditionalists and the New Left meant that the draft programme lacked clarity and force. Its major prescriptions were for the modernisation of the economy on environmentally safe lines, and a reaffirmation of West Germany's commitment to the Western Alliance, linked to NATO reform. In short it represented a carefully calculated 'greening' of social democratic principles. The 1987 election campaign exposed a certain shallowness in the new platform and its inconsistencies on issues like nuclear power; and subsequently the draft programme was withdrawn.

The SPD entered the election strategically bankrupt, with no convincing formula for a return to government. Relying on the threadbare illusion that it could win a majority on its own, the SPD vetoed any discussion of an opening to the Greens. In the election *post mortem*, Lafontaine launched a vigorous attack on this tactic in an attempt to establish himself as frontrunner for the 1990 chancellor candidacy and to reorientate the SPD leftwards, although subsequently he moderated his position. To the consternation of his own supporters and of the party's trade union wing, Lafontaine opened the issue of labour-market flexibility as an answer to unemployment. His advocacy of a theme usually associated with the coalition parties was interpreted as an overture towards the FDP. The apparent turnaround by this advocate of the left-majority strategy added to the confusion surrounding the SPD's strategic orientation.

## The Christian Union Parties

On the right, fragmentation was less dramatic but still served to weaken the political cohesion of the Union parties, accentuating long-standing divisions which had already begun to open up during Kohl's first term. The radicalisation of the party right was in part a reflex response to the rise of the New Left. Indeed, a number of 'New Right' issues – tougher laws relating to demonstrations, a more uncompromising Ostpolitik – could be interpreted as direct reactions to the radicalisation of the left. It was also bound up with the rhetoric of the *Wende* with its promises of an 'historical new beginning', and a spiritual-moral renewal. Largely unrealised in government programmes, the expectations fostered by this rhetoric fuelled the hardlines conservatism of CSU chief and Bavarian minister-president Franz Josef Strauss, CSU Interior Minister Friedrich Zimmermann, and CDU *Fraktion* leader Alfred Dregger. Their calls for a second *Wende* expressed frustrations at the Chancellor's rather bland 'more of the same' style of government, and his failure to set in motion a radical policy revolution. A further dimension of the radicalisation of the right was the rise of a new tide of German nationalism, partially endorsed by the CDU–CSU in the 1987 election campaign.

A contrary tendency, resisting the clamour of the right was the modern, progressive and pragmatic wing of the party personified by CDU General Secretary Heiner Geissler (Naumann, 1987, pp 167 – 71). Extrapolating from the trends of the 1987 election and the drift to the FDP, Geissler pointed to the electoral dangers of pandering to what he regarded as marginal groups on the right. Instead he advocated a policy reorientation towards the political middle-ground. His proposed programmatic renewal centred on a progressive social policy – the restructuring rather than dismantling of the social state, initiatives on family and women's issues – and the reaffirmation of an accommodative Ostpolitik.

Since the 1960s, when the Union parties emerged from Adenauer's shadow, they have represented an uneasy alliance between pragmatic conservatives like Geissler, and the hardliners. Most of the time pragmatism has dominated, and indeed the strength of the CDU–CSU and its success as a *Volkspartei* was due to its pragmatic character. The resurgence of the right threatened to alter the political balance, with implications for their capacity to act as *Volksparteien*. A more immediate threat was conflict and immobilism in the coalition which was profoundly dispiriting for the CDU. Kohl's uninspired leadership offered no answers beyond empty appeals for unity. A sense of purposelessness pervaded both party and government. If the CDU proves unable to impart a renewed sense of direction to the coalition parties there is a danger that the FDP will turn its attention to an alternative coalition pairing with the SPD.

## The FDP

The FDP has an apparently inbuilt capacity for survival in a shifting electoral landscape. Instability is endemic to a party like the Liberals which lacks a secure social base. Even without alignments with particular social groups, the party has developed the ability to carve out a niche for itself in the party system, based as we have seen on its functional role within the system. Its survival relies heavily on astute tactical calculation and flexibility – features the FDP has always cultivated. Perils abound, however, in the changes of course which this strategy entails, and particularly so in the manoeuvres involved in changing coalition partners. In 1982–3 the party experienced a massive turnover of members and voters and in six Landtag elections following the *Machtwechsel*, failed to achieve the crucial 5 per cent hurdle. Survival in the Bundestag election of 1983 and relative security in 1987 was due to its ability to 'borrow' second votes from its coalition partner. Loaned votes can easily be recalled and in spite of its recent revival, the FDP lives close to the electoral threshold. The party depends on being able to play its customary functional role in the party system.

To reassert its role as pivot in the party system the FDP must keep alive the long-term prospect of alternating coalitions – thus the possibility of a return to a Social-Liberal coalition with the SPD. This combination has become more difficult in the 'new look' party system. The departure of Martin Bangemann to the European Community and the candidacy for his post as Party Chairman of Irmgard Adam-Schwaetzer provoked speculation that under her leadership the coalition question might have been opened up. However, the victory for Otto Lambsdorff confirmed the FDP's centre-right orientation, and the party felt more secure in playing its other role as Liberal corrective to the CDU/CSU. Paradoxically perhaps, but in keeping with its history, the FDP inclined to the right on economic issues and to the left on social questions. Its advocacy of a radical reform of the tax system to favour wealth creation, and its resistance to the hardline conservative tendency in the CDU–CSU on foreign policy and civil liberties enabled the Liberals to play a distinctive and positive role. On the one hand the FDP pushed Kohl to tackle the contentious issue of taxation, on the other it protected the Chancellor from the 'hawks' in his own party. Significantly, surveys revealed a very high percentage (86 per cent) of Union party voters wishing to see the FDP remain in the Bundestag (Forschungsruppe Wahlen eV 1987, p 53), and by implication in the government. The FDP are likely to derive continued support from this source, acting against any impulse to change coalition partners. However, the party's flirtations with the SPD continue, and are reciprocated. In the long term it would be rash to rule out a restoration of the Social-Liberal coalition.

## The Greens

The major question accompanying the rise of the Greens concerns the prospect for their assimilation into the party system. Their distinctive characteristics make it difficult to answer this question decisively in view of the major differences between the Greens and the established parties. Their initial determination not to behave like an orthodox political party reflected their origins in the extra-parliamentary new social movements and suggested a low potential for assimilation. The axioms of *Basisdemokratie* (grass-roots democracy) were written into the party's founding programme: transparency in policy and decision-making, openness of hierarchy, and decentralisation of power were the principles on which the party was built. To guard against elite domination, bureaucratisation and the concentration of power, party statutes contained an elaborate system of checks and balances. Leadership was divided between three co-equal chairmen to prevent the emergence of a leader who was 'larger than the party'. The party Executive was given the role of secretariat rather than directorate, its members restricted to two-year terms of office and debarred from election to Land, Federal or European parliaments, an attempt to ensure against the growth of an entrenched and dominant elite, as was also the provision that Members of the *Bundestagfraktion* were to rotate in mid-term. At every level of elected office-holding, Green deputies were to be shadowed by a party committee exercising scrutiny and control. In questions of policy, open party conferences were given an authoritative role.

The policy of *Basisdemokratie* proved very difficult to maintain in practice. In particular the *Bundestagfraktion* grew to be independent of the extra-parliamentary party. Aided by financial support from the state, the *Fraktion* bureau come to employ around 100 research and administrative staff. Superiority in terms of resources, and the intermittent meetings of the committee intended to shadow the *Fraktion*, combined to undermine the supposed subordination of the parliamentary party to the extra-parliamentary arm. Green MdBs were reluctant to relinquish their posts through rotation, and although all but two did so in 1985, the practice of rotation has since been dropped. A number of MdBs quickly became prominent media figures, effectively freeing themselves from party control. Moreover, at the lower levels of party life the accountability of elected office holders to the membership, and broad participation in policy formulation was frustrated by apathy. Mass participation was not perceptibly higher than in other established parties. In short, as far as party organisation was concerned the Greens showed signs of assimilation into the parliamentary party system, following a well-worn path: 'Once inside the system, the party leadership is socialised into the realities and limitations of effecting political change and the need for compromise to achieve any progress. In time the lure of power and effectiveness may prompt the party to moderate its platform and broaden its appeal' (Flanagan and Dalton, 1984, p. 9).

It would be premature to claim that the Greens are irrevocably committed to this road. From the outset internal party life was characterised by fragmenting and unstable tendencies, from which two divergent factions have emerged. With their foundations in the *Bundestagfraktion*, the pragmatists (or *Realos*) tend to contain their demands within 'reasonable' bounds, conform to an extent with the protocols of parliamentary politics and show a willingness to cooperate with the SPD. By contrast, the fundamentalists (*Fundis*) emphasise the party's anti-system character and relate more readily to extra-parliamentary movements than to the SPD. Since 1987, the conflict between these two factions has escalated into intense acrimony. The balance between the factions has tended to fluctuate and remains quite evenly poised. There are clear affinities between the pragmatists and the SPD's New Left. Whether this common ground can be used to establish a bridge between the two parties, thus incorporating the Greens in the party system depends on the pragmatists gaining a decisive advantage which hitherto they have been unable to achieve: in 1989 they were clearly.

Although the Greens have not yet found a stable niche in the party system, their performance in federal and state elections suggests that they are a permanent feature of the system for the foreseeable future. They have, moreover, made a very significant impact on the political agenda, heightening the salience of environmental issues and increasing the sensitivity to gender in politics. The establishment of an Environment Ministry can be ascribed in large part to their influence as can the intensification of attention in the SPD to issues such as nuclear energy and chemical pollution. In all three of the established parties women have recently been appointed or elected to top posts and provisions made for their increased representation in the upper party echelons. The new social trends of the 1970s and 1980s are opening up the party system, and the old parties are being forced to respond to the political agenda which has accompanied post-industrial society (Flanagan and Dalton, 1984, pp. 7–23).

Change brings uncertainty, and all the parties have experienced self-doubt in the face of system change since the *Wende*. The established parties, however, have adapted to change without making a definite break with the past. Patterns of party behaviour associated with the old system show a surprising degree of persistence. In particular, the SPD and FDP have sustained the possibility of a future alliance in defiance of the 'logic' of the two-bloc party system. Moreover, the CDU and SPD have largely restrained the impulse to exploit fully the openings to the right and left resulting from a weakening of the mechanisms of system centrality. In short the parties have been reluctant to accept fully the implications of the new party system, which suggests that there may still be life in the old model.

## The Decline of Party Democracy

Political parties are ascribed a privileged status in the Federal Republic, even dating back to the formative years in the immediate post-war period. The experience of the Third Reich had destroyed the institutional framework of the state and discredited the political class which manned it. Political reconstruction began from a *tabula rasa* and the parties were singled out to play a key role in public life. However, the failed democracy of the Weimar Republic and twelve years of totalitarian rule underlined the weakness of the party tradition in Germany. The promotion of party government and party democracy consequently figured as a dominant consideration in the framing of the Basic Law. Article 21 outlined the conditions of party life and charged the parties with responsibility for 'forming the political will of the people'.

The parties became synonymous with the democratic state. Powers of patronage allowed (even encouraged) them to infiltrate wide areas of public life. 'The parties were the special instrument of democracy; the grip of democratic ideas was secured by party penetration of other institutions' (Dyson, 1982 c, p. 84). In particular, the bureaucracy, broadcasting and education were brought under party control. By the 1960s party oligopoly had so developed that it became common to refer to the 'party state'. The term carried negative connotations, suggesting that party democracy had turned from a source of strength to one of potential weakness. Its tarnished image reflected in a weakening of party legitimacy, culminating in the 1970s and 1980s in a syndrome of *Parteienetfremdung* (alienation from parties) stemming from an undercurrent of discontent with and loss of confidence in the parties.

Discontent had its source in the structure and character of the parties themselves. The structure of the established parties resembles a pyramid-shaped hierarchy. At its apex is a very narrow elite which has control of a vast bureaucratic machine employing hundreds of functionaries. Ordinary members have only limited opportunities to participate in internal party life. Amongst members of both major parties the demands for participation began to assume importance in the 1970s. In the CDU, frustration was caused by the limited opportunities for office-holding – a major motivation for joining the party (Kolinsky, 1984, pp. 144–6). Although the leadership responded by (artificially) generating new posts at local level, frustrations remained. In the SPD the problem was more acute. The influx of young, radical, middle-class members entering the party in the early 1970s proved difficult to assimilate. Their aspiration to participate and their radical policy goals were impossible to reconcile with the party's hierarchical structure and middle-of-the-road politics. The challenge which they posed for the party was contained by the power of the bureaucratic machine which effectively excluded them from decision-making. However, the effect of this sterilisation of internal party life was a loss of vitality in the lower reaches of the party. The functions of integration and communication, crucial to a party's capacity for electoral mobilisation, suffered badly. In fact, the SPD, the Union parties and the FDP all showed signs of malfunction in these respects, provoking searching enquiries into the character of the parties at local level. Attempts were made to revitalise the parties at the grassroots, but these centre-led exercises served to emphasise still further their 'top-down' hierarchical character.

A second malaise in party life concerns the so-called 'representation-gap'. The composition of the established parties diverges very markedly from the social profile of the population. Intimate party-state relations and party patronage in the state bureaucracy meant that large numbers of civil servants joined the parties for reasons of career opportunism. The SPD was particularly affected by this syndrome, earning it the unwelcome sobriquet of being *'Partei des öffentlichen Dienstes'* (party of the public service). Additionally, the premium attached to expertise has led to a professionalisation of party politics. Public administration, law journalism and the universities are the reservoirs which feed party membership, and the over-representation of these career groups becomes more pronounced in the higher levels of the party hierarchies. Another distorting effect

arose from the mutual embrace between parties and organised interests, a *Verfilzung* (interpenetration), meaning the over-representation among party office-holders of interest-group functionaries.
Parliament presents a microcosm of party life in which these tendencies particularly stand out. In the 1983–7 Bundestag 33.4 per cent of
MdBs were civil servants, while a further 13.5 per cent were the
employees of the parties themselves or of socio-economic interest-
organisations, a fact which underlines the narrow representational
base of party politics. Such a restricted social base was bound to
engender a similarly narrow political perspective which increasingly
broad sections of society no longer shared.

The crisis of participation and the representation-gap in the established parties led to a stagnation in internal party life and the growth
of political activity outside the parties. In the 1970s, the focus of this
activity was the *Bürgerinitiativen* (citizens' initiative groups). Small in
size, uncoordinated and diverse in political character, these included
ecology groups, municipal politics pressure groups and 'alternative
life-style' groups. Made politically active and brought under one
organisational roof by the campaign against nuclear energy in the
mid 1970s, these movements were the forerunner of the Green Party.
Epitomising the rejection of the established parties by a small but
significant section of the electorate, the Greens presented themselves
as an 'anti-party' party, striving to avoid the bureaucratic organisational format of the older parties.

A further dimension in the erosion of party legitimacy was the
perceived decline in ethical and moral standards, an issue which was
raised in the course of the Flick Affair which from 1982 brought a
flood of revelations concerning irregular and illegal practices in the
funding of the parties through corporate donations. As this affair
ran its course, the CDU triggered the opening of the Neue Heimat
scandal. Although the malpractices in this trade-union run housing
concern did not directly implicate the Social Democrats, the SPD's
union links meant a certain guilt by association. The culmination
of public disquiet over political morality came with the Schleswig-
Holstein election of September 1987. Revelations that campaign staff
close to CDU minister-president Uwe Barschel had employed an
array of dirty tricks to smear the reputation of SPD candidate Björn
Engholm sparked a train of events which ended in Barschel's suicide.
Conduct which suggested that the parties perceived themselves as
above or outside the law was bound to intensify the feeling of *Parteienentfremdung*.

*Parteienentfremdung* has compounded the effects of electoral
dealignment (see Chapter 6), with the main damage inflicted on the
*Volksparteien*. The combined vote of CDU–CSU and SPD reached

a peak at just over 90 per cent of votes cast in the election of 1972 and 1976 (see Table 7.2). In 1980 and 1983 that figure fell to around 87 per cent and in 1987 to 81.3 per cent. Parallel to this there has been a fall in electoral participation from a high point at around 91 per cent in 1972 and 1976 to about 89 per cent in 1980 and 1983 and a sharp fall to 84.4 per cent in 1987 (the lowest since the 1950s).

TABLE 7.2   *The decline in CDU–CSU and SPD share of the vote*

| Year | % |
| --- | --- |
| 1965 | 86.9 |
| 1969 | 88.8 |
| 1972 | 90.7 |
| 1976 | 91.2 |
| 1980 | 87.4 |
| 1983 | 87.0 |
| 1987 | 81.3 |

## Party Finance

The style of party politics in the Federal Republic is only sustainable through a very high level of finance. The large *Apparat* parties with large bureaucratic organisations drawn by intense electoral competition into enormously expensive election campaigns, generate an upward spiral of financial demands, the fulfilment of which is way beyond the capacity of the parties themselves. Income from internal sources such as membership subscriptions, covers less than half of the parties' requirements. The remainder is drawn from state subventions and from private, and more significantly, corporate donations. State finance was introduced, and subsequently stepped up, in order to reduce the reliance of parties on industrial and commercial donors, but increased state aid has not assuaged the thirst for corporate money. In the 1980s the Flick Affair subjected the shadow world of party finance to public attention, revealing the extent of malpractice in the financial nexus between parties and business.

State funding remains the largest single source of party finance. Introduced in 1959 in response to a ruling by the Federal Constitutional Court against the practice of tax concessions for business donors, the volume of state aid rose from DM 5 million per annum in the early stages to over DM 150 million by the middle 1980s. Relying on Article 21 of the Basic Law, funds were initially earmarked for the 'furthering of the political education work of the parties' (as opposed to general party activity). This led to the creation by the parties in the middle 1960s of foundations, ostensibly for the purposes of political education, but tending in reality to act simply as outposts of the party apparatus. The Party Law of 1967 established a new order for state party finance, relating it to electoral performance. The level of funding was tied to the number of votes cast for a party, using a formula of DM 2.5 for each vote, subsequently increased to DM 3.5 and in 1984 to DM 5.0. As previously, the move was a response to a ruling by Federal Constitutional Court; in accordance with the Court's judgement it widened the net to include parties which were not represented in the Bundestag. It also endeavoured to make the practices of party finance more open by obliging the parties to publish annual accounts of their income and to name large donors.

Attempts to wean the parties away from corporate patronage and to subject donations to public scrutiny were largely unsuccessful (Kolinsky, 1984, pp 33–8) Donations continued to increase, and means were found to circumvent the disclosure of donors' identities by subterfuges such as the channelling of money through the party foundations and through party-related organisations for the receipt of donations. The use of 'non-profit' intermediary organisations benefitting from tax exemption even allowed parties and donors to circumvent the 1958 ruling on tax liability. Other practices for tax avoidance included the passing off of donations as payment for purely nominal services such as advertising (offset against company taxation) performed by party-related organisations (Andersen and Woyke, 1986, p. 118) In 1979 an initiative by all four parties to relax the law on the taxation of donations was blocked by the Federal Constitutional Court, but the 'black economy' in party financing remained uncurtailed. Between 1969 and 1980, one Cologne-based, party-related 'collection association' alone directed some DM 220 million into the CDU–CSU and FDP (*Aktuell*, 1984, p. 482). The case in 1975 of a Lichtenstein company which had been used illegally to channel funds to the CDU brought the issue into the open for the first time, sparking off a wave of activity on the part of the judicial authorities. Between 1981 and the beginning of 1984, approximately 1,800 judicial enquiries were instigated by the Bonn public prosecutor. Among the subjects of these enquiries were the ministers, ex-ministers or state secretaries Otto Lambsdorff, Josef Ertl, Hans Friderichs (FDP); Wolfgang Vogt, Horst Waffenschmidt (CDU); Oscar Schneider and Friedrich Zimmermann (CSU). In all, fifteen Bundestag deputies were charged with assisting in tax evasion operations.

The most dramatic of the charges centred on Lambsdorff and

Friderichs, who it was alleged, as Economics Ministers, had sanctioned concessions on taxes payable upon a sale of shares by the massive Flick conglomerate. Flick, it transpired, has been a long-standing and substantial contributor to the funds of *all* the major parties through intermediaries. The company's general manager, Eberhard Brauchitsch was also arraigned. It was revealed that firms in insurance and pharmaceuticals had been making similarly illicit contributions to party finances. Beleaguered by legal process and public opinion, the CDU faced a further scandal. The Bundestag President (speaker) and former party leader, Rainer Barzel, was alleged to have received large sums of money in the 1970s to persuade him to make way for Helmut Kohl as CDU chief. The implication of Chancellor Kohl in questionable conduct recurred when it was alleged that he had lied to the Bundestag's special committee of investigation into the Flick affair.

In addition to the committee of investigation, a commission of experts was set up in 1983 to draft a new framework for party finance. Its main recommendations were embodied in a law passed in December 1983. Annual party accounts would henceforward have to include not only the source of finance but also the details of expenditure. Tax exemptions were granted to small donations and concessions allowed on contributions up to DM 1000,000. Payments through intermediaries were strictly proscribed, and financial sanctions introduced against irregular donations. A formula for the equalisation of tax advantages between parties was devised, and the vote-related state subsidy increased. In short the new law, which took the form of an amendment to the 1967 Party Law, sought to place party finance on an even-handed, legally-prescribed and transparent basis.

The reverberations of these tremors in the world of party finance are potentially far-reaching. Firstly, as para-state institutions, conformity with the norms of legal rectitude in party life is a paramount concern. Departures from these norms are bound to damage the parties' public standing, contributing to their estrangement from the electorate and ultimately threatening party democracy. Secondly, in spite of the appearance of affluence, the parties are financially stretched by the scale and intensity of their activities, and frequently have to resort to borrowing. Year-by-year comparisons of the volume of party donations are hazardous, because of the unreliability of party accounts at least before 1984 and because donations tend to fluctuate with political circumstances. However, a crude survey indicates that the level of donations was reduced quite considerably between 1983 and 1985 (*Jahrbuch der BRD*, 1985–6, p 412; 1987–88, p 347). A permanent loss of income resulting from the tightening of financial regulation would inevitably mean a contraction of party activities, with unforeseeable consequences for the parties.

## The Party System in the Länder

West Germany's federal system means that the government in Bonn is surrounded by ten 'satellite' administrations in the Länder. The vagaries of regional electoral geography determine the composition of these administrations. In some of the Länder a party's dominance at the polls has given it a near monopoly on state power. Thus the CSU's exclusive hold on government in Bavaria has been uninterrupted since 1962. The CDU has governed alone in Baden-Württemberg since 1972, in Rhineland-Palatinate from 1971 to 1988 and in Schleswig-Holstein from 1967 to 1987. Single-party SPD government is less common. The Social Democrats have monopolised power in Bremen since 1971 and ruled in Hamburg from 1978 to 1987. With these exceptions, government in the Länder has generally been based on coalitions.

When the arithmetic of election results permits, coalitions tend to reflect the Bonn model. A *Machtwechsel* in Bonn normally means musical chairs in the Länder too. In fact the mutation of coalition formation in Bonn is often preceded by changes in the Länder. The defection in 1966 of the FDP from its coalition with the CDU in North Rhine-Westphalia in favour of an SPD–FDP government was a signpost for the formation of the social-liberal coalition in Bonn three years later. In similar fashion, the break-up of social-liberal coalitions in Hamburg (1978) and North Rhine-Westphalia (1980), the formation of a centre-right coalition in Saarland (1977) and preparations by the FDP in Hesse for a switch from SPD to CDU, all pointed towards the 1982 federal change in coalition.

The 1983–7 Bundestag saw some significant changes in the party landscape in the Länder. It was a period of single-party government in an unusually large number of states. The party system had been thrown out of equilibrium by the displacement of the FDP from many state assemblies and their replacement by the Greens. In those states where elections failed to produce clear-cut, single-party majorities, government formation became acutely problematic. Whilst the FDP had been attuned to coalition-building, the Greens were ambivalent towards the very idea of co-option into government. Hesse was a case in point where neither of the major parties had an absolute majority. Although the FDP returned to the assembly (after a year in exile) in the 'emergency' election of 1983, the centre-right bloc still lacked a majority. As the largest party in the assembly, the initiative lay with Holger Börner's SPD either to form a minority government or to come to terms with the Greens. After a year of minority government and a period in which the Greens undertook to support the Börner administration without accepting ministerial responsibilities, a tenuous coalition was concluded in which the Greens' Joschka Fischer held the Environment Ministry. Lasting from December 1985 to February 1987, the red-green experiment merely underlined the incompatibility of the two parties and the potential problems of coalition formation in the new four-party system.

A similar stalemate in coalition formation occurred following the Hamburg state election of 1986 which left the major parties evenly balanced and the FDP absent from the state assembly. Neither the SPD nor the Greens was prepared to countenance a coalition, and negotiations for a grand coalition between the SPD and CDU proved abortive. An emergency election was necessary to enable the return of the FDP with a view to forming a social-liberal coalition. The re-emergence of an SPD–FDP–axis fuelled speculation over a possible opening to the left in the FDP. It was, however, more in the nature of a product of exceptional circumstances than a pointer to likely developments elsewhere.

The changing party landscape in the 1980s also signified a reversal of party dominance in some of the Länder. In the Saarland, the CDU lost the hegemony it had exercised since 1962, with the election of 1985 returning an unprecedented SPD majority. Similarly in Schleswig-Holstein in 1988 the SPD reversed four decades of CDU dominance. Conversely the 1970s and 1980s saw the CDU steadily overcoming the long-standing dominance of their rivals in Hesse. In part, these aberrations reflected singular circumstances (the Barschel affair in Schleswig-Holstein, the red-green 'chaos' in Hesse), but they also revealed an important underlying trend. The north-south divide had long been a feature of the party landscape with the predominantly Catholic south favouring the CDU–CSU and the protestant north inclining towards the SPD. In the 1980s the growing economic imbalance between the 'sunrise industry' states in the south and the northern 'rust belt' compounded the north-south axis in the party system. The identification of the affluent south with Union parties was intensified whilst the 'have-nots' in the north drifted towards the SPD.

Economic imbalance also generated conflict between the northern and southern Länder which sometimes crossed party lines. The SPD–led 'poor-house' states in the north successfully petitioned the Federal Constitutional Court for a change in the arrangements for the distribution of financial resources between the Länder. More significant, though, was the initiative of Ernst Albrecht, minister-president of Lower Saxony, a CDU enclave in the north. Albrecht's move took him into conflict with his party colleagues in Bonn as he threatened to join forces with the SPD to veto the Federal Government's tax reform bill in the Bundesrat. Although confrontation was averted through compromise, the episode showed how far the cohesion of the party system in the Länder has been eroded.

## End of the 'Frozen' Party System?

An inventory of party system change in the last decade should begin with the evident weakening of its centre orientation. A closed triangle of parties, in which electoral and coalition logic dictated moderation, was transformed into a four-party system with potential for polarisation. The new party formation reflected an elongation of the political spectrum resulting from underlying changes in the political culture. As the ideological trauma of the past faded into history the political constraints which it imposed have wakened perceptibly. At the same time the steady advance of post-industrial values added a new dimension to politics.

Party system fragmentation is another striking feature of the 1980s. Electoral and social change has meant that the parties can no longer count on absolutely loyal electors or stable voting patterns. Unable to structure the electorate as effectively as they once did, the parties have been forced to respond to electoral change, creating uncertainty over their position in the party landscape. Changing coalition permutations in Bonn and the Länder have compounded this uncertainty. The resultant reappraisals of party identity have intensified internal party conflict. The major parties have suffered from this loss of control and internal cohesion, whilst the minor parties have reaped the electoral benefit. This shift has implications for a party system built on the *Volksparteien*. Alienation of the public from the parties has also hit them hardest, possibly weakening the foundations of party democracy. Paradoxically, the steady increase in the role and function of the parties – the party oligopoly over public life and their capacity to shape and dominate politics – has coincided with a loss of relevance and esteem in the public's perception. Control over party finance tightens the reins on their activity somewhat. Moreover, negative public opinion, with its electoral implications, forces the parties to pay further attention to their image and to respond more sensitively to issues of public concern. The future of the party system depends in part on the capacity of the parties for responding to the cultural, electoral and social changes.

The prevailing atmosphere of flux and uncertainty has been heightened by re-emergence of the neo-Nazi NPD (National Democratic Party) and more particularly by the appearance of the Republicans, a new force on the radical right. First emerging in Land elections during 1986, the Republicans, led by Franz Schönhuber, won 7.5 per cent of the vote in elections to the Berlin House of Representatives in January 1989. The new party showed its potential on a federal-wide basis in taking 7.1 per cent of the West German vote at the elections to the European Parliament in May 1989.

This fragmentation inevitably hit the CDU–CSU hard: in the European election the CDU–CSU share of the vote fell by 7.9 percentage points, intensifying internal disharmony and adding to speculation about the future of Chancellor Kohl. In Bavaria, the CSU suffered especially badly: no less than 37 per cent of the Republican vote in the European election came from this one Land. In part, the success of the new party in Bavaria can be ascribed to the weakness of the CSU following the death of Franz Josef Strauss, who had been the party's charismatic and unifying leader. Neither his successor as party Leader, Theo Waigel (now also federal Minister of Finance), nor the new minister-president of Bavaria, Max Streibl, has been able to compensate for the loss of Strauss. Schönhuber, once a CSU politician, is a more convincing populist figure, and the lack of a clear social profile in the Republican vote in Bavaria confirms the impression that the 'Strauss legacy' may be lost by the CSU.

The success of the Republicans is due in large part to their ability to exploit the issue of foreign workers, asylum seekers, and German nationals from the East whose repatriation, they argue, has been encouraged by lavish state subsidies and social benefits. This theme is reinforced by expressions of German nationalism, and the radical right is much less inhibited than the CDU–CSU in this respect, although the Republicans are careful to distance themselves from the NPD and to avoid overt association with neo-Nazi ideology. Both the Republicans and the NPD can be seen as 'anti-foreigner' protest parties, but research shows that there is a more general sense of disillusionment with the established parties and with their incapacity or lack of political will to tackle the economic and social problems facing the 'small man'. Economic weakness and a perceived low social status are characteristics of the Republicans' electorate. Thus, the radical right plays on the mixture of resentment and *Angst* that the 'foreigner' issue arouses in vulnerable sections of society. It is too early to say whether this formula will provide the Republicans with a permanent base in the party system.

Potentially, the rise of the radical right has far-reaching implications for the party system, weakening its central orientation: in the European election some 18 per cent of voters supported a party to the left or right of the SPD and CDU–CSU. This polarisation creates problems for the *Volsparteien* and for the FDP, and it promotes a possible fragmentation of the party system. Multi-partism and a two-bloc party system are possibilities, but, on the left, the SPD/Green axis is not yet consolidated, and – on the right – the Republicans are beyond the pale of political respectability as potential partners for the CDU–CSU. The combination of polarisation and fragmentation may present acute problems for coalition-building, if neither of the two major parties can dictate the terms. One possibility would be a Grand Coalition of CDU–CSU and SPD. Ominously, however, the experience of this line-up from 1966–9 suggests that radicalism flourishes under such circumstances.

There is a danger of exaggerating the extent of party system change and of overlooking the strands of persistence and continuity. The old model is still recognisable in the 1980s. Despite the tendency towards a 'two-bloc' party formation, the three established parties may still be able to maintain their pattern of interaction. It may be premature, for example, to rule out an SPD–FDP coalition in the medium-term future. The *Volksparteien* exhibit less vitality than in the past, but their strength and resilience is by no means exhausted. For their part, the Greens, a party of a different kind, are coming to resemble their older counterparts in some respects. In short, a quite far-reaching change in the party system is under way but it is not complete, and the form the new system may take is not yet clearly discernible.

What is beyond dispute, however, is that the hyper-stability and inertia of the party system in the previous two decades is at an end. It is true that party system *stability* is a foundation for a stable political order, but *inertia* in the party system can lead to an ossification of political life, sapping the vitality of democracy and the effectiveness of government. The break-up of a frozen party system can thus also be judged positively.

# PART THREE

# Economic and Social Policy

# 8

# Economic Policy

KENNETH DYSON

A central characteristic of modern liberal democracies is the wide-spread belief amongst their politicians and the public's perception that the economic competence of a party will be decisive for its electoral success. This characteristic applies to West Germany with particular force. In West Germany the post-war economic 'miracle' played a key role in the re-establishment of a mixture of national confidence and pride after the excesses of the Nazi period and the deprivation of total defeat. It was vital to the stabilisation and legitimation of a new and precarious 'second' republic. The economic 'miracle' was also attributed to a particular economic policy formula – the 'social market economy'. And it was the particular strength of the Christian Democratic parties (CDU–CSU) to be able to identify themselves with the 'social market economy' and to secure for them-selves a long-term reputation as *the* parties of 'economic competence'. The 1980s were characterised by the return to power (in 1982) of the CDU–CSU, against the background of a crisis in public finances. In coalition with the FDP they succeeded in winning two successive federal elections (1983 and 1987) in which 'economic competence' remained a decisive issue.

## Key Themes of the 1980s

West German economic policies in the 1980s continued to be shaped by a legacy of critical historical events; the consequence is a pattern of policy responses that sometimes puzzles and occasionally infuriates other governments. Memories of the collapse of Weimar into Nazi tyranny combine with the harsh experience of political and

148

economic reconstruction to make 'social partnership' between both sides of industry a high political value. In this way the otherwise pervasive impacts of 'Americanisation' after 1945 have been qualified by complex arrangements to ensure codetermination at the higher levels of company decision-making and worker participation at lower levels in detailed social planning (e.g., for redundancies). Indeed aspects of these arrangements, notably the works councils introducing a measure of industrial democracy at the level of the firm, have their origins in the 1920s. The material and political consequences of hyper-inflation in the 1920s and experience of the realities of a 'barter' economy after 1945 have furthermore forced attention on price stability as the central aim of economic policy. The result is an unusually powerful role for the Bundesbank (Dyson, 1985).

Not least, there is the impact on economic policy of the circumstances of German unification and of political reconstruction under Allied supervision after 1945. West Germany has a dispersed and divided structure of economic policy-making, with wide-ranging influence and occasional dominance of provincial over metropolitan interests, reinforced by a federal structure of political authority. Ranged against this overall dispersal of powers is the creation in just one key area of public institution with the authority and capacity to make and enforce authoritative decisions – namely the Bundesbank in monetary policy. This contrast is decisive in explaining the particular character, strengths and weaknesses of West German economic policy. Also ranged against the prevailing pattern of dispersal of political power is the measure of integration and self-organisation within the private sector. This self-organisation of capitalism is enormously important in underpinning the functioning of the 'social market economy' (Dyson, 1984). In particular, the close, collusive, interlocking network of relations between banks and industry has provided its own 'crisis-management' mechanism (e.g., for the AEG-Telefunken crisis). Banks like the Deutsche and the Dresdner and companies like Daimler-Benz and Siemens are major national institutions in their own right. Once again economic history reveals its mark; the legacy of Germany's relative economic backwardness in the mid-nineteenth century was a powerful set of institutions to achieve modernisation.

This legacy of institutions and policies has faced an environment and problems common to other Western industrialised societies in the 1980s. A rapid rate of technological and structural change has led to new industrial competitors, the organisation of markets on a global scale, the emergence of new sectors and a spate of rapid innovations in old sectors. Inflationary pressures, particularly unleashed by the two oil crises of 1973 and 1978–9, have compounded problems of international competitiveness. There has also been the striking rise in real interest rates throughout the 1980s as a side-effect of the expansionary strategy of the Reagan Administration. Urgent need for industrial adjustment has in turn forced a reappraisal of the economic policy mix, particularly of the relevance of supply-side measures of deregulation. The consequence has been new tests for the policy-making capacity of the West German state in the 1980s; a new critique of policies for being too late, limited and ineffective; and a recognition that the explanation for this condition of inertia and *immobilisme* might lie in the characteristics of the West German state. Criticisms of policy failure focused in particular on the service sector, which, as American experience reveals, possesses major job-creating potential – notably financial and telecommunications services and transport and retail distribution.

Moreover, these sectors are a significant element in the cost structure of other sectors, making for a significant 'knock-on' effect from a failure to deregulate; whilst an undeveloped stock exchange system puts a major obstacle in the way of privatisation and the creation of a 'shareholders' democracy.' These new pressures and evidence of policy failure in key sectors for international competitiveness have helped in turn to illuminate the dominant interests within large areas of economic policy-making – the Bundespost and the banks in particular; the problems for economic modernisation engendered by the fragmentation of political authority in a federal system (e.g., in stock exchange and new media reforms); and the constraints posed by the strong institutionalisation of trade-union power (e.g., in telecommunications and reform of working hours). In short, the 1980s revealed a limited public capacity to insist on and drive through industrial change. Key characteristics of West Germany's political economy conspired to create high barriers to the emergence of coalitions of modernisers.

The major themes of the 1980s were ones of continuity and consensus. Old ways showed a remarkable power of survival in the face of a more turbulent international environment of innovation and change, notably in the safety-first, cautious approach to regulation of financial markets and telecommunications. The consequence was the high costs and lack of variety and flexibility of financial and telecommunications services. West Germany is a case study not of a breakthrough of new 'radical' market ideas, as in Britain, but of an established 'social market' ideology built into the political foundations of the new republic. The market had become a conservative rather than a radical ideology; whilst its emphases – in contrast to Reaganism and Thatcherism – were macro-economic, rather than micro-economic supply-side measures, and a strong social dimension. If the infrastructure of bank industry relations carried over from the nineteenth century served to provide long-term support for investment programmes (often denied by the stock market), the consequence was a failure to develop a variety of corporate financing methods like venture capital for new 'start-up' businesses.

This conservatism was apparent in the Christian-Liberal (CDU – CSU – FDP) coalition government of Helmut Kohl. The background to its formation was a mounting public debt crisis between 1979 and 1982; the failure to agree measures to tackle this crisis brought down Chancellor Helmut Schmidt's Social-Liberal coalition. Kohl's government gave political priority to a fiscal consolidation strategy. In turn this strategy focused attention on the roles of the Finance Ministry (under Gerhard Stoltenberg) and of the Bundesbank. In essence, the *Wende* of 1982 proved to be a return to traditional ideas on which the 'economic miracle' was presumed to have rested. It was argued that high public spending by the SPD – FDP coalition since 1969, and its consequences for the budget deficit and taxation, had crowded out private-sector investment, with major costs to economic growth and employment. By heavy cuts in public expenditure the federal government would also re-establish a good working relation with the Bundesbank in controlling inflation. Kohl was neither the master of economic detail (as Schmidt had been) nor able to provide a new economic vision; his skills were more in the realm of political tactics. Similarly, economic thinking had stagnated in the SPD since its acceptance of the 'social market economy' in its Bad Godesberg programme of 1959 (with the famous formula 'as much market as possible, as much planning as necessary') and the neo-Keynesian policy innovations during Professor Karl Schiller's period as Federal Minister of Economics (notably the Law on Stability and Growth of 1967).

By 1988 there had been no turning-point to match with those of Ludwig Erhard (notably with the 1948 currency reform) or Karl Schiller. At the same time new economic ideas were urgent; neither fiscal policy nor monetary policy, as pursued under Schmidt or by Stoltenberg, were able to deal effectively with changing economic circumstances. Prophets of change had yet to make their impact. Count Otto von Lambsdorff, former FDP Federal Economics Minister whose intervention directly precipitated the fall of the Schmidt government, was an assertive proponent of deregulation (but with diminished personal political credibility after the Flick affair); whilst in 1988 Oskar Lafontaine, a deputy chairman of the SPD and head of government in the Saar, sought to open up new radical perspectives against powerful vested interests in the party (Lafontaine,

1988). Yet neither has yet had a significant direct impact on the conduct of federal economic policy.

## From Modell Deutschland to Standort Deutschland

At the same time the climate in which economic policy was conducted altered during the 1980s. The self-confidence of *Modell Deutschland* – (The German Model) – proclaimed by Chancellor Schmidt during the 1976 federal elections – had given way to a new uncertainty (Katzenstein, 1982; Dyson and Wilks, 1983). Various developments combined to generate a new debate about *Standort Deutschland* (*Location – Germany*) in 1987–8 when it became a key media theme and was taken up by Kohl in his speech at the Hanover trade fair. The Kohl government appeared, after five years, to have failed to deliver the goods: structural crisis still afflicted the coal and steel industries; investment in new communication and information technologies was inadequate compared to the United States and Japan; hours of work were inflexible and short (the Japanese worked 2,138 hours per annum compared to 1,716 by West Germans); labour costs were the second highest in the world (after Switzerland), notably because of the costs of insurance, social security and paid leave; energy, telecommunications and transport costs were relatively high; the United States reduced its direct investment by DM 1 billion in 1987, whilst Japan had invested three times as much in the UK in 1986; and, meanwhile, West German direct investment abroad, notably to the United States, had doubled in the 1980s (notably Siemens, Nixdorf, Hoechst, BASF and Bertelsmann). Alarming statistics could be marshalled; in only three years since 1971 (1976, 1979 and 1980) had the growth of the West German economy exceeded the OECD average; the growth of fixed asset formation by business had slowed drastically from an annual average rate of more than 3.5 per cent in 1965–73 to 1.5 per cent in 1979–86; the deterioration in unemployment had been exceeded only in Spain and the UK (an eightfold increase since 1973); whilst the fall in domestic population had begun earlier (1973) and was projected to be greater than in any other OECD country.

Three developments in particular seemed to indicate the need for more radical measures: the dramatic fall in the value of the dollar (it lost over half its value in relation to the DM between 1984 and 1987) produced a wave of uncertainty in an economy based on the idea of export-led investment; the prospect of Japan's export onslaught being extended to mechanical engineering (with over one million employees, West Germany's biggest sector); and the political commitment to complete a single integrated EC market by the end of 1992, challenging West Germany's inherited regulatory standards and her service industries in particular.

External criticism mounted, with the OECD arguing that the Bonn government had failed to take adequate supply-side measures (deregulation) to revitalise the West German economy. Internal criticism focused on the absence of confident leadership in economic policy, on the short-term and reactive behaviour of the federal government (with its sensitivity to regular state elections and in 1987 the worst performance by the CDU in a federal election since 1949, fear of the voter was strong), and on the unwillingness to challenge powerful vested interests. The heads of IBM Deutschland, BMW, Daimler-Benz and the Deutsche Bank were notably prominent in the new debate. Thus the head of the supervisory board of Deutsche Bank, Wilfried Guth, spoke of the Chancellor as stronger on stamina than political courage; the former co-chairman of Deutsche Bank (F. Wilhelm Christians) pleaded for more deregulation (e.g., of shopping and banking hours, telecommunications and transport); and the present co-chairman (Alfred Herrhausen), noted as close to the chancellor, was critical of a lack of policy-making leadership and pressed for a new direction in Bonn.

At the heart of the debate was the question of whether economic competence and political leadership in Bonn could match the scale of the complexity of international problems. As mentioned earlier, Chancellor Kohl showed less interest in and understanding of economic issues than his predecessor; the Finance Minister, Stoltenberg, was a politician in the bureaucratic mould, stronger on figures than ideas, and by 1987 distracted by a messy and tragic scandal affecting the CDU (of which he was chairman) in Schleswig-Holstein; whilst Martin Bangemann, the Economics Minister, was overshadowed by his more combative predecessor Lambsdorff, the FDP's economic spokesman in the Bundestag, and was more committed to continuity in economic policy.

The dominance of the theme of continuity and consensus over that of *Standort Deutschland* and the calls for bolder and more radical leadership was not simply a function of the character of the political structure. It had much to do with the fact that, despite various alarming statistics and developments, the West German economy was still performing comparatively well in key areas (notably control of inflation and the balance of payments surplus, both highly symbolic figures in Germany) and still linked to a very high standard of living for the large majority. The pervasiveness of wealth and affluence helped to distract attention from structural problems. Also, the huge balance of payments surpluses reduced the pressures on government to revitalise the economy. The export share of GDP has grown faster, in both absolute and relative terms, than that of other OECD states and is notably concentrated on the manufacturing industries. In practice, the pressures on Bonn to use domestic policies to stimulate investment and growth have been reduced by the willingness of other countries, notably the United States, France and Britain, to pursue their own domestic expansions. In the view of some commentators, West Germany has been able to depend on the mistakes of others.

Of equal importance, West Germany can be said to have been less susceptible to simplistic and fashionable ideas about competitiveness. Quite simply, West German competitiveness was hit far less than expected by the falling dollar and currency turbulence; in 1987 the real, inflation-adjusted value of the DM barely changed, exports to the EC were up 6 per cent and a record surplus achieved (£39.8 billion). West Germany remained an international leader in investment in human capital, with a highly skilled, qualified and motivated workforce; expenditure on company-funded research and development was twice as high as in the UK; whilst, again compared to the UK, leading high-technology companies maintained a key role in patenting activity.

The economy benefited from a combination of product strategy with market focus. German industry specialised on high-value, distinctive products that were impervious to the effects of the falling dollar (machine tools, capital goods, textile machinery, pharmaceuticals, automobiles and vehicle engineering). Firms like Bosch, BASF, Hoechst, Bayer and Siemens were technology leaders. Despite OECD criticisms, its own figures showed that West Germany was the world leader in trade in goods with a high skill content, with a share of 20 per cent (Japan 17 per cent, US 15 per cent, France 7 per cent, Britain 6 per cent). Secondly, the EC had become *de facto* the home market well before '1992', taking just over half of West German exports (compared with 10 per cent to the United States). The EC was attractive as a relatively 'dollar-independent area' and because of the relative buoyancy of many of its markets. Correspondingly, West Germany enjoyed a soaring trade surplus with the EC. In 1987 she remained the world's top exporter (ahead of the United States and Japan and more than double the value of the UK's exports); had the highest value of exports per capita ($4,803 compared to $2,301 in the UK); and had the second highest foreign trade surplus after Japan ($65.4 billion compared to a UK deficit of $23.2 billion). Against this background it seems unsurprising that the European Management Forum should rate West Germany in fourth place on its 'competitiveness indicator' (after Japan, the United States and Switzerland).

On a global level West German industry was very profitable and very competitive. Between 1980 and 1987 wages and incomes had not risen in real terms (trade-union restraint was a continuing factor despite outbreaks of militancy); whilst corporate income was up 42.7 per cent. Whilst tax on undistributed profits remained relatively high, comparatively generous tax provisions made it possible to build up large reserves to cover possible risks and to allow depreciation provision against tax. Also, competitiveness was a function of unit costs rather than wage rates; and unit costs were helped by investment in automated plant, education and training of the workforce, and reduced import prices for oil and raw materials with the falling dollar.

The dominance of the theme of continuity and consensus has, accordingly, complex roots: in the resilience of the economy and a continuing capacity for self-adjustment, in the complexity of the economic policy making structures, in powerful vested interests and their capacity to veto change, and in continuing inhibitions about employing a bold and assertive style of leadership in a recently mature liberal democracy with a strong attachment to the institutions, procedures and aims that have so recently served to help establish and legitimise that democracy. Caution and prudence, stability and predictability, enjoy a pre-eminence in the value system of West German economic policy (Dyson, 1982a).

## The Party Political Context of Economic Policy

As indicated at the beginning of this chapter, during the life of the Bonn Republic the CDU – CSU has been more successful in setting the agenda of economic policy than its major rival the SPD. Its first Economics Minister Ludwig Erhard (1949–63) became the symbol of the social market economy; the SPD took on board this ideology in its Bad Godesberg Programme of 1959. In essence, the private sector was allocated primacy in industrial adjustment and the value of competition recognised. The public sector's role was to facilitate the functioning of the market, to deliver certain 'public goods' (like defence and railways), to correct market imperfections and to modify the outcomes of the market in the interests of social peace and solidarity. With Karl Schiller as Economics Minister after 1966 (till 1972), the SPD gained the initiative for the first time in the form of the idea of an 'enlightened' social market economy in which, via new arrangements for collaboration, the different levels of government (e.g., in the Financial Planning Council to coordinate budgetary strategy) and both sides of industry (notably in Concerted Action) would become better mutually informed and thus more capable of rational behaviour (Dyson, 1981). Also, the federal government's budgetary policy was given a new role in ironing out fluctuations in the economy in a neo-Keynesian manner. The Law on Stability and Growth of 1967 introduced these innovations and also committed the federal government to realising the 'magic square' of economic policy goals – full employment, price stability, external equilibrium, and growth. Schiller's role as an electoral locomotive for the SPD in the 1969 federal elections was widely recognised; the beneficiary in status and influence was, as earlier under Erhard, the Federal Ministry for Economics.

The Social-Liberal (SPD–FDP) coalitions of Willy Brandt (1969–74) and Helmut Schmidt (1974–82) inherited both a consensus about the 'social market economy' and a broader range of fiscal and monetary instruments to manage the economy. At the same time, the impacts of the two oil crises led to deteriorating relations between the coalition partners, focused on conflicts between the Finance Ministry (SPD) and the Economics Ministry (FDP). Electoral clientèles and policy priorities were different. The FDP Economics Ministers (Hans Friderichs, 1972–7, and Count Otto Lambsdorff, 1977–82) pressed for cuts in business taxes to promote investment and championed managerial independence and the rights of property against a major extension of worker codetermination in industry. Following the collapse of Concerted Action in 1977 (the trade unions walked out when the Federation of German Industry brought the new codetermination law to the Federal Constitutional Court), the management of the federal government's relations with the trade unions was undertaken directly by the Chancellor (Lehmbruch and Lang, 1977). By contrast, the SPD favoured the use of public investment more directly to stimulate employment and the development of an 'active' industrial policy (*Strukturpolitik*) under the auspices of the SPD–led Federal Ministry for Research and Technology (Dyson, 1981; Glotz, 1980). As the spearhead of the SPD's concept of 'modernisation policy' the budgetary share of the Research and Technology Ministry climbed rapidly. It was, however, the issue of fiscal policy that most divided the Social-Liberal coalition, particularly after 1977, and in the autumn of 1982 failure to agree the future course of action on the mounting budgetary deficit brought down the coalition.

From the outset the CDU–CSU–FDP coalition of Helmut Kohl made fiscal consolidation its top priority. It came to office against the background of an emotionally-charged debate about the budget deficit and the public debt. As a percentage of GNP the general government budget deficit had risen from an average of 1.7 per cent (1970–4) to 4.9 per cent in 1981; public debt has grown from an average of 18.8 per cent (1970–4) to 35.3 per cent in 1981. The impression that the government had lost control over public finance was widespread, although in comparison with other OECD countries the key factor was the rate of change in the budget deficit rather than its level. Quite simply, for historical reasons already referred to, West Germans place a particularly high value on the goals of price stability and sound public finances. By 1981–2 the Bundesbank and the Council of Economic Experts (*Sachverständigenrat*) were in clear conflict with the federal government over these issues. Hence in 1982 the new government came to office with the weight of economic 'authority' behind it. Fiscal policy was aligned with the monetary policy of the Bundesbank in the search for price stability and predictability, the aim being to stabilise expectations in a world characterised by high uncertainty. A break was made with a Keynesian policy of using budget deficits to fight recession on the grounds that this approach had had an adverse effect on expectations and thus investment and job creation in industry and commerce.

Correspondingly, new attention focused on the role of the Finance Ministry to which a CDU star was appointed – Gerhard Stoltenberg. Stoltenberg became a symbol of financial rectitude and enjoyed enormous public approval. Rather than raising taxes, the emphasis was on reducing the budget deficit by keeping a lid on expenditure growth. Between 1982 and 1986 this policy enjoyed considerable success. As a proportion of GNP the budget deficit fell from 4.9 per cent in 1981 to 2.1 per cent in 1985, with all levels of government contributing (the federal government and the states cut their deficits by 40 per cent and 37 per cent respectively).

Furthermore, West Germany was able to return to a leading international position in the league table of price stability. It was, as a consequence, able to assume a *de facto* leadership role within the EMS with respect to price stability. By pursuing a policy of aligning their currencies with the DM, other members of the EMS were able to legitimate policies for controlling inflation. In this sense West Germany 'exported' price stability within the EC. In fact, fiscal consolidation at the federal level was facilitated greatly by the Bundesbank's profit transfers. By law, the Bundesbank is obliged to transfer profits from its ordinary business transactions to the federal government. Beginning in 1982, these profits were exceptionally large (over DM 10 billion annually), helped by the high level of interest rates. Without them, federal government borrowing in 1985 would have been just 10 per cent below the record level of 1981.

Also, subsidies continued to grow despite a policy of reducing them. Total government subsidies amounted to DM 38 billion in 1985 compared to 29 billion in 1981.

By 1987–8 Stoltenberg's reputation was seriously in question: with the political scandal in his home state of Schleswig-Holstein over the 'dirty tricks' campaign by Uwe Barschel (the head of the Land government), the controversies over the tax reform, and the new escalation of the budget deficit and conflict about how to tackle it. Fiscal strategy seemed to be in ruins, not least with the impact of the dramatic fall of the dollar, higher West German contributions to the EC budget and the near disappearance of profits from the Bundesbank. The 1988 budget was formally in breach of Article 115 of the Basic Law which limits government borrowing to the size of its investment spending in any one year.

With growth stagnating, the prospects were for lower tax revenues and higher expenditure on subsidies and unemployment. New conflicts beset the coalition over the budget deficit. Stoltenberg delivered a controversial economic boost in December 1987 in the form of a DM 21 billion programme of additional lending (at subsidised rates) to local authorities and small businesses. A phalanx of actors attacked this measure as inadequate and second best to tax cuts for business: Lambsdorff, the Federation of German Industry, the Association of German Chambers of Commerce and the West German Banks' Association. Subsequent increases in consumer taxes were attacked by Franz Josef Strauss, chairman of the CSU and head of government in Bavaria, and by Lothar Späth (CDU), head of government in Baden-Württemberg. Both wanted more measures to stimulate the economy.

Coalition conflicts came to a head over the major long-term tax reform that was masterminded by Stoltenberg's ministry. Tax cuts worth DM 5 billion (2.5 per cent of GNP) were planned between 1986 and 1990. In the view of Strauss, this reform represented a piece of 'shoddy work'; according to Lambsdorff, the reforms were too cautious, slow and self-defeating in that, without a major economic boost, the budget deficit would increase thus diminishing the future room for manoeuvre in tax cuts; whilst Späth wanted tax incentives to promote industrial investment rather than income-tax cuts to fuel consumption. The sharpest conflicts were with the CSU. The CSU wanted to retain tax privileges for farmers, an end to the fuel tax on aeroplanes piloted for private and sports purposes (flying was a hobby of Strauss), and the continuation of the investment allowance law of 1973 (the subsidy to the construction of the Wackersdorf nuclear power plant was worth DM 800 million). In particular, the CSU objected to the proposed tax at source on the interest income of churches, charities, clubs and foundations whose income had been in effect tax free (the withholding tax). This latter measure was designed to stop tax evasion on a huge scale and to claw back revenue lost from income-tax reductions.

Banks and insurance companies joined in the opposition, stressing the threat of a loss of business abroad notably to Luxembourg and Switzerland. In addition to all the special pleading behind the tax reform conflict was a fundamental difference of priority. Stoltenberg wanted to begin with a programme of income-tax cuts and then move to reform corporate taxation; Lambsdorff and Späth argued that priority should be given to radical reductions in corporate taxation in order directly to promote industrial investment. The growing tension between employers and the CDU over tax reform became a major aspect of the mounting debate about *Standort Deutschland*.

Despite this outbreak of dissension, uncertainty and pessimism, the Bonn coalition was held together by the low credibility of the SPD on economic issues (not least with the general public). In some key areas, notably industrial relations and public investment, the SPD was closer to the centre-left of the CDU than to the FDP. The problem was how both to make the party's ideas relevant to the changed context of the 1980s and to make it a party with prospects for making coalitions. This problem was not properly addressed until after the defeat in the 1987 federal elections. A party commission set up under the chairmanship of the former general manager, Peter Glotz, to analyse the reasons for this defeat concluded that the SPD must develop a coherent and relevant economic programme that at once identified the party with the theme of the modernisation of economy and society and challenged inherited ideas and attitudes.

The pace-setter in the new public debate on behalf of a 'new revisionism' was Oskar Lafontaine,' a deputy chairman, chairman of the SPD programme commission and head of government in the Saar. In his attempt to pursue a new 'economic realism' Lafontaine attracted support from the former party chairman Willy Brandt, party treasurer Hans-Ulrich Klose and younger politicians like Gerhard Schröder (SPD leader in Lower Saxony) and Björn Engholm, head of government in Schleswig-Holstein. A new corpus of economic ideas began to emerge after years of stagnation since Schiller, including a new interest in small firms, venture capital, more flexible use of manpower and machines, reduction of corporate taxation on reinvested profits to encourage higher investment, and higher taxes on some forms of energy to fund new investment in ecologically-friendly technologies.

Lafontaine's most radical and controversial proposal was based on the idea that the 'insiders' in the formal labour market, including the trade unions, must take some responsibility for the 'outsiders' (the unemployed, part-time workers and many women workers) by a fairer distribution of existing work and the creation of new types of work. New jobs could be created only if the trade unions' demand for a reduction of working hours (the 35-hour week) was combined with a willingness to accept proportionate wage cuts on the part of higher-paid workers. Traditional SPD members and leading trade unionists protested vigorously, not least the public service union (ÖTV) and IG Chemie. As a consequence, at the SPD party conference in 1988 Lafontaine was re-elected a deputy chairman but with a substantially reduced vote. Lafontaine was, however, prepared to think long term, could count on the backing of such veterans as Brandt, Karl Schiller and Klaus von Dohnanyi and was able to note the enthusiasm of leading FDP politicians for his ideas. The challenge was radical. Both sides of industry were being told that productivity gains should not just be distributed amongst themselves but be used to create new jobs. Those in employment would have to share work, income and wages with the unemployed by creating a more flexible, 'post-corporatist' economy to integrate the disadvantaged (Lafontaine, 1988). The SPD must also not concentrate solely on the formal labour market but must recognise and revalue unpaid but 'socially necessary work' in the family, the voluntary sector, leisure and further education. This new concept of 'work' led on to the proposal for a basic minimum income. At the heart of this challenge was the attempt to identify the SPD with the vision of a more open, flexible and experimental society in which variety would be encouraged by spreading paid work, guaranteeing income and elevating the status of unpaid work.

## Power and Influence in the Policy Process

It will be clear from the previous analysis that the economic policy process in West Germany is much less centralised and concentrated than in the UK. Various factors play a part, not least coalition politics, federalism and the independence guaranteed to the Bundesbank. This disaggregated policy process makes radical reform difficult. Government takes the form of complicated political bargaining, within a CDU that encompasses a wide spectrum from centre-left to right, between CDU and CSU, with the FDP and with state governments whose veto power in the Bundesrat is considerable. On the one hand, multiple points of access are available for powerful organised interests to veto change so that politicians can soon become persuaded that the costs of radical proposals are too high. On the other, the combination of coalition politics with the regular role of state elections as barometers of the standing of the federal coalition government parties makes for cautious and short-term time horizons in economic policy decisions.

When these characteristics are set alongside a policy style that values stability, predictability and order (Dyson, 1982a), the result is a slow process of deregulation in sectors like transport and tele-communications and continuing high subsidies to sectors like aero-space and coal. From an external perspective, particularly that of OECD, supply-side measures lacked energy, speed and purpose. Similarly, the tax reform programme seemed to require lengthy and laborious negotiations, not just within the coalition but with the states whose approval in the Bundesrat was essential. It took seven-teen months to pilot the programme through the Bundesrat; the price was concessions to northern CDU states for more financial aid, thus driving up the budget deficit. Inside as well as outside West Germany the question was increasingly asked whether too high a price might be being paid for consensus and social peace. Was stab-ility being bought at the expense of government inaction and econ-omic rigidity?

The complex process of West German economic policy-making was affected by the rising issue of the North-South divide in the 1980s, an issue that was in turn fuelled by the regional concentrations of structural crisis – notably in the Ruhr and the Saar. By contrast, virtual full employment prevailed in Bavaria and Baden-Wür̈ttem-berg where the new industrial sectors and research and development expenditures were concentrated. These two states were the benefici-aries of a major 'brain drain' within the Federal Republic. In 1960 the North accounted for 52 per cent of GDP, the South for 48 per cent; by 1982 the North's contribution had fallen to 46.6 per cent, the South's risen to 53.4 per cent. The northern states received 3.7 billion less tax revenue, paid DM 6.4 billion higher debt charges and paid out DM 4.1 billion higher social policy expenditure. The sou-thern states benefited from contracts of the Federal Railways, Fed-eral Post Office and the armed forces worth DM 14.1 billion more and research contracts of the federal government worth DM 2.3 billion more. This issue began to threaten the passage of the tax reform programme when the CDU head of government in Lower Saxony, Ernst Albrecht, launched a 'coalition of the poor' based around the seven states of Bremen (SPD), Hamburg (SPD–FDP), Lower Saxony (CDU–FDP), the Saar (SPD), Schleswig-Holstein (SPD), North Rhine-Westphalia (SPD) and Rhineland-Palatinate (CDU). The aim was to draw the federal government into a new role in financing social policies at the state and local levels by paying half of the rising cost of supplementary benefit. Funding this policy in context of high unemployment was locking the northern states into a vicious circle of decline; resources for modernisation policies were being diverted. The problem was that a CDU state was pioneering a proposal that threatened to increase federal taxation.

A complex tapestry of cooperation and competition characterised federal-state relations in economic policy (Donges, 1980). The two SPD states of North Rhine-Westphalia (headed by the SPD chancellor candidate in 1987, Johannes Rau) and the Saar (captured by the SPD in 1985) were particularly hard hit by crises of the coal and steel industries (Dyson, 1984). Despite a subsidy of DM 2.6 billion between 1978 and 1985 the Saar steel industry's employment fell from 22,000 to 12,500. By 1985 Arbed Saarstahl was threatened by bankruptcy. Lafontaine's government took three measures: it removed the bankruptcy threat by buying out 76 per cent of Arbed Saarstahl for the symbolic price of DM 1; it appointed the former CDU Economics Minister in the Saar as executor, thus incorporating the opposition and improving contacts to Bonn; and it established a Saar Steel Foundation to guarantee high redundancy pay and thus pacify the trade unions.

In 1987 heavy cuts were agreed by the unions in the Ruhr coal and steel industries: 30,000 jobs in coal by 1995 and 35,000 jobs in steel by 1989. In the steel industry, however, social partnership was fractured by the disclosure of Krupp's plan to close the gigantic Rheinhausen works. Televised scenes of chaos followed: mass protests, traffic blockades and the storming of the Villa Huegel, the dynastic home of the Krupp family. This episode was followed by a Ruhr conference and a five-year federal programme for the Ruhr which Chancellor Kohl presented as an expression of solidarity with the coal and steel workers. An additional DM ½ billion was made available, with a large range of infrastructure projects including transport and major research centres (like the new German space agency). Management of the structural crises in the Ruhr and the Saar continued to exhibit a strong commitment to a consensual policy style and a new degree of interdependence between regional and sectoral aid policies.

At the same time an increasingly fierce competition between Länder and between local councils has developed in the field of new technology and industrial policy initiatives. This competition has been intensified by a shortage of private investment, by the assumption that new investment depends in many cases on siphoning off investments from another state and the loss of comparative advantage of the North to the South. The pioneers were CDU in Baden-Württemberg, whose government started to support new technologies in 1976, and SPD in North Rhine-Westphalia and Hamburg which followed in 1978. In addition to substantial subsidies and credits (typically covering 33–60 per cent of the costs of a project), information and advice services were established on a large scale. Notably between 1985 and 1986 there was a major boom of technology centres, most of them in Baden-Württemberg, North Rhine-Westphalia and Lower Saxony. These centres tend to focus support on small and medium-sized firms, although Baden-Württemberg also promotes collaboration with big companies like Daimler-Benz. The consequences of this process are twofold: firstly, local and regional policy initiatives have expanded in scope and influence; and, secondly, a conflict has emerged between states like Bavaria and Baden-Württemberg which claim the leading role for themselves in technology policy (they enjoy in any case regional economic booms) and poorer states (CDU and SPD alike) which seek to promote an active role for the federal government.

Within this complex, disaggregated policy process the independence and authority of the Bundesbank has continued to guarantee a major element of continuity in West German economic policy. With a statutory obligation to 'safeguard the currency' (memories of hyperinflation and its consequences directly inspired the legislation establishing the Bundesbank), the central bank's interest-rate, open-market and minimum-reserve policies have been operated both with independence (of the federal government) and to great effect in controlling inflationary pressures (Dyson, 1979 and 1984). The Bundesbank operates on the assumption of a clear distinction between its own responsibility for monetary and currency policies and that of the federal government for financial and economic policies. Despite being drawn into the Financial Planning Advisory Council (*Finanzplanungsrat*) and the Counter-Cyclical Economic Council (*Konjunkturrat*) established by the Law on Stability and Growth of 1967, the Bundesbank has always denied the proposition that fiscal policy had priority over monetary policy. Accordingly, it was hardly surprising that conflicts could erupt between SPD ministers in Bonn and the Bundesbank, notably early in the 1980s. Earlier the fall of the Erhard government in 1966 and of Karl Schiller in 1972 took place against the background of conflict with the Bundesbank. These outcomes reflected its authority and prestige. With only four presidents in 30 years (Karl Otto Pöhl since 1980), and an average period in office of its directors of 11.2 years in 1987, the Bundesbank had been able to accumulate its own expertise and identity. The possibility of a party-political polarisation of the central bank council has not been in evidence.

Following recommendations of the Council of Economic Advisers from 1972, the Bundesbank began the practice of setting and publishing annual money supply targets in 1974. However, since then the Bundesbank had continued to reject the idea of medium-term money supply targets in favour of a pragmatic approach. 'Moderate monetarism' has remained the approach, with stress on flexible policies in the pursuit of currency stability. Between 1979 and 1985 the Bundesbank was the only central bank in the OECD states to achieve its money supply targets. Heavy currency inflows in 1986 and 1987 led the money supply targets to be exceeded by a wide margin and produced a new conflict between a money supply-oriented policy and a currency-oriented policy. Interventions by the Bundesbank in foreign exchange markets to achieve stability of the DM put achievement of money-supply targets at risk. The outcome of this conflict was a recommitment to cautious pragmatism: annual money-supply targets would be retained to ensure credibility of price-stability policies but were still seen as just one element in the central bank's operations.

## Corporate Stability and International Pressures

Increased international controversy has surrounded the aims and methods of West German economic policy in the 1980s, with particular stress being placed on the 'complacency' of this policy. At the end of 1987 there was an unprecedented public row between the OECD and Bonn; the OECD's *Economic Outlook* (OECD, 1988) pointed to the failure of the Bonn government not only to stimulate domestic growth in order to cut its huge balance of payments surplus and relieve pressure on the dollar but also to improve domestic economic performance through supply-side measures of deregulation. These comments were strongly echoed by the American government which saw West German attitudes as the root cause of a lack of international policy coordination.

Tensions between the EC Commission and the Bonn government surfaced over the amount of regional and industrial aid distributed by the federal and state governments, seen as in breach of EC competition rules (here the EC gained a victory in 1988); over measures to reduce expenditure on the Common Agricultural Policy (CAP) (The Agriculture Ministry was a staunch defender of farming interests); and over the future of EC steel output controls (Norbert Blüm, CDU chairman in North Rhine-Westphalia and Minister of Labour in Bonn, wanted an extension; the FDP Economics Minister Bangemann argued for their termination). In the early 1960s Bonn, and Erhard in particular, used to be suspicious of the EC's bias towards bureaucratic 'planification'; now, in the late 1980s, the EC – through its Single European Market programme – was a stimulus for a liberalisation that was not notably evident in Bonn. Abroad, West Germany's government seemed divided, irresolute and self-preoccupied in its economic policies, incapable of matching its international economic significance with an appropriate measure of statesmanship.

As this chapter has stressed, the aims, methods and style of West German economic policy reflect the extent to which the past haunts the present and the role of historical sensitivities in contemporary economic debate in West Germany. The inter-war period's continuing presence is embodied in the priority accorded to stability and predictability as principles of economic policy and to consensus and solidarity (despite their economic costs in terms of labour-market flexibility and redundancy pay). In particular, as we have seen, the Bundesbank's independence and power respresent an attempt to exorcise the ghost of the Weimar Republic's failure in economic policy and to impose an 'objective' discipline on a society whose historic 'fragility' is still widely assumed. The contrast between the scale of the West German economy and the political behaviour of its government remains sharp and has its roots in memories of earlier German attempts to assert a world role. Politicians have preferred to stress the limited room for manoeuvre in economic policy and even their helplessness (e.g., Stoltenberg in 1987) rather than assume a leadership role commensurate with the economic prominence of West Germany. This political style sits somewhat oddly with the enormously important role of the economy, and the export drive in particular, in helping Germans to regain their international respect in the post-war period.

The preference for caution, pragmatism and consensus has also been easier to sustain in the absence of a decade and more of desperation about relative economic decline (as in the UK). As we have seen, the debate about *Standort Deutschland* has revealed new concerns in the late 1980s – about high public subsidies (e.g., coal consumed a subsidy of DM 24 billion between 1980 and 1987), about the very slow pace of deregulation (especially in services), about sluggish investment and about low growth. Despite new tensions between the Bonn government and industry over domestic growth and tax incentives, a 'traditional' attachment to fiscal consolidation strategy was associated with rapid export expansion, particularly within European markets. As earlier, the Bonn government could rely on an efficiently organised corporate network within the private sector to mobilise a response to the new challenge of international competitiveness. 'Flagship' companies like Siemens, Daimler-Benz and Hoechst could play a role on their own: thus in 1985, by taking over AEG (electronics), Dornier (aerospace) and MTU (engines), Daimler-Benz was able to create West Germany's largest industrial grouping. The consequence of new corporate assertiveness in an altered international context was to rupture some traditional cosy relationships: thus in 1986 the Bosch and Siemens representatives resigned from Daimler-Benz's supervisory board in the wake of its new, competitive acquisitions.

The structural bedrock of West German economic policy remained the bank-industry nexus, with the 'universal' banks (like Deutsche, Dresdner and Commerzbank) having a privileged 'insider' position amongst the top 100 German companies and in contacts to government (Kreile, 1978 and Dyson, 1985). These banks are traditionally investment as well as deposit banks; exercise (mainly by proxy) extensive shareholder voting rights in major companies; are represented in key supervisory board positions within industry; and, as 'house banks', offer comprehensive services to industrial companies (including the management of stock issues). Accordingly, they pursue an active relationship with some industrial clients and, at times of crisis, act as instruments of discipline (e.g., the AEG crisis of the early 1980s). The consequences are fourfold: government is insulated from many of the pressures of industrial crisis management, and thus better able to sustain its ideology of the 'social market economy' in industrial affairs; West Germany continues to lack a hostile 'takeover' culture as in the United States and Britain, and maverick personalities tend to be distrusted; shareholder rights are relatively weak (with only about 500 publicly traded companies and the presence of worker representatives on supervisory boards); and long-term bank loans play a more significant role in industrial finance. The industrial benefits have been notably apparent in German performance at developing and applying technologies. This solid business structure is in turn reinforced by codetermination and in particular the close cooperation of both sides of industry in a highly developed system of occupational training that guarantees skills, quality and reliability. In total, these characteristics have lent a stability and predictability to West German corporate structure that matches the stability and predictability at the level of macro-economic policy. At both levels, the contribution of government has been to sustain the mechanisms that promote stability and predictability, in the form of the bank-industry nexus and worker codetermination and support for and cooperation with the Bundesbank. The consequence is also a measure of rigidity.

These subtle and complex mechanisms that underpin the operation of the West German economy have been subjected to increasing international political and economic pressures in the late 1980s. The political commitment to complete the Single European Market by the end of 1992 is a direct challenge to West Germany's regulatory culture, not least in banking and financial markets, and implies that the 'takeover' culture will spread to West Germany. In this respect stability and predictability may be less in evidence at the industrial level. At the level of industrial behaviour West Germany seems to be set for greater assimilation into the international economy. By contrast, the European Monetary System (EMS) has become the symbol of West German strength and influence. In practice, contrary to the expectations of its founders, the EMS has developed into a sort of DM zone rather than an Ecu zone. Many other EMS members have preferred to use the DM as a standard of stability for themselves in order to be better able to implement their own counter-inflationary policies. In other words, West Germany has provided its European partners with the public good of price stability. The EMS has operated in this respect as an extension of West German economic policy: not as an engine of growth but as a provider of stability. Supported by Chanceller Kohl, the Bundesbank was able to insist that further development towards European monetary and economic union with West German participation would depend on the creation of an independent central bank at the European level. At this level, West Germany was in a powerful position to shape the future development of economic and monetary union in Europe.

# 9

# The Politics of Welfare

STEEN MANGEN

## The New Policy Climate

In common with its neighbours the Federal Republic experienced a
rapid expansion of social budgets during the 1960s and early 1970s.
From 1969 to 1975 welfare expenditure broke loose from economic
growth rates, rising sharply from 24 to 33 per cent of GDP, as the
SPD strove to fulfil its mandate as a progressive social party. After
the oil crisis of the previous decade, successive German governments
have implemented policies of retrenchment. The present Chancellor
tightened an austerity programme already instituted by his predecessor. But throughout the 1980s the mainstream of the SPD and
the Union parties have pressed for a consolidation, rather than a
full-blown dismantlement of the German welfare system. The intention was to avoid fundamentally disturbing existing institutional
arrangements, although it was conceded that some of the system's
benefits would in future be less generous.

What has been new under Kohl has been the policy climate in
which cuts were implemented since, although the new government
resorted to a similar range of *ad hoc* measures designed to curb
budgetary increases as did its predecessor, social policy debate has
gradually acquired a new vocabulary. Whilst the right has made the
now familiar calls for a 'new subsidiarity' of the state, echoing those
elsewhere in Western Europe, radical debate on the left has moved
somewhat away from the traditional forum within the SPD into the
fast growing Green movement where issues have been reformulated
in the language of 'socio-ecology'. To some extent, these developments have undermined the bipartisan consensus on welfare that has

existed in the Federal Republic since the 1950s, although, as we shall see, the effects should not be overstated.

The wide-ranging concerns that have emerged in the 1980s will undoubtedly influence West German social policy well into the next century. Discussion here is limited to the implications for health expenditure and social security (particularly pensions). At issue are: the appropriate divisions of public and private responsibility for providing welfare; citizen participation in the planning and management of welfare services; and the long-term unemployment and an ageing population. Self-help, privatisation, social symmetry, efficiency, citizenship and the generational contract are key concepts in the debate. Some, of course, have been well-aired elsewhere in Western Europe; others are peculiarly German pre-occupations.

After more than a decade of retrenchment relying on short-term tamperings with the system, the search in recent years has been for longer-term stability, particularly in the two policy areas discussed here. This chapter reviews outstanding problems and the approaches of the main parties to resolving them, but first there is a brief description of the workings of the German welfare system. At this stage it is worthwhile reminding the reader not to lose sight of the fact that social policies are part of a broader government programme, most critically its macro-economic strategy of reducing public expenditure and its plans for tax reform, both of which are analysed in Chapter 8.

## The German Welfare System: Funders and Providers

Among OECD countries West Germany is a medium welfare spender, the social budget consuming almost one-third of GDP. Social security accounts for almost two-thirds of this expenditure, health care one-fifth and education much of the remainder. The greater part of the social budget is financed by social insurance schemes and by the Länder and local authorities.

Post-war German *Sozialpolitik* (social policy) has conventionally been conceived within the framework of the social market economy, in that welfare policies are understood as contributing to the achievement of wider societal goals (*Gesellschaftspolitik*), rather than being narrowly interpreted in terms of a moral imperative of the state to provide directly for the welfare of individuals. It is for this reason that labour market policies are also closely identified with *Sozialpolitik*. In German conceptualisation, then, the state is not itself a universal provider but, rather, a guarantor and overseer of certain social rights that are mostly fulfilled by other agencies: for instance, by social insurance which, to a large extent, is funded by employers and employees. This is an essential principle of the German 'Social State' (rather than 'welfare state') and is enshrined in a code of impartial laws that are supervised by the Constitutional and Social Courts.

In the German constitutional system a clear distinction is made between the welfare responsibilities of each tier of government – federal government, Länder, and communes. Crucially, the subsidiary principle enshrined in the constitution allocates to various citizen initiatives a primary role for many welfare functions, the public sector in these cases being the provider of last resort. These charitable and voluntary agencies – the so-called 'free agencies' (*freie Träger*) – then, administer many of West Germany's health and social services.

A summary of the major divisions of responsibility in this complex welfare system is attempted in Table 9.1.

Although the role of the federal government has been growing over the last twenty years, particularly with the attempts at macro-economic management, the prime responsibility for much social policy-making lies at the Länder level, with Bonn retaining certain reserve functions. To improve what are still poor social planning capacities, there has been an emphasis since the 1960s on 'concerted federalism', through which Bonn sponsors conferences of Länder ministers holding various social policy portfolios in an attempt to promote some degree of national uniformity of provisions. The growing infringement of Bonn in policy areas traditionally understood as within the remit of the Länder has led to conflict on several occasions in recent years, not least because of the existence of opposing party regimes at federal and Land level. The Länder employ several strategies to fight off these advances. First, there is the resort – or threat of resort – to the Federal Constitutional Court to obtain rulings on political responsibilities. More important as a routine watchdog is the Bundesrat which, as the preserve of the Länder, has been critical in maintaining the their powers. It is thus essential to bear in mind that the federal government's capacity to push through policies in areas which are not directly its preserve is formally restricted.

As already outlined, the powers of the federal government to implement key elements of social policy are further limited by the fact that many social provisions are administered outside the state or local government sector. The *'freie Träger'*, which manage a large proportion of these services, are organised in five politically powerful, sometimes competing, associations. Similarly, social insurance is not a national unified system predominantly offering universal flat-rate benefits along British lines, but is organised

TABLE 9.1 *Health and welfare: policy-makers, funders ad providors*

**Federal government**
* Oversees the social insurance system
* Contributes to capital costs of services
* Retains certain reserve functions: e.g. medical education, research in health and welfare, promotes 'model' services, regualtes the 1961 Federal Social Assistance Act
* Has an exhortative role: e.g., commissions enquiries, 'concerted federalism'

**Länder**
* Have major responsibility for policy-making and planning
* Contribute to capital cost of services
* Provide certain services: e.g., some hospitals
* Largely fund 'last resort' means-tested social assistance

**Communes**
* Undertake local policy-making and planning of social services
* Contribute to capital costs of services
* Provide certain services: e.g., some hospitals and preventive health and welfare services
* Administer and partly fund social social assistance

**Voluntary sector**
* The many separate agencies are organised into five 'Spitzenverbände' peak-lever organisations): two are denominational, one is allied to the trade union movement, one is the German Red Cross and the other an association of small agencies
* Planning by these agencies is largely dictated by the availability of funding, with the result that there is no overall planning strategy
* Contributes to capital costs of services
* Each agency negotiates operating fees with the social insurance schemes and, where necessary, social assistance
* Administers hospital services (37 per cent of all in-patient beds) and are the principal providers of a wide range of welfare services

**Private sector**
* Provides capital costs of services
* Profit is dominant planning criterion
* There are few restrictions on the establishment of services
* Maintains some health and welfare provisions (e.g., 10 per cent of all hospital beds)
* Doctors in 'office' practice are the major providers of outpatient treatment.

**Social insurance**
* Sickness insurance funds operational costs of health services on a daily fee for occupied beds and fee for 'item of service' basis
* Pension schemes fund operational costs of rehabilitative services for the disabled
* Social assistance partially funds operational costs of welfare services and, where liability is not accepted by social insurance schemes, funds health and rehabilitation treatments for some patients
* Fees are negotiated separately with hospitals, medical practitioner associations and welfare agencies

**Private individuals**
* Liability for the costs of certain medical treatments and welfare facilities falls in part or whole on individuals and/or their families

according to each contingency (e.g., sickness, old age, disability), these schemes being variously administered at local, Land and federal level. Apart from the unemployment fund, which was first introduced in the 1920s, the features of German social insurance are essentially those instituted by Bismarck one hundred years ago. As semi-autonomous public corporations, self-administration of the schemes is the fundamental organisational principle. Table 9.2 provides details of the main components of the insurance system.

TABLE 9.2   *The social insurance system: major agencies*

| Contingency | Agency |
| --- | --- |
| Sickness | Over 1500 sickness funds, including company schemes, special occupational schemes and 'contracted out' schemes largely for white-collar employees |
| Industrial accidents | Separate industrial schemes funded by employers |
| Old age, survivors and disability | 'Blue-collar' pension schemes administered by each Land |
| | Certain separate occupational schemes |
| | 'White-collar' pensions managed by Federal Insurance Agency |
| Unemployment | Federal Employment Agency |

Social insurance entitlements are closely regulated by the equivalence principle: that is, the benefits paid to those temporarily or permanently out of the workforce should provide an equivalent standard of living to that attained in periods of working life. Insurance benefits are therefore earnings-related and are among the most generous in Western Europe, even though certain cuts have been introduced over the past ten years or so. Where claimants have no right to insurance benefits, they may be entitled to social assistance administered by local authorities which is means-tested according to stricter regulations than, say, has been its equivalent of supplementary benefit in Britain.

The social insurance system is highly prized by Germans who are aware that they fare rather better than many of their European neighbours. The very popularity and high expectations the electorate has of the system does impose constraints on politicians' ability to enact reforms, as will be demonstrated later in the case of pensions. Despite its widespread appeal, there are several negative social consequences produced by the nature of the insurance system. They arise from the fact that social insurance is closely tied to the world of work: those with poor previous employment status do rather less well out of it, as is evidenced by the inferior financial position of women pensioners when compared with men. Because the equivalence principle rather than a strong redistributive element predominates, the goal of status preservation, with its inevitable transfer of the inequalities of the labour market into the welfare system, exacerbates 'two nation' tendencies.

In fact, until recent years redistribution, which has been a prime concern of British social policy theorists, has received comparatively little attention, for high economic growth rates meant rising standards of living for all with very little unemployment, particularly among the young. In the 1980s this has no longer been the case. Outside the government some politicians with a major interest in social policy – the so-called '*SoPos*' – argue that social need has played second fiddle to the equivalence principle in the operation of social insurance. For them, there is a moral as well as an economic crisis of the welfare state, since they see in West Germany today a 'new social question' replacing nineteenth century concerns about relations between capital and labour. Rather, their concern is for the millions of marginalised people who are relatively poorly served by the welfare state – the long-term unemployed, the handicapped, single parents and many of the elderly. On the other hand, right wing authorities (e.g., the *Kronsberger Kreis*) reject any redistributive role for social insurance, arguing that such efforts, when appropriate, are better achieved through fiscal policy.

In its operation, the welfare system relies on a heavy bureaucracy and rigid legalism to govern the many contractual agreements between a myriad of autonomous funders and providing agencies. The fundamental decentralisation of decision-making has tended to afford access to power to highly organised and 'establishment' pressure groups, leaving smaller and newer bodies relatively out in the cold. Critically, as Heinze and Hinrichs (1986) note, the overriding need for sustained high levels of consensus at various points in this political system acts as an impediment to much needed innovation in social policy (for an example see Mangen, 1985). The 'crisis' of the welfare state in Germany is thus not merely economic but, as elsewhere in Western Europe, reflects growing disillusionment with its large-scale, insensitive and bureaucratic nature.

There is no easy way out of these problems, because the German welfare system offers few incentives either to be more responsive to the needs of clients or to plan across services. Indeed, there are perverse incentives for each agency to hold its ground, since there is little gain in making concessions in the interests of overall efficiency or of controlling rising costs. German governments have devoted considerable attention to these problems but, as we shall see in the case of health care, they have not been noticeably successful in devising feasible solutions.

Before examining present party positions on health and social security, some essential context for the policies pursued in the preceding decade is now provided.

## Social Policy in the 1980s: A Strategy of Retrenchment

Most commentators agree that the 1982 *'Wende'* was not meant to herald a dismantling of the German welfare system, despite some of the rhetoric. Cuts – and they have been considerable – have broadly followed the spirit and the direction of Schmidt in his later years: 'consolidation' has been the byword of both chancellors. In fact, the long series of cuts began in 1975, with efforts to curb sharp increases in the public debt. They have continued through the deepest recession in the early 1980s, when negative economic growth rates were recorded and both governments were grasping at immediate budgetary palliatives, although Schmidt had earlier been criticised by some SPD economic advisers for precipitate and over-reaction. The adverse economic effects were still evident in the social budgets of 1983 and 1984. However, better economic performance in the mid-1980s, coupled with CDU setbacks in Länder elections at that time, encouraged the government to call a halt to further substantial cuts. Indeed, there have been some extensions of welfare rights, particularly in the field of family policy and relaxation of benefit rules for the older unemployed.

A summary of the most important cuts in health and pensions is given in Table 9.3; it will be evident that many of these strategies have been employed by other Western governments whatever their political composition. Table 9.3 shows the range and frequency of *ad hoc* tampering with service provisions, although on occasions cuts have also been accompanied by 'sweeteners', such as the temporary reduction in the pension insurance contribution in 1981 and the reduction in the qualifying period for a pension in 1982. Cuts have taken many forms: reductions in level of entitlements as related to income, tightening of eligibility rules, postponing the updating of benefits, and so forth. Bäcker and Naegele (1986) estimate that, in total, there have been more than 250 fiscal and welfare measures which, in one way or another, have reduced entitlements. The apparent lack of 'fairness' – or what Germans refer to as 'social symmetry' – in the cuts has been a sensitive issue, as the left has exploited the fact that the poor and unemployed have had the dubious privilege

TABLE 9.3 *Retrenchment strategies in pensions and health, 1977–1985*

| Strategy | Enacted |
|---|---|
| **Pensions** | |
| * Delays in indexation | 1977, 1982 |
| * Substitution of guaranteed indexation for discretionary increases | 1978 |
| * Tightening of entitlement criteria | 1977, 1983 |
| * Insurance contribution increases | 1978, 1983, 1985 |
| * Federal subsidy to pension funds reduced | 1981, 1982 |
| * Pensioners liable for own health insurance | 1982 |
| * Progressive increses in pensioners' health insurance contributions | from 1984 |
| **Health** | |
| * Corporatist 'concerted actions' by providers and funders for cost containment | From 1977, reformed 1981 |
| * Prescription fee increases | 1977, 1981, 1982 |
| * Certain dental fee increases | 1977, 1981 |
| * Restriction in coverage of optical fees | 1982 |
| * Stricter criteria for cure coverage | 1981 |
| * Daily charge for in-patients and cures | 1982 |
| * Non-coverage of costs of comfort drugs | 1982 |
| * Social insurance contribution levied on sickness benefit | 1983 |
| * Incorporation of one-off payments in calculation of insurance contribution | 1984 |

Source: Alber (1986); Backer and Naegele (1986).

of bearing the brunt of them. It is partly for these reasons that in recent policy announcements on health and pensions, for example, ministers have been anxious to stress that curtailments must be shared by all: by those in employment, by suppliers of welfare, such as doctors and drugs companies, and by current pensioners, who up to now have suffered rather less than other social security recipients from the cuts (see below).

The upturn in the economy in the last few years has failed to make any appreciable dent in the numbers of long-term unemployed and regional inequalities in unemployment rates have worsened. This, together with the problem of the growing numbers of elderly, has encouraged the government to direct greater effort towards long-term stabilisation of the system, particularly with regard to the future of pensions. A further and vital factor guiding the government's search for stabilisation is its commitment progressively to reduce public expenditure ratios in the short run from the current 46 per cent of GDP to under 40 per cent, the level of the late 1960s before Brandt came to power.

In an era of retrenchment German governments, like their counterparts elsewhere, have had to learn how to present their social policies to the electorate as progressive or, at least, prudent. This is a strategy which, to say the least, requires careful political management. Both Schmidt and Kohl can claim some measure of success, for Germans have been willing over the past decade or so to re-elect them despite their imposition of unpopular cuts. Furthermore, the present governing parties have been particularly skilful in reducing people's expectations, and they have also managed to discredit the SPD as spendthrifts in the past who would offer more of the same in the future. It is true to say that sections of the electorate have been compliant partners in these processes: surveys in the early and mid-1980s indicated that many respondents were willing to sacrifice the level of benefits (often of other people) for curbs on their own taxation and social insurance levies. Nonetheless, there are counter-currents, some of which have emerged only recently.

Political scientists in the past few years have been pointing to the constraint on governments imposed by a growing 'welfare constituency'. Alber (1986), for example, estimates that one-quarter of the German electorate now derives its primary source of income from welfare benefits. Furthermore, a growing number of the workforce is employed in the administration and provision of welfare services. When the potential strength of this combined constituency is assessed in the light of the fact that current non-recipients in the population, and particularly younger employees, are starting to be rightly concerned about the quality of their entitlements at the end of their working life, one can begin to appreciate how welfare issues could achieve a higher profile in future elections.

## Current Party Positions on Welfare

### The CDU–CSU

The *Wende* promised by Chancellor Kohl placed emphasis on supply-side stimulated growth and, in his prescriptions for the state, a return to a traditional reliance on the subsidiarity principle. Both strategies were eagerly urged on him by the junior FDP partners who had been progressively distancing themselves from Schmidt's social and economic policies in the last years of his government. Some politicians within the current coalition have reformulated ideas about subsidiarity, imputing to the Social State damaging effects on economic performance and the moral fibre of the nation. This reformulation of the subsidiarity principle departs from the traditional social catholicism both Union parties traditionally espouse. The Church's teaching arose from its mistrust of the secular state and a desire to restrict its influence over the everyday lives of individuals whilst, at the same time, imposing certain social obligations on it; the views expressed in the relevant papal encyclicals did not sanction a wholesale withdrawal of the state's responsibilities for collective welfare (Richter, 1987).

In the event a *Wende* in the welfare state has not occurred. Both the CDU and CSU, as *Volksparteien*, have a strong tradition of commitment to social action which is reinforced by important internal pressure groups. In contrast to many conservative parties elsewhere the CDU–CSU can claim an above-average performance in welfare provision, although many within the Union parties retain their ambivalence about how 'social' the Social State should be (for further discussion, see Michalsky, 1985). Apart from social Catholicism, other factors have influenced their position on welfare: cultural and political competition with the GDR; the fight for the middle ground with the SPD, not only in federal but also in the regular round of Länder elections; and, not least among the *SoPos* in the party, an old etatist tradition. The *SoPos* have continued to argue the conservative notion of social responsibility, with emphasis on the family and community support. Those on the right favour more targetting through increased selectivity in provisions, the privatisation of many social services, an element of commercialisation in those remaining in the publicly-funded sector and greater responsibility for individuals to provide for their own welfare. These latter views are heartily supported by the FDP. On several occasions in past years tensions have built up within the coalition on issues such as tax reform, social security and the health services, the general line taken by elements of the Union parties being that new proposals go too far and by the FDP that they do not go far enough.

Schmidt (1985, p.47) makes the important point that tensions over social policy are bound to be ever-present within the coalition, since 'it would seem unlikely that a government dominated by a catch-all party . . . would run the risk of dismantling [the welfare state]' for 'the political risks . . . seem too high' (Schmidt, 1985, p. 47). For these reasons and given the incompatibility of goals in such a broad area as welfare, as witnessed in the government's current taxation and family policies, compromise on views about the future of social provision is inevitable.

## The SPD

Historically, the SPD's strength over the Union parties in welfare policy arises from its adoption of a programmatic approach to social reform. Nowhere is this more in evidence than during Brandt's chancellorship. The budgetary retrenchments initiated by Schmidt broke this tradition and, with it, fractured the broad party consensus on welfare issues that had prevailed after Bad Godesberg when the SPD abandoned its more radical policies. In the latter years of his office Schmidt failed to convince both the rank-and-file within his party and the DGB (the trade union movement) that his 'middle way' was more than an attempt to appease the FDP which, in the person of Count Lambsdorff, was ever more vocal in rejecting expensive social policies and in arguing for a renegotiation of the welfare system. Schmidt's departure deepened dissension within the party which was increasingly aired in public. There were concerns among radicals that the SPD had discredited itself as a party of the democratic left by penalising many within its own constituency among the working class in order to retain the support of its bourgeois junior government partner. The split between left and right in the party has led to a identity crisis from which the SPD has not yet emerged. Its abandonment by certain radical elements for the Greens, the failure to attract the young voter and the decline of its traditional areas of support in the industrial heartland in the north and Rhineland have merely served to exacerbate the party's chronic problems.

The left wing of the SPD, forced to respond to the radical social policy alternatives proposed by the Greens have largely joined their bandwagon, if not formally their movement. The talk now is of grass-roots welfare utilising 'new social movements' which are community-based and have local expertise. Self-help and a challenge to bureaucratic services and the power of the professional have thus captured their imagination. Greater access to welfare funding for newer, small 'citizen' associations is to be energetically encouraged. For the left, the Social State must be retained, for it represents a real victory of the working class. But it must be recaptured by that class through greatly improved public participation in the organisation, planning and delivery of welfare.

Party moderates want to preserve as much of the present system as possible and, more conventionally perhaps, see the Social State as a means of stimulating economic growth. Furthermore, their support for innovative grass-roots reform is moderated by their concern not to alarm their allies among the *freie Träger*, particularly the *Arbeiterwohlfahrt*, which is a large-scale provider of welfare services.

The 1986 report of the SPD Social Policy Commission clearly expresses the tremendous difficulties involved in reconciling party differences over the future of welfare. Its proposals are cautiously radical: whilst wishing to initiate reform of social insurance, which would include incorporating civil servants who at present enjoy non-contributory benefits, the authors seek to reassure the electorate that the system's essential features, particularly the earnings-related element, will be retained. The report stresses the need to harmonise the different insurance schemes in order to guarantee greater viability of the funds and to promote equality of treatment among recipients. The Committee also argued that the costs of social security should no longer be so closely tied to occupational status, because such a system excluded too many people, but rather that it should be funded by a tax on company turnover. To relieve pressure on locally-funded social assistance, a federally-funded basic benefit for the unemployed and job-creation measures were advocated, as was a policy to introduce an insurance scheme to cover the costs of institutional care for the elderly and long-term disabled.

The Commission's main response to demands for greater public participation in the welfare system is largely confined to resurrecting the 1950s idea of the 'social community' embodied in local committees comprising representatives of insurance scheme and welfare providers under whose auspices a range of social services could be coordinated (Tennstedt, 1986).

## The FDP

The FDP is the principal advocate of post-oil crisis neo-liberalism, campaigning for individual responsibility and less reliance on collective welfare, which it argues is both economically inefficient and stifles initiative. For the FDP, social services are to be organised in such a way as to give every incentive for individuals to make provisions for themselves. For this reason the party is a strong proponent of self-help, which it regards as a means of substantially replacing more formal efforts, since its guiding principle is that the state's task must not extend beyond guaranteeing a basic welfare minimum. As for those health and welfare services that will continue to be collectively funded, the FDP sees an urgent need to promote competition in order to achieve greater operational efficiency. Thus, unlike the SPD, a more effective system is not to be attempted through a unification of the pluralist system, but by an even wider pluralism through the fostering of new agencies that have sound ideas on how to attain value for money in the delivery of welfare.

## The Greens

The most innovative ideas on social policies to be canvassed in the 1980s have come from the fledgling Green movement. Indeed, many social issues that have gained currency in recent years – self- and mutual help, community participation, grass-roots welfare, and so forth – have, to a large extent, been the brainchild of the Greens. *SoPo* elements in the other parties have therefore felt themselves forced to respond to this radical, fresh appeal.

Although there are important factional differences between the more radical *'Fundis'* in the constituencies and the pragmatist *'Realos'* in the Bundestag, both share a strong ecological emphasis in social policy: the promotion of welfare should not be at the expense of environmental concerns. Both factions subscribe to a strong compensatory welfare model in which victims of technological and social change should receive benefits to offset the social, economic and psychological costs imposed on them. Under their slogan 'work differently, distribute differently, live differently and help differently', the Greens have proposed a radical alternative to existing social provisions. The movement regards welfare as essentially a grass-roots affair but, although distrustful of large bureaucratic state-supervised services, Greens insist that their approach does not exonerate the state from its responsibilities. Theirs is a moral crusade seeking to infuse the population with a spirit of collectivism embodied in the 'community' as the integrative socio-ecological unit. However, the movement is not oblivious to the fact that the welfare bureaucracy is deeply entrenched, though how far to accommodate this reality is one of the main points of contention between the *'Fundis'* and *'Realos'* (Kvistad, 1987; Opielka and Ostner, 1987).

The Greens want to see a move away from preoccupation with the rationality of the welfare system and the requirements of the economy to a deeper consideration of the ecological damage imposed by the persistent striving for greater economic growth. Social policy for the Greens should be explicitly redistributive and based on notions of citizenship, which is why they support the idea of a non-means tested minimum income for all. In employment policy they propose job sharing and a guarantee of work for everyone. The movement has also put forward plans for a flat-rate minimum pension, supported by a compulsory supplementary pensions fund offering earnings-related benefit. Women – and particularly widows, according to the Greens – are entitled to a better pensions-deal. Reflecting the past experiences of many of their membership in the mental health movement, they propose a radical deinstitutionalisation programme that would render most large establishments housing the mentally ill, the handicapped and the elderly superfluous by the mid-1990s.

Perhaps the Greens are at their most articulate in expressing their policies on the position of women. '*Fundis*' in the movement see the securing of equal opportunities as feasible only through an unequivocal policy of a 50–50 quota of training and employment places. The Greens attach greater importance to protecting and promoting the interests of women and children rather than to conventional 'family policy'. Among the ranks of the '*Fundis*' are feminists who see an equally important cultural struggle.

## Political Issues in Health Provision

The German health system is characterised by high quality services that enjoy popular electoral support but which suffers from an inequality of distribution by geographical area and clinical specialism and a lack of effective planning machinery. There has been serious overprovision in some sectors – particularly in acute hospital beds – matched by patchiness in the supply of other services, notably community care facilities. The alarming increase in the numbers of doctors in training is exacerbated by a lack of planning capacities to eradicate the existing maldistributions alluded to above.

Health expenditure has increased by 900 per cent since the late 1960s, and today West Germany is near the top of the league of Western European spenders. Sickness insurance contributions, which are shared by employer and employee, now average 13 per cent of salaries. They have risen sharply over the years and are a significant non-wage cost that entrepreneurs complain handicaps German industry's international competitiveness. Moreover, on some well-publicised indicators, such as infant mortality rates, the health service's performance is unimpressive. The main political issues, then, concern value for money in a service which Germans hold in high regard and the comparative absence of strategic planning of the system.

Despite the consumption by health care of a large share of public expenditure, the federal government has few direct powers, apart from the supervision of the sickness insurance schemes. Indeed, Bonn's involvement in health planning has actually declined recently and the government now allocates federal block grants to the Länder to spend as they wish. Whilst the Länder retain the major policy-making responsibilities, many services are managed by the voluntary or private sector (see Table 9.3). Financial reform has been on the political agenda since the first 'Concerted Action' was launched in

1977 with the aim of controlling ever-rising costs. The root of the problem is the system of reimbursing suppliers of health care. Doctors receive a fee for each 'item of service' they perform. Although there is a policing system to check gross abuse, by and large, the more clinical interventions a doctor carries out on each patient, the greater is his total fee. Hospitals receive a fee for each day a bed is occupied, a method of funding that provides a positive incitement to hospital administrators to see that all beds are continually filled, with the consequence that average in-patient spells are over twice as long in West Germany as they are in Britain. Although there has been some discussion on the left of an integrated health budget to circumvent these problems – something akin to the 'global budget' introduced by the first socialist government in France under Mitterrand's presidency – such a solution has never seriously been on the cards, in view of the objections of the influential medical lobby that has powerful friends in Bonn, particularly among the FDP.

Cost containment, then, has dominated the political debate in the last decade. The two corporatist 'Concerted Actions' (the second was in 1981) which were formulated by representatives of major providers and funders and whose recommendations were not binding on the parties concerned, could claim only short-term effects. Rather, the limited impact of cost control measures has come about through the implementation of the series of cuts illustrated in Table 9.3. The continuing problem confronting politicians stems from the simple fact that there are weak links between demand for health care and its costs to the individual. Moreover, as stated above, the present funding system provides little incentive to the many, often competing suppliers of health care or their clients to economise; indeed, there is every incentive for health services to oversupply. Essentially, the German health service is 'a bargaining system with the medical profession in the driving seat' (Zapf. 1986). Those who pay – in general, the sickness insurance funds – have, argues Murswieck (1985), almost no influence over the quality, quantity or distribution of the services supplied.

## Present Health Proposals

Employment Minister Blüm has recently secured a tentative agreement within the coalition for restructuring the finance of health services. He has shrunk from a radical structural reform and, instead, has put forward a carefully constructed package that retains the essential features of the system and appears to offer something to everyone. Under his proposals certain dental work, non-essential medicines and spa cures will henceforth be paid for by the consumer. For a transitional period, until the sickness insurance funds have balanced their books again, patients will have to pay up to 20 per cent of the cost of drugs on the approved list. Significantly, of the projected 14 billion marks to be saved, half will go in a 1 per cent reduction in insurance levies. The rest will pay for the renewed effort to provide long-term community care for the elderly and severely handicapped. Informal carers are to be offered tax incentives, an attendant's allowance, and up to 25 hours a month of professional support supplemented by four weeks' relief a year with a guarantee of a replacement carer.

Blüm's proposals have met with sharp criticism from the SPD, the Greens and the employers' organisation, the BDA. The Greens and SPD accuse the Minister of shirking the necessary structural reform, the absence of which is merely storing up problems for the future, particularly in view of the ageing population that will further inflate demand for health care. His political opponents have castigated him for merely cutting costs and transferring the burden to patients and their families, views which recent surveys indicate are shared by a majority of the electorate. There is concern that increased economic, social and psychological costs will accrue to home carers, despite the improved benefits. The Minister has responded to accusations about a lack of social symmetry in these reforms by insisting that doctors and the drugs industry will have to accept their share of cuts too. Yet it remains to be seen how successful he will be. The powerful pharmaceutical companies, for example, have already threatened court action against the idea of state-imposed prices for their products and have obtained the support of FDP politicians.

There are also disputes within the coalition about some of the details of Blüm's plans that are still unresolved and, at present, it is uncertain how much of the projected savings will actually materialise. The FDP would have liked stricter measures, the CDU *Sopos* and BDA fewer, and some in the CDU are worried about the implications of these and other policies that might be in the pipeline for Länder constitutional primacy in health affairs. For his part, Blüm has made it clear that he is prepared to allocate to the community care programme only the amount saved elsewhere in the health system: in other words, there is no new money involved here. The insurance funds are doubtful that these savings will accrue in reality and there are also fears that, once in operation, the government would be unable to resist calls to subsidise the community care programme from general taxation.

## The Crisis of Pensions

Because the Federal Republic has an extremely low birth rate (1.3 per woman) which is falling faster than elsewhere in Western Europe, demographic factors loom large in social planning. And no more so than in the case of pensions. Planning horizons in this field are necessarily lengthy and politicians are currently searching for ways of avoiding the projected situation which will obtain in 2030 when, because of a sharp decline in the proportion of workers to pensioners, the contribution rate to the pension funds would have to double if the current level of benefits is to be maintained.

Ministers are only too aware that pensions policy requires careful handling for it has proved a serious headache in the past. It was, for example, the most important domestic issue of the mid-1950s and its resolution then gave the CDU–CSU the only absolute majority in the history of the republic. The success of the government of the day lay in guaranteeing Germans pensions at a high proportion of their previous salaries, and this is what people have come to expect from the state supervised schemes, private pension funds accounting for less than 10 per cent of relevant expenditure. There are some pensioners who have fared less well. Because they are earnings-related, pension inequalities are considerable. Women have an unfavourable pensions-income profile when compared with men and widows, in particular, have been even less generously treated. Consequently, some pensioners have had to rely on top-up social assistance payments from local authorities. Their numbers have been increasing and, as later discussion indicates, this has caused conflict between Bonn and certain Länder.

The demographic problem is gaining increasing attention from the popular media which have been quick to point out that the long-standing 'generational contract' is breaking down. In a pay-as-you-go pension scheme like Germany's the present workforce pays for the pensions of today's elderly in the expectation that the next generation will pay for theirs. The declining birth rate means that there will not be sufficient numbers of workers in the next century to honour this contract, not unless they are forced to pay a crippling contribution rate. As younger Germans are becoming progressively aware, they are therefore extremely unlikely to recoup what they are currently paying out. Quite simply, if things stay as they are, tomorrow's pensions will bear no comparison with today's.

Concern about the long-term viability of German pension schemes is not new, although it is fair to say that the sense of urgency is now more strongly felt. The security of pension funds has, in fact, featured prominently in federal elections since 1976, when their financial difficulties were first becoming apparent. In several years federal subsidies have had to be paid and in the last ten years various retrenchment measures – in particular, the suspension of indexation – have been implemented, despite previous assurances to the contrary (see Table 9.3). Merklein (1986) in a series of articles in *Der Spiegel* claimed that in no other area of social policy have there been 'so many lies and broken promises'. It is understandable that the government has been playing its cards close to its chest as, indeed, have SPD politicians.

Late in 1987 the CDU announced proposals for discussion within the coalition. Unlike the urgent situation of sickness insurance, the government does have some little time to play with, as it is calculated that pension schemes are currently guaranteed sufficient resources until the early 1990s.

In the past few years Minister Blüm has been devoting energy to educating the public, speaking of the need to restore the balance in the generational contract and pointing out that current pensioners have been relatively favourably treated. In a Bundestag debate on the subject he stressed that the situation was simply getting out of hand when a country with an epidemic of childlessness was allocating more than three times the proportion of its social budget to pensions than it was to children and youth.

There has been no shortage of solutions to the pensions dilemma. For a time FDP Minister Bangemann canvassed the idea of a national flat-rate scheme, similar to several proposed by specialists in the CDU, with private pensions providing supplementary income. The FDP officially favoured the idea of incentives for private insurance for those who have made forty years' contributions to the state supervised schemes. The SPD, supported by the DGB, have urged that as much as possible of the present system should be retained, but that its funding should change from an employer's contribution, which could be construed as a tax on jobs, to a contribution based on company turnover. The Greens want an ecologically sound pensions scheme incorporating a 'machine tax', a solution that has also been considered by the SPD. The Greens' basic pension, more generous than the one proposed by the CDU, would be supplemented by a compulsory additional earnings-related pension, along the lines of the current Swedish model. Both the SPD and Greens have advocated that pensions should be underpinned by a safety-net, basic social-security benefit in order to reduce reliance on social assistance.

A 1987 commission on pensions has not adopted any of these innovative models but has advised a more pragmatic approach, recommending an increase in federal subsidies, changes in indexation criteria and the introduction of incentives for a longer working life.

Since most of the coalition, including Blüm, and the SPD do not favour a unitary pension and wish to retain the earning-related principle, reforms along these lines are likely to secure the widest support in the Bundestag. Indeed, some minor amendments to the pensions system have already been passed, such as the introduction of the so-called 'baby year' whereby elderly women (or their male survivors) are attributed one year's contribution to the pension fund for each child they have had.

In September 1988 the CDU finally announced reform proposals for consideration within the coalition. Predictably, the essential structure of the pensions system is to remain but, innovatively – and largely due to Health Minister Rita Süssmuth and the Baden-Württemberg minister-president Späth – reforms are to be harnessed to serve wider objectives in family and health care policy. Three 'baby years', a policy originally supported by the Greens, is to be conceded. Family and friends caring for the elderly or severely disabled at home are also to be credited with pension contributions for periods during which they provide this support. In both these cases, the CDU is aiming to resolve certain long-term problems: they hope the 'baby years' will lead to an increase in the birth rate, thus providing a larger workforce to pay for pensions in the next century; and they argue that credits for carers will diminish their call on social assistance, thereby reducing the financial burden on the Länder and local authorities. If these proposals are eventually approved in parliament, there will also be a new pensions calculation formula and an increase in the federal subsidy to the funds. The age for full pension entitlement is to be raised progressively in the late 1990s to 65 for both men and women, a policy that will particularly affect women who currently retire at 60, but partial pensions for early retirement will be available. Finally, the calculation rate of pension credits for students in full-time education is to be reduced, as is the length of time for which credits can be attributed.

The CDU General Secretary Geissler maintains that these proposed reforms will modernise and stabilise the system. But colleagues within his party, such as Biedenkopf, who some years ago presented his own pensions plan, believe that the CDU has taken the soft option and may be placing a tremendous burden on successive generations. Despite these internal dissensions, the CDU is taking a firm line on its plan and apparently is in no mood to compromise with its partners in government. The aim is to see their proposals passed before the next election in 1990.

Earlier in the summer of 1988, before these proposals were announced, action was forced through by the Länder on the related and growing problem of social assistance. Expenditure has been rising sharply in the 1980s as more and more pensioners have made calls on it. Their ranks have been joined by the long-term unemployed whose entitlement to unemployment benefit has expired or who have insufficient contributions to qualify for benefit. The increasing dimensions of the problem may be adduced by the fact that it is currently estimated that over one-third of the unemployed are no longer entitled to full benefit and are dependent on social assistance. This situation has come about despite government attempts to relieve the burden on social assistance by prolonging older workers' entitlement to unemployment benefit.

Since social assistance is funded by the Länder and local authorities, the issue forms part of the general problem of growing north – south divide. In some of the larger northern cities there has been a 40 per cent increase in expenditure in the 1980s. Here, rather than being a last resort, social assistance has moved to the centre ground of welfare provision. The problem will be exacerbated by Stoltenberg's tax cuts planned for 1990 which will reduce the revenue of the Länder. Northern states fear that if they raise the company tax they control, even more jobs would be lost to the south.

Matters were brought to a head when the CDU Lower Saxony Minister-president Albrecht threatened to join the other northern states and vote against his party's tax reforms in the Bundesrat, unless federal concessions on social assistance were forthcoming. Since the 1988 victory of the SPD in Schleswig-Holstein, Albrecht's desertion would have given the opposition victory in the Bundesrat. The more prosperous Länder were unwilling to countenance a financial reform of social assistance, which Albrecht and his allies proposed. However, a potentially embarrassing defeat for the government was eventually averted by the sanctioning of a federal package of regional aid which, although frustrating Stoltenberg's plans for public expenditure, has at least saved his tax reforms.

## Problems of the 'Welfare Mix'

More than in any other EC country demographic concerns are pre-eminent in the planning of social provisions. The issue is complex for there are both gains and losses accruing in the middle term: whilst expenditure will be saved on education and, taking account of current household formation rates, the demand for housing will decline, there are the intransigent problems of how to secure the funding of pensions, how to control rising health expenditures and how to overcome the labour shortages that are projected for the turn of the century.

German politicians have been eagerly espousing self-help and citizens' initiatives as the appropriate solution to certain welfare problems. These attractive slogans take on different meanings as one moves through the political spectrum. For many Greens they form the basis of a new welfare state; for the SPD and CDU '*Sopos*' they are valuable supplements to a system that will continue to need a large public input; for others in the Union parties and in the FDP they represent a renegotiation of the responsibilities of the state towards its citizens, restoring a real sense of agency to the individual. This rediscovery of the benefits of the small scale has occurred because of a growing disenchantment on all sides with large bureaucratically administered services. There is, therefore, much discussion of the appropriate distribution of responsibilities among the various sectors: the so-called 'welfare mix'. However, current policies here, as elsewhere in Europe, remain poorly specified. Unanswered are questions of how far these alternative forms of delivering welfare provide functional equivalents to the present system. To what extent will the community step in, will families be able or want to cope, will private enterprise be eager to supply services?

There are those who have serious reservations about the long-term viability of policies for social insurance now being implemented or in the pipeline. Elements on the left argue that the equivalence principle is no longer a basis for stabilising the system but, on the contrary, exacerbates social inequalities and dualistic tendencies in society. for them a 'citizenship' model of social security offering a guaranteed minimum and funded through general taxation is more appropriate, since it is more firmly based on notions of social solidarity; only in this way can the 'new social questions', above all 'new poverty', be addressed. Elsewhere in social policy there are many politicians, even among the governing parties' own ranks, who are pessimistic about the new strategies for controlling health expenditure. They have reservations that sufficient savings will materialise to maintain the community care programme which, once launched, will have a momentum of its own that may make future subsidisation unavoidable.

In his speech to the 1988 CDU Annual Conference Chancellor Kohl warned of the difficult decisions that lay ahead. He alluded to an unpleasant possibility that other politicians, such as Norbert Blüm, have been speaking of for several years, namely the need not for reductions in working hours and working life, but for increases in order to make good the labour shortages expected at the turn of the century. Referring to the reformulation of social policies he hinted that certain proposals to be implemented in coming years were bound to be unpopular. But they were necessary. For, as he warned, unless growing social security burdens on the working population were curbed, demographic trends could endanger social stability. And that has been the perennial bugbear of a republic that has only just celebrated forty years since its foundation.

# PART FOUR

# Germany and the World

# 10

# Foreign and Security Policy

**WILLIAM E. PATERSON**

The creators of the Federal Republic were determined to fashion a set of institutions and policies which would not be subject to the process of internal collapse that had brought down the Weimar Republic. They were also aware that both the Imperial and Nazi regimes had collapsed because of foreign policy failures which had united overwhelming forces against them. There was widespread consensus on the institutions and policies of the internal policy agenda. Dissensus, unusually for Western Europe, was concentrated on the external policy agenda. The key division was between those who stressed that priority must lie in complete integration with the West and those who wanted to assign priority to the achievement of reunification. Consensus on foreign policy goals has been much harder to achieve than on domestic policy, and the old question of the degree to which West Germany's foreign and security interests are identical with those of the Western alliance is once again an area of impassioned debate. The debate itself is now a more complex one. At issue now is not only the degree to which resolution of the German question – whether in the form of reunification or, more usually, closer German-German relations – should take precedence over wider Western goals, but divergent responses to the Gorbachev agenda on arms reduction.

## The Security Imperative

At its creation the Federal Republic possessed neither indigenous military forces nor defensible frontiers. One-quarter of its population had fled from areas under Soviet control. The Soviet Union was held to be an expansionary power. These factors added up to a massive security deficit and Adenauer's central priority on becoming chancellor in 1949 was to provide for West German security.

The available options were severely restricted. A neutralised reunified Germany as suggested by the Soviet Union would neither, in Adenauer's view, have guaranteed the maintenance of West German democracy and the social market economy, nor would it have provided the physical or psychological security so desperately sought by the population of the Federal Republic. This security, he argued, could be found only in an unequivocal identification with the West and explicit dependence on the military power of the United States and ultimately its nuclear deterrent. Reliance on the American nuclear deterrent could not provide the whole solution, however. In return, West Germany would have to make a contribution to its own defence.

Adenauer's policy was certainly a correct reading of American imperatives but was much less welcome to the immediate Western neighbours of the Federal Republic or to domestic opinion in the Federal Republic where the twin sentiments of '*Nie weider*' (never again) and '*Ohne mich*' (without me: count me out) characterised the popular views of the older and younger generations respectively. The years between 1950 and 1955 were taken up with finding an acceptable formula for West German rearmament. Adenauer's preferred 'European solution' was rejected by the French parliament in 1954, a measure of how strong West European suspicions continued to be, but nevertheless the Federal Republic joined NATO in 1955.

## The Federal Republic and NATO

The position of the Federal Republic in NATO has often been described as a double containment. The primary and manifest benefit of NATO membership for the Federal Republic is an alliance containment of the Soviet Union. Less obvious, but vital to securing the agreement of other West European members of NATO, were the constraints accepted by the Federal Republic as the price of NATO membership. Under the Western European Union Treaty of May 1955 the Federal Republic is barred from manufacturing or possessing biological, chemical or nuclear weapons of its own – a markedly inferior status to Britain or France. All West German forces are assigned to NATO, it has no independent planning function and German armed forces cannot operate out of the NATO geographical area. The employment of West German military force was conceived exclusively in alliance terms; a constraint reinforced by the presence of troops of six allied states on the territory of the Federal Republic.

## Between Deterrence and Detente

The Federal Republic's exposed geographical position and the long-term Soviet superiority in conventional forces has given successive West German governments a vital interest in the maintenance of the credibility of the alliance deterrent though conversely the total dependence on the American nuclear deterrent makes West German governments uniquely nervous about any changes in American nuclear doctrine, and West German governments have responded with some alarm to every innovation in nuclear strategy from the doctrine of flexible response in the Kennedy administration onwards.

Throughout the 1950s and 1960s West German security policy was squarely based on an unequivocal and exclusive attachment to the concept of nuclear deterrence, and the advent of an SPD–led government in 1969 did not alter this stance since the SPD had conformed to the general security policy consensus since 1960. Deterrence was however now increasingly flanked by detente though deterrence remained far more central. The inherent tension between a policy based on the maintenance of military capabilities (deterrence) and one stressing intentions, confidence-building measures and arms reduction (detente) hardly arose at that time since deterrence continued to enjoy such a broad spectrum of support.

These tensions began to become tangible during the period when Helmut Schmidt was chancellor (1974–82). The Federal government continued to place its central emphasis on deterrence and to devote its policy attention to strengthening the credibility of the deterrent and to inhibiting any tendency by the United States to de-emphasise its commitment to defending Western Europe.

## The Intermediate Nuclear Forces Debate

Disillusioned with the quality of American leadership, Helmut Schmidt began to adopt a more assertive role and to loosen the mental constraints that had induced the Federal government always to wait for an American lead, and in a speech to the International Institute of Strategic Studies in London in 1977 Helmut Schmidt drew attention to a growing imbalance between the capacities of the Warsaw Pact and NATO in medium-range nuclear systems and suggested that steps be taken to remedy this disparity. Schmidt's initiative was taken up by NATO and in 1979 NATO adopted the so-called 'twin-track' resolution. This envisaged negotiation with the USSR to persuade them to remove their SS–20 missiles from Eastern Europe, with the threat that should these negotiations fail, then NATO would deploy intermediate-range nuclear missiles in Western Europe.

In initiating the modernisation of theatre-nuclear weapons policy Helmut Schmidt had been pursuing the two central goals of West German security policy: the maintenance of the credibility of the alliance deterrent strategy and the prevention of American decoupling. These goals took precedence over the pursuance of detente. The Soviet Union did not respond at that time to the NATO offer and Cruise and Pershing Missiles were stationed in West Germany in the early summer of 1983.

The priority of deterrence over detente, while still commanding majority support in West German society, then faced its first sustained challenge from a burgeoning Peace Movement. The threat posed by the Soviet Union which had been a central experience for the post-war generation seemed much less real to a younger generation which had grown up in a period dominated by Brandt's Ostpolitik. The radical left who had broadened their support through sponsorship of environmental movements built upon that experience to play a key role in the Peace Movement.

More immediately worrying for Schmidt was the fact that this opposition was now widely shared inside the SPD. The SPD had opposed nuclear weapons in the late 1950s but the new opposition by significant sections of the SPD had a novel character. In the 1950s the SPD protest was largely a moral one against nuclear weapons. The opposition to the stationing of Cruise and Pershing II missiles was closely linked to preservation of detente. Opposition to the stationing of the weapons became increasingly bound up with accusations that the Reagan presidency had brought detente to an end. Opposition thus continued to increase particularly as negotiations proved fruitless and plans for deployment went ahead. A demonstration in Bonn against the imminent stationing of the missiles in October 1981 was the largest in the history of the Federal Republic and was supported, much to Helmut Schmidt's anger, by almost a quarter of the SPD Bundestag *Fraktion*.

A possible defeat for government policy at the conference of the SPD in Munich in April 1982 was staved off by a compromise which left the decision to a special conference in November 1983. The collapse of the Schmidt government put enormous pressure on the official SPD policy of support for the 'twin-track' decision. At the special party conference on 18–19 November 1983 in Cologne the delegates voted overwhelmingly to reject the deployment of the new missiles in the Federal Republic. The isolation of Helmut Schmidt by then on this issue became brutally apparent. Despite what many considered to be his finest speech, his arguments in favour of deployment were rejected by 400 votes to 14.

The missiles were in fact installed in early winter 1983 with rather less public protest than had been predicted given the size of the Peace Movement. In the period immediately preceding deployment, Erich Honecker, the GDR leader, introduced a new theme in the debate. Since the late 1960s, the SPD and, to a lesser degree, the FDP had argued that the German past laid a special responsibility on the Federal Republic to encourage detente. In a letter to Chancellor Kohl in Autumn 1983, Honecker introduced the concept of a *'Verantwortungsgemeinschaft'*, a shared responsibility of both German states to safeguard peace and to ensure that 'war never again starts from German soil'. This tactic was unsuccessful in inhibiting the chancellor from supporting deployment, but it struck a responsive chord among a wide section of the West German population.

## Nuclear Difficulties

The security policy of the Federal Republic is based on two premises – that the external threat comes from the Soviet Union and a total identification with a reliance on the security provided by the United States and its nuclear capability. This policy was supported from 1960 by a parliamentary and societal consensus. The societal consensus began to show signs of erosion from the mid-1970s. Ostpolitik modified the popular perception of the threat potential of the Soviet Union especially among younger age-groups. The parliamentary consensus remained, though a significant minority in the SPD parliamentary party now distanced themselves from a pro-nuclear policy.

Despite the advent of a CDU–CSU–FDP government in 1982, committed to strengthening or as they saw restoring the old certainties of security policy (especially the close relationship to the United States), public support for the central positions of West German security policy has shrunk dramatically. Popular identification with the United States, once almost total, is now at a historically low level for the Federal Republic. On the far left, lack of identification with the United States quickly shades into anti-Americanism, and opposition to the capitalist character of the Federal Republic is projected on to the United States. The lack of identification with the United States goes much further than the left, however, and there has been a widespread popular cooling off towards the United States since the advent of the Reagan presidency. By contrast, perceptions of the Soviet Union have been very significantly altered by Mikhail Gorbachev. Changed perceptions emerge clearly in a poll conducted by Sinus, a Munich based public opinion research firm, in October 1988: 70 per cent of better educated West Germans have a favourable view of current Soviet policies, while 52 per cent have a negative attitude to American policies. The perception of the Soviet threat has also changed. The Sinus poll found that 44 per cent of West Germans now believe that NATO and the Warsaw Pact are of approximately equal strength compared with only 24 per cent who thought this way in 1981.

At the parliamentary level the consensus has broken down. The Greens are opposed to West German membership of NATO and reject all features of the established West German security policy. Since 1983 the SPD has changed the relative weighting it accords to deterrence and detente in its security policy. In its revised security programme for the 1987 election, it played down the Soviet threat, advocated a reduction in defence spending and the length of national service and in general argued for the adoption by NATO of a more explicitly defensive posture. In all its security proposals since 1983 it has given increasing weight to detente and greater European autonomy. It has cultivated relations with the Soviet Union and the GDR and has concluded a draft agreement with the SED on a Chemical Weapons-Free zone in Central Europe.

## The INF Treaty and the Singularity Debate

The conclusion of the Soviet-American agreement on the scrapping of Intermediate Range Nuclear Missiles in early 1988 opened up wide differences within the Federal government. Foreign Minister Genscher welcomed it as a Soviet-American contribution to detente and as the late fruits of the twin-track policy which had been intended to secure the removal of the SS–20s from Eastern Europe. Chancellor Kohl, Defence Minister Manfred Wörner and the Chairman of the CDU–CSU parliamentary party, Alfred Dregger, were much less enthusiastic about the development. They accorded detente a lesser priority than the maintenance of the credibility of the alliance's capacity to deter – a capacity which, given the imbalance of conventional forces, continued to rest almost exclusively on the nuclear element. They were also concerned, as Mrs Thatcher was initially, that an INF argument might presage an American decoupling from Europe. The position of the Federal government quickly became untenable. The British government withdrew its reservations and this left the chancellor and his supporters opposing a proposal which appeared to foster detente and which was supported by the other principal NATO allies and the Foreign Minister. Internally, the CDU–CSU appeared to be isolated and in two Land elections in Hamburg and the Rhineland-Palatinate in mid-May 1987 public disquiet on this issue, especially marked in Hamburg, was a major contributory factor in electoral losses for the CDU. Shortly thereafter the government indicated its agreement with the proposals although it signalled its desire to maintain its own Pershing I missiles, a position which it then also later abandoned.

In the wake of the INF Treaty a new debate broke out on alliance strategy in which the Federal government stood out against the strongly held policy preferences of her principal allies and the leading figures in the NATO command. Their preference was to move on from the INF Treaty to a treaty on strategic missiles. In this scenario the capability of deterrence would be preserved by the modernisation of short-range and battlefield nuclear weapons in Europe; a policy most closely identified with Mrs Thatcher. These priorities were publicly and fiercely rejected by then Defence Minister, Wörner, and by the Federal chancellor. Agreement on strategic nuclear weapons would, it was argued, significantly reduce the risks for the United States and might encourage limited nuclear war. Shorter-range missiles were very heavily concentrated in the two Germanies and their presence is a constant reminder to the West German population of their terribly exposed position, 'the shorter the range, the deader the German' (Volker Rühe). Removal of long- and medium-range missiles would largely leave those that were based in and targeted on the Federal Republic. Modernisation and a stress on short-range missiles would, the Federal government feared, be unacceptable to the population of the Federal Republic since the risks inside NATO would manifestly be spread unevenly and it would underline the 'singularity' of the FRG – i.e., the dangers posed by the unique concentration of shorter range missiles on German soil.

> Therefore we Germans reject the option of declaring ourselves in agreement with conversion from medium range nuclear missiles to shorter range missiles. On the contrary we are of the view that the zero option in middle range nuclear weapons has not rendered arms reduction in short range missiles superfluous but more urgent. We, the CDU/CSU, are not requesting a third zero option but rather a drastic reduction of nuclear missiles

with less than 500 km range to the minimum point necessary in order to inhibit the massing of conventional attack forces (Dregger).

The American nuclear deterrent still continues to be accepted by the majority of the population of the Federal Republic, but West German policy-makers fear that support for a nuclear policy would be drastically eroded by the policy favoured by the Western allies and now also by Manfred Wörner in his new role of Secretary General of NATO. In the long run the government argued this might lead to denuclearisation which would leave the Federal Republic hopelessly exposed given the overwhelming preponderance of Soviet conventional forces. In the short run the Federal Government had to fight the federal election of November-December 1990. The issue has so far been fudged, with the government maintaining that its Lance missiles could last until 1995. The allies have been keen to press ahead, however, and Manfred Wörner has argued strongly for the implementation of the modernisation programme.

Until President Gorbachev's speech to the United Nations Assembly in December 1988, it looked possible that the advocates of modernisation might eventually prevail. President Gorbachev's unilateral arms reduction of 500,000 men and his promise that much greater reductions could be negotiated had, as he undoubtedly calculated, a major impact on West German public opinion and it looks very unlikely that modernisation will now go through. In the longer term, further Soviet unilateral reductions would put great pressure on NATO, including the Federal Republic, to match them with the attendant danger that this would preserve existing Soviet superiority. The preferred strategy of the Federal Republic of asymmetric arms reductions to reduce the disparity between the Warsaw Pact and NATO forces now looks much more difficult to maintain, particularly when the demographic difficulties of maintaining the Bundeswehr at present levels into the 1990s are also considered. President Gorbachev's initiative has also given an added impetus to a West German public mood of impatience with the burdens attendant upon the presence of NATO forces – demonstrated, for example, in the massive protests against low flying military aircraft.

Tension between the Federal government and its leading NATO allies on the modernisation issue deepened considerably in 1989. A succession of poor election results increased the electoral vulnerability of the Kohl government and, by raising the possibility that the FDP might not attain 5 per cent in the 1990 election, has paradoxically increased its leverage in the coalition. Both developments increased the pressure on Chancellor Kohl not to yield to Anglo-American demands for modernisation of short-range missiles. In

April 1989 Chancellor Kohl went much further and called for negotiations with the Warsaw Pact for the removal of short-range missiles
altogether. This move was supported by some smaller NATO allies
but gravely alarmed the British and American governments who
took the view that there should be no negotiations on short-range
missiles until the Warsaw Pact's superiority in conventional and
chemical weapons is eliminated.

## The European Alternative

Whilst the United States retains its pre-eminence among the allies of
the Federal Republic, the difficulties of recent years have refocused
attention on a possible security relationship with France. The most
surprising and prominent advocate of this view who has recently
been unkindly characterised as a 'late Gaullist' (Baring, 1988, p.
175), is the former chancellor, Helmut Schmidt. Schmidt was preoccupied during his active political career with the maintenance and
strengthening of NATO, even when, as in the case of the twin-track
resolution, it led to severe tensions with his own party. This late
conversion appears to have two explanations. His period as chancellor very largely coincided with that of the Giscardien presidency in
France and the relationship with France was exceptionally harmonious. By contrast, Schmidt had a very negative view of Carter and
Reagan and, despite his admiration of the United States, his relationship with successive administrations was very strained. He has also
become increasingly concerned about the possible early use of
nuclear weapons in an East-West conflict and argues that a fusion
of French and German forces under French leadership would inhibit
this by greatly increasing the strength of the conventional forces
available to the West. Schmidt and many others in the SPD are
arguing not for the replacement of NATO but for the creation of a
strong European pillar within NATO, in effect to make France, 'the
most important as well as the closest ally of the Federal Republic'
(Schmidt, 1987).

The difficulties of Schmidt's project seem overwhelming. If such
a proposal were to be adopted, it would be likely to encourage the
American decoupling from Western Europe that Schmidt has been
so concerned about. There is little evidence that the French government is seriously interested in creating a European pillar and, if
some future French government were interested, it seems unlikely
that it would be a more comfortable alliance leader than the United
States. Above all the Federal Republic is, and will remain, a con-

sumer rather than producer of security and France is simply much less credible in the role of security producer than the United States.

Helmut Kohl's oft-stated claim to be the inheritor of Adenauer's political legacy carries some conviction in security policy where, like Adenauer, he argues for a reliance on American protection. Again like Adenauer, the relationship with France is more than an interest, it is also a core value. Kohl has therefore encouraged closer Franco–German defence cooperation with the creation of the Franco–German Council on Security and Deterrence and the establishment in late 1988 of a Franco-German Brigade.

At first glance the intention of strengthening the European pillar of NATO is unambiguous, but there is some ambivalence about the motives on the German side. Publicly, the Federal government argues the intention is to bring French forces more closely within the NATO framework. Privately, the view is sometimes expressed that this is the beginning of the Franco-German security cooperation that will be increasingly necessary as the United States, the latest victim of 'Imperial overstretch' begins to wind down its commitment to the defence of Western Europe. From the French perspective, closer security cooperation offers an additional constraint over West German policy in case the Gorbachev era permits even closer 'inner-German' relations. The joint security council thus serves as a counter-balance to the progress in inner-German relations surrounding the visit of Herr Honecker in September 1987. Wherever the balance lies between these three interpretations, the initiative is limited in nature. The German contingents are territorials, and the site of the headquarters of the new Brigade, Böblingen, is in the rear area of a US corps which both reduces its importance and probably also signifies that it would most likely come under US command in the event of hostilities. The Federal government proposal for a multi-nation airborne division in December 1988 has been widely regarded by other member states as impractical.

## Ambiguities of Ostpolitik

The creation of the Federal Republic was a product of German defeat and superpower rivalry rather than a reflection of the autonomous will of the German people. West German governments were therefore in the uncomfortable position of advancing and trying to make credible the claim that they could represent the interests of areas in the GDR and the areas beyond the Oder-Neisse line over which they exercised no actual jurisdiction. This *Alleinvertretungsanspruch* (claim to sole right of representation) was based on the argument that only those Germans living in the Federal Republic have been able to vote for a freely elected government. The Federal government was thus the only legitimate government on German soil and its primary duty, constitutionally anchored in the Basic Law, was to work for German reunification. The Federal Republic has thus continually proclaimed a national interest of the Germans in self-determination, an aspiration which it alone can legitimately represent. This concept was buttressed after 1955 by the Hallstein doctrine which argued that recognition of the GDR would be considered an unfriendly act by the Federal government. Only the USSR was permitted, because of its centrality to any possible reunification negotiations, to maintain dual diplomatic relations.

In the bipolar international system of the 1950s and early 1960s the Hallstein doctrine, with the support of the United States, prevailed and no non-Communist state recognised the GDR. This whole complex, in which, for some foreign policy purposes at least, the Federal Republic proclaimed itself as the spokesman for a German national interest, came under extreme pressure in the late 1960s. Following the move to detente by the superpowers in the early 1960s, the West Germans had to give up their insistence that German reunification should precede detente and they had to accommodate themselves to a less bipolar international system. In this new system the Hallstein doctrine became more and more expensive to uphold and, from the late 1960s onwards, it began to be breached. The erection of the Berlin Wall in 1961 did not herald the long awaited collapse of the GDR, but helped by closing off alternatives to consolidate the regime.

In differing degrees these developments led to the Ostpolitik of the Brandt-Scheel government, which first took office in 1969. At the heart of Ostpolitik lay the view that recognition of the territorial status quo in Europe and the establishment of diplomatic relations with the GDR would unfreeze relations between the two halves of Europe and set free forces which would transcend the status quo. The hope was that recognition of the territorial status quo would make possible a long-term transition to a European Peace Order, though the contours of this 'peace order' were left indistinct.

Brandt's resignation in 1974 after the discovery that his assistant, Günter Guillaume, was an East German spy, underlined the lack of progress towards these rather utopian goals. His successor, Helmut Schmidt, continued to pursue a policy of Ostpolitik and detente, but on a much more pragmatic basis, and he used the freedom of manoeuvre gained by his predecessor principally with regard to a much more assertive Western policy.

Ostpolitik was formulated and implemented in a climate of superpower detente. Towards the end of the Schmidt period the super-power detente began to break down and many observers assumed that the Federal government would reflect this change in climate. By now, however, detente was too central to West German policy to be abandoned. It was the buckle of the increasingly frayed coalition; the major policy on which the SPD and FDP were agreed. It was also the one policy common to all the factions in the SPD. There were important economic interests at stake with the Federal Republic exporting more to the USSR than Britain, France and the USA combined. Although the total volume of exports to the East was tiny in comparison with those to the West, it was quite significant in some sectors (e.g., steel). Finally, and crucially, close German-German relations appeared to depend on the maintenance of satis-factory relations with the USSR.

Schmidt's insistence on maintaining detente brought him into con-flict with other Western allies. His meeting with Honecker in December 1981 in Werbellin coincided with the declaration of mar-tial law in Poland, and Schmidt was widely criticised in other Western countries for putting German-German relations above considerations like alliance solidarity and the support for greater liberty in Eastern Europe. The projected construction of an oil-natural gas pipeline from Siberia led to a bruising encounter with the United States administration, who feared that such a development would make the Federal Republic too dependent on the USSR.

## The Kohl Government

Relations with the Soviet Union deteriorated very badly in the first years of the Kohl government. Helmut Schmidt's 'twin-track' policy had failed to persuade the USSR to remove the SS–20s from Eastern Europe and the advent of the Kohl government coincided with the necessity of fulfilling the second track – i.e., actually installing the Cruise and Pershing missiles. The Soviet government attempted to isolate the Federal government on this issue and made the restoration of good relations conditional on the non-installation of the missiles. This was not an option open to the Federal government given its commitment to the maintenance of close relations with its Western allies.

Relations with the Soviet Union were further jeopardised by the Kohl government's endorsement of the Strategic Defence Initiative (SDI), often called Star Wars, through which the United States hoped to make itself invulnerable against missile attack. Hans-Dietrich Genscher, who had continued as foreign minister, was opposed to West German support for SDI because of the damage it would inflict on detente, but was overruled by the chancellor who gave first priority to the maintenance of close relations with the United States.

The CDU–CSU had opposed the ratification of all the Eastern Treaties and had also been critical of Helmut Schmidt's policy of detente. Once in government they changed their position on day to day German-German relations and became enthusiastic advocates of closer relations with the government of the GDR. Franz Josef Strauss, hitherto the most bitter critic of a detente policy towards the GDR took the lead in arranging very large-scale bank credits for the GDR in 1983. Despite tensions associated with the implementation of twin-track resolution, the GDR government responded positively to these overtures.

Although the CDU–CSU changed its policy in relation to the GDR at an operational level, it did not change its rhetoric. This had only a minor impact on German-German relations given the overwhelming importance of these relations to both governments. The impact on the Soviet government and other East European governments was much more profound. The stress by the Federal Government on the 'openness' of the German question was sometimes accompanied by the suggestion that this also applied to the former German territories. This naturally aroused considerable anxiety in these states which had thought that issue had been taken off the agenda by the Easter Treaties. There was a decidedly national tone to many of the pronouncements of the CDU–CSU ministers and to the actions of the Federal chancellor – e.g., his visit to the Silesian Refugees' Convention in 1984. Kohl deeply offended the Soviet government in 1986 by an interview with *Newsweek* in which he compared the public relations skills of Gorbachev with those of Joseph Goebbels.

Hans-Dietrich Genscher tried to blunt the impact of this rhetoric by endless diplomatic visits and by his declaration in the Bundestag on 12 September 1984 that the Federal government regarded the borders of all European states as inviolable. Genscher's efforts did little to ease Soviet displeasure, and this was made clear by the Soviet intervention in the cancellation of a projected visit by Erich Honecker to the Federal Republic.

## The Thaw in Eastern Relations

The period of cool relations between the governments of the Federal Republic and the Soviet Union lasted approximately five years and detente has now been re-established. The conclusion of the INF Treaty and the re-establishment of harmony between the super-powers removed the major impediment to good relations. The Soviet Union now seems to place a high priority on good relations with the Federal Republic. This is part of a wider policy in which, by stressing the European vocation of the USSR (our common European house), Mikhail Gorbachev wishes to loosen the bonds between the Western European allies and the United States. The economic weakness of the USSR and the centrality of economic advance to the Gorbachev project dictate a close relationship with the Federal Republic, and closer economic relations were at the centre of the visit by Kohl to Moscow in October 1988. Agreement was reached for the German banks to provide a massive DM 3 billion credit to the Soviet Union and on a range of other initiatives, including the export of nuclear reactors where the troubled German nuclear industry could recoup some of the losses created by the lack of orders in the Federal Republic.

Whilst the Federal government has responded to the new climate in the USSR, the Chancellor has been at great pains to restate the commitment of the Federal government to the openness of the German question and to avoid the impression of equidistance between the two superpowers that would be created by a too enthusi-astic espousal of the Gorbachev initiatives, though many Western allies believe that foreign minister Genscher is too close to the USSR.

The central goal of Ostpolitik has been to improve the conditions of Germans living in the GDR, and to a lesser degree to assuage the conditions of those German communities which had been left in Eastern Europe after the mass expulsions of Germans in most East European countries in 1945. The easing of the condition of Germans outside the GDR has very largely taken the form of arranging for their emigration to the Federal Republic. Throughout Eastern Europe most of the remaining German communities have opted for emigration; this has been a very expensive policy for the Federal Republic which first has to persuade the East European governments to allow the would-be emigrants to leave by means of financial inducements and then to provide facilities for them in the Federal Republic. There are some signs in relation to the very large numbers of would-be emigrants from Roumania that public support for the policy is beginning to be strained given the massive investment in infrastructure that has to be made to receive them.

## The Making of Foreign Policy

The foreign policy-making process in the Federal Republic, as elsewhere, is even more clearly executive-centred than the domestic
policy process. What differentiates the Federal Republic from other
states is the manifest centrality of foreign policy decisions reflecting
the Federal Republic's genesis as more a foreign policy in search of
a state than a state in search of a foreign policy. The key questions
in West German politics – security and the prospects for the economy
– continue to be viewed in the context of the relationships between
the Federal Republic and the international environment. This means
that the Foreign Ministry, which was not created until 1951, has
never enjoyed the unchallenged pre-eminence in the taking of
decisions on foreign policy enjoyed by some foreign ministries in
long-established West European states. Instead it has had to share
responsibilities with other ministries. This has been especially true
in relation to Westpolitik, where the Economics Ministry plays a
major role in policy towards the European Community, and the
Defence Ministry is a major actor in the formulation of alliance
policy. In a sense this inter-ministerial rivalry has become less distinctive as similar pressures have also eroded the competences of foreign
ministries elsewhere in Western Europe. Arguably, the more distinctive feature of West German foreign policy-making, reflecting its
political centrality, has been the degree to which foreign policy has
also preoccupied successive chancellors. This chancellorial interest
has reflected both its centrality as an issue and the fact that in this
area the chancellor can operate with fewer constraints in 'determining the guidelines of policy' (Article 65). The normal constraints
flowing from the departmental principle and the imperatives of
coalition government still apply, but the departmental principle is
weakened by the absence of the pressure from interest groups in
the relevant ministries that characterises policy-making on domestic
issues, the major exception being agriculture.

### Helmut Schmidt

Throughout the entire period between 1974 and the collapse of the
Social-Liberal government in September 1982 Helmut Schmidt was
chancellor and Hans-Dietrich Genscher foreign minister. Helmut
Schmidt was an unusually forceful, competent and popular chancellor. Moreover, he had ministerial experience at the highest level in
both economics and defence. Helmut Schmidt came closer than any
chancellor since Adenauer to making a reality of Article 65 and to
determining 'the guidelines of policy'. He was constrained by the

coalition nature of the government, by Genscher's success in office, and by a growing distance, especially on defence, between himself and his own party, the SPD, which often made him dependent upon the support of the FDP. His intervention in foreign policy was thus necessarily selective. He had a major impact on West German policy towards the EC where he cultivated a Paris-Bonn axis and stressed inter-governmentalism at the expense of supranationalism. The introduction of the European Monetary System (EMS) was the most notable outcome of the close cooperation between Schmidt and Giscard. His other major area of intervention was in European-American relations. Here he intervened constantly to attempt to correct what he saw as a failure of American leadership, especially in the monetary field, but he was also very active in alliance issues and launched the debate on the modernisation of theatre-nuclear weapons which led to the NATO dual-track resolution of 1979. Policy towards the East was largely dominated by Genscher and the foreign ministry.

## Helmut Kohl

Despite his fondness for seeing himself as Adenauer's political heir, Kohl has been unable to emulate Adenauer's dominance in foreign policy decisions and the advent of the CDU–CSU–FDP government has seen an increase in the influence of the Foreign Ministry. Helmut Kohl has displayed relatively little interest in policy details and lacks the interventionist bent or broad policy grasp of his immediate predecessor as chancellor. His has generally been a government run on the *Ressort* (departmental) principle. Moreover, Hans-Dietrich Genscher has been in a very strong position. He has been foreign minister since 1974 and has an unrivalled experience in the area. The FDP is also central to Chancellor Kohl's governmental strategy. Without the FDP there would be no majority and, almost as importantly, the FDP can act as an ally of the chancellor against the pressures imposed by the CSU. Hans-Dietrich Genscher and the Foreign Ministry have thus dominated the making of foreign policy in this government.

The chancellor has sporadically attempted to intervene and he established a foreign policy unit in the Chancellor's Office under the direction of Horst Teltschik. Differences between the chancellor and the foreign minister have surfaced most frequently on questions of alliance policy. The chancellor was much more favourable to SDI and West German participation than the Foreign Ministry who have been very determined backers of Eureka and Esprit, the European-based schemes for scientific and technological collaboration. Sharply divergent views were also apparent in the reaction to the arms negotiations between the US and USSR in 1987, where the chancellor for a time insisted that the Federal Republic hold on to its 72 Pershing IAs, while the Foreign Ministry was much more prepared to give them up in the interests of a negotiated settlement.

The dominance of the Foreign Ministry in foreign policy has been challenged but not seriously threatened by the desire of the Länder, especially Bavaria, to participate in foreign policy decisions. Most of the Länder minister-presidents have in recent years undertaken foreign tours and some German commentators have spoken of a *Nebenaussenpolitik* (shadow foreign policy). This is to accord it an importance it does not warrant, since they are constitutionally barred from concluding agreements. In two areas, however, they can play a role. The association of the individual Länder with Länder banks gives them an access to German-German relations by virtue of their ability to extend credit to the GDR. Franz Josef Strauss was notably active in this area. Much more worrying for the Foreign Ministry and the Federal government as a whole has been the desire of the Länder to increase their involvement in the formulation of West German policy towards the EC (see Chapter 11).

## Future Uncertainties

Alone among past and present German states, the Federal Republic has been successful in relation to both internal and external policy. The original aim of aligning the Federal Republic firmly with the emerging international structures of the West was convincingly achieved by the mid-1950s, and has not been seriously challenged. It is an alignment that has brought the Federal Republic rich dividends. Its security – a prime concern given its perceived vulnerability – was for a period exclusively and still today is largely provided by the efforts of other states: 'The Federal Republic's security was essentially provided by others. Hence, it could neither threaten nor be threatened. Instead of having to embark on an autonomous defence policy – traditionally the most important source of conflict among nations – the Federal Republic could reap the merits of tutelage' (Joffe, 1982, p. 66).

Economically, the results have, if anything, been more spectacular. The Federal Republic's primary goals were the lifting of production restrictions imposed by the occupation authorities and access to markets. These goals were achieved almost immediately by West German acceptance of the various West European institutions. The West German economy dominates the European market space and the EC provides an almost ideal vehicle for West German economic aspirations. The EC provides access to its most important markets. It also means that the Federal Republic, like other members, avoids the damaging effects of unilateral trade disputes with external countries, particularly the United States.

Despite often aired public anxieties about American withdrawal and the floating of ideas for a European Defence Community by figures like former Chancellor Schmidt, it appears unlikely that the security context of the Federal Republic will change dramatically overnight. It will continue to depend on NATO and its own forces will continue not as an instrument of an independent West German policy but as the price of a NATO security guarantee – a guarantee that few West German policy-makers would be prepared to exchange for a French guarantee, even supposing it were available.

The successful record in relation to Westpolitik was perhaps predictable. The success in managing relations with Eastern Europe, were feelings of fear and bitterness were much more intense, was harder to foresee. Normal relations with the Soviet Union having been achieved, the indications are that the Federal Republic will press hard to capitalise on the economic opportunities now available. These are, however, very small in relation to the Federal Republic's trade with the West and the indications are that, contrary to often expressed fears by Western neighbours, the Federal Republic will continue to give priority to Westpolitik.

In the longer term imponderables and difficulties abound, especially in the defence and security area. One of the difficulties resides in the degree of suspicion in other Western capitals about German motives and intentions. In the months before the Gorbachev-Kohl summit in October 1988, there was continuous speculation that Gorbachev might come to some arrangement with the Federal Government on German reunification. No such offer was made or was ever likely to be made and established positions were simply restated, but fears of a Gorbachev plan on reunification have simply been replaced by endlessly repeated doubts about the strength of foreign minister Genscher's ties to the West.

Real difficulties do exist, however, and they were greatly exacerbated not by a Gorbachev plan on reunification but by his proposals for arms reduction in December 1988. The relationship between the Federal Republic and NATO has been shaped by a common perception of a Soviet threat. By changing the threat perception of so many West Germans, Gorbachev has indirectly created the potential for enormous stress in the relationship between the FRG and NATO, since the cement of the Federal Republic-NATO relationship lies in a widespread acceptance of the view that West Germany suffers from a security deficit that can be made good only by NATO.

Modernisation of nuclear missiles now appears to be excluded. Further strains have been placed on the public acceptance of allied forces and West German willingness to respond to increasing American expectations with regard to contribution to alliance expenditure has been reduced. Moreover, there are already signs that the reduction of a perceived Soviet threat might lead to longer-term consequences.

In late December 1988 Admiral Schmähling, head of the Bundeswehr's Office for Studies and Exercises, apparently prompted by the Gorbachev speech, argued that the interests of the Federal Republic and the United States were not identical, that nuclear weapons should be withdrawn from the Federal Republic, and that the long-term aim should be replacement of NATO and the Warsaw Pacts. Such views are commonplace among Greens and in sections of the SPD, but their articulation by a very senior military planner gives them quite a different weight.

Requiems for West German membership of NATO are decidedly premature, and much will turn on the political future of Mikhail Gorbachev, but the period when the NATO relationship could be treated as immutable does appear to be passing. The old certainties are dead and we appear to be entering, as the Schmähling episode suggests, a phase of questioning and speculation even if the changes on the ground remain slight for the moment. We are a very long way from the early days of the Kohl government, where a frosty relationship with the USSR was complemented by a very warm relationship to the United States and it looked for a short time as if the 1980s could be the 1950s after all.

# 11

# The European Dimension

## SIMON BULMER

### Significance of European Integration

European integration has been of central importance to the Federal Republic's existence. The post-war division of Europe excluded the possibility of German reunification and presented the new state with the need for acceptance into the new international order. Initially, policy was heavily dependent on the attitudes of the Western allied powers, which held responsibility for the foreign affairs of the FRG. The inducement that they in effect offered to the FRG was the granting of sovereignty in return for commitments to good behaviour in multilateral frameworks such as the European Coal and Steel Community (ECSC). European integration was thus a major component in the FRG's development from a position of dependence to one of interdependence. Independence, by contrast, was never an option after 1945, due to the strategic importance of the FRG and the unacceptability to the French of unchecked West German power.

Any account of the development of West Germany's economic and political development in the subsequent period must closely examine the basis provided by European integration and cooperation. This study tackles the task in four main parts. The initial concern is with how European integration came to play such an important role as an arena of political cooperation for the FRG. Attention is then focused on the nature of West German interests in the European Community (EC). Two particular sets of issues are of importance in this context: the EC's programme following the ratification of the Single European Act (SEA); and the difficulties of reforming the EC's budget and its agricultural policy. It will be shown that West Germany has a diverse set of interests and that these create contradictions in the federal government's European policy. The sectorised nature of policy-making, its federal dimension and the resultant problems of policy incoherence have begun to raise questions about German reliability in the coalition-building process of such importance to EC policy-making. Questions have also been raised in West Germany itself, as in 'Liegt Bonn in Europa?' (*Die Zeit*, 10 April 1987). These aspects will be examined in a fourth section.

## The Europeanisation of West German Politics

For the FRG there was little real choice about the Europeanisation of West German politics. It was actively encouraged, albeit in differing ways, by all three of the Western allies, who retained formal controls relating to the new state's foreign and defence policy until 1955. Nevertheless, it should be pointed out that Western Europe was by no means the exclusive framework of West Germany's orientation, for an Atlantic framework was important for economic reconstruction and was vital to defence interests, although membership of NATO came only in 1955. Why, then, was European integration of such importance?

A basic explanation lies in the ending of Germany's traditional Central European role due to the Cold War. This necessitated a fundamentally changed role for the new state. It was reinforced by the fact that the division of Europe resulted in a major dislocation to pre-existing German patterns of trade; new markets had to be found. Clearly these markets were not restricted to Western Europe, especially given American encouragement of an open international economy. Nevertheless, meeting American aspirations on national and international economic reconstruction was not an adequate solution, even when defence issues are placed to one side. America was doubtless West Germany's most important ally but an accommodation had to be reached with neighbours, particularly with France.

Accommodation with France came in the form of the Schuman Plan (9 June 1950), an attempt to ensure some French influence over West Germany's strategic industries of war – coal and steel – by means of placing them under supranational control. From the West German government's perspective, the plan's main attraction was that of obtaining international acceptance, as an equal of France, while gaining some, if not complete, control over the coal and steel industries which had been under allied control. When the European Coal and Steel Community came into operation in 1952, with membership extended to six states, it marked the start of the Europeanisation of West German politics.

There were two separate components to this process. First, there was the external dimension: the anchoring of the West German foreign policy in the framework of European integration. Second, there was the acceptance of integration by the major political forces and by all government bodies. These two components are examined in some detail because they are of central importance to understanding more recent developments.

## External Aspects

Of foremost importance is the fact that European integration signalled the priority given by Chancellor Adenauer to integration into the West. This policy envisaged European integration as offering the Federal Republic an arena of political cooperation. The policy was characterised by the support of successive governments under Adenauer's chancellorship for integration projects: the ill-fated European Defence Community and the successful European Economic Community (EEC) and the European Atomic Energy Community (Euratom). These political objectives remained prominent throughout Adenauer's chancellorship and were pursued even to the extent where, by association with President De Gaulle's support for a Europe independent of the United States, they almost conflicted with West Germany's security imperatives. In fact, it was not until the chancellorships of Erhard (1963–6) and Kiesinger (1966–9) that the economic aspects of the integration process came to predominate over the political ones. The reason for this was the stalemate which developed between de Gaulle's France and the other EC member governments over the form that European Union should take. The result was that progress towards political integration ceased for the time being, and its value as the impulse to the FRG's European policy was much reduced.

It should be noted that it was during Adenauer's policy of making the politics of integration a priority that German readiness to disregard questions of sovereignty was at its greatest. There were a number of reasons for this attitude. Of greatest importance was the fact that the new state was seeking international acceptance and was thus on probation. It is no surprise that it has been seen as the *Musterknabe* or model of support for integration. Symbolic of this was the constitutional provision, in the Basic Law, Article 24, for the transfer of sovereignty to international organisations. Retention of sovereignty is characteristically the concern of mature nation states. It could not, therefore, be a concern for the FRG, since it bore the historical burden of the Nazi nation state's recent atrocities, and it claimed to represent all of a divided nation and regarded its own state boundaries as temporary in nature pending reunification. On three counts, then, the FRG was not a mature nation state.

A second core element of European integration was its Franco-German basis. This has proved to be the very foundation of both advances and setbacks in the European Communities. Whether in the negotiation of the Rome treaties, launching the EEC and Euratom or, more recently, in the creation of the European Monetary System (EMS), there is evidence to support the view that, 'if a Franco-German deal could be stitched together even on issues difficult for one or both, the other participants in the negotiations would generally fall into line' (Wallace, 1986, p. 162). The two-month delay in the introduction of the EMS provides evidence of Franco-German disagreement causing a setback, albeit only temporary.

One of the rare examples of Franco-German agreement failing to provide an impulse for all member states relates to the period in the early 1960s when Adenauer and De Gaulle sought closer political cooperation, largely on the latter's terms. For the other four member states the Political Union initiative was perceived as a threat to the Atlantic Alliance and was not acceptable without British participation as a safeguard. This case is interesting on two counts. Firstly, it was out of the failed Political Union initiative that the 1963 Franco-German Treaty of Friendship emerged which, although not initially fruitful, provided scope for joint EC initiatives from the 1970s onwards. Secondly, there were divisions within the FRG – and, indeed, in the Federal government over the suitability of following the 'Gaullist' foreign policy favoured by Adenauer. Those concerned at the incompatability of such a policy with the FRG's dependence on American security guarantees proved to be in the majority in the Bundestag. These 'Atlanticists' inserted a preamble into the treaty at the ratification stage and ensured that it was not a suitable instrument for De Gaulle's European policy aspirations.

The importance of the Franco-German relationship to European integration can be overstated, however. This is because there is a third component to the Europeanisation of German politics: the indirect relationship between the 'German Question' and European integration. The policy of integration was pursued by Adenauer because international circumstances excluded the possibility of reunification. However, as relations between the FRG and the East have changed, especially the improvements following the treaties of the early 1970s and also in the Gorbachev era, so the importance of, and implications for, the European Community are highlighted. The importance of the EC is that it serves as a forum for allaying concerns about the Federal Republic drifting into Central European neutralism. The potentially destabilising nature of West German Ostpolitik was minimised by the strong commitment to the EC. In addition, there is some evidence to suggest that the EC member states, particularly France, try to counterbalance advances in the Ostpolitik by increasing the FRG's commitment to Westpolitik. The decision in January 1988 to strengthen Franco-German defence cooperation, including the creation of a joint brigade, maybe seen as a counterbalance to the improvement in relations with East Germany at the time of the visit of Herr Honecker in September 1987. In other words, the unresolved German Question serves as an external factor encouraging close Franco-German relations, both bilaterally and within the EC.

*Internal Aspects*

Hitherto Adenauer's policy of support for integration has been presented as German policy, but it is important to note that there was initial opposition to membership of the ECSC from the Social Democrats on the grounds that it would obstruct German reunification. There was also opposition to German membership of the projected European Defence Community on similar grounds, but with particular criticism of rearmament. By the time of the negotiations leading to the establishment of the EEC and Euratom, the SPD had modified its position to one of support for integration, a development mirroring the general removal of socialist ideology from the party's policy (Paterson, 1974).

The Free Democratic Party, by a somewhat different route, had joined the consensus of support for European integration by the mid-1960s. Despite voting for the ratification of the ECSC Treaty, the strengthening of the national liberal wing of the party led to a majority of Bundestag deputies voting against the ratification of the Rome treaties. The primary reason for this vote was the fear that strengthened integration would obstruct reunification, a view similar to that held earlier by the Social Democrats. However, by the time of Walter Scheel's election as party chairman in 1968, the FDP had also joined the prevailing consensus.

The two Christian Democratic parties' policy had been one of support for integration. During the 1960s, however, there were divisions, as identified above. These separated the 'Gaullists', led by Adenauer and Strauss, who saw integration leading to a political union with an identity of its own, and the Atlanticists, who were unwilling to contemplate any development that might conflict with security dependence on the United States. These differences were ultimately decided in favour of the Atlanticists when it became clear that de Gaulle's political goals lacked support from other member states and were obstructing the process of economic integration.

By the end of the 1960s, therefore, party politics in West Germany had been Europeanised. Difference on European policy were matters of nuance, or derived from differences over the substance of domestic politics. This broad consensus has shown continuity up to the present, although challenged by the parliamentary representation of the Greens in the 1980s (see below).

A similar picture prevailed among interest groups. Initially there were suspicions among West German industrialists from the coal and steel sectors about French motives in the Schuman Plan, and there was even opposition to the ECSC membership from some quarters. By the time of EEC membership these fears had been largely eliminated. The position of industrialists was matched by support from the Federation of German Trade Unions (at the time when the Social Democrats were still in opposition). The main interest group opposition came later from the German Farmers' Union (DBV), which adopted a very critical stance towards the creation of the Common Agricultural Policy (CAP) in the mid-1960s. This position was scarcely surprising because German farmers, as the highest-cost producers, suffered a 10 per cent cut in cereals prices with the 1965 establishment of common pricing under the CAP. From 1969 the DBV began to play a more constructive role, although the impact of even limited CAP reforms has placed this role under severe pressure from the mid-1980s. Nevertheless, the broad consensus of support among interest groups for European integration remains through to the present.

The final dimension of the Europeanisation of West German politics lies in the way EC membership was absorbed by the governmental system. As a federal system, the addition of a supranational level of policy-making presented no serious challenge because government was already multi-tiered in nature. Similarly, the strong principle of ministerial autonomy at the federal level suggested that most matters of European integration should be distributed to the locus of expertise in the federal government. As a result, European policy is overwhelmingly a matter for policy specialists.

The Economics Ministry took charge of coordinating matters relating to the ECSC; it was only from 1957, at the time of the EEC's establishment, that the Foreign Office became responsible for coordinating matters of integration policy. This situation has been counterbalanced, however, by Adenauer's personal involvement in integration policy during his chancellorship.

The main advantage of this easy assimilation of European policy into governmental structures was the minimal disruption of existing responsibilities at the federal level. The impact of ECSC membership upon the vertical distribution of authority in the federal system was very limited because it was concentrated upon one state, North Rhine-Westphalia, at least until the Saarland became part of the FRG in 1957. The impact of the EEC Treaty was greater but, because of its framework form, the effect upon the federal structure was creeping encroachment, which the Länder tolerated because of their support for European integration.

Increasingly in the 1980s, it will be seen that the assimilation of EC business has created problems. In the case of the Federal government, there have been problems in presenting coherent policy, as departmental interests have predominated over the collective one. For the Länder governments, the creeping loss of powers specified in the Basic Law came to a head with the Single European Act (SEA), signed by EC foreign ministers in 1986. This reform of the EC treaties in effect proposed a formal transfer of significant further Länder responsibilities to the EC. As a result, it proved to be a disruptive factor; all the accummulated grievances of the Länder about inadequate consultation on EC matters raised the issue into a challenge to the state's federal structure (see Chapter 3).

## The Federal Republic as an 'Ordinary' EC Member

West Germany's emergence as an 'ordinary' member of the EC did not occur overnight. It was the product of developments in international relations, in the EC and in the FRG itself; all of these factors were interrelated.

At the international level the climate of detente at the start of the 1970s brought important developments. For the FRG it offered the opportunity for some normalisation of relations with Eastern Europe and East Germany in particular. Chancellor Brandt's Ostpolitik was the response to this opportunity. Its significance for European integration lay in the fact that it opened a new policy resource to the FRG. There was no longer the need to rely on allies to act as intermediaries in relations with some East European states. This development was symbolic in cutting through one of the final bonds of West German dependence. It also paved the way to membership of the United Nations in 1973.

During the period of detente the nature of the international political agenda changed. The Yom Kippur War (1973) and the subsequent oil embargo and price escalation compounded the international economic instability that had commenced in the currency markets at the end of the 1960s. The resultant international recession presented major challenges. For the EC there was the question of whether it could escape the stalemate of the late 1960s and tackle the key issues of the day. For the FRG, with its priority given to counter-inflationary policy, the recession reduced margins of manoeuvre in EC policy-making.

The impact of these developments was to increase German preparedness to be assertive in the bargaining between member governments in the EC. Symbolic of this was the '*Zahlmeister*' (paymaster) question. This arose during the negotiation of the European Regional Development Fund (ERDF) in 1973. Isolated in the negotiations, the federal government refused to back down as had often been the case in the past. Instead it refused – for a few weeks, at least – to agree to a more generously funded ERDF, on the basis that it would largely be financed by Germany (Bulmer and Paterson, 1987, Chapter 9). The role of 'paymaster' of the Community was rejected, although in practice West Germany has been the main contributor to the EC budget from the 1970s. The defence of national interests was now being pursued explicitly. Ironically the European Commission, traditionally immune from gratuitous criticism by German politicians, found itself described by Helmut Schmidt in 1975 as 'people who could not even run a tram company for two years without making a loss' (quoted in Carr, 1985, p. 96). There was also a marked reduction during Schmidt's chancellorship in the number of ritualistic pleas for European Union.

Towards the end of the 1960s the EC, although bicephalous by design, had been acting with all the purpose of a headless chicken. However, in the aftermath of the 1969 meeting of government heads at The Hague, moves were initiated in a number of different policy areas including budgetary policy, economic and monetary matters and foreign policy cooperation. The latter, normally known as European Political Cooperation (EPC), was a further development enabling the FRG better to play the role of an ordinary member state. From its creation in 1970, EPC enabled the FRG to gain wider support for its Ostpolitik and greater freedom in foreign policy.

At the domestic level the priority that Chancellor Brandt gave his Ostpolitik replaced the earlier precedence given to European integration. The European Community came to serve as an area for economic competition. Apart from the EC's failure to make a quantum jump towards deeper – as opposed to wider – integration, this development was also the result of the Federal Republic having been accepted as an equal in the EC. As a result, the political necessity of integration lost precedence to the need to defend economic and social interests in the diverse activities of the EC.

## West German Interests in the EC

*Economic Interests*

Of vital importance has been the high degree of correspondence between the economic principles favoured by the EC and those embodied in the West German social market economy. The foremost West German economic interest in the EC has been the latter's importance as an export market for manufactured goods. As a result, successive German governments (and particularly economics ministers), regardless of party origin, have served as advocates of free trade principles within the EC. The logic of this situation is clear, for the EC is West Germany's most important trading partner. In 1986 50.8 per cent of German exports went to EC states, while 52.2 per cent of its imports originated from them. These figures have added significance when it is taken into account that about one-third of German GNP is accounted for by the export of goods and services (to all markets) and approximately one in every four jobs is dependent on exports. With this level of export dependence, West German interest groups and the federal government are vigilant in ensuring that EC policies do not obstruct free trade in manufactured goods.

The vigilance is reflected in two ways. First there is the almost ritualistic rehearsal of free market ideology when interventionist EC policies are under construction. For example, in the late 1970s the Commission sought to use its important powers (set down in the ECSC Treaty) to attempt to bring order to the EC market for steel. The then economics minister, Count Otto von Lambsdorff, used a variety of tactics in the EC Council of Ministers to attempt to forestall the almost inevitable decision – given the possibility of using majority voting in this policy area – to intervene in the steel sector. Although there were genuine concerns about the unfairness for some German steelmakers of the proposed quota system, Lambsdorff's policy was based on the view that any deviation from competitive markets would inevitably work against the interests of the member state with the most competitive manufacturing industry. Interventionism was perceived as a threat not only for the steel industry but also, by setting a precedent, for other industries as well.

Vigilance is also reflected in a reluctance to support the use of protectionist measures by the EC in its extensive trade relations with non-member states. The FRG has important markets in industrialised countries outside the EC and thus does not wish to provoke retaliation from them. There was, in consequence, clear opposition to French attempts, in the early years of the Mitterrand presidency, to recapture the domestic market by raising defences against imports from non-members.

A different form of vigilance was demonstrated in Chancellor Schmidt's initiation of the European Monetary System in 1978. The EMS aimed at minimising the disruption that volatile international exchange rates were having on trade with those EC states, such as France, that were not in the existing arrangement, known as the 'Snake'.

The wish to increase the EC markets would appear to have gained support from the Community's objective of completing the internal market by 1992. This target, essentially liberalising the deregulatory in nature, was set down in the Single European Act (SEA). However, there are several important qualifications to the assumption that this objective will be of universal benefit to the FRG. The competitiveness of its economy within the EC has begun to be questioned. For example, at a time when the EC steel market is recovering, the West German industry is suffering serious problems. Paradoxically, in 1987–8 it has been seeking continuation of the quota system in order to facilitate domestic restructuring at a time when other states were favouring an end to quotas. Free market rhetoric is easier at a time of economic success!

Another qualification relates to questions about West German competitiveness in some of the service sectors and newer industries where the internal market initiative gives particular impetus. Two examples will serve to illustrate this point. The telecommunications sector in the FRG has been protected by the Bundespost's monopoly and by its heavily regulated nature (Humphreys, 1989). With the EC making progress towards increasing competition in this sector during early 1988 (under the German presidency of the EC Council of Ministers), it is legitimate to ask what the impact of these changes will be. Will the German industry prove to have been poorly served by this relatively protected and regulated framework? Or will industrial upheaval be minimised by it? Another sector where similar questions may be raised is in insurance. As a further area where the EC is pursuing deregulation, the relatively inefficient German industry has traditionally been protected by regulatory barriers to market entry by foreign concerns (Dicke *et al.*, 1987, pp. 107–14).

A final qualification relates to how West German industrialists react to the creation of the internal market. The theoretical ease with which business will be able to relocate within the enlarged 'domestic market' of the EC may make it attractive for German employers to set up manufacturing subsidiaries in other member states which have lower wage costs. It is considerations such as these that have led to a debate about West Germany's attraction as a location for industry (*'Standort Bundesrepublik Deutschland'*).

These reservations about the impact upon the FRG of completing the internal market indicate that market principles are not as widely practised as the federal government's preaching of the rhetoric. Nowhere is this more graphically illustrated than in the German agricultural sector, which is among the highest-cost producers of the EC. In fact, there are significant regional variations, and it is the south German producers that are the least efficient. Moreover, despite the social market economy's principles, this sector was highly protected before the creation of the CAP, and remains so within it. It has been argued, with some justification, that it has been German agriculture rather than that of France that has led to the high cost of the CAP (Weinstock, 1987). Two agricultural ministers – the Free Democrat, Herr Ertl (1969–83), and Herr Kiechle (1983- ) of the Bavarian Christian-Social Union – succeeded in protecting German farmers. This was done initially through Ertl's pursuit of high-price policy. Kiechle, by contrast, has had to contend with mounting EC pressure to bring the costs of the CAP under control. This protection has been achieved by a fierce rearguard action against radical reform on the one hand, and national compensatory payments on the other. These payments have served to minimise the impact on German farmers of CAP reform, while further undermining the pretence of a *common* agricultural policy by renationalising it. All this from the state that used to be regarded as the model supporter (*'Muster-knabe'*) of integration.

What is particularly striking about German interests in the CAP is that they not only were inconsistent with the free market rhetoric in industrial and trade sectors but also ran counter to the financial interest of the FRG. With the CAP accounting for approximately two-thirds of EC expenditure, and with the Federal Republic as the major contributor to the EC budget, it follows that the high prices supported by the agriculture ministry were imposing increasing burdens on the German taxpayer. For some partner governments this has been regarded as a peculiar policy on two counts. Firstly, West German agriculture is a very small part of the economy as a whole. Secondly, on other matters, such as the establishment of the ERDF, the German Finance Ministry proved much more able to minimise financial commitments to what is perhaps a more worthwhile cause, namely that of balanced economic development in the EC.

The inconsistency between German agricultural interests and those concerning EC expenditure has presented the EC with some diffi-culties during the 1980s. Most notably, the finance ministry's support for reducing farm expenditure has contradicted the agriculture ministry's resistance to such cuts. Similarly there have been contradictions between specific criticism of proposed EC policy and the avowed political objectives of the federal government.

*Political Interests*

The establishment in 1970 of EPC enabled the FRG to pursue a foreign policy role more in keeping with its economic stature. The EPC has served several different interests of the FRG as shown by Rummel and Wessels (1983). In the early period of EPC it acted as an emancipation factor, allowing West Germany a stronger international voice before relations with East Germany were put on a sounder footing in the Basic Treaty of 1972 and before membership of the UN in 1973. This interest has come to be of less importance in the 1980s, although the Federal Republic is still not able to pursue an unconstrained foreign policy role due to memories of the Nazi era.

The EPC has also served as an alibi in a few foreign policy areas where the Federal Public is vulnerable. One example is policy on the Middle East, where Israeli memories of the holocaust linger. Other examples are where the EC states distance themselves from American policy, especially from President Reagan's 'Cold War' stance during NATO rearmament, despite heavy security dependence on the United States. In such cases it has been possible for West Germany to hide behind EPC. The EPC has also been an area where German interests could be pursued without the costs and controversies associated with the Community's activities. Finally, of course, it has enabled the Federal Republic to gain wider support for its policy towards Eastern Europe: the Ostpolitik.

So how do these diverse, and sometimes contradictory interests in the EC and EPC fit in with integration policy more generally? The overwhelming impression is that they do so only with difficulty and for two reasons. European integration remains an article of faith for West Germany because, as was seen earlier, it has been internalised by all the key actors in the policy process. But in practical terms this commitment is much less open-ended than in the early years. Since many of the political objectives of integration have been achieved with acceptance of the FRG as a mature state, the terms of integration have become at least as important as the principle itself. This is not to argue that Germany is uncommitted to integration. On the contrary, the verbal commitment has enjoyed a revival under Chancellor Kohl. In addition, initiatives are still being made: foreign minister Genscher's initiative in the early 1980s for strengthening integration, and the Franco-German draft treaty on EPC, tabled in

1985. These examples are counterbalanced, however, by others where governmental agencies specify conditions for further sectoral integration: the prerequisites of the West German Federal bank for any strengthening of the EMS, or the Länder governments' (initial) objections to the introduction of the Erasmus scheme to facilitate students spending periods in the higher education systems of another member state.

The second reason is that the predominance of such conditions places the responsible federal ministry (or Länder ministries) in a strong position *vis-à-vis* the Foreign Office, which has formal responsibility for integration matters. The Foreign Ministry may thus support both the development of the EMS and the creation of the Erasmus programme, but is not empowered to deliver German agreement to the EC Council of Ministers until the constitutionally responsible authorities are satisfied. This proviso is important, especially where EC proposals bring new burdens to the budget. On such matters, the Finance Ministry's approval is vital. Of course, this is true of all member states to some extent. What is different in the case of the FRG is that policy coherence is constrained by a series of constitutional provisions as well as the more normal constraints, such as coalition politics.

## Policy Style and Policy Coherence

In the previous section the Federal Republic has been seen to have a diverse, and somewhat contradictory, set of interests in EC and EPC activities. These contradictions are not restricted to debate within the Federal Republic about European policy but spill over into EC negotiations causing uncertainty among partner governments.

The most striking case of incoherence occurred in 1985, when the EC was beginning to address the problems of its slow-moving decisional process. With a summit meeting in the offing to discuss this and other issues, Chancellor Kohl and foreign minister Genscher came out in favour of greater use of majority voting in order to speed up decision-making in the Council of Ministers. At the same time agriculture minister Kiechle decided to make the first ever German use of the veto, in the Council of Agriculture Ministers. Kiechle's decision was taken with a view to obstructing proposed cereals price-cuts because they would compound the effects of (already) falling farm incomes in West Germany. This position was logical enough but it cut straight across the integration policy just advocated by Genscher and Kohl. Despite the obvious blow to the credibility of German integration policy, Kiechle's position was actually approved by the federal cabinet. And the matter developed into something of a farce when the German government allowed itself to be outvoted in the Council of Ministers on the cereals issue. To the cynic this had all the signs of German European policy disappearing into an ever increasing spiral of inconsistencies.

So how is such inconsistency – illustrated here by an especially pronounced case – to be explained? The answer lies in some of the general features of West German policy-making. There is nothing special about the subject-matter being European policy for, as indicated earlier, West German politics has assimilated integration by the late 1960s. Nevertheless, the situation raises problems for the EC because of its dependence on coalition-building between (reliable) partners and across policy sectors.

The real explanation lies in the sectorisation inherent in the federal government and compounded by the vertical distribution of power between Bonn and Länder. Sectorisation is enshrined in the Basic Law Article 65, which guarantees the principle of ministerial autonomy. There is only one constraint upon such autonomy, namely that the overall guidelines of governmental policy are set by the chancellor and these take precedence. However, because of the Europeanisation of politics, as outlined above, European policy does not have high priority in the governmental programme, partly because of the lack of party political controversy. As a result, it does not tend to feature in the chancellor's policy guidelines, thus clearing the way for specialist ministers to take responsibility for it as a matter of their concern.

This situation has prevailed under both Helmut Schmidt's chancellorship and that of Helmut Kohl. Schmidt proved to be just as unable to bring agricultural policy (i.e., including his agriculture minister) under control in the interests of CAP reform as Helmut Kohl has been more recently. The one clear example of chancellorial authority being exerted by Schmidt came with the launching in 1978 of the Franco-German proposals for what became the EMS. Significantly, much of Schmidt's endeavours had to be spent in convincing other domestic executive agencies, in particular the Federal Bank, with its constitutionally guaranteed autonomy for exchange-rate policy. This was in addition to his efforts to convince other EC governments.

Helmut Kohl's style of chancellorship has been less attuned to providing European policy initiatives. Instead he has tried to act as an 'honest broker', akin to his cabinet role more generally. Under both German presidencies of the EC, Kohl has been involved in seeking package deals at summit meetings. In 1983 he had two attempts at making progress in reform of the CAP and the EC budget but both summits failed to achieve a deal. In February 1988, by contrast, Kohl did preside over a package deal aimed at restructuring the EC's finances, partly through CAP reform. This was a significant achievement for Kohl, given that his own agriculture minister had been one of the main opponents of the European Commission's reform proposals.

Kohl's consensus-building skills have been based on the coalition politics of the FRG. Coalition dynamics are also important in domestic European policy because they may serve to reinforce its sectorised nature. This applies particularly to the Agriculture Ministry, which throughout the period from the mid-1960s has been held by a junior coalition partner, eager to demonstrate its importance in the government. Moreover, the last three agriculture ministers have all been from Bavaria, the most rural state in the FRG. However, of the three influences – sectorisation, party politics and federal politics – it is argued here that the first influence has predominated (Bulmer and Paterson, 1987, Chapters 4 and 6).

Federal politics play an important role in those areas of European policy that affect the powers of the Länder. West Germany's federal constitution serves to give regional concerns institutional status. In general terms this has not created serious conflict, for the essence of the federal system is its need for consensus-building between layers of governmental authority. Moreover, the Länder have been consistent supporters of European integration. Despite this there has always been a concern that the Federal government, as the only formal representation of German interests in EC meetings, should be open to instructions from the Länder governments. This whole issue became of major importance during 1986–7, and eventually an agreement was reached in December 1987 providing for formal consultation of the Länder where their exclusive powers are affected by EC proposals (for further details on this matter, see Chapter 3).

The importance of federalism, therefore, is that the federal government does not hold exclusive competence for all the policy areas addressed by the EC. As a result, the federal government has to carry out vertical policy coordination in addition to that on a horizontal plane. In the case of the EC's Erasmus proposals – referred to earlier – the federal government blocked negotiations in Brussels for a while on behalf of the Länder, which are responsible for education matters.

It is clear then that West Germany's European policy style is sectorised in nature, with further lack of coherence deriving from the federal structure of the state. The four key ministries involved in European policy – Economics, Agriculture, Finance and Foreign Affairs – have considerable autonomy from each other and from the chancellor. Only on EPC business is there a case of one ministry –

the Foreign Office – having clear policy responsibility. Yet to take an excessively critical view of West Germany's European policy style is inappropriate. It is the product of the Europeanisation of West German politics. None of those criticising German incoherence would wish to see changes to the external dimension of Europeanisation, namely the FRG's anchoring in the West.

## New Developments in German European Policy

If the Federal Republic has come to be rather routinised in its dealings with the EC, what are the prospects for future developments? There are in fact some emergent difficulties stemming from both domestic politics and from the evolution of the EC itself.

The decline in popular support for integration is beginning to cause serious concern to the federal government. Chancellor Kohl's efforts to rekindle enthusiasm for the ideal of integration represented a change of atmospherics from Schmidt's pragmatic approach and a return to earlier rhetoric. Apparent public disenchantment represents a serious mis-match both with his efforts and with the renewed vigour in the EC itself. In the aftermath of the 1988 German presidency this led the government to devote serious attention to the problem. At the time of writing (1988) the outcome remains unclear. There is a generational element to the problem, symbolised by the questioning of values undertaken by the Greens. Their attachment to integration remains ambiguous because of their criticisms of individual policies. The CAP, for instance, is seen as environmentally damaging; the contribution of integration to European peace tends to be overshadowed by their concerns about NATO policy. All this highlights a growing question about continued public support for integration in the future. Any further decline in the level of turnout at the 1989 European elections would again point up this issue.

In addition, some economic groups are encountering problems which they are able to attribute to the EC. The most striking case is that of farmers, who associate falling incomes with the EC. This development has generated some movement towards electoral abstention on the one hand, or support for the radical right on the other. The response of the Christian Democratic parties, fearful of radical right-wing parties, has been to seek to pre-empt such developments through special payments to farmers.

The evolution of the EC will also have an impact on German attitudes, depending on the success of implementing CAP reform and completing the internal market by 1992. The latter, it has been suggested, might actually add further German 'losers' from inte-

gration, to rank alongside the farmers. Of course, all this depends
on whether, and to what extent, the internal market is completed
by 1992. However, it was striking that in 1988, no campaign of
publicity on '1992' had commenced in the FRG despite those in
France and the United Kingdom. This is doubtless due in some
measure to the fact that West German industrialists already regard
the EC as the domestic market, but there is a suspicion of complacency.

Two possible side-effects of completing the internal market need
mention. First, there is a possibility that the less developed member
states will be prepared to tolerate EC competition only if there is
greater protectionism against imports from the Far East. Pressures
of this nature would run counter to West German interests. Secondly, and an alternative scenario, these states may demand
increased regional or industrial aid to gain or retain competitiveness.
This would place further strains on already burdened West German
budgets.

Another development from within the EC is a concern that the
Federal Republic is not playing the leadership role that is appropriate
to the EC's strongest economy with the strongest currency as well.
Calls for leadership are greeted in the FRG with little enthusiasm.
This is scarcely surprising since European integration was motivated
by a wish to escape from the continental turmoil wrought by the
last two attempts at German leadership this century. And, more
specifically, the West German policy style acts as a formidable constraint in its own right. The new procedure for the consultation of
the Länder may make it even more so. There is a tendency, therefore, for West German economic strength to be used in a negative
way; specific sectoral interests may hinder EC initiatives while there
is also a lack of 'leadership' from the Federal government.

In the past it has been the development of Franco-German initiatives that has allayed these fears. The record of the 1988 West
German presidency also allayed them with the agreement reached
on budgetary and agricultural matters in February 1988. There was
also satisfactory progress on the internal market with some important
agreements, such as on liberalising capital movements. Nevertheless,
it could be argued that the latter achievements were merely in line
with the Community's own timetable towards 1992 and that the
German agriculture minister had been one of the obstacles to an
earlier settlement than that in Brussels.

Finally, there is the likely impact of any possible loosening in
Soviet control over its East European allies, in particular East Germany. This possibility is highly speculative in nature. However, any
move towards pan-German neutralism seems unlikely. The FRG has

a highly penetrated political system, and this is most apparent in its relations with the East. On the one hand, support would be necessary from EC partners. On the other, the Western allies retain an interest by virtue of their responsibility for Berlin. Some very fundamental changes in international politics will be necessary for any Central European accommodation.

# 12

# Inter-German Relations

## A. JAMES McADAMS

### Transformation of a Relationship

On 2 February 1973, Helmut Kohl, then the CDU minister-president of the Rheinland Palatinate, used a Bundesrat debate on the admission of East and West Germany to the United Nations to list his party's well-known grounds for refusing to support ratification of the Basic Treaty of 1972, the signing of which only months before had begun the normalisation of relations between the two Germanies. The treaty, he declared, had seriously weakened his country's ability to preserve the grounds for eventual national reunification, since its proponents now accepted the GDR – while not fully recognising it diplomatically – as a *separate* German state. In so doing, the Social Democratic-Liberal majority had needlessly endangered the FRG's historical right, as the only freely elected state on German soil, to speak for all Germans, including those living in the GDR. At the same time the East German regime, now emboldened by its growing international stature, would no longer feel constrained to give in to the FRG's demands for an improvement in the human rights situation on the other side of the Elbe.

How different Kohl sounded, then, on 7 September 1987, when he received the General Secretary of the East German Socialist Unity Party (SED), Erich Honecker, for his first official visit to the FRG. Now Federal chancellor Kohl welcomed the GDR's leader *in the name of* the Basic Treaty, underscoring the manifest progress which had taken place in inter-German relations in the past fifteen years and noting that absolutely nothing had happened to change his country's commitment to restoring Germany's unity in 'free self-determination'. Two states now existed on German soil, he admitted, whose daily affairs needed to be practically addressed. But, he stressed, the commitment of all Germans to the national cause and the will to protect it were as strong as ever.

Kohl's seeming about-face on the merits of the Basic Treaty might be explained by appealing to political expediency alone. Whereas in 1973 he was speaking as a representative of the leading opposition party, the Christian Democratic Union (CDU), which had seen the inter-German treaty just squeezed through parliament, by 1987 his party was once again in power, ready to make political capital of every sign of progress between the Germanies. But there was also considerably more to Kohl's transition, for in the Basic Treaty's first decade in the 1970s one could hardly have been so optimistic about inter-German prospects. Even many of the treaty's staunchest advocates found the allure of detente with the GDR diminished by the mire of tedious and excruciatingly technical negotiations with East Berlin.

By the 1980s, however, all this seemed to change overnight, as new prospects with the East were suddenly discovered and politicians on both sides rushed to expand relations. In the SPD–FDP coalition's final years, a major initiative was taken to put the countries' ties on a new footing when Helmut Schmidt paid his first official visit to the GDR in December 1981. But even greater surprises came with the formation of the new CDU–CSU coalition with the FDP in late 1982. Instead of overburdening the inter-German relationship with unfulfillable demands, as many critics of the CDU had feared, the conservative members of the new government followed the urgings of their Free Democratic coalition partners and essentially adopted the pro-detente line of their predecessors. In 1983 and 1984, Bonn assisted East Berlin in securing two massive loans from West German banks, totalling nearly DM 2 billion. In the following years, city partnerships between the Germanies were arranged for the first time, a treaty on cultural exchange was signed, and from 1984 onwards unprecedented successes were registered in the number of East German citizens allowed to visit the FRG, or even to emigrate. Then, in 1987, Kohl fought off any remaining opposition within his own party and paved the way for Honecker's visit to the Federal Republic.

For its part, the SPD, hardly a party to play the role of the disinterested observer, responded to every CDU gesture by seeking to outdo its conservative competitors in opening up new dimensions in the inter-German relationship. Far from limiting itself to the development of day-to-day ties between the Germanies, the party leadership initiated regular working groups on security questions and ideological affairs with East Berlin, leading it in 1985 and 1986, along with the SED, to propose the creation of chemical and nuclear weapons-free zones in central Europe. Naturally, such alliance-transcending gestures have been applauded by the SPD's rivals, the Greens, who since their entry to the Bundestag in March 1983 have proposed simply to take the process of inter-German rapprochement one step beyond that which even the authors of the Basic Treaty dared to go: the exchange of conventionally styled ambassadors and the full diplomatic recognition of the GDR.

What can such changes mean both for the FRG's future relationships with the GDR as well as for its own self-conception of its place in European affairs? To understand these issues, it is necessary first to demystify the inter-German relationship by looking at the varied causes behind the dramatic improvement in Bonn's ties with East Berlin in the 1980s. This will then put us in a position to see not only that a great deal has changed in inter-German relations since the signing of the Basic Treaty, but also that there are still distinct limits to the kinds of tie with East Germany that even the most liberal West German politicians are willing to accept.

## The Development of Inter-German Ties

Why is it that in contrast to the explosive development of inter-German ties in the 1980s, Bonn's relations with the GDR were so comparatively slow to develop in the Basic Treaty's first decade? West German officials often answer this question by paraphrasing Egon Bahr, the treaty's principal architect on the Western side: 'Before 1972,' Bahr concluded, not long after finishing negotiations with East Berlin, 'we had no relations with the GDR. Now we have bad relations.'

In one sense Bahr was absolutely right. Because the FRG insisted on seeing itself as the rightful heir to the German nation and because it regarded the East German state as an illegitimate creation of the Soviet Union, Bonn had for decades refused to entertain any official ties with the GDR. Since the founding of the two Germanies in 1949, Konrad Adenauer's CDU government had propagated the notion – the so-called 'policy of strength' – that the best way of keeping hopes for national reunification alive was by ignoring the GDR and concentrating on the strengthening of the West German state; eventually, so the reasoning seems to have gone, East Germany's prospects were to have grown so dim, politically and economically, that reunification would be its only alternative. In the meantime, however, the practical principle guiding West German thinking was that nothing should be done that might lead to a deepening of the inter-German divide. From 1955 onwards, West German leaders took this principle of holding open the German question to the point of enunciating a policy, popularly known as the Hallstein doctrine, under which West Germany threatened to sever relations with any country apart from the USSR which established diplomatic ties with the GDR.

To maintain that Bonn refused to open official relations with East Berlin is not to say, however, that it had no relations at all with the East German state. For while West German authorities argued on one level that the GDR was not even a state worthy of *de facto* recognition, the practical demands of inter-German division, and above all the fact that the West German leaders did not wish to do anything that might increase the burdens on the population of Eastern Germany, led to at least three kinds of contacts between Bonn and East Berlin.

Most prominent among these was a complex network of economic and trade ties, first vouchsafed by the Interzonal Trade Agreement of 1951 under which trade with the GDR was granted preferential treatment; with the signing of the Treaty of Rome in 1957, West Germany was even able to get its Common Market partners to treat East German exports coming into West Berlin and the FRG as domestic trade, freeing them from tariffs. No doubt, such unique economic advantages have been crucial for the development of the GDR. Just as important, their existence has demonstrated the West German government's readiness to pay a high price to maintain the 'special' character of contacts between the Germanies. For, with the exception of a short period in 1960 when Bonn temporarily abrogated the Trade Agreement in retaliation for East Berlin's harrassment of transit into West Berlin, the German-German economic relationship has prospered even in the times of greatest political tension. Whereas in 1952, each of the Germanies exchanged roughly DM 200 million in goods, by 1960, this figure stood at DM 1 billion each, and by 1970 at more than DM 2.5 billion for the FRG and nearly DM 2 billion for the GDR.

The existence of West Berlin, isolated in the centre of East Germany, provided the second reason for Bonn's maintenance of unofficial links with the GDR. When the Berlin Wall was erected on 13 August 1961, it not only brought an end to the long-standing flow of refugees out of East Germany, but it also signalled a new stage in *West* Berlin's history. If one wanted to re-establish contacts with now-separated friends and families in the eastern sectors of the city, so West Berlin's SPD–dominated city government reasoned, the only choice available was to deal in some way with the government of the GDR. Naturally, the FRG resisted East German demands that it formally recognise the GDR in the process. However, with the support of the city's popular mayor, Willy Brandt, and the grudging acceptance of the Christian Democratic government in Bonn, West Berlin officials began back-door negotiations with East Berlin, which by late 1963 led to a series of agreements permitting Christmas and Easter visits for hundreds of thousands of West Berliners to the East. Such humanitarian concerns were also at the root of a third kind of regular West German contact with the GDR: from 1963 onwards, Bonn routinely negotiated the release to the West of thousands of East German political prisoners, in the process demonstrating its desire to take responsibility for all Germans by paying tens of thousands of Marks for each person freed.

In retrospect, one might say that the Basic Treaty of 1972 continued the tradition first established by these economic and humanitarian contacts with the GDR. When Brandt himself finally assumed the chancellorship in 1969, following the national victory of a new Social Democratic-Liberal coalition, he was of course careful to stress that the FRG's Basic Law forbade its leaders from recognising East Germany as a foreign country. But it did not keep them from coming to the realistic conclusion that the GDR certainly was a state in its own right and, as such, had to be taken seriously. After all, the Berlin Wall afforded the East German leadership not only a means of restraining its own population; it could also be used to shut out West German influence and thereby minimise any hopes that the FRG might have in keeping inter-German commonalities alive.

However, the institutionalisation of such official and unofficial ties with the GDR in the 1970s was never a smooth or easy task. This may be one of the reasons why many of the early enthusiasts of the Basic Treaty found themselves quickly disenchanted with the slow pace of negotiations over such mundane topics as the demarcation of the inter-German boundary, the division of common waterways, garbage disposal, and the regulation of postal communications and telephone services.

For one thing, East Berlin itself turned out to be a wary participant in the formalisation of the two states' dialogue. The GDR's first party chief, Walter Ulbricht, had been an outspoken critic of Soviet moves which had led to the normalisation of the USSR's relations with the FRG in 1970 and to the 1971 four-power agreement on the status of Berlin. Although Ulbricht was deposed in 1971, the East German government's apprehensions about its population's readiness for an upgrading of relations with the FRG continued even under the new leadership of Erich Honecker. Hence many West Germans were disappointed to find that there was no sudden opening of the GDR to the West. To be sure, after the Berlin accord and the Basic Treaty were signed, citizens of the Federal Republic and West Berlin could now travel more easily to the GDR, but travel by East Germans to the West increased only slightly between 1972 and 1973, and only a very small percentage of these trips was made by GDR citizens below the retirement age.

Domestic misgivings about the expansion of inter-German ties also played a role in Bonn, since the CDU and particularly its Bavarian sister-party, the CSU, subjected the SPD–FDP coalition to constant criticism for ostensibly selling out the German nation with its new Ostpolitik. In 1973, the state of Bavaria even took its case against the Basic Treaty to the Federal Constitutional Court to test its legality. Although the Court upheld the treaty, such pressures put the Bonn government in a difficult position. On the one hand, to maintain domestic credibility, the SPD–FDP coalition was constantly forced to assure the West German population of its commitment to the cause of national reunification and the maintenance of a 'special' inter-German relationship. But, on the other hand, what complicated matters was that its representatives had to convince their East German counterparts that they were still capable of negotiating in good faith.

Of course, the final difficulty which influenced inter-German talks in the 1970s was simply the fact that the two states came to their meetings with very different priorities. The West Germans wanted to do everything they could to emphasise what the Germanies, and particularly their populations, still shared in common, while the East Germans stressed, at least for the most part, the divisions between East and West. This situation was complicated by the fact that both German states, not to mention their superpower patrons, had – and still have today – very different notions about the status of Berlin questions in their negotiations. This was in part due to ambiguities in the language and interpretation of the 1971 four-power accord, which allowed Bonn to argue that it had a legal right to broaden its political and economic relationship with West Berlin, while the GDR in contrast took the opposite position, contending that matters affecting either the city of the FRG should be treated as totally separate concerns. The result was that negotiations which touched on Berlin tended at times to exacerbate inter-German differences. This was of no small consequence, since well over half of the talks conducted by the FRG and the GDR in the 1970s directly concerned the divided city.

## The Expansion of Inter-German Detente

Many of the participants involved in the development of ties between the Germanies during the Basic Treaty's first decade will now say that the plodding, seemingly mundane accomplishments of that era actually played an instrumental role in laying the foundations for Bonn's and East Berlin's enormous successes in the 1980s. In essence the Germanies learned how to cooperate with each other. Through countless negotiations, East and West German mediators acquired a familiarity with the goals (and fears) of their adversaries, something which had been impossible in previous times of mutual isolation. Most importantly, each side also learned to distinguish between the maximal objectives of its opponents – which neither Germany was bound to realise anyway – and their minimal expectations of the relationship. To an extent, this made simple compromises in each side's interest possible, such as that exemplified by the construction of a new Autobahn between Hamburg and West Berlin in 1978.

Yet, while the inter-German contacts of the 1970s may have been a necessary condition for progress between Bonn and East Berlin in the 1980s, they alone can hardly account for the intensity with which these ties later developed. To understand the foundations of today's qualitatively better relationship between the two states, it is necessary to put these ties in their proper international context. From late 1979 onwards, at least three developments outside of the Germanies emerged to cast relations between Bonn and East Berlin in an entirely new light. On 12 December 1979, NATO ministers meeting in Brussels responded to the stationing of Soviet SS–20 intermediate-range nuclear missiles with a plan to deploy their own mid-range weapons in Western Europe by the autumn of 1983 should negotiations with Moscow fail to remove the new Soviet threat. Only two weeks later, the USSR began a long and bloody intervention in Afghanistan. Finally, in the summer of 1980, worker-unrest in Poland led to the formation of the first, organised independent trade union movement in Eastern Europe and the added threat that the Soviets might decide to use force to quell the disturbances and restore socialist authority.

As these prospects of a new Cold War between the superpowers loomed over the Europeans, inter-German ties acquired a salience that they had not had before. In part, this was because each of the German states was compelled by the situation at hand to review the accomplishments of the preceding decade and, in effect, to ask whether even seemingly mundane achievements could be sacrificed to the competitive instincts of the superpowers. The risks of any rise in East-West tensions were spelled out for the West Germans in late

1980 when the GDR's leaders, fearing that their own population might imitate the independent initiatives of the Polish working class, took offensive measures to insulate their country from the uncertaint-ies around them. These steps included a drastic increase in the amounts of Western currency which West German visitors were required to exchange when visiting the GDR. Predictably, in the following months, the number of visits from the FRG to East Ger-many declined by almost one-half. The West German government immediately protested against these measures as a violation of the spirit of the Basic Treaty. But the lesson of such developments was not lost on the Bonn leadership, which began to ask itself what steps could be taken to shore up the many practical links which had been established between the Germanies. One might even say that it took *just such* a clear threat to good relations between Bonn and East Berlin for many West German politicians to appreciate what they now stood to lose.

The FRG's sensitivity to the challenge of maintaining positive inter-German contacts was repeatedly demonstrated in Bonn's sub-sequent dealings with East Berlin. When, at the height of the Polish tensions, Honecker tried to raise the stakes by making his country's full diplomatic recognition by Bonn a precondition for further dia-logue, the West Germans may have refused to give in, but they also persisted in seeking less provocative avenues for German-German compromise and accommodation. In fact, the growing tensions between the superpowers had much to do with Helmut Schmidt's decision to arrange his December 1981 visit to the GDR, following years of indecision on the part of his government. In his talks with the East German general secretary, both public and private, Schmidt deliberately emphasised his respect for the GDR's sovereignty, even seeming at times to go out of his way to solicit Erich Honecker's opinion on the resolution of pressing bilateral and international prob-lems. When the imposition of martial law in Poland occurred, incon-veniently for Schmidt on the last day of his trip to the GDR, the West German chancellor was so concerned to avoid offending his host that he merely joined Honecker in calling on the Poles to solve their problems without outside interference.

Yet, while the Germanies were clearly interested in safeguarding their own relationship from the rising tensions around them, it would be a mistake to think that specifically inter-German concerns were always at the heart of their motivations. In fact, in Bonn's case, much of the publicity given to the cause of FRG-GDR detente was really about West Germany's larger relationship with the USA and about its own role in the Western alliance. Schmidt made this point very clear when, after the Soviet invasion of Afghanistan, he noted that his country's main contribution to world peace could be found in its ability to offer an alternative to the *Sprachlosigkeit*, or 'speechlessness', which had descended upon the superpowers. The FRG's ties with the GDR provided at least one appropriate vehicle for this task.

Furthermore, there is good reason to think that many of the members of the governing SPD–FDP coalition who rushed to endorse an upgrading of their country's relations with the GDR in the early 1980s were really using their expressions of concern about the fate of inter-German ties as a convenient way to voice even greater frustrations with the security policies of the American Reagan administration and the apparent unwillingness of the USA to compromise with Moscow on the impending stationing of NATO's intermediate-range nuclear forces. Hence, following the fall of the Schmidt government in October 1982 and the SPD's decision as an opposition party to withdraw its endorsement of the INF deployment, a number of prominent Social Democrats, including Egon Bahr, sought to stake out their opposition to American policy by calling for a 'second-phase' in the FRG's Ostpolitik, in which not only humanitarian questions but also security concerns might become a focus of German-German dialogue. Indeed, in 1984, to the dismay of many observers, the SPD initiated the first of its talks with its counterparts in the East German SED on a proposed chemical weapons-free zone in central Europe.

## Domestic Change in the FRG

The other key change necessary for an upgrading of West German relations with East Berlin must be seen in the FRG's internal politics. While few onlookers may have been very surprised to find the SPD and its Free Democratic coalition partners endorsing at least a continuation of the rudiments of inter-German detente in the 1980s, most political observers were unprepared for the unabashed enthusiasm with which the CDU and even Franz Josef Strauss's CSU took up the cause of good ties with the GDR. Certainly, there was good reason in 1982 and 1983 for expecting the contrary. As we have seen, throughout the previous decade the two parties had been harsh critics of the Federal government's Eastern policies, even to the point of refusing to accept the Helsinki accords. Members of the FDP admit today that when they entered the new governing coalition with the CDU–CSU in 1982, even they were uncertain how the conservative majority would vote on matters relating to policy toward the East, in no small part because prominent members of the two parties' right wings, such as Herbert Czaja and Herbert Hupka, had publicly called for a return to a tough-minded stance on all ties with East Berlin. Not surprisingly, many East German authorities were convinced that the new government, in conjunction with the 1983 deployment of the NATO missiles, was sure to lead to a new 'ice age' in inter-German relations.

From almost the first days of the new coalition, however, the Kohl government showed that it had little interest in abandoning the basic policy lines already established by its predecessors. Key spokesmen for the chancellor, such as the first head of the Chancellor's Office, Philipp Jenninger, and his successor, Wolfgang Schäuble, stressed that any changes, were they to come, would emphasise only the CDU–CSU's long-term commitment to the cause of German unity. But all part understandings with the GDR, *including* the FRG's acceptance of the Basic Treaty, would be respected; as the CSU's Strauss himself now repeatedly put it, '*pacta servanda sunt*' (agreements are to be kept).

Had West Germany's conservatives simply changed their views overnight about the value of the inter-German agreements of the 1970s and early 1980? In part, some had. It was one thing for a party in opposition to criticise the Social Democrats for being too eager to accommodate the East German Communists or for failing to be tough enough on human rights issues and the primacy of national reunification. But when finally in power, many Christian Democrats found the challenge of responding to the practical day-to-day problems of the inter-German relationship – the facilitation of travel between the two states, the freeing of political prisoners in the GDR, the negotiation of economic agreements and cultural exchanges – so complex that the appeal to political catchwords and clichés alone was not sufficient.

Another reason for the change in thinking of West German Christian Democracy has less to do with the question of inter-German relations itself and more with the broader history of the CDU between 1969 and 1982. It was during this period that the party found itself for the first time out of power. As a new generation of politicians took over the CDU leadership, including Kohl and his influential general secretary, Kurt Biedenkopf, they were naturally inclined to ask themselves what the party could do to avoid its past mistakes, win the confidence of the West German electorate and regain control of the government. The *Deutschlandpolitik* (Inner-German policy) was one – but only one – of the many policy questions in which the new party leadership was inclined to think that it had overplayed its hand in the early 1970s by being too inflexible. Even at the time of its inception, the Basic Treaty had been supported by the majority of West German voters, and throughout the decade the CDU had unquestionably lost credibility for having opposed it and the subsequent Helsinki process. It was only logical, therefore, that as the party sought to reorient itself in the public mind as a party of the middle, and not of the extreme right, its leaders tried to use such questions as the future of the inter-German relationship as proof of a new capacity for moderation and compromise. Naturally, such tactics were not only useful for getting votes but also for convincing sceptics in the FDP that the CDU would be an agreeable coalition partner.

Whatever the cause of the turnaround among West German conservatives, however, it is important to recognise that the Christian Democrats' acceptance of the Ostpolitik meant more in practice than the mere emulation of the example already set by its predecessors in the SPD. As we have seen, the Social Democrats always operated under one key constraint: the presence of incessant criticism from the ranks of the conservative opposition. But when the Christian Democrats themselves became the government, the number of likely opponents to any new initiatives towards the GDR was thereby reduced. This was certainly one of the reasons why the Bonn government was able to support the two controversial bank loans of 1983 and 1984 to the GDR, initiatives which the Social Democrats might have had a hard time selling to their critics during their days in power. Of course, the CDU still had to worry about right-wing critics within its own ranks and in the CSU. But this was one of the reasons why in 1983 Kohl's regime was eager to enlist Strauss himself in the credit negotiations, as a way of fending off any remaining criticism. Naturally, Kohl's decision to receive Honecker in 1987 during his visit to Bonn was an even more controversial step in the process of inter-German accommodation, one which some West German conservatives still found difficult to accept. But who can doubt that had the SPD tried to stage a similar visit during Schmidt's tenure the public outcry might have been even greater?

Ironically, the consequence has been that the Christian Democrats have at times proved even more successful than their Social Democratic successors in extracting concessions from the GDR. In a tacit exchange for the good economic relationship with Bonn and for such goodwill gestures as the Honecker visit, East Berlin has shown itself to be manifestly forthcoming in facilitating the flow of inter-German contacts. Whereas the East German leadership once hesitated to receive many representatives of the CDU publicly in East Berlin, now prominent conservative spokesmen, such as the leader of the CDU's Bundestag *Fraktion*, Alfred Dregger, and the deputy *Fraktion* chairman, Volker Rühe, have become part of a routine stream of official West German guests in the GDR. The most staggering achievements in the area of German-German contacts have been registered in the movement of average citizens between the two states: in 1984, the GDR government allowed an unprecedented 34,982 citizens to emigrate permanently to the FRG, up from only 7,729 the previous year; and in 1987, following a year of upward movement, over 1.3 million East Germans under the retirement age were allowed to make short-term trips to West Germany, a huge contrast with the approximately 100,000 visits of 1985.

## Differences Among the Parties

While a broad consensus has thus been reached among the West German parties about the need for a good working relationship with the GDR, there are of course still some differences about the way in which business with the other Germany should be conducted. But, with the passage of time, even these differences – over approaches to the national question, over expectations of the GDR, and over the subjects of proper negotiations with East Berlin – have become more and more subtle, so that it is increasingly difficult to ascribe a single, fixed position on the management of inter-German affairs to any of the major parties.

Consider, for example, the debates which used to rage over the question of Germany's national destiny. One can still say that there are at least two poles of West German elite opinion on this question: at one extreme, some members of the CDU and the so-called 'national liberal' wing of the FDP still maintain that everything should be done to keep the issue of national reunification uppermost in the public eye, even if this might mean offending East Berlin and temporarily holding up progress in inter-German relations. At the other extreme, one finds members of the SPD and Greens who argue that the national question has become anachronistic and that the best strategy for the Federal Republic is simply to abandon the trappings of any special relationship with the GDR and recognise East Germany as a foreign country.

The great majority of party members, however, now tend to congregate between these two extremes, preferring the safe middle ground. On the one hand, conservatives seem to have learned the practical and electoral lessons of adhering too fervently to hard-line nationalistic positions, which have not only threatened the health of the inter-German relationship, but have also occasionally worried West Germany's neighbours. Thus, to placate the fears that some countries like France and the Netherlands have of a resurgent, unified German state, CDU leaders now speak only very vaguely of realising the goal of German unity after Europe *too* has become united; in a spring 1988 document on the goals of the CDU's foreign and German policy, the party leadership did not even mention the word 'reunification'. To be sure, at the CDU's 36th Congress in June 1988, Kohl later emphasised his government's commitment to the goal of eventual German unity. But many observers left the congress with the impression that he was primarily trying to appease his party's right wing, but not at all interested in making the reunification issue a CDU priority.

On the other hand, it would probably be wrong to think that the major West German parties are moving in the direction of the abandonment of national themes altogether. For one thing, the Basic Law commands the government to work toward the 'completion of the unity' of Germany, a position that was upheld by the Constitutional Court's decision of 1973 and which still enjoys broad support. When in 1985 the Bundestag's deputy opposition leader, SPD member Jürgen Schmude, called for a revamping of this goal, he was not only met by a storm of criticism from the CDU but also from his own party. In part, the persistence of such national themes also its roots in the unique problems associated with the division of Germany, above all those tied to the fate of West Berlin. If one were to accept the nation's division as final, most West German politicians argue, one would risk undermining the FRG's claims in that city. Even the Greens do not argue that West Berlin should be turned into a full-fledged Bundesland, thus sealing the division.

Continuing interest in national themes is also reflected in the kinds of expectations that West German politicians have of East German behaviour. Here, too, one can speak of a general continuum of elite opinion, which seemed particularly pronounced during the 1970s. At that time, at one extreme, spokesmen for the Social Democrats argued that progressive changes in the GDR were best assured by first winning the confidence of the East German leadership rather than overburdening it with unrealisable demands for domestic reform. As we have seen, the Christian Democrats took the other extreme, often to the point of contending that internal changes in the GDR should be made a precondition for further progress between the Germanies.

Yet in this case, too, inter-German progress in the 1980s has led to a blurring of these positions, as all of the West German parties have become sensitive to the problem of balancing their own hopes for change against the realities of their country's relationship with the GDR. The complexity of this challenge was spelled out in late 1987 and early 1988, when West German politicians were forced to grapple with a series of widely-unpopular SED measures designed to limit the autonomy of the East German churches and to crack down on the country's small dissident community. The CDU government responded in a manner that mirrored that of the previous SPD–FDP coalition, overtly condemning the SED's actions but privately using its back-door contacts with East Berlin to resolve the conflict and limit the damage to inter-German relations. In contrast, the East German measures unleashed an internal debate within the Social Democratic Party, in which the party's young Turks castigated the old-guard SPD leadership for ostensibly taking a greater interest in maintaining good ties with the East German establishment than in defending the rightful claims of its critics. This latter position was seconded by the Greens, who accused all of the larger West German parties of selling out the East German populace to the cause of *Realpolitik*.

If there is one area in which party divisions tend to be more clearly defined, however, it is in the appropriate subject of negotiations with the GDR. Since the mid-1980s, the Christian Democratic-Free Democratic coalition has been quick to accuse its counterparts in the SPD of pursuing a *Nebenaussenpolitik*, a 'shadow foreign policy', in its talks on security questions with the SED, and of coming dangerously close to alienating the FRG and its NATO commitments. Similarly, the Social Democrats were subjected to widespread criticism in the autumn of 1987, when a party commission negotiated a common paper with the SED on ideological values, calling for the development of a 'culture of political contest and dialogue' between East and West.

It still remains to be seen whether the SPD would advocate such a far-reaching dialogue with the SED were it to come to power. But even here, despite the clear differences separating the Social Democrats from the West German government, the practice of the CDU–FDP coalition on such questions has at times differed somewhat from its public criticism of the SPD. In private discussions, members of the FDP and even some representatives of the CDU concede that the SPD–SED common document, while highly idealistic, served a useful function in clarifying the two sides' differences and bridging the inter-German divide. Moreover, while the West German government still insists that the FRG, and particularly an opposition party, has no business conducting negotiations on such sensitive issues as the elimination of nuclear or chemical weapons from central Europe, this has not stopped Christian Democratic leaders from regularly sharing their views on a host of arms control questions with their East German counterparts. During Honecker's visit to the FRG, for example, conventional arms reductions and the impending INF Treaty played a prominent part in German-German talks. For that matter, Hans-Dietrich Genscher's FDP–dominated Foreign Ministry has since 1981 routinely promoted discussions on security questions with the GDR Ministry of Foreign Affairs, as a means of exchanging information and building East-West confidence. The crucial distinction between the governing parties and the SPD, however, still appears to lie in the subject of actual arms negotiations, which the ruling coalition views as the proper domain of the superpowers.

## The Future of Inter-German Relations

What, then, can we expect of the inter-German future? The cardinal distinction that one needs to draw is between a basic continuity in FRG-GDR affairs and the development of qualitatively new domains of German-German cooperation akin to the dramatic achievements of the 1980s.

On the one hand, the argument for basic continuity is easy to sustain. The consensus which now exists between Bonn and East Berlin on the rudiments of inter-German cooperation is so strong that all of the major parties have an interest in perpetuating it. Paradoxically, this is true not only because the West German government has so much to offer East Berlin in the form of economic ties and the international recognition that comes with visits like that of Honecker to the FRG. Implicitly, West German politicians also recognise that they depend on the GDR as well, both for allowing East German citizens to travel and even emigrate to the West and for simply keeping regular contacts alive. All of this is necessary, if the FRG wants to keep German issues in the public mind.

On the other hand, Bonn's greatest challenge in the future may be to find new areas within which the tempo of inter-German progress can be maintained. The question here is whether the two Germanies can avoid being victims of their own success. It is always easy to find fault with the Basic Treaty of 1972 for failing clearly to resolve outstanding questions between the two states: some liberal politicians complain that the FRG and the GDR do not exchange full ambassadors and that Bonn could do much more to recognise the sovereignty of the GDR, while some conservative politicians bemoan the Treaty's vagueness on West Germany's commitment to national unity. But most of the participants in inter-German dialogue recognise that a better treaty is not to be had. The same can be said for still-unresolved disputes over Berlin. Occasionally, proposals are made to upgrade the city's status, perhaps turning it into an inter-

national cultural centre; and West German officials continually protest against what they regard to be unjust limitations placed on their
authority over West Berlin by the city's four occupying powers. But,
as with the Basic Treaty, the successes of the past two decades in
resolving tensions over Berlin have led many observers to conclude
that no major new initiatives need to be taken.

This leaves only two prominent areas in which the East and West
Germany might still seek a qualitative development of their relationship. The first possibility is in the expansion of economic ties.
Throughout the early 1980s, the growth of the GDR's economy was
impressive by East European standards, with the country attaining
annual levels of growth hovering around 5 per cent. By the end of
the decade, however, the GDR seems to have been afflicted with
many of the problems that have long beset its socialist neighbours –
diminishing factor productivity, declining investment, and an
inability to maintain the high rates of consumer spending; to which
its population has become accustomed. As East German growth has
declined, many West Germans involved in the maintenance of inter-
German ties have asked themselves what contribution the FRG
might make to stabilise the GDR's economy. A greater reliance on
inter-German trade, which has largely levelled off in recent years,
seems an unlikely solution; West German businesses and manufac-
turers complain that while they would like to do more business with
the GDR, the East Germans simply do not produce the quality
goods capable of competing in Western markets. This leaves the
possibility that the FRG might take an active role in arranging further
bank credits for the GDR or that it might even seek new means of,
indirectly or directly, subsidising the East German economy. In times
of budget-cutting in the West, such a proposal becomes as much a
political as an economic issue. Are West German voters, in fact, so
interested in further enhancing their country's ties with the GDR that
they will be willing to make it one of their government's priorities,
to the potential detriment of some of West Germany's domestic
commitments? The answer to this question depends on the prevailing
mood of the coming political generation of the 1990s. West Germany's future leaders might indeed be open to innovative solutions
to pressing East-West problems, but given the time that has elapsed
since Germany's division and lacking their predecessors' personal
and psychological attachments to the other German state, they may
simply lack the motivations of past generations.

The other possible area in which FRG-GDR ties might be
developed is in international affairs. Logically, there is very little to
inhibit the two states from playing increasingly active roles within
their respective alliances. Like the GDR in the Warsaw Treaty

Organisation, the FRG has become a pivotal player in NATO, and as we have seen in both of their actions in the early 1980s, Bonn and East Berlin are quite capable of using their own special relationship as a counter-example to that of the superpowers in times of rising East-West tensions. In particular, the SPD's initiatives taken with the SED demonstrate that West Germany could seek to use its unique links with the East to play a greater role in setting NATO agendas on such controversial questions as the control of chemical weapons, particularly if the Social Democrats are able to convince their rivals in the FDP or even the CDU that such independent gestures are consonant with alliance goals.

Yet here, too, one needs to ask whether the challenges of the 1990s will influence inter-German relations in the same way as the challenges of the 1980s. As we have seen, much (although not all) of the impetus for the dramatic increase in FRG-GDR ties of the last decade came from the Germanies' mutual revulsion at the sudden escalation of superpower tensions, this in turn led such parties as the SPD to seek new and innovative solutions to the surrounding problems. Most recently, both German states have had good reason to rejoice at the relaxation in these international tensions, signified by the ratification of the Soviet-American INF accord of 1988. Yet in the absence of common fears of a new Cold War, one might also wonder whether inter-German contacts will lose some of their sense of urgency. While politicians in both the FRG and the GDR might agree that a good working relationship is well worth maintaining, it remains to be seen what new grounds they might discover to justify ever-closer ties with their counterparts in the other German state.

# PART FIVE

# Current Issues

# 13

# Generation and Gender

EVA KOLINSKY

In the first half of the twentieth century, the German political environment was changed too often to allow for continuities of political expectations and behaviour. West Germans now in their eighties have experienced the feudal industrialism of Imperial Germany, the Weimar Republic with its extremist challenges to democratic politics, the National Socialist dictatorship, and – for longer than any of its predecessors – the democratic polity of the Federal Republic. Each of these system changes demanded adjustments and shaped behaviour, expectations and attitudes especially of those who were young enough then to gather their first and arguably formative political orientations. The political development of West German democracy relied on integrating the various generations and winning them over to support democratic politics even though many had rejected democracy in the past or had little knowledge of it. This process occurred largely in the 1950s and was dominated by an emphasis on conformity and system support. After that, the generations whose formative experiences lay in the post-war era began to set their own priorities – a search for more democracy in the 1960s, for self-realisation in the 1970s. This chapter examines this integration into democratic politics and the new diversity of generations in West Germany as well as with a special focus on women and the contemporary remnants of a gender gap in politics and society.

## The Makings of Democratic Conformity

The Second World War and the ideological and political impact of National Socialism, deeply affected the outlook of pre-democratic generations. In the 1940s, German adults professed to be occupied with survival; the majority took little interest in the recasting of their political system which went on around them during the occupation period. The young generation felt that their trust had been betrayed: National Socialism not only collapsed but was shown to have perpetrated crimes against humanity on a hitherto unknown scale; they professed that they would remain aloof from all ideologies (Schelsky, 1957). The generations – young and older – who were initially reluctant to welcome democracy have since become stalwart supporters. When the study by Fischer and others compared the views of young adults in the 1950s with those held by the same generational cohort thirty years later, they had become more liberal, pluralistic and participatory (Fischer *et al.*, 1985).

These changes were facilitated by improved social and economic conditions since the 1950s which allowed individuals opportunities and a wider choice of lifestyles than their parents or grandparents could have known. Despite their diverse backgrounds in non-democratic environments, the generations which constituted the West German citizenry in the 1950s have since developed democratic political preferences and a strong commitment to democratic norms.

The commitment to the Basic Law is a case in point: the early indifference towards its origins and intent soon gave way to its emphatic acceptance as the normative framework for the whole political process. In a similar way, party pluralism, parliamentary decision-making, electoral participation, all of which had had their critics in the founding years of the Federal Republic or had inspired little interest, have won approval as cornerstones of a stable democracy. The personal popularity of the first Federal chancellor, Konrad Adenauer and the successes of his government in improving living conditions and in gaining international acceptance for the new democratic state were further important integrative factors. Given the apparent changes for the better on so many levels, West Germans adopted the political behaviour which was expected of them. From a contemporary perspective this 'democracy by the book' approach (Edinger, 1968) seems too concerned with system stability and undervalues expressions of conflict and the freedom of the individual to participate at all levels of political life.

The founding generations of the Federal Republic were, of course, concerned with the stability of institutional structures in order to preclude a repetition of National Socialist control, or to avoid the deficits of democratic legitimacy and authority which had undermined the Weimar Republic. In a more immediate sense they were determined to escape the dislocation and economic deprivation of the post-war years. The persuasive force of economic prosperity coupled with a pragmatic approach to democracy, understood as conforming to the system, neutralised the uncertain generational experiences of the founding years and allowed the new polity time to take root through growing stability, affluence, and political consolidation both internally and in the international sphere.

## Conformity and Negative Integration

Two further factors favoured political conformity. The first relates to the geopolitical position of West Germany seen as the bulwark of democracy against Communism in East Germany and the Soviet bloc. Well into the 1960s, acceptance of democratic politics was deemed to be identical with rejecting its Communist counterpart. The assumption that they were constantly under threat of conquest and of losing their liberty served to stifle internal debate and a critical interest in the democratic qualities of West German political life. (Berg-Schlosser and Schissler, 1987). This 'negative integration' served to integrate the various generations, with their mixed political values and views of democracy, in a defensive posture. It also encouraged an understanding of democracy as providing a stable rather than a participatory political environment and thus sowed the seeds of the contemporary generational divide.

The second factor relates to the National Socialist past and the tacit resolve to let bygones be bygones. (Mitscherlich, 1963) In the 1950s and early 1960s it was considered unseemly to probe into the possibly unsavoury past of the pre-democratic generations, and it was deemed no less unseemly to question the broad political conformity with the rules of democratic politics which had emerged. The politics of conformity survived into the 1980s, and still constitute the core of the contemporary political culture.

## From Conformity to Diversity

As the post-war generations reached political adulthood, they began to challenge the conformity culture with new issues and policy styles (Baker *et. al.*, 1981). Since the 1960s, young people whose only political environment has been West German democracy, have been less fearful of change and less concerned with stability. Conforming to the rules of the system which inspired the political behaviour of the founding generations, has been displaced among the children of democracy by an interest in innovation, personal participation and, above all, by self-realisation in private and political life (Inglehart,

1977). As increasing numbers of young people are staying at school beyond the minimum leaving age, they defer their full integration into the labour market and experience an interim period of adolescence which allows for the development of personal preferences. Young people today are also more likely than older generations to obtain further and higher educational and vocational qualifications (Jugend '81, 1982).

If affluence and a range of opportunities have fostered a variety of lifestyles and distinctive youth cultures, then education has fostered new political orientations. Educated young people, in particular those who completed advanced secondary education and attended universities, have begun to question the conformist patterns of West German democracy and to advocate more innovative approaches and greater chances of participation for the individual. Education can be regarded as a divide between generations, and also within the young generation. In the past, educated Germans tended to opt for the political right, now they appear more inclined towards the left. Low levels of education, which had traditionally fed into left wing or working class politics have begun to show a new affinity towards the right, in particular among the young generation.

Generation, seen as a formative stage in shaping social values and political orientations, has gained a new relevance and is perceived as an opportunity to explore alternatives and create personal allegiances against the grain of the surrounding political culture. The contemporary generation-gap separates the under-forties from their elders, and concerns the balance of stability and change in politics. For the young generations whose formative political experiences relate to the Federal Republic, the need for system stability has not been as paramount as for those who had recast the German political order after National Socialism. Freed from the concern about system stability, the post-war generations could focus on individual preferences, the democratic qualities of the political process and even opt for protest to make their mark.

Two aspects in particular have contributed to redrawing the map of contemporary German politics along a generational divide: the first concerns electoral choices and the second the articulation of political issues. As the post-war generations reached voting age they began to break away from inherited party allegiances and cleavage lines. Party preferences became more personal and thus more volatile than had been customary in the past (Klingemann, 1985). Initially, the Christian Democrats attracted the majority of voters under the age of 25. The electoral mobility of young voters since the 1960s has helped to redress the party balance and enabled the SPD to rise from a decade of opposition into government (Hofmann-

Göttig, 1984). In 1972, and with the voting age lowered to 18, the SPD for a brief spell became the strongest party in the Bundestag. It was perceived as competent to enhance the democratic qualities of the West German polity and to broaden the avenues of partici- pation and equal opportunities. In government, the SPD could not meet all the expectations of democratic innovation which the younger generations had invested in the party and lost some of their electoral support. Those who valued economic stability turned to the Christian Democrats while those who valued innovative change turned to the new party which seemed committed to changing the very agenda and the style of West German politics: the Greens. With nearly 70 per cent of their electorate under the age of forty, and seats in most regional parliaments and in the Bundestag, the Greens have become a visible manifestation of the generational divide in contemporary political life (Bürklin, 1988).

The second development to change the generational balance and redraw the political map of West Germany concerns the articulation of specific issues, whether inside or outside party-political agendas. By the mid-1960s, the two major parties, CDU–CSU and SPD had become *Volksparteien* intent on appealing to all social groups with broadly based, multi-thematic programmatic platforms. Party agendas had, of course, reflected public sentiments, but they ulti- mately arose from within the party organisation. Moreover, the two largest parties had become similar in their policies and styles to collaborate in a Grand Coalition between 1966 and 1969. While the founding generations of the Federal Republic looked for strong institutionalised political ties between parties and politicians to tackle social and economic instability, the younger generations entered their political adolescence and adulthood with different notions as to how governments, parties and people should be linked. In their view, the similarity between catch-all parties and the control they retained over the issues on the political agenda were the political equivalent of cartels and designed to curtail the rights of the citizens to be heard and to play a part in shaping their political environment. Whereas the founding generations had been willing to delegate to the powers-that-be the right to select the relevant issues and to supply the political agendas, the post-war generations claimed a stake in selecting the issues that should matter, and were inclined to doubt that political parties, politicians or governments were suf- ficiently attuned to their specific concerns.

## Self-Realisation and Protest

The post-war generations who grew up in affluent and democratic surroundings are more likely than their parents to value personal participation and choose priorities which reflect their own personal experiences or concerns. In the German context, the general trend towards post-materialist values and self-realisation in contemporary democracies commenced at a time of generational and political culture change. The institutionalised political culture of the early decades came increasingly under pressure from young West Germans who had accepted the principles of democracy during their political socialisation and now set out to measure the realities of political life against these principles. Young and educated West Germans were inclined to be the most ardent democrats and also most sceptical about the democratic nature of the West German polity. Many maintained that National Socialist structures had never been abolished but were hidden behind a façade of democratic rituals. In established democracies, the transition to post-materialist orientations and assertive self-realisation encouraged a varied and participatory culture of initiatives, action groups or political parties which added informal and unconventional avenues of participation to existing ones, and created new channels for influencing decision-makers from outside traditional political frameworks (Roth and Richt, 1987). The post-war generations have grown up expecting that their wishes can be put into practice, even if this might mean remodelling the established political culture and institutions.

The new confidence in the potential relevance of individual actions broadened conventional participation in political parties and spurned unconventional action and extra-parliamentary opposition movements. In both types of participation the young generations, the children of democracy, have played a prominent part since the early 1970s. Party membership, for instance, doubled within the decade from one to two million and potential membership increased from around 6% to 15% of the adult population. Citizens' initiatives and localised action groups attracted some two million members, and three in four West Germans declared they might join if a relevant issue arose in their personal environment. Similar tendencies towards a participatory culture have been observed in other advanced industrial societies (Barnes, Kaase *et al.*, 1979). The special sting of the participatory culture in West Germany lies in the assumption that protest is needed to unmask authoritarian or even fascist practices which are said to have survived into the present; that confrontation is needed to shake up the institutions and make them responsive to individual expectations; that violence has to be used to coerce 'the system' from stability into change. The protest culture among the young generation in West Germany displays a strong distrust of democratic procedures and is prone to disregard democratic conventions in favour of confrontation and polarity (Kolinsky, 1989). To that extent it echoes the anti-democratic heritage of Germany's troubled past.

## Agendas of Protest from the Left

The student movement which arose in the mid-1960s (and collapsed at the end of the decade into an array of left-wing orthodoxies and political terrorism) was the first and arguably the most influential of the social movements which have since characterised extra-parliamentary politics in West Germany. To this day, the '1968 generation' is regarded as a cohort with a keen interest in political participation and a propensity to challenge established priorities inside and outside parties and parliaments. Although many are now in their fifties, and occupy positions in the political, intellectual or economic elites, others have retained the oppositional orientation and detachment from mainstream politics which constitute the contemporary protest *milieu* and from which the new social movements and the Green party have drawn most of their support (Veen, 1989).

Initially the student movement advocated university reforms at a time when higher education appeared wedded to an ethos, curriculum design, and structure of authority unchanged significantly since the nineteenth century. The qualifications universities could offer seemed unsuited to the needs of the modern world, and conditions of study deteriorated alarmingly as student numbers increased. Demands for more participation in decision-making in higher education mingled with concerns that university education was out of touch with reality and could not create the career opportunities West German students had come to expect. While the majority of students sought more participation and also reassurance about the adequacy of their training, the activist core interpreted the participatory deficits of the university system as shortcomings of capitalism, consumerism and class society. For them the target of any protest action was Western 'imperialism'.

The concluding phase of the student movement consisted of street battles and violent confrontations with the West German police on issues as far apart as the war in Vietnam or press reporting in West Germany. By that time, regional governments and political parties had already begun to reconsider their attitude toward educational reforms, to develop policies to broaden access to advanced secondary schooling and universities, and to modify the autocratic decision-making processes which had survived in the tertiary sector. While the student movement and subsequent protest cultures have assumed that the established political institutions would reject the new issues and ideas raised at extra-parliamentary level, the opposite has been true: in many instances, parties, parliaments and governments have incorporated key demands into their own policies; they reacted in a flexible rather than a confrontational manner and took up those themes of the protest culture which were also relevant for a wider public.

This capacity of West German *Volksparteien* to incorporate some of the issues of the new social movements has been interpreted as a threat to the aims and effectiveness of the movements themselves. To remain distinctive in the face of pragmatically adaptable *Volksparteien*, movements have opted for radical and often confrontational action. It seems that the very flexibility of the *Volksparteien* has exacerbated the tendencies among the young generation towards political radicalism. For example, the student movement with its search for equality and fair opportunities was radicalised into left wing terrorism at the very moment when under the social-liberal coalition government welfare policies and equal opportunities were higher on the political agenda than at any point in the past.

A similar link between a new social movement, mainstream parties and political radicalisation has been evident in the field of ecology. Against a background of popular concerns about pollution, the uncertain safety of nuclear power, and general unease about the potentially destructive impact of modern technologies on people's lives, the early 1970s brought a rapid rise of citizens' action groups to address themselves to local problems, to petition administrators and to lobby politicians and parties. These groups could draw on the participatory political culture and the willingness of the younger generations to play an active role in politics and society. Since environmentalism had become a priority issue among West Germans across all age groups and political persuasions, the particular strength of the ecology movement lay in its socio-economic breadth and its links with local communities. And since environmentalism was so popular, none of the political parties could afford to ignore it, and they all developed detailed ecology policies. Not only were these policies similar, they also absorbed most of the ecological concerns and demands which had first been voiced by the extra-parliamentary movement. In a climate of electoral mobility and uncertain majorities, the West German *Volksparteien*, whose consensus-structure has favoured a panoramic approach and militated against a decisive focus on specific policy fields, had no choice but to respond to the movements and issues of the young generation (Flanagan and Dalton, 1984). The movement, however, which had given prominence to new issues such as environmentalism, nuclear energy, and missiles resorted to attacking installations, and purported to confront the political system itself whether at a perimeter fence, construction site or military barracks (Kolinsky, 1987).

Despite some links between *Volksparteien* and new social movements, a generation-gap of protest has remained clearly visible. Similar to the radicalisation which turned the tail-end of the student movement into terrorism, themes and policy styles of the new social movements have been radicalised as soon as segments of their original issues had been taken up by mainstream politics. Although the radicalisation has always cost movements their potential mass-support, it has remained potent throughout the 1970s and 1980s and has sustained a protest culture with left-wing overtones among the educated, young generation.

## The Protest Culture of the Right

On the right of the political spectrum, generational change has also developed distinct political overtones. The 1950s saw the decline party-based extremism and its electoral integration into centre-right politics. First signs that young people might be susceptible to aspects of National Socialism appeared in the late 1950s during a brief wave of anti-semitic daubing at a time when acute prejudice against Jews seemed to have been silenced if not by a change of attitudes then at least by an effective social taboo (Kolinsky, 1984). When the right-extremist National Democratic Party (NPD) enjoyed temporary electoral success in the mid-1960s most of the right-extremist support emanated from the older generations although the party attracted some young protest voters. In the 1970s, the extreme right became factionalised and radical, with a small but young clientèle. Enmity against Jews, against *Gastarbeiter* (guest-workers) and against people seeking asylum in West German drew inspiration from the racist actions of the National Socialists, and the groups adopted their language, as well as many of their aggressive and intimidating tactics, including violent assaults on individuals and communal institutions. Within the extremist right, a generational rift divides the young neo-Nazis with the activist radicalism from the more conventional right extremists whose leanings towards the National Socialist past usually stop short of physical assault. Attempts to explain why young people turn to the right, although their political socialisation should have fortified them against National Socialism and its ideological derivates, have tended to focus on two points: some argue that right-extremism continues to be latent in contemporary German society and can surface at any time. Among young people, it seems to have surfaced in the 1970s at a time of increased unemployment and the uncertainties connected with it (Silbermann and Schoeps, 1986). Others have argued that the recourse to National Socialist language, symbols and actions which has characterised neo-Nazism has to be seen as a provocative gesture intended to shock the burghers and command attention (Stöss, 1986). In this view, the young recruits to neo-Nazism are not converts to ideologies of the past, but utilise them because they carry the stigma of unacceptability. These neo-Nazis may not simply be chips off the old block but their mode of articulating their dissent indicates that they expect little from democratic practices and are willing to abandon them in favour of more fundamental change. In their radicalised detachment from political conventions and from democratic participation, the young protesters of the far right resemble the radical fringe within the alternative culture and the new social movements which we discussed earlier.

## Social Opportunities and Political Orientations

At first glance, it appears that the socio-economic circumstances and experiences which encourage left-wing and right-wing orientations among young West Germans today are distinctly different from the earlier periods. The divide is educational and occupational. Young people with left-wing preferences today tend to be academics or educated to advanced secondary level. Many have trained as teachers, social workers, sociologists, educationalists, and in a range of social sciences, humanities and caring professions, which all feed into new middle class white-collar occupations, often with civil servant status. Young people with right-wing preferences, by contrast, tend to be relatively poorly educated, work in unskilled or semi-skilled occupations usually in small firms and in small towns; those who gained qualifications have normally completed a craft apprenticeship.

The political orientations of these two clientèles can be linked to their socio-economic expectations and experiences since the early 1970s. Having been raised in a society with apparently unlimited opportunities, young people grew up expecting that in the transition from childhood to adolescence and again to adulthood they would be able to choose and obtain any training, career, lifestyle they could wish. The reforms of the 1960s and 1970s had transformed advanced education from an elite path for some 5 per cent of an age cohort to an option for an increasing number of young people. In the 1980s, 50 per cent of an age group attended grammar school, at least one in four obtained university or other tertiary qualifications. At the more immediately vocational end of the labour market, legislative changes in the early 1970s extended the range of accredited training programmes while the number of places on offer rose from near 400,000 to over 750,000 in the mid-1980s.

Despite the apparently favourable socio-economic trends the 1970s and 1980s have been decades of unfulfilled expectations for a substantial proportion of the young generation. Those in higher education were hit by the collapse of the teaching profession where recruitment has practically ceased and by the decline in entry to the civil service after graduation. Unemployment among academics had been virtually unknown in West Germany but has now risen to near 10 per cent in certain fields of expertise. Although economic forecasts show that prospects for university educated personnel are excellent, this is not true for humanities and social sciences students where opportunities have dwindled and are not likely to improve (von Rothkirch and Weidig, 1985; 1986). The response of potential students and graduates in these fields has been varied: some have opted for vocationally more secure careers in management or in technical fields and undertaken retraining after their studies. Many, however, have reacted in a post-materialist fashion and placed personal inclinations before the constraints imposed by labour market integration. From them 'not working' has become an aspect of leading an alternative lifestyle, an option which every second young West German under the age of thirty would favour. This generational cohort of non-integrated young people, for whom education failed to deliver the opportunities they had expected, has reacted to the situation by opting for an alternative culture, in which non-employment carries no stigma and social, economic and political norms or conventions bear little significance. The radical confrontations which can be part of the protest culture within the new social movements are rooted in this distance from opportunities and integrative structures.

At the opposite end of the labour market – that is, among artisans, craft apprentices or the unskilled, changes in the technological environment have made it more difficult to extend vocational training into skilled employment. In West Germany, small business enterprises provide the largest number of training places, but can offer permanent employment to only a fraction of those who qualify. Moreover, small businesses have been hit particularly hard by insolvencies and the impact of new technologies on labour processes. Although craft training continues to exist in over four hundred skills, most cannot be utilised in the sector in which they have been acquired. Instead, buoyant opportunities appear to exist for non-traditional skills such as computing, technical expertise, or administration. For young West Germans who turn to apprenticeships and vocational qualifications, employment has not become affected by post-materialist notions of alternative living, but continues to be valued as an essential dimension of a person's life (Allerbeck and Hoag, 1985). With being or remaining in work no longer certain, with loss of skill a danger or an experience for many, with the social and economic role of traditional crafts and small businesses declining, right-wing ideologies and especially their National Socialist packaging can offer an affirmation of national or racial superiority and biological certainties to counteract personal perceptions of socio-economic demotion. As has been shown for the rise of National Socialism, the most susceptible groups have not been the unemployed but those who perceive their contemporary situation as one of decline and marginality. The protest culture of the extreme right among the young generation can be traced to these discrepancies between expectations and opportunities at the vocational and unskilled sectors of the world of work; in a similar fashion, the protests to the left can today be linked to generational responses to opportunities and shortcomings in education.

## Gender, Politics, and the Participatory Culture

For the post-war generations of young West Germans, educational opportunities and choices of occupation laid the socio-economic foundations for greater political participation, expectations about democratic politics and the new value orientations with their stress on self-realisation and individual satisfaction discussed above. Whilst older generations had looked for stability, younger generations have begun to regard change and innovation as a *precondition* of democratic political life. The contemporary climate of flexibility, with issues arising at extra-parliamentary level and parties or parliaments responding with innovative adjustments of their policies, suggests that political agendas in West Germany today are set by elites, organisations and leaderships, as they have always been, but that they are also set by informal influences, action groups, individuals, public opinion and not least the radicalised actions of the protest culture. Women have been the most interesting newcomers to the participatory culture, and they are about to remodel the organisational structure of West German policy-making.

Women entered the post-war era with a special legacy of pre-democratic practices. Weimar politics were dominated by men;

although women had won active and passive voting rights in 1918, and had held 10 per cent of the seats in the National Assembly in 1919, they could not hold let alone enhance their political presence in the Reichstag, or rise to hold positions in government, in party leaderships or at other levels of the political elite. Women were largely confined to the women's sections of political parties or to the women's movements which were divided, like society as a whole, along sectarian and partisan lines.

The brief encounter with political participation came to an abrupt halt when the National Socialists seized power in 1933 and banned women from parliamentary or political office. Although the National Socialist women's organisations were headed by women who tried to salvage some of the spirit and participatory goals of the bourgeois women's movement, their brief was more limited: not to encourage participation but to enforce the ideologies of motherhood, of subordination to the purposes of state and party, of rendering service without regard for personal likes or dislikes. Women were to display loyalty and obedience, not exercise choice. Although the government attempted to recruit women into the labour force once industrial labour was in short supply and most girls had to complete compulsory periods of work, the majority of working women were channelled into the least skilled fields such as domestic or agricultural work which held few prospects of advancement and attracted the lowest pay.

Even in the post-war years, when women were often in sole charge of their families and also in paid employment they filled the gaps in a men's world and did not make gains in qualifications, status, leadership positions or, indeed, raise their aspirations. For the average West German woman of the 1940s and 1950s, normal living meant a life in the private sphere where a woman could rely on a family and husband, and afford not to work. Since many, of course, had been widowed or remained single, employment began to emerge as an important aspect of a woman's life, but in the founding years of the Federal Republic it was not regarded as a social and personal goal and a step towards equality for women in general.

In the political sphere the focus on normalisation in the private sphere meant leaving the matters of state largely to the men. Women in the 1940s and 1950s were less interested in politics than men, and they were more reluctant to turn out to vote, to join political parties, or even to hold political opinions. In politics, men seemed to be the competent citizens, women the non-comprehending ones who looked to their man to take the lead.

First signs of change in political orientations appeared in the 1960s. Women who had hitherto followed the Weimar pattern and opted for the centre-right in elections, began to consider party preferences as a matter of individual choice, not of traditional allegiances. The electoral mobility of West German women can be linked to generation, but also has to be connected especially to education and occupational qualifications. Since the mid-1960s, West German women rapidly reversed the qualification deficits which had seemed endemic in the past: girls today obtain better school results, are less likely than boys to attend the lowest level of schooling – *Hauptschule* – and have caught up with boys in advanced secondary education and *Abitur* (matriculation). In tertiary education and in professional and vocational training some women's deficits have remained, but they are on the decline and the gender gap of qualifications which had kept women in a subordinate place for so long is less and less in evidence. Instead, discrepancies have begun to emerge between women's qualifications, their expectations about work, status and advancement, and the opportunities for women in contemporary German society (Kolinsky, 1989).

For the young generations of educated and qualified women, political choice depends on how competent they personally perceive a political party to be. The CDU–CSU had entered the post-war era with a women's bonus of unquestioning support and with a majority among women voters across the age groups. Among older women, little has changed here. Among younger women, however, the SPD began to gain ground in the 1960s as it was perceived as an advocate of women's equal rights and opportunities. In the 1970s, the Social Democrats could build their position in government on the electoral support of women as the Christian Democrats had done in the 1950s (Hofmann-Göttig, 1986). In the 1980s, the expectations of equal opportunities had not been met, and none of the parties could rely on the electoral support of the educated young generation of women. The SPD lost credibility when the Schmidt government seemed to make any kind of social reform dependent on economic growth and prosperity; the CDU continues to suffer a deficiency of support among women under the age of forty; here the Greens made some gains but fell far short of a women's bonus among the young and educated, an electorally mobile generation.

Among young women, gender is no longer the barrier to the interest in political participation which it had been in the 1950s and 1960s, and which remains, albeit in a modified form, among the older generations. The traditional lower levels of electoral turnout have crumbled in particular for the age cohort between 25 and 45. The gender balance of political parties where women accounted for less than one in four members, is changing as up to 40 per cent of new members are women (Hoecker, 1987). No longer a barrier to political participation, gender has itself become an issue in politics. Growing up in conditions of affluence, socio-economic choice and personal opportunities and without the lack of qualifications which had tied their mothers or grandmothers to traditional family roles and a back seat in political life, women of the post-war generations expected to find equal opportunities where few had existed before. They began to see themselves to be on a par with men in their competence to hold political office but found equal access an elusive target in the ossified party organisations and in the face of established avenues of elite recruitment.

Where women had been reluctant in the past to join a party, or had done so only alongside their husbands, an increasing proportion of young women today is interested enough in political participation to be motivated towards membership. However, women in particular want to make a personal and visible contribution. While political parties had no difficulty in the past in containing the political activities of women in separate women's groups, wings or associations, this is no longer easy. In the SPD for instance, women had always been more numerous than in other parties but their prime function had been regarded as creating the *milieu*, the family environment in which future generations of Social Democrats would be reared. The younger generation of women who joined in the 1970s defined the party political role of women more assertively as meaning equal representation in parliaments and in party offices, and regarded the women's organisation as a pressure group to achieve those aims. After years of pleading for equality, and in the face of an increased dependence of the SPD on women's electoral support, the party has now moved towards quota regulations designed to guarantee that by the mid-1990s no less than 40 per cent of parliamentary and party offices should be held by women.

As on other issues, the Greens have taken the lead in the quota debate when they altered their party statutes in 1985 to make parity between men and women obligatory. Since then, the issue of women's equal political opportunities has become more pressing and more specifically linked to the introduction of numerical quotas. The 1987 elections at federal and regional level were the first to be dominated by a quota debate; even the CDU–CSU and FDP who oppose formal quotas, nominated more women than in the past and are slowly increasing their share of women office holders and parliamentarians. In the SPD, parliamentary representation of women has risen by 30 per cent since the mid-1980s as the new emphasis on equal access began to bite. Overall, 40 per cent more women held parliamentary seats in 1988 than in 1985; with their rule that no less than half the parliamentary candidates should be women, the Greens have made a major contribution to reducing the gender imbalance of parliamentary representation.

Competence to advance women's equality may not be a priority issue for all generations and the socio-economic groups, but it is of considerable importance among those among the female electorate who have at once been the most politically motivated and the most likely to change party preferences in line with their expectations and policy concerns. For these educated, qualified, urban, new middle class women under the age of 45, equality of opportunity is a sufficiently salient issue to determine their party orientations. And here, the Greens are regarded as the party which could turn intentions into political realities while the other parties appear less committed to equality – or, in the case of the SPD, less capable of translating the intentions of their own women members into policies and practices against the barrier of a cumbersome and hostile party organisation and an entrenched tradition of male dominance.

In the contemporary political culture, the Greens have mobilised the women's vote. To be more specific: women of the war and pre-war generations are hardly drawn to the Greens and many have remained loyal to the Christian Democrats. The very youngest, who were born around 1970 and reached voting age in the late 1980s, appear to be more detached from all parties, including the Greens; in the 1987 federal elections, about 40 per cent of this group did not vote. It is the middle-generation, women who experienced the 1960s and 1970s as adolescents and young adults and initially saw the Social Democrats as the party of democratisation and equality who now look towards the Greens as a party which might live up to its promises. This is not to say that the whole of the age cohort has swung to the Greens; rather among this age cohort, the Greens have won some ground as a trail-blazer for the right of women to equality. Some women have changed party preferences in favour of the Greens or chose the Greens once they were old enough to vote. A decade earlier these women would have looked towards the SPD for very similar reasons.

## Organisation or Participation?

The new emphasis on equal opportunities and the women's bonus of the Greens cannot be fully explained by the failure of the SPD–FDP coalition government to overcome gender imbalances in the West Germany polity. The generation of women who began to articulate their expectations and carve out a social, political and economic role for themselves in the 1970s were children not only of democracy but heirs to the participatory climate which had commenced in the 1960s. While they looked towards parties and established institutions to make their voices heard, they preferred action groups or informal movements. If women in the 1950s had shied away from formalised organisations because they felt unsure of their social status or uncertain how to compete in them effectively, the young generation of women have viewed organisational structures themselves with misgivings. They no longer feel socially ill at ease, although complaints about party meetings being held in smoke-filled back-rooms of pubs are as old as women's party membership itself. Young women today feel competent to compete but unwilling to do so on the terms set by the organisations, and that means by the men who have created them and shaped their norms. Within the young generation of women, expectations about equal opportunities encompass social, economic and political rights and positions, and this is the level which has influenced party policies. The expectations, however, also extend to the style of policy-making itself, the mode of communication between people and the scope allowed to individuals to bring their own self-realisation to bear.

In the young generation, confidence has grown that women need not adjust to existing organisations, hierarchies and competitive pressures, but that their participation should be on women's terms, should heed their preferences for consensus-based and non-hierarchical decision making, and that there is a need for a visible impact of the individual on political decisions. The notion that women need *more than* 'equal rights' gained ground in the 1970s through the women's movement, and the focus on women's issues this entailed. The movement has allegedly been born during the days of the student movement when some female protagonists of the left upstaged an SDS (Socialist Students) congress by accusing the male elite of having thoroughly reactionary attitudes towards women whom they exploited socially and sexually while denying them the right to participate on equal terms and retain their own identity.

It was only in the mid-1970s that the nascent women's movement developed a broader social and political momentum and became, for a time at least, a protest movement. Abortion was the issue which mobilised women, and it contributed significantly to sensitising the West German population to the reality of unequal opportunities. The SPD–FDP government had attempted to pass legislation to legalise abortion on demand while the CDU–CSU opposition appealed to the Constitutional Court to curtail the scope of the new law, and restrict abortions. From the vantage point of younger generation women, the controversy concerned the rights of women to determine their own affairs; the issue symbolised the demand that a woman should be free to decide over her own body.

Although the women's movement was short-lived as a mass-based protest movement, it continues to exist in a myriad of action groups, safe houses for battered wives, refuges, and other women-specific small-scale institutions and actions. It also continues to exist in public awareness of the shortfall of women's equal rights, which is higher now than in the 1950s and 1960s when the gender gap had been much more substantial. The women's movement has also sensitised the West German population, and young women in particular, to their right to be different as women, and to preserve their own identity in and through their social political or economic participation. The women's issue is no longer one of access, but one of changing the nature of institutions and the socio-economic priorities which govern them in order to accommodate women's personalities.

The focus on the personal aspects of participation is part of the broader change in the political culture towards new politics and the emphasis on specific issues and qualitative dimensions of the political process. We saw earlier that among the educated young generations new political orientations have altered the way in which young people see their place in West German party democracy. The stability of institutions is judged as less important that the articulation of specific issues and an emphasis on what has been called the 'qualitative dimension' of politics. These orientations among the young have given rise to the protest culture of extra-parliamentary opposition. Among women the generational focus on new politics is, above all, a focus on the individual, on the quality of communication, on non-hierarchical patterns of organisation and on remodelling political participation in style and, therefore, in substance. The Green party is perceived as the political party most competent to address the women's issue. We can now be more specific and outline what is meant by this: for all its parliamentary, organisational and administrative offices the Green party has instituted a 50 per cent quota. For a time, the parliamentary group in the Bundestag was led by an all-women team, and early in 1989 only women represented the Greens in the Hamburg Land parliament. In the Greens, the women have considerably more say and public prominence than in any other political party.

The majority of first-generation women members and activists were recruited from the women's movement. These women, who prided themselves in being independent of institutions and organisations, regarded the Green party as an ideal framework for putting their political views into practice. The draft anti-discrimination legislation of 1986 which calls for an abolition of the gender-gap in all walks of life, and demands preferential treatment for women until the gender imbalances are ironed out, extended the expectations of the women's movements into the parliamentary arena. Within the party organisation, Green women have pressed for new patterns of communication and new personal styles. These subjective dimensions proved destabilising in a young party which interpreted its commitment to participatory politics as a commitment to stem professionalisation and encourage a rotation of offices, the regular involvement of members and affiliated movements and engage in other experiments of organisational *glasnost* – all of them doomed to fail in the face of the need for parliamentary efficiency and the strong impact of personalities in a party with so few organisational constraints (Hülsberg, 1988; Kolinsky, 1988). The women's plea to have their individuality accepted as the basis for Green party communication and policy-making shifted inner-party attention from issues or strategies to personal behaviour. The absence of agreed organisational channels already meant that personalities could wield undue influence in the Greens; the personal slant of the women's issue intensified the acrimonious climate of interpersonal rivalries, bickering and in-fighting.

The hopes to set up the Green party as a haven for alternative expectations, lifestyles and attitudes have not been fulfilled. Instead, the perception of the Greens as a vessel for partisan issues and partial protests by sections of the multi-faceted protest culture have weakened the role the party might play to innovate West German party politics and parliamentary decision-making by means of a new and specific focus on neglected aspects of social, economic or political change. The swing to self-realisation has sidestepped this challenge by stipulating that people and their attitudes need to change before issues can be tackled in substance and innovative improvements attempted. The manner in which the issue of women's opportunities was articulated in the women's movement and in the Green party has shifted it from a reform of circumstances to a rebirth of people's nature. This cul-de-sac of self-realisation enhances the attractions of the Greens as a protest party, but seems to return the initiative for policy changes to the more established forces in the party system.

# 14

# Environmental Politics

## WILLIAM E. PATERSON

*Der sterbende Wald* (the dying forest), the expression used by Germans to describe the plight of Germany's forests has become the best known German catchphrase of the 1980s outside Germany. its ubiquity is eloquent testimony to the saliency of environmental concerns and their political resonance in the Federal Republic. The growth in environmental consciousness since 1970 has had a major impact on public policy priorities and underpinned the emergence of the Greens as a parliamentary force. An analysis of its causes and effects therefore is central to any judgement about the future trajectory of the political and economic systems of West Germany.

## The Organisation of Environmentalism

A people of social movements (Joachim Raschke).

Environmentalist groups have existed in Germany since the late nineteenth century. Their appeal was often based on the articulation of explicitly anti-industrial value. These values sometimes attracted considerable support, especially in periods of recession as at the end of the 1920s and part of the electoral success of Hitler and the NSDAP is to be explained by their success in tapping anti-industrial sentiments. Environmental groups were only slowly re-established after 1945. The territory of the Federal Republic included Germany's core industrial areas and the stark imperatives of post-war reconstruction imposed a much less equivocal endorsement of industrial values. All the major parties were committed to an industrial society. Environmentalist groups also suffered from the parallel that was often drawn with the views of the National Socialists. That their anti-industrialism very largely applied to their period in opposition and that once in power they had been eager industrialisers was less often mentioned.

The *Deutscher Naturschutz-Ring* (German nature conservation circle), the first post-war national environmentalist organisation, was not founded until 1950. It was concerned with the protection of the interests of the hunting, shooting and fishing fraternity and with minimising the impact of industry upon the countryside rather than confronting industrial society head on. It was and remained a fairly ineffective organisation on the right of the political spectrum which attempted to cultivate an 'insider' status with the Federal government.

The strong identification of environmentalist positions with the right began to alter in the 1960s and a plan for dealing with air pollution in the Ruhr ('Blue skies over the Ruhr') was a major plank in the SPD's electoral programme of 1961. Despite the 1961 election programme, the left in the Federal Republic remained overwhelmingly committed to policy positions designed to encourage unrestricted economic growth. By the end of the 1960s a strong counterposition, emphasising ecological positions, had emerged even if the existing priorities had not yet been displaced. This counter-position strongly reflected generational cleavages. The post-war and its immediate successor generation reacted to extreme economic scarcity. The generation which came to maturity in the late 1960s had enjoyed a long and sustained period of prosperity and, unsurprisingly, did not assign such a high priority to maintaining it. They embraced rather post-material quality of life issues like environmental protection. The emergence of so-called 'sunshine' politics was also a product of the massive expansion in higher education in West Germany during the 1960s (Baker, Dalton and Hildebrandt, 1981).

The new saliency of environmental positions was reflected in the creation of two national environmental organisations, the Bund (Environmental Protection Federation, 1970) and the BBU (Federal Association of Citizens' Initiatives in Environmental Protection, 1972). The Bund most nearly approximates to the Anglo–American model of environmental interest groups with individual members and has consistently been concerned to negotiate with government in the style of an orthodox interest group. It is significant that it was founded in Bavaria, at that time the only Land to have a separate Environmental Ministry. The BBU by contrast is the peak association of citizen's initiatives active in environmental policy. Citizens' initiatives emerged in the early 1960s. Unlike the established political parties, citizens' initiatives were not primarily concerned with the electoral battle but were groups of concerned citizens who had banded together to oppose unwelcome developments by official agencies or by the private sector. The commitment of the established parties to economic growth and the interdependence between the parties and the bureaucracy rendered them unsuitable vehicles of protest. The established parties and interest groups concentrated in parliamentary action while citizens' initiatives were prepared to employ a whole battery of strategies and had few reservations about direct action. They were almost all locally based.

The foundation of a peak-level association, the BBU, at first made little difference and the initiative remained at the local level with the BBU being relatively little known before 1975. The turning-point was the series of demonstrations against the building of a nuclear plant at Wyhl in the Rhineland Palatinate. This episode had the effect of greatly increasing the visibility and popularity of the citizens' initiatives or the new social movements as they were just beginning to be called (see the section 'The Politics of Nuclear Power', below).

The success of the demonstrations at Wyhl coincided with a crisis of the radical left in the Federal Republic. The prospects of the radical left were significantly reduced by the introduction of the *Radikalenerlass* (Radical's Decree) against the employment of radicals in the public service in January 1972. This was designed to, and did, reduce the reservoir of support for the radical left by imposing potential penalties on those who identified with it. The *Radikalenerlass* was directed particularly strongly against the so-called *K. Gruppen* (K-groups) a bewildering array of unorthodox communist groups, largely Maoist in inspiration. The Young Socialists or *Jusos* were also affected by the introduction of the *Radikalenerlass* but they were much more immediately affected by the transition from Willy Brandt to Helmut Schmidt in June 1974. Willy Brandt had encouraged former members of the extra-parliamentary opposition (APO) to come into the SPD after 1968 and was indulgent towards the *Jusos* while according them little influence on governmental policy. Helmut Schmidt, coming to power after the oil price crisis, made no secret of his distaste for, or impatience with, the *Jusos* and the party leadership swiftly set about reducing the resources available to them and their role in party discussion.

Both the K-Groups and the *Jusos* had up until then regarded the environmental issue as a diversion from more important issues and had shown little interest in it. The K-Groups pursued Maoist goals and the *Jusos* were preoccupied with the factional struggle inside the SPD. The *Jusos*' fondness for highly academic discourses on capitalism and the state had severely reduced their capacity to mobilise support. Both groups were attracted by two aspects of the demonstrations at Wyhl: firstly, the political awareness that site occupations and 'repressive' police behaviour aroused. Secondly, they perceived the political resources which could be mobilised through a focus on Wyhl and the anti-nuclear cause: 'The events at Wyhl had been met with considerable public sympathy for the local opposition movement. Public opinion on nuclear energy shifted markedly. *"Bürgerinitiativen"* (citizens' initiatives) had acquired a very positive public image. Public trust in them was higher than in most other political institutions and groups, including political parties and governments. In the nuclear case, the commitment of established political parties and governments to nuclear energy and the identification of citizens' initiatives with the anti-nuclear cause provided the left with a new chance. None of its campaigns had been particularly popular. The anti-nuclear cause suddenly presented an opportunity to change this' (Rüdig, 1986, pp. 276–7).

Henceforward the K-Gruppen and many *Jusos* invested a great deal of their energy in environmental movements. They were joined in this by the less organised radical left, the *Spontis* who were attracted by the possibilities for direct action and confrontation with the authorities. Environmental politics was now moving much more strongly away from its location on the right of German politics and was increasingly identified with the radical left.

The reduced willingness of the SPD–FDP government to introduce more far-reaching environmental policies after Helmut Schmidt became chancellor, coinciding as it did with the new-found interest of the *Jusos* in environmental and especially anti-nuclear policy, deepened the cleavage between the *Jusos* and the party leadership. During Schmidt's leadership they were consistently, though often narrowly, defeated on environmental issues and more and more they dropped out of activity inside the SPD and transferred their political energies to the environmental movements.

The late 1970s and early 1980s were a golden period for environmental movements in the Federal Republic. The Federal Environmental Agency reported 1,500 citizens' initiatives with 5 million members registered with it in 1981. The BBU was enormously active in this period. It had been very skilfully led by Hans Helmut Wüstenhagen, Chairman from 1973–7. His successors included the very able Jo Leinen who became environmental minister in the Saar from 1985. One striking development was the increased ability of the citizens' initiatives to mobilise sympathetic expert opinion from within the scientific community to challenge industrial opinion on issues like the correct standards to be adopted in relation to the Federal Emission Law. Some of the scientists working for the Federal Environmental Agency were very sympathetic and an Öko-Institut (ecological institute) was founded in Freiburg in 1977 to provide further scientific backing for environmentalist parties.

The environmental movements continue to exist, but they have lost much of their centrality. The BBU in particular is much less active than it was and is plagued by continual financial and personnel crises. By 1985 the number of affiliated organisations had sunk to around 350 from a high of over 1,000. The environmental groups have to a large extent been displaced by the political parties. The Greens-Alternatives, both at the parliamentary level and through myriad ecological projects, provide a rival rather than a complementary pole of attraction. The electoral success of the Greens was a major factor in transforming the SPD to a more ecological position (see the case studies below) and ecologists have found the SPD a much friendlier environment since the end of the Schmidt government. The transition of the SPD helped weaken the BBU since it precipitated endless disputes between those, like Jo Leinen, who argued that the BBU should support ecological initiatives in all parties, and those who wanted to have an exclusive relationship with the Greens. Environmental movements have not disappeared but attention is now focused much more on the German section of Greenpeace, which is hooked into an international network, than the BBU, and on a splinter movement from Greenpeace which adopted the name 'Robin Wood' to dramatise its fight to control air pollution and rescue 'the dying forest'. Local initiatives continue to be extremely active, however, when threats to the environment emerge.

## The Emergence of the Greens

The decision to found the Green Party in 1980 occurred only after years of extra-parliamentary activity by a very wide range of groups articulating the various issues that together make up 'the new politics'. By 1977 there was considerable tension within the environmentalist movement between the radical left, who saw environmental protest as part of a wider rejection of the capitalist system, and who were more prepared to contemplate violent political protest, and environmentalists, who wanted to co-operate with established parties and institutions where possible. Right wing and left wing environmentalists began forming rival lists to compete in Länder and local elections.

The competition between right wing and left wing ecological groups was clearly a major impediment to surmounting the 5 per cent electoral threshold and in July 1978 right and left wing groups combined in Bavaria to fight the Bavarian Land election of October 1978 as *Die Grünen* (the Greens). The Bavarian Cooperation Model quickly became the rule in other Länder.

Potential support for the Greens increased markedly in 1979 with the dramatic growth in the Peace Movement attendant upon the adoption by NATO of the dual-track resolution which provided for the large-scale stationing on German soil of Cruise and Pershing Missiles should the Soviets fail to withdraw their SS–20s from Eastern Europe.

The catalyst for the formation of the Greens was provided by the first Direct Elections to the European Parliament in 1979. Participation in the election held out the promise of enough financial support to maintain a permanent organisational infrastructure since any party competing in the election would receive DM.3.50 from state subsidies for every vote it gained. A federal congress of the Greens was held in Frankfurt in March 1979 at which it was agreed to launch a proto party 'Die Sonstige Politische Vereinigung (SPV): Die Grünen' (the alternative political association: The Greens). In order to conform with West German electoral law the party elected an executive committee but no agreement was reached on an electoral programme or a formal organisation framework.

The SPV achieved 3.2 per cent in the European election and at a Conference in Karlsruhe in January 1980 a decision to form a Green Party was taken by over 90 per cent of the delegates, though it took a further conference at Saarbrücken in March 1980 to adopt an agreed formula. During these discussions the left, who argued in favour of a party that was both ecological and adopted a generally left wing stance on other issues, triumphed and the final programme clearly placed the Greens to the left of the SPD on the party spectrum.

The successful entry of the Greens into the Bundestag in 1983 and their increased support in 1987 has transformed the role of environmental concerns in the making of public policy in the Federal Republic. Ecological issues are only one of the sets of issues that are articulated by the Greens, but they are the most electorally salient and those which other parties, especially the SPD, cannot afford to ignore. There has been some variation across sectors but in the two central sectors of nuclear energy and chemicals control that we shall look at in some detail there has been a considerable impact.

The organisational philosophy of the Greens with its stress on 'openness' and the fluctuating nature of participation at party conferences means that any consistent strategy to realise environmental goals and to build upon policy gains already made is extremely difficult, and this sets a limit to the effectiveness of the Greens in transforming environmental perspectives into long-term policy victories.

## Governmental Policy

Governmental policy during the first two decades of the Federal Republic gave a fairly low priority to environmental measures. No major statute was introduced between the Nature Protection Law (*Reichsnaturschutzgesetz*, 1935) and a series of major enactments in the SPD–FDP coalition. Priority in these years was given to the restoration of production and the expansion of exports.

### The SPD–FDP Governments

The advent of the Brandt-Scheel government in 1969 marked a clear break with previous practice. The government saw itself as a reform government not in terms of redistribution between capital and labour but as articulating a number of issues in external policy, education and environmental policy alongside the basic consensus which had developed in the first two decades of the Federal Republic.

In environmental policy, as in other policy areas, the two Brandt governments (1969–74) were in favour of more far-reaching reform than the three governments led by Helmut Schmidt. The Brandt government issued an Emergency Programme for Environmental Protection in 1970 and the First Environmental Programme in 1971. These initiatives stressed the 'polluter pays' principle (*Verursacherprinzip*, modified however by the criterion of economic responsibility (*Kooperationsprinzip*). These first laws were in general not sector specific and were calculated not to impose too heavy costs on industry. The junior coalition partner, the FDP, has always seen itself as the most 'industry friendly' of the established parties. The FDP held the two most important ministerial portfolios in relation to environmental policy, those of Economics and the Interior. The desire of Hans-Dietrich Genscher, the interior minister, and some of his leading civil servants, notably Günter Hartkopf, one of the two state secretaries, to institute ambitious reforms, was checked by the Economics Ministry which sees itself as an attorney for German industry. The most important of these early laws were the *Abfallbeseitigungsgesetz* (Waste Disposal Law, 1972) and the *Bundesimissionsschutzgesetz* (Emission Protection Law, 1972).

A much more threatening development as far as industry was concerned was the move towards a more open, more anticipatory mode of decision-making in this policy sector. An *Arbeitsgemeinschaft für Umweltfragen* (working group for environmental questions, AGU) was established in 1971 to act as a source of policy advice for the federal government on environmental issues. the AGU incorporated all the relevant interest groups, including the environmental groups who expanded rapidly after 1975. These groups were in a small minority in the AGU but they developed good relations with the Interior Ministry, the Ministry responsible for environmental policy. Further nervousness on the part of industry was occasioned by the foundation of two new institutions, The *Sachverständigenrat für Umweltfragen* (Expert Commission on Environmental Questions) in 1972 and the *Umweltbundesamt* (Federal Environment Agency) in West Berlin in 1974. The establishment of these bodies appeared to be a signal that the government was no longer going to depend exclusively on 'the closed circle of experts' for advice on the formulation and implementation of environmental policy, but was going to go beyond industry and the established scientific community for advice.

These gains for the environmentalist position were largely dissipated by the advent of the Schmidt government in 1974. The oil price rise of 1973 and the ensuing difficulties for the Western economies led to the reassertion of a relatively narrow view of economic priorities and a move away from anticipatory, participatory mode of decision making to a rather narrower focus on crisis management. The reassertion of economic priorities was a major theme at the so-called Gymnich discussions in 1975. Schmidt gave unequivocal priority to economic goals and his views on environmental questions were much influenced by conversations with top union and management officials from Bayer Chemicals. Schmidt's position was energetically supported by Count Otto von Lambsdorff, the economics minister (1978–84), who was a major constraint on the environmental enthusiasm of his FDP colleague, Gerhart Baum, at the Interior Ministry (1977–82). The pace of legislative enactments slackened and the *Abwasserabgabengesetz* (Waste Water Tax Law, 1976) and *Bundesnaturschutzgesetz* (Federal Natural Conservation Law, 1976) were notably weaker than their immediate predecessors. It also became increasingly clear that whatever legislation was enacted industry was in a position to ensure that its interests remained protected at the implementation stage and disappointed environmentalists began to use the term '*Vollzugsdefizit*' (implementation shortfall) (Richardson and Watts, 1985, p. 28).

Schmidt's decision to reduce the priority given to environmental goals coincided with a steady rise in environmental consciousness. The result was growing tension within the SPD and a strengthening of the environmentalist movements which provided the basis for the establishment of the Greens and a long-term strengthening of the priority given to environmental policy.

## Environmental Policy of the Kohl Government

The advent of an industry-friendly government in 1982 might have been expected to reduce the displacement of environmental policy in the legislative programme of the Federal government. The electoral success of the Greens and the continued electoral saliency of environmental policy has ensured that this has not been the case. Moreover, a series of incidents or environmental damage, some like Chernobyl in foreign countries, have kept environmental protection measures high up on the political agenda. The parlous state of much German woodland focused environmental attention on the alleged environmental effects of car exhausts. Whilst the 'dying forest' is illustrative of the way in which long-term environmental damage can affect environmental consciousness, the Chernobyl nuclear accident in May 1986 and large-scale spillages by the German chemicals companies into the Rhine in Winter 1986 demonstrates the degree to which dramatic incidents force environmental control still further up the political agenda.

In its first six years the Kohl government introduced few totally novel environmental regulations but has concentrated on updating and extending existing environmental legislation (e.g., the Federal Emission Law). The increased importance of environmental issues has been reflected less in new legislation than in the creation of a Ministry for Environmental Protection and Reactor Safety (*Ministerium für Umwelt, Naturschutz und Reaktorensicherheit*). The creation of an Environment Ministry has been informally considered by earlier governments but it quickly ran up against the problem of coalition balance. Environmental questions were largely handled by the Interior Ministry which was headed by an FDP minister. Creating a new ministry, unless it were to be headed by a minister from the FDP, would have been unacceptable to the FPD and such a solution would have been unacceptable to the SPD. In CDU–CSU–FDP governments since 1982 the Interior Ministry was headed by a CSU minister. This reduced, but did not entirely eliminate, the barrier to the creation of a new Ministry since the CSU can be regarded for some purposes as more of a coalition partner and less a part of the same party as the CDU.

The stimulus needed to create a separate Environmental Ministry was provided by the Chernobyl nuclear disaster of May 1986. This coincided with a vital Land election in Lower Saxony. Faced with the prospect of losing considerable electoral support as a result of public disquiet on the nuclear issue, the response of Chancellor Kohl was not, as in the case of the SPD leadership, to think about a change of policy in relation to nuclear power, but to create a Ministry for Environmental Protection and Reactor Safety which would hopefully be enough to preserve the electoral position of the CDU without making policy concessions. The position of Friedrich Zimmermann, the CSU incumbent had been weakened by a very unconvincing handling of public information and safety standards in the wake of the Chernobyl disaster. In the event the CDU secured a one-seat majority in the Land election.

Walter Wallmann took over the newly created Ministry in June 1986. The Ministry inherited the competences which had formerly belonged to a number of ministries, principally the Interior Ministry. The prestige of the new Ministry, and Walter Wallmann in particular, was dented by the chemical spillages into the Rhine in Winter 1986 since shortly after coming to office he had endorsed the chemical industry's view that it was better able than the state to provide environmental protection in its own area. Wallmann resigned in Spring 1987 after the CDU won the Land election in Hesse and was replaced by Klaus, Töpfer, the environment minister in the Rheinland-Palatinate and a respected environmental expert. The changes at the Federal government level had been anticipated by the Länder beginning with Bavaria in 1970. The creation of the Ministry also led, followed normal German practice, to the creation of a Bundestag Committee to shadow the Ministry. Under Klaus Töpfer the Ministry has gone some way to establishing itself. It is handicapped by a rather restricted budget (1.8 per cent of the Federal budget) but the saliency of environmental issues means it cannot be ignored. There has been continued tension with the Research Ministry which has made itself a more outspoken supporter than the Economics Ministry of an 'industry-friendly' approach to a number of environmental issues including reactor safety and biotechnology and which has the financial resources to sponsor a large number of research projects in the general area of environmental protection.

## The Politics of Nuclear Energy

In any explanation of the growth of environmental consciousness in the Federal Republic anti-nuclear sentiment is normally accorded a central role (Rüdig, 1986). This fear of civil nuclear power is a relatively recent phenomenon, however, though there have been a series of extra-parliamentary movements against nuclear weapons since the mid-1950s. The assumption, in the Federal Republic as elsewhere, that the generation of nuclear power carried little environmental risk was almost unchallenged and there was little dissent from this view within the German scientific community. This was crucial given the 'socially invisible' character of the environmental threat posed by nuclear power. Scientific worries about the safety of nuclear power did not surface in Germany until the early 1970s, and then only in the reporting and translation of US scientists (Rüdig, 1986, p. 179). The first expression of expert dissent by Klaus Traube, a senior scientist in the West German nuclear industry, occurred only after the anti-nuclear movement had taken off in 1975.

## Growth of the Anti-nuclear Movement

The high energy dependence of the Federal Republic and the potential markets in nuclear technology led the Federal government to create the Ministry for Atomic Questions in 1955. The purpose of the Ministry was to encourage and oversee the development of a West German nuclear industry by the private sector. Some progress was made but the availability of cheap oil supplies meant that it was not seen as an overriding priority. This situation was dramatically altered by the oil price rise of 1973 and the increased effectiveness of OPEC. Chancellor Schmidt presided over a programme which envisaged a very major expansion in the proportion of national energy needs to be supplied by nuclear power. The formulation of this programme was relatively uncontentious, but its implementation was to trigger off the growth of a mass anti-nuclear movement.

The catalyst for the anti-nuclear movement turned out to be the siting policy adopted for the construction of the many new nuclear reactors required by the programme. The indigenous production of nuclear weapons in the Federal Republic was forbidden under the Paris Treaty (1955) and this precluded the option of using sites originally developed for military purposes. In Britain, France and the United States development on former military sites has been associated with an absence of local opposition. Unlike Britain or the United States, the Federal Republic possesses almost no wilderness, and the option of siting in a really remote site like Dounreay in Northern Scotland was unavailable. The third option less likely to provoke dissent initially was to expand at existing sites. The large number of electricity utility companies (12) and the desire at that time of individual Länder governments for potentially cheaper energy in their area precluded development on existing sites and favoured a policy of dispersed siting.

*The Wyhl Effect*

> While in France the issue-making process extended over years, in West Germany there was one incident above all which made nuclear energy a national issue, the conflict between policy and local people at Wyhl early in 1975 (Rüdig, 1986, p. 191).

The decision to site a nuclear reactor at Wyhl in Baden-Württemberg was to prove a fateful error on the art of those responsible for implementing the nuclear programme of the Federal Government. Wyhl is a sleepy village near the Kaiserstuhl, a major wine-growing area. Local wine-growers were worried by the extension of industrialisation into what had been an almost exclusively agricultural area. They were worried initially not so much by the issue of reactor safety but the effect of the cooling towers on the micro-climate and therefore ultimately on their product.

Wyhl also lies close to Freiburg and its large university. Once the first demonstrations occurred student support arrived quickly, but it took very insensitive police tactics in clearing the site to turn it into a major issue and ten days after the site had initially been occupied by local residents, it was reoccupied by 28,000 people. At that point the Land government abandoned plans to clear the site and less than a month later an administrative court withdrew the construction licence.

The events at Wyhl persuaded the radical left to become deeply involved in the environmental issue and the Wyhl tactics were widely imitated. It was Wyhl which really launched the environmental movement which was henceforward to be a factor of major importance in the implementation of the nuclear programme.

*Impact of the Anti-nuclear Movement 1975–86*

In a very influential article Herbert Kitschelt (Kitschelt, 1986) uses the concept of political opportunity structures to examine the impact of anti-nuclear movements across four systems. Kitschelt views political opportunity structures as being 'comprised of specific configurations of resources, institutional arrangements and historical precedents for social mobilization, which facilitate the development of protest movements in some instances and constrain them in others (Kitschelt, 1986, p. 58).

The concept of political opportunity structure is not new but it is normally used only in relation to the input processes of political decision cycles where a distinction is made between open and closed systems. Kitschelt refines it to include political outputs – i.e., how a political system actually implements a decision (p. 63). This distinction is especially useful in relation to the Federal Republic where political input structures appear relatively 'closed', but political output structures are relatively weak (see Table 14.1).

TABLE 14.1 *Political opportunity structures in France, Sweden, West Germany and the United States*

| | | Political input structures | |
|---|---|---|---|
| | | Open | Closed |
| Political output structures | Strong | Sweden | France |
| | Weak | United States | West Germany |

Source: Kitschelt (1986) p.64.

## Political Inputs and Outputs

Social movement theorists categorise a system as 'open' when the legislature has the capacity to develop and control policies independently of the executive, where patterns of interest intermediation between interest groups and the executive are 'pluralist' and fluid and where new policy demands are taken up and find their way into the policy consensus. By contrast, the West German system is relatively 'closed'. The Bundestag has little capacity to operate independently of the executive and policy in this area was almost exclusively made by a closed circle of experts from the executive and industry. The Ministry primarily responsible for regulating this area, the Interior Ministry, was shadowed by a Bundestag Committee but its expertise lay in the more traditional areas of the Ministry's interest. The tight and relatively harmonious relationships between established interest groups and the executive in the Federal Republic looms large in any examination of the Federal Republic but the establishment of the AGU and the access it gave to environmental groups must slightly qualify our perception of the West German system as 'closed'. The close links between established economic interest groups and the dominant peoples' parties and the continued economic success of the West German model made it very difficult to get new demands on the policy agenda.

The predominantly 'closed' nature of the West German system had clear effects on both the tactics and impact of the anti-nuclear movement. The 'closed' nature of the input system encouraged confrontation strategies against the political process and this was to be the *leitmotif* of political action by the anti-nuclear movement from

Wyhl onwards. This did not mean that more conventional attempts at influencing policy were not pursued, however. A sustained attempt was made to change the policy of the SPD and after 1983 to exert some influence on policy through the Greens' parliamentary party.

The results were on the whole not very encouraging from the anti-nuclear perspective. The confrontation tactics did succeed in mobilising a great deal of support, but it proved very difficult to transform this into greatly increased influence at Federal level. A parliamentary commission on nuclear energy convened in 1979 produced an ambivalent report in the election year of 1980 but after the election in 1982 a majority of the commissioners very largely supported the planned nuclear programme.

The SPD federal leadership successfully resisted attempts to alter the party's pro-nuclear policy though with increasing difficulty and in some areas such as Hamburg the local SPD leadership became anti-nuclear. The formation and electoral success of the Greens was clearly a gain for the anti-nuclear movement and provided a platform for further advance.

## Blocking Mechanisms

While the relatively closed character of the formation process was unpromising terrain for the anti-nuclear movement, the implementation process was much more promising and offered a number of opportunities for successful blocking tactics. Two aspects of the process were of particular importance.

### The Licensing System

The licensing system faithfully reflects the federal nature of the political system. The laws which govern the licensing arrangements are framed by the Federal government and Länder governments have to follow Federal regulations although free to develop additional guidelines. The granting of building permits and operating licenses is however in the first instance a Land responsibility. Local opposition to a project thus had a potentially greater impact than it would have done if licensing had been exclusively a Federal responsibility since Land governments have found it more difficult to ignore the potential electoral effect of opposition. The Land decision can be overturned if the relevant Federal minister (till 1986 interior, then environmental minister) overrules it on the grounds that it does not correspond to Federal guidelines. The result has been a pattern of delay at the Land level followed on some occasions by Federal intervention. Federal intervention was constrained after 1979 by the Federal-State 'Declaration of Principles' which instructed regulators not to licence additional nuclear plants until satisfactory arrangements existed for reprocessing and waste management (Campbell, 1988, p. 175). The result has been focused and often successful pressure by the anti-nuclear movement on projected reprocessing and waste disposal sites. In this connection the CDU government of Lower Saxony was caught in 1979 between the SPD–FDP federal government's desire to have it grant a licence to the plant in Gorleben and a Green Movement which burgeoned after Three Mile Island. The Land government refused a licence and the federal government had to fudge an interim solution (Rüdig, 1986, p. 312).

The licensing procedure provided for public hearings of a decidedly constrained and formalistic character. Only local citizens are allowed to make statements; no opportunity is allowed for cross-examination and they are of very limited duration. Reasonable doubt existed about their impartiality. Campbell cites the case where the official in charge of licensing was also the acting vice-chairman of the electricity utility that had commissioned the reactor (Campbell, 1988, p. 163). The restricted opportunities for public participation stimulated confrontational strategies on the part of the anti-nuclear movement. The streamlining of the licensing procedures by the Federal government in 1981–2 did nothing to lessen this tendency.

*The Courts*

The courts probably constituted the major barrier to the implementation of the nuclear programme and the anti-nuclear movement made frequent and often successful recourse to them. By 1979, three of the eleven plants under construction had lost their construction permits and four more had been halted because of actual or threatened suits (Campbell, 1988, p. 164). In 1984 the average construction delay had risen to 42.4 months in the Federal Republic (Kitschelt, 1986, p. 80).

The cumulative effect of the anti-nuclear movement had been to delay and greatly increase the cost of the nuclear programme. It had also been able to greatly slow down the rate of ordering of new plants. Against this all the established parties and economic interests remained in favour of the programme and the very high costs of energy in Germany meant that the steep increase in the cost of the programme was not quite the decisive blow to the prospects of the nuclear industry it would have been elsewhere.

## After Chernobyl

The disaster at the Chernobyl nuclear plant in the Ukraine in May 1986 made a dramatic impact on the nuclear policy debate in the Federal Republic. It coincided with a crucial Land election in Lower Saxony where public consciousness of the environmental risks associated with nuclear power had already been heightened by repeated controversies about the Gorleben plant and the Greens seemed set to do well. The response of the Federal government was to create a new Ministry for Environment and Reactor Safety. Opinion inside the SPD had been turning increasingly against nuclear power since the late 1970s while the party policy continued unaltered. Under the impact of Chernobyl and the need to compete with the Greens, the SPD reversed its policy to one of complete withdrawal from nuclear power within ten years. The German nuclear industry was so worried by the effect of Chernobyl on public opinion and the SPD's *volte-face* that it spent over DM.25 million on publicity during the Federal election campaign of 1986–7.

The conversion of the SPD and the Greens' increased electoral success brought about an increasingly parliamentary focus to anti-nuclear activity. This tendency was encouraged by the creation of a full Bundestag Committee on the Environment and Reactor Safety to shadow the new Ministry. Demonstrations against nuclear sites especially at Brokdorf and at the proposed reprocessing plant in Wackersdorf in Bavaria continued. The increasing level of violence associated with these demonstrations was generally held to be counter-productive.

The Federal government has remained committed to nuclear power and has tried to defuse the issue by bringing out a series of regulations to tighten nuclear safety. Its position has been weakened by the continued failure of the nuclear industry to develop arrangements for waste disposal and reprocessing. The industry's already poor image was weakened by a series of scandals involving nuclear-waste transport companies in early 1988.

It has also led to a series of running battles with SPD–led Länder governments – e.g., the new SPD energy minister in Schleswig-Holstein cancelled the operating licence of Brokdorf in Summer 1988. This decision was then reversed by the Federal environmental minister Töpfer. More worryingly for the government, Lothar Späth, minister-president of Baden-Württemberg, conveyed to Chancellor Kohl in Summer 1988 his worries about the nuclear programme and his decision that the two large electricity utilities in Baden-Württemberg would no longer make a financial contribution to the completion of the fast breeder reactor at Kalkar.

The very high price of German coal and the fears of energy-dependent sectors of German industry like chemicals of a major rise in energy prices if there is a withdrawal from nuclear power which now supplies about 40 per cent of German needs, preclude any speedy decision.

The future prospects for the German nuclear industry on the other hand appear fairly restricted. No new nuclear power stations are scheduled to be opened before the year 2000, and it seems fairly unlikely that the industry can expect many new orders from domestic clients, though the USSR government agreed to purchase a number of German nuclear reactors during the Kohl visit of Autumn 1988. In a little over a dozen years, helped by the Three Mile Island and Chernobyl accidents, the anti-nuclear movement has succeeded in splitting a very well established consensus in favour of nuclear policy and so inhibiting and constraining the implementation of the West German nuclear programme as to rule out the development of a successful German nuclear industry.

## The Politics of Chemicals Control

The reactive processes involved in chemicals production carry with them some risk of environmental damage. At the time of the large-scale expansion of the industry in the nineteenth century a central process, the Leblanc process for the production of alkalis gave rise to very visible pollution through the large-scale emission of clouds of hydrogen chloride. The response of the Imperial government was to introduce legislation controlling emissions from chemical plants into the air and the aquatic environment. The regulatory regime was not very restrictive, however, and the profitability of the German chemical industry meant that it was easily able to bear the costs of compliance.

Subsequently, the balance tilted very strongly towards self-regulation by the industry. The industry's spectacular scientific and technological achievement, aided by the requirements of the German state in two world wars, led to a much greater dependence of the state on the chemical industry. Technical advances and the replacement of the Leblanc process meant that the pollution created by the chemical industry, as in the nuclear industry, was often 'socially invisible' – i.e., its effects were not noticeable by the general public. Questions of environmental protection in relation to the chemical industry were settled in an expert dialogue between industry and the bureaucracy which emphasised self-regulation by the industry and almost completely excluded environmental groups and political parties.

This pattern very largely persisted throughout the SPD–FDP government. Very little of the environmental legislation enacted was sector specific. One major exception was the Chemicals Law of 1980 which attempted to regulate the entry of new chemicals onto the market. This Chemicals Law was the German implementation legislation of an EC Directive (Grant, Paterson and Whitson, 1988). Those political forces inside the Federal Republic, principally environmental groups, especially the BBU and the Interior Ministry, which would have liked a more stringent law were easily overwhelmed by the chancellor, the Economics Ministry and a parliamentary opinion which was predominantly sympathetic to the expert testimony of the chemical industry mediated through the VCI (*Verband der Chemischen Industrie*, Chemical Industries Association).

The break with self-regulation in the ensuing legislation was only minimal, however. The Chemicals Law is essentially a notification procedure where the firms carry out the great bulk of the tests on the new chemicals and the state regulatory agencies function as backstops. In this sense it is best seen as an example of 'regulated self-regulation'.

The chemical industry had to make surprisingly few concessions to environmentalist pressures in the SPD–FDP period and its major policy principle of self-regulation was more or less intact. It is interesting at this point to compare it with the nuclear industry. Where the nuclear industry had been the subject of furious demonstrations since 1975, the chemical industry attracted much less attention. A number of explanations suggest themselves. The chemical industry was a very long established and economically successful industry. It was expanding in the 1970s but almost exclusively on the basis of existing sites where people in the surrounding areas were very likely to be employed by the industry. Unlike the nuclear industry there was almost no expert dissent within the scientific community. The result was that environmentalist groups like the BBU devoted relatively little attention to the chemical industry. Within the SPD and the wider labour movement, IG Chemie (the chemical workers' union) played a very effective role in keeping the environmental effects of the chemical industry off the political agenda.

## The Changing Political Climate

Paradoxically the political climate for the maintenance of the self-regulation model in relation to environmental policy has significantly weakened since the 'industry-friendly' CDU–CSU–FDP government came to power in 1982. The principal reason for this is the entry of the Greens into the Bundestag after the federal election of March 1983. The success of the Greens reflected, and very much reinforced, the political salience of environmental issues in the Federal Republic. The impact of the Greens was felt first on the SPD, which felt the need for a much stronger profile on environmental issues in order to compete with the Greens. Its most important initiative in relation to the chemical sector was its so-called chemicals policy (*Konzept für eine Umwelt und Gesundheitsverträgliche Chemiepolitik*), which it announced in April 1986. This policy was basically concerned to tighten up the procedures for the introduction of new chemical substances. Its major, and very unwelcome innovation to the chemical industry, was the concept of 'social net benefit'. This concept specified that new products should be introduced only if their production represented the minimal possible danger to plant workers and the environment, if their introduction would lead to the use of fewer resources in production, and if their production represented the least possible danger to health and the environment.

## The Greens

The entry of the Greens into the Bundestag in 1983 posed significant potential problems for the chemical industry. In practice, however, the Greens concentrated on nuclear energy and peace issues in the Bundestag, and the major conflict between the Greens and the chemical industry occurred at the Land level when a leading Green, Joschka Fischer, became environmental minister in Hesse in December 1985. Fischer concentrated on much stricter implementation rather than new legislation, and was able to exert considerable pressure on Hoechst Chemicals, who have their main plant in Frankfurt, during his incumbency of just over a year. His decision to concentrate on the implementation stage, his disinclination to proceed in a 'cooperative' manner, and his readiness to hire new officials less sympathetic to industrial needs all seemed very ominous to the VCI.

Given the changing political climate, the VCI executive felt the need to develop a set of guidelines (*Leitlinien*) which would restate the VCI's commitment to self-regulation in a much strengthened form. The *Leitlinien* committed VCI members to the safe production, use and disposal of chemicals and their byproducts. The VCI restated its traditional position that it was committed to protect the environment 'on its own initiative and responsibility even in the absence of legally binding regulations'. The most novel and strongest declaration relates to the balance between economic advantage and environmental risk:

> If required in terms of health care and environmental protection, it will also restrict the marketing of products or stop their production, irrespective of economic interest.

These principles were seen as morally binding on VCI members, but the VCI did not commit itself to the sanction of exclusion from membership to firms that did not live up to them.

### The 1987 Federal Election and Control of the Chemical Industry

In the year preceding the Federal Election of 25 January 1987 both the advocates and the adversaries of state regulation had prepared their dispositions accordingly. The SPD intended to campaign on the basis of the *Chemiepolitik* (Chemicals policy) in the election. The Greens campaigned on a less specific more emotionally anti-chemicals platform. The VCI developed its *Leitlinien* and the Federal Environmental Minister, Walter Wallman, had expressed his satisfaction with the VCI's approach.

These carefully laid preparations of the various actors were thrown into complete disarray by a series of chemical spillages into the Rhine and Main just as the campaign got under way. The original spillage at the Sandoz plant in Switzerland on 1 November was accompanied by a spillage from Ciba-Geigy in Basle. The Swiss spillages were a very severe embarrassment to the VCI but much worse was to come. In November and December all three major German firms registered spillages into the Rhine and Main. Hoechst allowed 850 grammes of benzole chlorine to escape through a rainwater canal into the Main.

Bayer had two separate accidents. Large quantities of disinfectant escaped from its plant at Krefeld-Uerdingen and 800 kilogrammes of methanol were accidentally allowed to flow into the Rhine at Leverküsen. BASF also had two separate incidents, one involving two tonnes of pesticide, the other two tonnes of ethylglycol. These incidents led to a great deal of public alarm and to the cessation of the use of the Rhine for drinking water for a period. Environmental issues gained rapidly in importance. It had been only the fifth most important theme in the public mind in the 1983 election; by the end of the campaign in 1987 it was the second most important theme and at some points in the campaign it threatened to overtake combatting unemployment as the most often cited theme.

The Rhine incidents affected the strategies of both advocates and adversaries dramatically. The Greens with their more emotional less inhibited attacks on the chemical industry profited most from the incidents. The spillages caught the SPD on the wrong foot. Its '*Chem-iepolitik*' was largely concerned with updating the Chemicals Law and this meant that it had invested a lot of time and energy in a programme which did not seem to be of central relevance. Volker Hauff, the SPD environmental spokesman, tried hard to regain the initiative and the SPD peppered environmental minister Wallmann with parliamentary questions but it was unable to extract nearly as much political capital out of the issue as the Greens.

The VCI and the chemical industry was thrown on the defensive. They pointed to the high level of safety which was obtained at German plants and played down the seriousness of the incidents. This could not disguise the fact that the spillages were a serious reverse for the chemical industry and its advocacy of self-regulation. They very seriously undermined the position of Walter Wallmann who had been an important ally.

Despite the repeated 'own goals' in the Winter of 1986 the environmentalist pressures on the chemical industry remain much less than on the nuclear industry. Very few, even of the most extreme environmentalist groups, call for abolition of the industry though many echo the Greens' call for the industry to move out of pesticides and some of the more hazardous product lines into so-called 'soft chemicals'. The pressures are nevertheless much greater than in competing countries of the European Community. The policy of the chemical industry is to push environmental policy out of the national framework up to a European level. This has a number of advantages. The environmental standards arrived at will probably be less onerous for industry than those that would emerge in a purely German context. This would impose the same environmental costs on competing countries and German industry now has a comparative advantage in clean technology and would therefore profit from the adoption of higher environmental standards throughout the community.

## Four Stages – and the Future

The rise of environmentalism in the Federal Republic has traversed four stages. From the late 1960s post-material issues, including the environment, begin to displace earlier values among educated critical youth. Established parties and interests organised around existing values could accommodate these generational value-shifts only to a very limited extent. The margins were further reduced by the oil crisis of 1973 and the ensuing economic difficulties which reasserted existing priorities. In the third stage dissatisfied environmentalists withdrew either partially or totally from the major parties and

invested their energies in environmentalist and other social movement. This led finally to the creation of the Greens and the conse-
quent adoption by the other parties, especially the SPD, of more
environmentalist values. The term 'post-material' suggests that the
adoption of these values has a permanent character. At present it is
certainly the case that the environmentalist tide shows few signs of
slackening and it was given a further impetus by the Greens'
increased share of the vote in the 1987 election. less often remarked
upon is the decline in the number of 18–24-year-olds who voted
Green in 1987. The behaviour of young voters at the 1990 election
will therefore be a crucial indication of whether the environmental
dynamic can be sustained.

The advent and strength of the environmentalist movement has
been a considerable challenge to the West German model. Considerable fears were expressed by leaders of German industry about its
potential impact on West German economic performance. It has
certainly affected energy costs and, were it to be successful in its
aim of closing down the nuclear industry, energy costs would arguably rise considerably. It has made West Germany a less attractive
location for some industries (e.g., Bayer and BASF are developing
gene technology in the United States because of the possibilities of
strict environmental legislation in this area). The overall impression,
however, is how little West German competitiveness has been affected by the environmental movement. The major economic difficulties
in the 1980s (see Chapter 8), the high labour costs, the absence of
deregulation and associated high service costs flow directly from the
old politics of the organised interests and parties rather than from
the demands of the new politics.

# 15

# The Trade Unions

## ANDREI S. MARKOVITS AND CHRISTOPHER S. ALLEN

For the West German unions, events in the mid- and late 1970s brought to an end a kind of 'golden era'. This period was even worse for unions in most other European countries. Gone were the days of virtual full employment, annual increases in real wages, and extension of social and workplace benefits that had been first won, and then extended during the 1960s and early 1970s when sympathetic Labour and Social Democratic parties were in government throughout Northwestern Europe. In the course of the last decade, however, various internal and external challenges profoundly changed labour's world both in the Federal Republic and the rest of Europe. These changes centred first and foremost on the altered states of solidarity for the unions both in the labour market and the political arena. Throughout Western Europe one could unmistakably detect major challenges to the solidarities of labour and the 'old' left which had dominated progressive politics since the beginning of the century when the dual development of mass production in the industrial sphere and large-scale political participation in the political realm created what we have come to know as modern society.

This chapter will place the case of the West German unions in the context of a more general attack on unions in industrialised countries. Whilst the West German unions may not have faced the 'labour bashing' policies of the Reagan and Thatcher governments in the early and mid-1980s and may have withstood these challenges from 'above' (more aggressive employers) and 'below' (the new or 'alternative' social movements such as the Greens) better than most other European union movements, they clearly have not escaped them.

## A Brief Overview of the Post-war Era

As is clearly visible in Table 15.1 we distinguish five time-periods, each with its own implications for the formation of union politics in the industrial and political arena respectively. The first period, comprising the immediate post-Second World War era, we character- ise as 'reconstruction' since it was in these five years that the basic foundations of the post-war order were initiated. Union activism was high virtually everywhere with labour seizing the opportunity in the face of a bruised and discredited capital to reshape Europe's post- war industrial and political order. Under the leadership of Hans Böckler, the first leader of the DGB (German Trade Union Feder- ation), West German organised labour formed a peak organisation that represented virtually all unionised workers, comprising today nearly 40 per cent of all German workers. Yet unlike the prolifer- ation of often competing craft unions in Britain and the United States, the DGB (German Trade Union Confederation) originally comprised only 16 (since 1978, 17) industrial unions (see Table 15.2 for membership figures in the 1980s).

Much of this effort, however, fell well short of labour's original hopes, as is depicted in the box of Table 15.1 labelled 'Rollback and Consolidation'. For reasons having much to do with the rapid proliferation of the Cold War and its ramifications affecting the domestic politics of virtually every European country and particularly the Federal Republic, labour lost a good deal of its earlier reformist élan concentrating instead on short-term accommodation with a con- servative *Zeitgeist*. Unions learned to live within the constraints of post-war West German capitalism instead of their earlier attempts at maximising their position in society. With the exception of Austria and the Scandinavian countries, labour parties bided their time in opposition where, more often than not, they devised accommo- dationist strategies which, so they hoped, would help them return to governmental power. This, in short, was the 'end of ideology' era where, with the notable exception of some Communists, labour became fully integrated into a successful capitalist order.

Following this decade of accommodation and relative lull, we witnessed by the late 1960s a rapid reversal and radical change in most of industrial Europe. Entitled 'mobilisation and system reforms', this era comprised the third periodisation in Table 15.1. Spurred by students' protests and their continued extra-institutional strategies in quest of radical reforms – in many ways the direct precursors of the contemporary 'new' social movements – unions and their allies successfully deployed labour's market power to gain major concessions from capital both in terms of pay increases and

TABLE 15.1  *Periodisation of post-war shifts in the political economies of Western Europe*

| | 1945–1950 | 1950s–mid-1960s | Late 1960s–early 1970s | Mid 1970s–early 1980s | Early 1980s–present |
|---|---|---|---|---|---|
| Union politics | Reconstruction period | Rollback and consolidation | Mobilisation and system reforms | Attempted rollback, consolidation and austerity | Decline of conventional macro-economic policies and strategies in favour of global and micro alternatives |
| Industrial Action: shopfloor strategies and plant level activities | High everywhere Unions trying to reshape capitist economics | Low on the whole A settling-in period. unions learning to live with existing conditions | High everywhere Unions successfully using labour's market power to gain major concessions from capital | High everywhere As opposed to previous period, actions and aims are defensive and protective, not offensive and reformist | Scattered and receding Defensive and protective Diffusion of old allegiances and compacts in the wake of 'flexibilisation,' 'new technologies,' new solidarities. |
| Political action; relations with political parties, the state, and society | High everywhere; unions have access to state via left wing parties, even Communist parties | Labour exclusion prevails in most countries with the exception of Scandinavia and Austria | Where labour inclusion exists there is high reform activity. however, inclusion is also used to constrain labour. In labour exclusion situations, status quo continues | Increasing disillusion with parties and state everywhere. Labour inclusion and exclusion start to blur and merge | Disillusion with old allegiances continues with no new lasting one on the horizon |

TABLE 15.2   *Membership of DGB unions, 1983 and 1987*

| Union | 1983 | 1987 |
| --- | --- | --- |
| IG Metall (metalworkers) | 2,535,644 | 2,609,247 |
| ÖTV (transport and public service workers) | 1,173,525 | 1,202,626 |
| IG Chemie (chemical workers) | 635,276 | 655,776 |
| IG BSE (construction workers) | 523,129 | 475,575 |
| DPG (postal workers) | 457,929 | 463,757 |
| HBV (commerce, banking and insurance workers) | 360,372 | 385,166 |
| IGBE (mine workers) | 366,328 | 347,528 |
| GdED (railroad workers) | 379,534 | 340,095 |
| GTB (textile-clothing workers) | 263,920 | 254,417 |
| NGG (food-processing workers) | 263,525 | 267,555 |
| GEW (education and science workers) | 185,490 | 188,861 |
| GDP (police) | 167,572 | 158,888 |
| GHK (wood and plastic workers) | 149,724 | 143,139 |
| IGDRUPA (printing and paper workers) | 144,344 | 145,044 |
| Leder (leather workers) | 50,864 | 47,659 |
| GLF (horticulture, agriculture and forestry) | 42,249 | 43,253 |
| Kunst (artists and musicians) | 46,668 | 28,440 |
| DGB total | 7,745,913 | 7,757,039 |

Sources: Markovits (1986) p. 450; *Die Quelle*, vol. 39, no. 5 (May 1988) p. 312.

'qualitative' reforms. Especially where its political representatives were in government, the labour movement also attained major gains by means of legislation and governmental intervention. Yet, already during this period, problems were apparent which later came to the fore in the wake of the economic crisis of the mid-1970s, and basically immobilised the labour movement and created both challenges 'from above' and 'from below'. Anchored in the contradiction inherent to the situation in which a labour party (co)determines the political fortunes of a capitalist system, the unions and their parties formed the vanguard of reformism. At the same time these very same parties curtailed the unions with various incomes policies and other 'corporatist' schemes lest the unions' ambitions and the militancy of their rank and file threaten the basic pillars of capitalist production and accumulation.

It is in the transition to the fourth period that we see the most significant break in our periodisation scheme in Table 15.1. The beginnings of a definite qualitative change in the texture and content of labour's politics *vis-à-vis* the state, the employers and its own constituency clearly became visible. Best seen as the first or 'social democratic' phase of the crisis, labour's gains from the previous period were contained by various austerity measures often implemented by labour parties. Faced with the increasingly urgent dilemma between being the party of order or that of the movement, most decisions assumed by labour parties favoured the former to the direct detriment of the latter. In this period the rift between party and union became more pronounced with each blaming the other for undermining labour's overall solidarity. Indeed, that is exactly what happened. With the onset of a major crisis in the world's economy in which growth became at best sluggish and unreliable, the old Keynesian formulae, centred on demand management and pursued by virtually every labour movement in the political economy of post-war Europe, ran into serious trouble. Thus began the dissolution of the Keynesian compact which was accompanied by a crisis of labour's overall strategy and a threat to its traditional structures of solidarity. However, it was not until the early 1980s that we witnessed a full-scale challenge to labour's solidarity on all conceivable fronts.

Whereas it should be clear from the preceding analysis that we would date the precursors of the *Wende* (change of course) in the Federal Republic and similar developments in other European countries (as well as the United States) to the mid- to late 1970s – i.e., in the social democratic period – there can be no doubt that the head-on attack against all things 'red' by 'black' from above and 'green' from below occurred in the course of the 1980s, the fifth period of our schema in Table 15.1. Whilst some of these measures were clearly purposive strategies explicitly designed to weaken labour, most were, in fact, part of a global restructuring of world capitalism which will continue to alter every aspect of labour's reality for years to come. The last periodisation in Table 15.1 comprises roughly the decade of the 1980s in which we have witnessed the definite demise of the wisdom and validity of conventional macroeconomic policies and strategies and the social compacts supporting them. These models, which were by and large predicated on the sovereign functioning of the nation state, have been increasingly challenged by various micro- and meso-level approaches (i.e., sectoral and/or regional) on the one hand and global strategies on the other. Although this period clearly has featured the emergence of right-wing resurgence as a solution to the crisis, it is perhaps best characterised by an eclecticism and catholicity in problem-solving defying conventional labels and approaches.

Rather than witnessing the emergence of a new hegemony in policy, this period has stood only for the definitive delegitimation of the old. This pertains especially to the left and the labour movement. Various schemes to increase 'flexibility' – the catch-word of the

1980s – fostered by the rapid proliferation of new technologies have permanently altered the conventional solidarities on the shop floor which defined labour politics for nearly a century. In addition to the creation of new cleavages at the work place, this decade has also introduced a new scepticism by some – but not all – workers *vis-à-vis* technology and growth. The sociological shifts and technological changes which have decisively challenged old solidarities on the shop-floor as well as in the political arena have yet to create new ones in more than a few plants and industries such as machine tools and portions of the automobile industry.

Whilst it has proceeded less far in West Germany, this erosion of labour's solidarity has been a ubiquitous phenomenon. The speed and extent of this process varies immensely from one country to the next, thus telling us much about the history of the particular country's political economy and the efficacy of the policies and strategies pursued by its labour movement. Yet despite national variations, one can nevertheless observe virtually everywhere attacks upon this traditional solidarity both 'from above' as well as 'from below'.

More specifically, the attack from 'above' centres on an array of right-wing attempts to privatise social relations and thus 'roll back' the state as a major actor in, and arena for, adjudication of societal conflict in favour of the market. There has developed a partial shift towards a privatisation of key areas of public life in West Germany, many of which had generally come under the auspices of the state as part of the post-Second World War labour-inclusive settlement. The partial erosion of one of the fundamental political arrangements that usually dissuaded labour unions from directly challenging management prerogatives has not only weakened labour's traditional solidarity, but was often designed to do just that.

The attack from 'below' constituent of the so called 'new' social movements (comprising the women's movement, peace movement, anti-nuclear movement, ecology movement, neighbourhood movements just to mention some of the better known participants in this diverse and loose coalition), has also challenged some of the major tenets of labour solidarity, though with a very different intent from its neo-conservative counterparts. Often perceiving the union hierarchy and the SPD as being overly bureaucratised, much too timid and lacking in courage and imagination, this challenge 'from below' has become a major threat to labour's (and social democracy's) hegemony as the dominant progressive force in European politics throughout much of the twentieth century. The new social movements, while often allied with labour's cause though seldom with its organised representatives, have unquestionably impinged on labour's hegemonic position in Europe's 'reform space'. Briefly put, in the course of the last decade, the labour claim to constitute the only progressive force advocating viable reformist strategies in the politics of countries dominated by the exigencies of capitalist production and concomitant class rule has lost much of its force. Undoubtedly, the political constellations for the collective solidarity 'labour' have undergone major changes since the onset of the economic crisis of the mid 1970s. There are few signs of any abatement of this turbulent process in the near future.

Whilst the Old Left offers increasingly no option, the New Left – i.e. Green and/or 'alternative' forces – still remains too marginal and extra-institutional to influence strategies and policies in a decisive manner, or to connect with the small number of innovative policies being initiated by segments of the metalworkers' union (IG Metall). In short, the 1980s represent for labour a decade of definitive change whose outcome still remains largely uncertain.

## Proliferation and Intensification of Trade Union Problems

In the following sections we highlight both some traditional and some recent problems with which the West German trade unions have had to confront this era of flux and uncertainty. In one sense, these challenges are in a chronological progression, yet a closer examination suggests that there is also an increasing complexity to the difficulties that the unions face. More specifically, the chronologically earlier problems remain while being augmented by ones more characteristic of the 1980s. Taken together, they have presented the West German trade unions with their most fundamental challenge since the end of the war.

## The Unitary Trade Union Movement

After disastrous divisions among competing politicised working class movements during the Weimar years – there were separate socialist, Communist, Catholic, and liberal trade union confederations during the 1920s and early 1930s – a much more unified trade union structure, *Einheitsgewerkschaft*, emerged in post-war West Germany. Under the principle of 'one industry – one union' and significantly, 'one plant – one union', the DGB created both a dominant presence as a voice for all of organised labour. Specifically, its member unions did not face rivals for organising workers in their designated industries. In practice, this means that individual unions can respond as the representative of all workers in a given industry when employers

– who are equally unified on an industry-by-industry basis – take action that affects the entire sector. It also means that there are no jurisdictional battles on organising new members among competing trade unions within the same factory as often happens in Britain and the United States. There are two very small trade union groupings that represent some Catholic workers and some salaried, white-collar workers, but the vast majority of West German trade union members belong to DGB unions.

Whilst there can be no doubt that this main pillar of the Federal Republic's industrial relations system has benefited labour immensely, it is also obvious that this comprehensive arrangement has led to a serious 'de-politicisation' in key circumstances. Especially under conditions of the 'social democratic crisis' of the 1970s, the unions could never attain sufficient leverage *vis-à-vis* the SPD to pursue with vigour policies favoured by the unions. Because of the existence of the unitary trade union structure, the SPD could never really be held accountable for its actions affecting labour's existence. The significant minority of the unions' membership that is allied with the CDU–CSU has repeatedly impeded mobilisation in the political arena. It has been precisely this Christian – conservative presence inside the West German labour movement which has prevented the Kohl governments of the 1980s from pursuing anti-union policies similar to those in the United States and Britain during the same period. However, whilst the unitary trade movement may have given West German labour organisational strength, it failed to translate this strength into commensurate political power. To be sure, a large number of West German trade union members are also SPD members, but the principle of the *Einheitsgewerkschaft* means that neither the DGB nor the individual unions can take political positions that explicitly endorse the SPD. As outlined below, this factor sometimes allows the party to take positions on issues that the unions oppose.

## Unions as Voluntary Membership Associations

The 'free rider' problem has always been a serious bane of the West German unions' existence, as West German unions have represented only between 35–40 per cent of the workforce during the post-war period. Especially in the boom years of the late 1950s and early 1960s, many potential union members refrained from joining the unions because they derived all the advantages and benefits attained by the unions for their members without having to pay union dues and submitting themselves to other collective obligations necessitated by union solidarity. There thus developed a culture of parasitism which has not been to the unions' solidaristic advantage in periods of boom or bust. In an era of increased societal flux and new, flexible forms of shop-floor organisation, unions could be perceived as dispensable, if not yet as irrelevant as they have been viewed in other advanced capitalist countries.

Against this so-called 'free rider' tendency, the West German trade unions have used two lines of defence, one old and one new. The old response – one that the DGB unions have stressed since the 1950s – has been to argue that the unions speak for all workers and not just those who already belong to unions. In fact, the industrial union structure mentioned above (one union – one industry), rather than the craft union structure more common to Britain and the United States, has prevented the West German unions from assuming that they represent a narrowly-defined small group of easily identifiable workers. The fact that the West German unions have not faced intra-union competition in organising new workers has meant that the West German unions have faced no *organisational* impediment to recruiting new members. The new response to 'free riding' by non-union members has been to stress that the introduction of more 'flexible' working arrangements has taken place at management's direction. Thus, the unions argue, without an organisational entity to help workers throughout a given industry resist management-imposed flexibilities and to redefine new forms of workplace organisation on terms favourable to workers, the individual 'free riders' will be unable to stand up to management-imposed changes on their own.

## The 'Juridification' of Industrial Relations

Many laws and regulations in West Germany govern the organisation of the workplace, relations between employer and employee, procedures for conducting a strike, among many others. Taken together, this pattern of mutually reinforcing rules regulating industrial relations is known as 'juridification'. Whilst these mechanisms have lent considerable strength and stability to labour in the form of calculability of conflict and regularisation of communication among all parties, it has impeded the unions ability to mobilise in the political arena as well as on the shop floor. This system encourages the depoliticisation of conflict and turns the unions into parties engaged in legal disputes instead of political struggle. The labour courts have wide powers to address issues which, in many other industrialised countries, would probably provoke unions to go on strike. Moreover, there are sharply defined areas within which unions can act and can not act, as well as specific procedures that unions must take before engaging in a wide range of actions. For example, before unions can go on strike, there must be a vote by 75 per cent (plus 1) of the members that authorise this action. Correspondingly, a vote by 25 per cent (plus 1) is enough to ratify a settlement and bring striking workers back to work. This juridification of industrial relations has a number of concrete results: the leadership cannot lead a union on strike without overwhelming support of the membership; West Germany has both a low strike rate as well as work stoppages of short duration; and wildcat strikes are rare and illegal. All of these points contrast sharply with the British and American systems.

Another major form of the juridification of industrial relations – one which contrasts sharply with Anglo-American patterns – is the West German system of codetermination (*Mitbestimmung*). Providing for the institutionalised participation of workers – specifically, union members – on the supervisory boards of directors of all medium-sized and large firms, codetermination gives unions an inside look at the workings of the most powerful firms in West Germany. Unions can thus understand – if not control – how and why major corporate decisions are made on such issues as investment and application of technology. Based on laws passed in the early 1950s and expanded in the 1970s, codetermination gives workers (and unions) up to 50 per cent of the members of these company boards. The problem for the unions in challenging management positions on contentious issues is that – with the exception of the coal and steel industries – the laws always provide management with an extra, and hence the likely tie-breaking, vote.

In sum, a legally regulated labour relations system may provide considerable protection for German workers, but it also inhibits their ability directly to challenge issues that are not easily administered by the elaborate legal structure regulating labour relations in West Germany. This problem is closely associated with the next issue, one that provides for additional forms of worker participation.

## The Dual System of Worker Representation

There are two institutional structures that represent West German workers: one is the trade union movement under discussion in this chapter (through which labour's participation in codetermination takes place). Comprising between 35 and 40 per cent of all workers in the Federal Republic, the trade unions represent the West German organised working-class *vis-à-vis* employers, the state, and society. In notable contrast to the trade unions' 'external' role of representation, all shopfloor and plant level affairs are the exclusive domain of the works councils (*Betriebsräte*). These 'internal' bodies of worker representation exist in a large number of West German firms numbering five or more full-time employees. The trade unions have historically addressed collective bargaining issues while the works councils have concentrated on social and personnel matters. Before the present period of more 'flexible' workplaces, these lines of demarcation were much clearer than they have become in the 1980s.

Despite the 85 per cent overlap in personnel between unions and works councils, and despite a structural intermeshing between these two major pillars of labour representation in the Federal Republic, the mere fact that there are two distinct and separate bodies definitely entails rivalries, periodic rifts and different representations of interest. Briefly put, whereas the unions' legitimation derives from a country-wide, multi-industry representation of a large number of diversified workers, the works councils owe their primary allegiance to their local plants and firms. Especially in a period of general flux and plant-related, management-imposed flexibility, there is plenty of evidence that the inherent centrifugality of this dual system of representation lends itself to 'mini-corporatist' tendencies which clearly undermine the large-scale, all-embracing solidarity claimed by the unions. The unions have by and large successfully avoided the proliferation of any plant-level syndicalism, although there have been some significant exceptions. For example, the powerful works councils in the big three chemical firms of BASF, Bayer, and Hoechst impeded the ability of the chemical workers' union (IG Chemie) during the early and mid-1980s to forge industry-wide union positions on key issues. The case of industrial relations in the chemical industry is simply the most visible manifestation of a tendency toward a culture of dual loyalties that has caused West German labour some organisational and strategic problems in this era of 'flexibility' and economic uncertainty.

## Intra-union Rivalries and Clashes

Echoing the tradition of the European left, the West German labour movement reflects the struggle between 'radicals' and 'moderates', or – as we have elsewhere (1980a, 1986) termed them – 'activists' and 'accommodationists'. The first group, largely – though not exclusively – centred around the metal workers', printers' and retail, banking and insurance workers' unions, perceives the role of unions to be in the vanguard of societal change well beyond the immediate confines of factory life. Especially in a period of flux and uncertainty, these 'activist' unions see it as their mandate to create a progressive political coalition around issues pertaining to collective bargaining, economic policy and societal reforms reaching beyond labour's immediate clientele. 'Activist' unions view their task in reaffirming the solidarity of labour as a class which is to be augmented by elements of the 'new' social movements in their joint quest towards major systemic reforms of a progressive nature.

As to the 'accommodationist' unions, represented by the so-called 'gang of five' comprising the chemical workers', construction workers', miners', restaurant workers' and textile workers' unions, their view of the world centres on a maximisation of their members' wellbeing in the here and now. Rather than see themselves as vanguards of a progressive movement based on universalistic principles of solidarity, these unions emphasise the primary of particularistic plant-related interests over those of class and movement. In contrast to their 'activist' colleagues who see their role as a constant challenge to all facets of the dominant system, the 'accommodationist' unions want to adapt to existing conditions. They see this strategy to be the best course of action to maximise benefits for their own immediate clientèle. This approach leads to very different political coalitions for the 'accommodationists', who – in contrast to the 'activists' – rely a good deal less on alliances with the 'new' social movements concentrating on established political parties (notably the SPD) instead.

## Organised Skilled Workers – Unorganised/Unskilled

There exists a large representational deficit in the West German labour movement outside the traditional union clientèle of male, German, skilled workers. This problem has always plagued the German labour movement since its inception in the nineteenth century. White-colour workers, women, youth, civil servants, workers in small firms have consistently been under represented in German union life. For example, while nearly 40 per cent of the workforce is organised, there is a wide difference by industry. The core sectors – metal working, chemicals, and industrial electronics – have anywhere from 60 per cent to 90 per cent levels of organisation. Yet workers in small firms and in much of the service sector are well under the national average. Not until very recently have there ever occurred any major attempts by the West German unions to reach out to these under-represented groups and gain their participation in labour politics. The universalistic self-perception of the West German trade unions who always saw themselves as representing *all* (i.e., even non-unionised) workers reacted against such an aggressive proselytising among non-unionised workers. The Federal Republic's constitutional ban against any form of involuntary membership also impeded the unions' movement in that direction. 'Closed shops' are legally banned in the Federal Republic. The period of increased 'flexibility' in the 1980s has meant new challenges to the old bastions of union strength, particularly with the decline of such 'male' industries as steel and shipbuilding in the more heavily unionised north of the country and the increase in jobs in the less-unionised southern Länder of Baden-Württemberg and Bavaria.

Yet one should not read the West German pattern of worker representation as one which had produced a dramatic loss of union members as has been the case in Britain, the United States and several other industrialised countries. In fact, after a small decline in 1982 and 1983 there was an absolute increase in union membership in West Germany, rising from 7,745,913 in 1983 to 7,757,039 in 1987 (see Table 15.2). How did West Germany swim against the tide of falling rates of international unionisation? First of all, industries such as automobiles, chemicals, machine tools, and industrial electronics remain exceptionally strong in the Federal Republic. This has produced increased unionisation in these sectors, even though these industries remain populated largely by male, blue-collar, skilled workers. Secondly, there has also been increased effort on the part of West German unions to recruit larger numbers of female workers. Women represented only 16.5 per cent of all union workers in 1973, but this figure had grown to 23.1 per cent in 1987. Whilst these results are laudable in international comparison, women will continue to grow as a segment of the West German labour force and increased 'flexibility' could challenge the unions' position in the above-mentioned core industries. Unions thus need to maintain and extend their numerical strength and gender mix via increased organisation drives by the unions among the more under-represented segments of the workforce if the unions wish to maintain and extend their organisational strength during the 1990s.

## Persistent Unemployment

Whether it is in a cyclical/conjunctural or structural variant, the continued presence of major unemployment has been the largest blemish on the West German economy throughout the 1980s. Many have worried that this seemingly intractable problem is symptomatic of a potentially larger social malady, namely that West Germany could become a 'two-thirds' society, with one-third of the population permanently unemployed or structurally underemployed. After unemployment dropped to near 1 per cent during the 1960s and early 1970s, and rose to only 4 per cent during the late 1970s, it has hovered between 8 per cent and 9 per cent since the early 1980s. This persistent problem has not only weakened labour's position in all aspects of the country's political arrangements but has further aggravated the unions' already precarious position by introducing two additionally detrimental factors. First, unemployment has been regionally skewed, with the Federal Republic's northern Länder suffering disproportionately as compared with the southern regions. Traditional industrial bastions such as the Ruhr and coastal areas have suffered from severe unemployment as a consequence of a global industrial restructuring which rendered steel and shipbuilding – their areas' leading products – largely uncompetitive in world markets. This has led to the unenviable situation for the unions in which areas where the unions had traditionally enjoyed a significant presence and where they had helped create and sustain a strong social democratic milieu, have developed into the country's most structurally disadvantaged regions. The unions and the SPD thus find themselves with the cumulative disadvantage of geography accentuated by industry.

Second, unemployment has exhibited a technological dimension which few, if any, experts predicted correctly. Some observers in the United States criticised West Germany's inability to develop a 'high tech' industry to match the and American and Japanese challenges. Whilst these observers have been looking in vain for a German micro electronics industry, the Federal Republic has chosen to emphasise high technology processes and new products in such traditional industries as automobiles, chemicals, machine tools and industrial electronics. The massive deployment of new technologies in virtually every sphere of modern life has thus suddenly confronted most unions with a problem which they could not easily counter with newly-developed strategies. Some unions – such as IG Metall the huge metalworking union – have responded more aggressively than others, as will be seen below. It is, however, in this area of responses to unemployment that the intra-union debate has become most intensified with various worktime reduction measures slowly being initiated and implemented in some industries. Some West German unions are hopeful that these developments will continue to find their way into the unions' practical strategies of collective bargaining.

## Proliferation of New Technologies

By the mid-1980s, there was simply no doubt that the so-called 'third industrial revolution' was about to change virtually all modes of production. These new technologies have begun to create new work conditions which indeed have led to a reconceptualisation of work itself. Work anchored in the world of simple technology mass production has rapidly been replaced by more 'flexible' forms of production which require both new process and product technologies as well as new work skills.

West German unions have responded to this dazzling development in two ways. Workers in the more well-positioned industries – automobiles, machine tools, industrial electronics and chemicals (comprising major portions of IG Metall's and IG Chemie's membership) have continued to take German labour's traditional view: that the furthering of technological development was a *sine qua non* for economic growth which in turn was a necessity for any kind of distributive justice. Although IG Metall and IG Chemie are located on different sides of the 'activist'-'accommodationist' axis, they both believe that most of their members can still benefit from these innovations in product and process technologies. Precisely because West German firms must remain internationally competitive, they must rely heavily on very specialised, highly value-added products requiring a highly-skilled workforce. Since unionised workers in these core industries do not seem to be adversely affected by these developments, the unions in West Germany have less to fear than elsewhere. In fact, some observers of the West German labour movement believe that the employers' need for highly-skilled workers – most of whom are also trade union members – has prevented the direct frontal attacks on trade unions that have taken place in Britain and the United States.

Unions and workers in industries that are much more hard-hit by these developments have taken a more critical view of new technologies. Within this group – centred on industries that had heavily relied on mass production, notably steel, shipbuilding, mining, and portions of textiles – there has been a definite growth in labour's scepticism *vis-à-vis* the beneficial aspects of these new technologies for workers' lives. With the erosion of the strength of these industries, unions in these sectors have remained rather helpless in terms of formulating appropriate strategies to counter these new technologies. And, since many of these declining industries also present environmental problems, they – and their unions – have been attacked by the 'new social movements' as obstacles to progressive change. While presently in the process of groping for appropriate answers, unions on this side of the technological divide are left with many insecurities and uncertainties. These are accentuated by developments now to be discussed.

## New 'Alternative' Lifestyles

One of the most profound changes since 1970 has been the consistent blurring of previously clear relationships between labour and leisure, or more specifically, between wage labour as part of the capitalist system and 'alternative' forms of labour largely outside it. Partly due to the massive cultural and behavioural changes wrought by the important presence of the 'new' social movements and their political institutions in the 1980s, there is a profound challenge to traditional working class culture and to the old social democratic milieu. Parallel to similar developments in most advanced capitalist countries where – just as in the Federal Republic – Old Left allegiances are losing their importance both in the workplace and in society, sections of the West German labour movement increasingly face a situation in which working class culture is eroding.

Part of what has been called 'post-modernism' entails precisely this decline of traditional working class culture on the shop-floor as well as in the home. The technological and organisational challenge to mass production methods has altered social relations inside the factories. Gone is the simple acceptance of management's autonomy in determining the specifics of how the production process is organised. This has lead to the formation of new solidarities that stress the desire for greater control over employees' working and non-working lives. Similar changes have occurred in the realm of social reproduction as well. Places of traditional working class socialisation such as the neighbourhood bar, the football club, the union's lounge, the SPD district's reading room, even the parish church, have all but disappeared in favour of a globalised youth culture (mainstream *or* counter), television and other forms of electronic entertainment. Horizons have drastically changed, as has geographic mobility. Add to this the profound changes in living arrangements which have proliferated virtually everywhere in the advanced capitalist world since 1970, and we see the establishment of new solidarities which have completely altered the meaning of the term 'family'. To round out the picture, it is important to mention the far-reaching effects which feminism has had on the collectivity of labour both on the job and in the home. Perhaps no other single legacy of the post–1968 world will eventually prove to have contributed as significantly to the 'post-modern' challenge of all established solidarities as has the feminist movement. Labour's world certainly does not remain exempt from this challenge.

As dramatic an impact as these new lifestyles have had on the labour movement, they should not be seen as a fundamental obstacle to the forging of solidarities and links between the Old and New Lefts. If there is a unifying theme that unites the various strands of the 'alternative' new social movements, it is the desire for a greater amount of control of their working and non-working lives. Yet, if one then compares the demands of the most 'advanced' segments of the trade union movement – those workers in the core industries whose skills give them a much greater measure of control over their working life than workers in traditional mass production industries – then the gulf between the Old and New Left may be less wide than is currently perceived. One core concept that unions in most industrialised countries seemed to lose as forms of mass production overtook earlier forms of craft production was the Marxist idea that workers produce value in society. Elements of both the Old and New Left may be striving toward greater control over the forces that shape their respective lives, but from different directions. These links, however, have yet to be solidified.

## Strained Relations: Unions and the SPD

As has been already discussed in this chapter and schematically depicted in the accompanying Table 15.1, rifts between unions and labour parties are nothing new. This applies also to the situation in the Federal Republic where the trade unions and the SPD have remained loyal but uneasy allies since the beginnings of the German labour movement over a century ago. Party interests have always diverged from those of the unions, and vice-versa. Yet, as the acerbity of the most recent row between the unions and the SPD's rising star, Oskar Lafontaine, amply demonstrates, the differences between party and unions have sharpened to an extent rarely seen in the Federal Republic's labour history. Lafontaine has attempted to distance himself from traditional blue-collar union voters while simultaneously making appeals to the 'new' social movements. He also suggested that reduced weekly working hours by all those employed – a major demand by the trade unions in the 1980s to help reduce unemployment – should be accompanied by a corresponding reduction in pay. Although Lafontaine's proposal may have been geared to making the SPD more attractive to non-working class voters, it created a storm of opposition among the unions, the SPD's most important voting constituency. The acuity of the tensions is closely bound up with the changes previously discussed which profoundly affect both institutions and their arena of operation. Just like the unions so, too, does the SPD struggle to overcome its deeply divisive crisis of identity which it has suffered since the mid-to-late 1970s. Whilst the eventual outcome of this struggle is far from clear there simply can be no longer any guarantee that the party will once again opt to protect its trusted union wing as the most secure strategy to maintain its claim to be the Federal Republic's major source of progressive politics. Since the advent of the Greens in the early 1980s the SPD has forfeited this claim. However, this does not mean that the social democrats will abandon their century-long ties to the unions. In fact, whilst approximately 1,000,000 union voters deserted the SPD to vote for other parties in 1983 – mostly for the CDU–CSU but also smaller numbers for the FDP and for the Greens – virtually all of these union voters came 'home' to the SPD in the 1987 election. These volatile changes suggest that under present conditions of domestic politics in the Federal Republic, coupled with the fundamental changes occurring in Europe and the global political economy, the unions' and the SPD's interests will probably remain in flux and more insecure than in the past. Both sides can no longer take the tradition of stable and mutual support for granted.

## The Future

All of the problems discussed here show that the unions in the Federal Republic will be increasingly confronted by the disintegration of their old and trusted solidarities and the concomitant rise of new ones. Unions will have to devise strategies to make them attractive to these new solidarities, and actively help create them. Labour simply cannot continue to claim sole guardianship over political reforms and progressive politics by virtue of its past hegemony. Neither unions nor labour parties still possess such autonomy. Both have to be on their guard lest their claim to be in the vanguard of reformist politics prove empty phrases.

The unions will succeed in this difficult endeavour only if they can readily adapt one of their greatest historical contributions to current conditions of public life: the unions' phenomenal success in having collectivised risk-taking on the job and even in the home. After all, the unions' very *raison d'être* was to make the risk borne by the individual workers a shared burden assumed by a collective via an organisation established in the name of a whole. Risks, of course, have changed with the times, and they are quite different today from what they were two decades ago. If the unions and the left can successfully identify such contemporary and future risks and sub-sequently mobilise people at least to contain – if not overcome – them, both will have contributed immensely to restoring labour as the core participant in the space of progressive politics. Whether the West German unions can ever rise to such ambitious levels remains to be seen.

# 16

# Public Order and Civil Liberties

GERARD BRAUNTHAL

The strength of a democratic government can be gauged by the degree of civil liberties it allows its citizens, even when faced by threats to the public order. This chapter examines the question whether the Federal Republic's guarantees of civil liberties based on the rule of law and written into the Basic Law of 1949 have become a reality for all citizens and permanent foreign residents or whether the habits of authoritarianism persist and the state seeks to repress dissenting opinion.

To gain an answer to this highly disputed question, we must examine the concept of the *Rechtsstaat* (literally, 'rule of law state'), the constitutional provisions on public order and civil liberties, the controversy over the 'Decree against Radicals' of 1972 barring political extremists from the public service, the government surveillance agencies, political protests leading to confrontations, and terrorism and anti-terrorist legislation. We must also examine the related civil liberties question of how the government and the population treat the country's minorities, especially immigrants and those seeking political asylum.

## Guarantees of the *Rechtsstaat*

Civil liberties in the Federal Republic are based on a 1794 Code and on Roman Law, which granted private, civil, and political rights to individuals if these rights did not contravene state power. Unlike other Western states where individual rights were won at the expense of state power, in nineteenth century Germany the rights were linked to the strong state, which expanded the sphere of liberty sparingly. As a result, the development of a democratic society and a civil libertarian tradition was stunted. Under the rule of law, citizens were considered 'free' only when they obeyed the government's rules and regulations. Despite legal codes and laws defining an individual's rights and duties and limiting state power, the narrow interpretation of the codes and laws constricted rather than enlarged individual freedoms. No wonder that tolerance of political views hostile to the established order was low and political repression of such dissenting views was high during periods of German history.

After the Second World War, the drafters of the Basic Law, cognisant of this development, symbolically put twenty basic rights and freedoms, found in other Western liberal democracies, at the beginning of the document. They include freedoms of speech, press, religious belief, association, and movement; equality before the law; freedom of information; privacy of mail; the right to petition; and the right 'to resist any person or persons seeking to abolish the constitutional order, should no other remedy be possible' (Article 20). These guaranteed and inalienable rights are binding on the three branches of government and cannot be amended.

Yet Parliament did enact laws dealing with national security, after heated debates, which some critics contend have curtailed individual freedoms. One was the passing of the National Emergency Act of 1968, bringing to an end the reserved emergency powers of the allied occupation powers. Its provisions refer to a 'state of defence' (i.e., an attack against Federal territory), a 'state of tension' (i.e., the first stage of a state of defence in an international crisis), and a 'state of internal emergency' (i.e., a natural catastrophe or an endangering of 'the free, democratic basic order'), in which individual rights would be limited.

## Concept of 'Militant Democracy'

The drafters of the Basic Law believed that the guaranteed civil liberties would become meaningless if the democratic system collapsed. To prevent a repetition of the situation when Nazis and Communists undermined the Weimar Republic, they included three articles that are the basis for the concept of 'militant democracy' (*streitbare Demokratie*). Articles 9, 18, and 21 grant the government the right to deprive political parties, associations, and individuals of their freedoms and rights if they abuse these rights in order to destroy the 'free and democratic basic order' (*Freie Demokratische Grundordnung*, FDGO).

The Federal Constitutional Court has defined the FDGO as the rule of law (responsible government, legality of administration, and judicial independence); separation of powers; popular sovereignty and democratic decision-making based on the majority principle; guaranteed human rights; and a multi-party system granting equal opportunities to all parties, including the right to form a parliamentary opposition.

Article 21, typifying the spirit of militant democracy, stipulates that political parties judged by their 'aims or the behaviour of their adherents to impair or abolish the FDGO or to endanger the existence of the Federal Republic shall be unconstitutional'. It grants the Constitutional Court the right to decide on the question of unconstitutionality upon petition of the parliament or government. In the 1950s, the Court, in controversial decisions restrictive of civil liberties, banned the German Communist Party (KPD) and the neo-Nazi Socialist Reich Party.

The concept of militant democracy became a contentious political issue in the 1970s when many radical university graduates sought employment in the public sector (see below). Conservatives feared that the radicals would undermine the public sector and endanger the democratic system. The CDU–CSU coined such slogans as 'no freedom for the enemies of freedom' and 'tolerance except *vis-à-vis* intolerance'. It hailed the 1970 decision of the Court, which ruled that the militant democracy articles signified that citizens must defend the FDGO and not misuse basic rights to abolish the system.

Many radicals, social democrats, and liberals took issue with the CDU–CSU's interpretation of militant democracy. They contended that the constitutional articles were included in the Basic Law in order to wage a campaign not against the left but against the right that had been responsible for the rise of fascism. In the 1950s, they warned about the dangerous rise of right wing radicalism in the emerging Cold War atmosphere and the government's circumvention of laws meant to purge old Nazis, while prosecuting Communists. They warned that left wing criticism of the existing system would be curbed by conservatives to crush the left, ostensibly to safeguard freedom and democracy. Then militance becomes intolerance.

## Controversy Over the 1972 Decree Against Radicals

These sharply clashing views about the meaning of militant democracy manifested a deep ideological gulf separating radicals and conservatives that could not easily be bridged. The gulf widened when left wing radicals received teaching, social work, and other public service positions in the aftermath of the 1968 student unrest. In a country with a fear of a Communist takeover from the East, a residue of ex-Nazis, a sizable number of bourgeois voters, and a deep strain of anti-Communism in its political culture, the CDU–CSU raised the alarm. It asked parents, already upset by proposed progressive educational reforms in some Länder: 'Would you want your child to be taught by a Communist who would introduce theories of social conflict into the classroom?' Chancellor Willy Brandt's SPD–FDP government was put on the defensive. It did not want to be accused by the CDU–CSU of being soft on Communists, especially when Ostpolitik was at stake. Brandt and the ten minister-presidents of the Länder thus signed a decree in 1972, labelled by its opponents as a *Berufsverbot* (ban on admission to professions), prohibiting left-wing and right-wing political extremists from entering or staying in the civil service, and reiterating the duty of public servants to uphold the FDGO. The decree, intended to provide a common standard for civil servants' loyalty at federal, Länder, and local levels, would have been less controversial if it had been restricted to sensitive civil service posts, but it included all 3.5 million public servants, ranging from school teachers and railroad conductors (who in other countries would not enjoy civil service status) to judges and top ministerial career servants. In the period from 1972 to 1987, it resulted in the loyalty screening of millions of applicants and many civil servants, and an estimated 1,250 rejections of applicants on political grounds, 265 dismissals from the service, and 2,100 disciplinary proceedings against public servants.

Criticism of the decree came not only from those affected, primarily members of the small, reconstituted and legal German Communist Party (DKP), but from the *Jusos* (Young Socialists) in the SPD and the Young Democrats in the FDP. They noted that in the postwar era many Nazis were retained in the civil service, including the judiciary and the police. They insisted that the decree constituted political repression against dissidents who rejected the existing political, economic, and social order. If the dissidents were permitted entry into the public service, they would not become a threat to the state. Moreover, a democratic state must assume the loyalty of its citizens unless it has compelling evidence to the contrary. They cited as a notable instance of repression the case of Silvia Gingold, a young DKP member who was refused a career teaching post in Land Hesse, even though her Jewish parents had been persecuted by the Nazis and her father had been active in the French resistance movement.

Despite a wave of protests against the decree, in 1975 the Constitutional Court affirmed its constitutionality; the court ruled that membership in a party with unconstitutional objectives may be considered sufficient reason not to grant someone civil service status. The court's ruling reassured authorities in the CDU–CSU–governed Länder that their hard line position against political extremists was correct, even when rejected applicants appealed against a negative decision in court and won their case for entry into the public service, as happened on many occasions.

SPD and FDP officials became more liberal in their administration of the decree when they realised that the German penchant for legalism and public order had produced ridiculous excesses. One was the case of a young SPD law student in CSU–controlled Bavaria who was barred from the bench because she once had been an executive committee member of a progressive organisation to which Communists also belonged. The SPD could not remain immune from criticism pouring in from socialist parties in other European countries, especially France, where Socialist Party chief François Mitterrand formed a civil rights defence committee. In addition, the Bertrand Russell International Tribunal, meeting in the Federal Republic, criticised the decree's civil service job ban, and urged the government to promote a climate of freedom of expression.

In May 1976, in response to foreign and domestic criticisms, Chancellor Helmut Schmidt and his SPD–FDP cabinet adopted new guidelines for appointments to the federal civil service. The guidelines omitted a provision in the 1972 decree that in effect barred members of a party pursuing anti-constitutional goals from the public service. The liberalised guidelines were accepted by the SPD–FDP governed Länder, but not by the CDU–CSU governed Länder, which have maintained to the present that membership in an extremist party is sufficient ground for barring an applicant.

In the late 1970s, the governing coalition became alarmed about university students' increasing alienation from a system that encouraged denunciations and snooping to ferret out radicals and discouraged signing petitions, writing seminar papers on radical topics, or speaking out on controversial issues. As a result of a political climate reminiscent of the McCarthy era in the United States, the cabinet decided in January 1979 to abandon routine loyalty investigations into the background of all federal jobseekers. Most SPD–FDP governed Länder again followed suit.

In the 1980s, the controversy over the decree abated, primarily because few radicals applied for the few available vacancies. Chancellor Helmut Kohl's CDU–CSU–FDP coalition government has abided by the SPD–FDP government decisions of 1979 not to screen all applicants for the federal public service. On the other hand, the CDU minister of post and telecommunications has been successful in ousting a number of DKP members from their permanent positions.

His hardline policy, initiated earlier by his SPD predecessor in the Social-Liberal government, was one reason why the International Labour Organisation (ILO) noted in a 1987 report that the government and the CDU–CSU–led Länder had not adhered to ILO convention (No. 111). It prohibits discrimination in employment on the basis of a person's political views, unless a person engages in activity against the security of the state. The commission recommended that loyalty screenings should be restricted to top civil service and to police and other security positions, but not to the entire public service.

The government did not accept the ILO report; it contended that it had an obligation to protect the FDGO and to keep out of the public service persons intent on eliminating human rights. It cited European Court of Human Rights decisions supporting its position.

The protracted controversy over the 1972 Decree against Radicals, one of the most heated domestic policy issues, epitomised the continuing confrontation between, on the one hand, conservatives who put priority on the maintenance of public order and on limiting the rights of dissenters and, on the other, liberals and radicals who advocated maximum rights for dissenters and urged legal restrictions be confined to the few guilty of sabotage, conspiracy, or espionage.

## Government Surveillance Agencies

This schism in orientation and policy was reflected also in the reaction of political parties and groups to an expansion of the government's surveillance agencies. As in other countries, public order is maintained by the police, which is supported by the Federal Criminal Investigation Bureau. In 1950, the Federal and Länder Offices for the Protection of the Constitution (*Verfassungsschutz*) were established to keep subversive activities in the FRG under observation. According to statute, the offices are responsible for compiling dossiers on left wing and right wing extremists and their organisations' attempts to undermine the constitutional system.

Controversy has arisen about the methods used by the *Verfassungsschutz* to collect materials for its voluminous files. Civil rights activist critics insist that the agency has exceeded its legal restrictions. In addition to gaining information from open sources, it has engaged in covert surveillance, concealed photography, mail opening, telephone tapping, and has used *agents provocateurs*. It receives much information from 20,000 to 30,000 contact persons and informers active in political groups, as well as from police, state registrar's offices, universities, and other administrative bodies. Some of this evidence is based on hearsay evidence, malice, or mistaken identities. According to a former Constitutional Court judge, 'Often the files of the intelligence service are not worth the paper on which they are written'.

The *Verfassungsschutz* has been especially interested in the political views of university students. Its use of informants had a dampening effect on academic freedom and led to students being afraid to voice dissenting views openly. Radical students knew that their names would then be stored in an intelligence file, diminishing their chances of obtaining a position in the public, or even private, sector. To gather and process the mass of data, the agency received increasing budgetary and personnel support from Parliament. The critics charge that the creation of a powerful secret service might lead to the emergence of an authoritarian state crushing freedoms. They contend that the growth of the intelligence service does not correspond to any great danger to the FRG, and that parliamentary control over it has not been too effective. Defenders maintain that it has not exceeded its powers; the Ministry of the Interior, under whom it operates, was closely monitoring its operations.

Civil rights activists have also been concerned about the proliferation of data banks set up by the surveillance agencies, Länder, and cities. Shades of George Orwell's fictional 'Big Brother' society (in his novel *1984*) are visible as government officials compile ever more information on every resident in the FRG. Citizens have become increasingly concerned about the misuse of data and the names of innocent persons stored in intelligence computers systems. As terrorism increased in the 1970s, surveillance of radical groups and border controls intensified. The authorities insisted that more identity checks and the use of data banks enhanced the security of all, but civil rights activists replied that existing procedures sufficed to capture terrorists and other offenders who might use forged passports or identity cards.

To protect citizens, the federal and Länder parliaments created the posts of commissioners for data protection and passed legislation restricting the use of information in the data banks. But when, in 1983, the Federal Commissioner for Data Protection, Hans-Peter Bull, was too critical of the government's policy on data collection, the minister of the interior, Friedrich Zimmermann (CSU), summarily dismissed him.

Closely linked to the debates concerning data bases was the emotionally-laden debate over the 1980 census, postponed for budgetary reasons until 1983. The Green Party and citizens' initiatives protested against its scheduling, viewing it as another intrusion of the state into the private lives of its citizens. They objected to provisions in the law that would permit police and security agencies to compare the census data with individuals' registration data, already on file with local authorities, and petitioned the Constitutional Court to halt the pending census. In 1983, the Court concurred; it ruled unanimously that the law's language had been too open-ended and did not set sufficient limits on the state's authority to question its citizens. It noted, for instance, that the government cannot force people to reveal information, such as their telephone number, in a census. It rejected a single identification number for each citizen, which could then be used to retrieve personal data from different computer bases.

The court's decision resulted in the cabinet approving revisions in mid-1984 to the bill to provide for further protection against the unlimited collection, storage, use and transfer of personal data. After lengthy deliberations, Parliament gave its approval in late 1985. The government launched a massive and costly propaganda campaign for the census, held in 1987, after one public opinion poll published in 1985 indicated that 30 per cent of respondents, including many voters for the governing parties, would refuse to fill out a census questionnaire. Most leaders of the Greens called for a boycott, but it fizzled because of police harassment of census opponents and the threat of heavy fines for those refusing to fill out the questionnaire.

## Political Protest as Confrontation

Orwell's *1984* society was beginning to be visible not only in the government's increased storage of information in its data banks about its residents, but in its surveillance of political demonstrations, many of which from 1967 onwards turned confrontational. At the root of the demonstrations was the rise of new social movements – ecology, anti-nuclear energy, and peace, among others – protesting against an array of government policies, from the construction of new airport runways (at the expense of forests) and nuclear plants to the deployment of US intermediate-range missiles. Most demonstrations remained peaceful on the premise that non-violence is the best tactic, but some turned violent when small groups of demonstrators did not abide by the premise or reacted to police brutality.

Once the police or *Verfassungsschutz* agents began to film the demonstrators to identify radical leaders or to have evidence on participants using violence, a number of demonstrators began to wear ski-masks to hide their identity. Often they were members of anarchistic groups ('*Chaoten*' and lately '*Autonomen*' – those who act on their own authority) who have no links to terrorists but who have turned against a society that in frequent instances has not provided them with jobs or much hope for the future. Many travel from one demonstration to another, wearing at them masks, black helmets and black clothes, often resulting in confrontations with the police whom they hate. The *Verfassungsschutz* estimates that of the approximately 6,500 '*Autonomen*', from 1,500 to 2,000 are militants who are ready to use force.

Until 1982, the CDU–CSU, in opposition in Bonn, put pressure, in vain, on the SPD–FDP government to support legislation prohibiting the wearing of masks (except at carnival times). In June 1985, the Bundestag, by then with a CDU–CSU–FDP majority, passed a bill to this effect. The bill also made it a criminal offence to carry 'protective' weapons or to refuse a police order to disperse if a demonstration turns violent. On the other hand, peaceful protesters were guaranteed the right to demonstrate, even if authorities had reason to anticipate violence. In the same month, the Constitutional Court ruled unconstitutional a ban that local authorities had imposed in 1981 on a planned demonstration at the construction site of the Brokdorf nuclear power plant (see Chapter 14).

In November 1987, an unknown demonstrator killed two policemen during a small demonstration at the Frankfurt airport, marking the sixth anniversary of the police razing of a shantytown that had been put up as a protest against the new runway. The demonstration turned violent when the riot police tried to disperse the crowd, containing some *Autonomen* members. The shooting of the policemen, the first ever in a political demonstration, precipitated calls by Zimmermann and other CDU–CSU ministers for still sterner legislative measures against violent demonstrators. The CSU, for instance, demanded, unsuccessfully, the right of police to use rubber bullets. FDP ministers, aware of the party's tradition of upholding civil liberties, were initially reluctant to back any change in legislation, but in May 1988, desirous of avoiding a confrontation with the CSU, supported the cabinet bill, less tough than originally envisioned. Among other provisions, the bill changed the law banning face masks from a misdemeanor to a felony.

## Terrorism and Anti-terrorist Legislation

In the late 1960s, the rise of left radicalism was paralleled by the rise of primarily left terrorism. Andreas Baader and Ulrike Meinhof led one terrorist group, known since the 1970s as the Red Army Faction, which with other groups never numbered at one time more than 200 persons. The Baader-Meinhof group members, belonging originally to one small German Socialist Student Federation (SDS) faction, had become enraged by police violence against student demonstrators in Berlin in 1967 and 1968. As a reaction, they were intent on producing societal upheavals by illegal acts, including bombings, arson, bank robberies, burglaries of weapons, taking hostages, and occasionally, assassinations of representatives of the government and business communities whom they identified as agents of imperialism.

The Red Army Faction consisted of a small group of even more fanatic terrorists who were not inhibited from committing assassinations; and for this reason they had less hope of gaining the support of the bulk of radicals. Most terrorists were caught and sentenced to prison terms. From 1970 to 1978, 215 persons were convicted of terrorism, 94 were under investigation, and 42 were still being hunted. They had been responsible for the assassination of 28 people, injuries to 93, the seizing of 15 hostages, as well as other indictable acts.

Although the scope of terrorism was small when compared with that in the Weimar era, conservative leaders and newspapers exaggerated its menace to the public order, partly to use as a weapon against the few hundred left wing sympathisers, partly to assail the governing parties. CSU chief Franz Josef Strauss stated, 'The SPD and FDP let criminals and political gangsters take over this government'. He and the CSU thereby also tried to create a illiberal atmosphere among the public, which would then be receptive to undoing the government's domestic reforms – including an expansion of civil liberties – and to vote CDU–CSU.

The SPD–FDP government, aware of the favourite reception the public gave the CDU–CSU calls for 'law and order' but also intent on projecting an image of toughness, requested Parliament quickly to pass new legislation designed to curb terrorism. The precipitating factor came when left wing defence lawyers were accused of having violated the Code of Criminal Procedure by passing communications between jailed terrorists and friends on the outside, among other acts. Parliament from 1974 to 1978 enacted a number of amendments to the code, such as allowing a lawyer to defend only one client at a time, permitting a judge to see written notes between lawyers and clients, and requiring a glass barrier between a lawyer and a client accused of terrorism (necessitating conversation by telephone).

In September 1977, in the aftermath of the kidnapping of Hanns-Martin Schleyer, the president of the employers' association, and prior to his murder in October, the federal and Länder ministers of justice ordered the isolation of about a hundred accused terrorists in prison. They could no longer receive or send mail, and talk to or correspond with their lawyers. This practice was swiftly legalised by parliament, which passed the Contact Ban Law, popularly known as the 'solitary confinement law'. Shocked by this limit on the civil liberties of individuals, a number of government deputies abstained or voted against the bill, but it was passed.

In 1978, new anti-terrorist legislation authorised the police to ask persons in public buildings and public transport for identification, even if there was no suspicion of their having committed a crime. Failure to show identification could mean being held up to twelve hours, during which time persons would be fingerprinted and their pictures taken to establish their identity. The police also received authorisation to search all apartments in a building in which a terrorist might be hiding, to engage in wiretapping, and to stop and search motorists at control points. To cope with the mounting duties, the police force and federal border guards were increased substantially in numbers and became more heavily armed.

Terrorism produced popular fear and near-hysteria, fuelled by the mass media and government overreaction, leading to a virtual national emergency. Police and intelligence agencies committed abuses, as shown in the 1975 illegal entry and wiretapping of the residence of atomic scientist Klaus Traube, who was summarily dismissed from his post when suspected of aiding a terrorist. The government lost its case in court when wiretap records exonerated Traube from the charge.

In the 1980s, terrorism waned, partly because of the arrest of most leaders. Yet when a Foreign Officer career official was murdered in 1986, the Bundestag governing parties (CDU–CSU and FDP) passed another package of anti-terrorist laws, including longer prison sentences for terrorists – over the opposition of the SPD and the Greens, which called the laws too sweeping and unnecessary for the maintenance of public order. Radical critics also had opposed a 1976 amendment to the Penal Code, repealed in the 1980s, that had instituted censorship of materials recommending unlawful violent acts. The law led to police confiscation of 'subversive' books, to harassment and arrest of radical bookstore owners, to cancellation of 'provocative' plays or films on television, to border guards registering the names of West German travellers carrying leftist publications, and to other acts of censorship.

This overreaction on the part of the Establishment to terrorist acts was counter-productive because it did not reduce terrorism and enhance public order. Rather, it reinforced the critics' view that the Establishment was only too ready to repress dissident views in the name of fighting terrorism, thus damaging the reputation of the Federal Republic as a bastion of democracy.

## Treatment of Minorities: Immigration and Political Asylum

One test of the strength of a democratic system is its treatment of minorities. In the late 1950s, when the West German economy was booming and a labour shortage developed, the government actively recruited workers from the less developed countries of southern Europe – Greece, Portugal, Spain, Turkey, Yugoslavia, and Italy – where job opportunities were more limited. In 1961, there were 686,000 'guest workers', as they were euphemistically called, even though the bulk of them became permanent residents. By 1974, their number had grown to over 4.1 million, including family members who had joined them. That year, the government, plagued by a recession stemming from the oil crisis, stopped all recruitment efforts and encouraged foreign workers and their families to return home. Yet despite this partly successful effort, assisted in 1983–4 by government bonus payments to the returnees, in 1986 there were even more resident foreigners in the FRG than prior to 1974 – 4.5 million (7.5 percent of the total population), of whom about 1 million were under 16, the maximum age under which children are allowed to join their working parent. (The government favours a reduction to a maximum age of six.) The chief reason for the growth, expected to continue, is the continued immigration of family members, the number of children born to foreigners in the Federal Republic, and an influx of refugees.

The largest foreign contingent in 1986 was Turkish, constituting about 1.4 million persons (32 per cent of all foreigners), followed by 591,000 (13 per cent) Yugoslavs, 537,000 (12 per cent) Italians, 279,000 (7 per cent) Greeks, and 150,000 (3 per cent) Spaniards. (Workers in European Community states, such as Italy, Greece, and Spain, can freely move to and work in other EC states, including the Federal Republic.) In the West German manual labour force, the foreign workers have accounted for about 15 per cent of the total. They have thus represented a significant work force in the automobile, textile, and semiconductor industries; in restaurants and hotels; in street cleaning and garbage collection – jobs that Germans often shun. They have received unemployment insurance, welfare payments, and subsidised housing, putting strains on Länder and municipal budgets.

When the economic miracle vanished and unemployment rose to more than 2 million from 1983 on, foreign workers and their families were disproportionately affected. Competing for scarce jobs and scarce housing, they became the target of increased hostility on the part of many Germans. Right wing groups, such as the small but vocal NPD, contended that almost precisely the same number of jobs were held by foreigners as there were unemployed Germans. They urged that money 'wasted' on social security for the foreigners be spent on creating jobs for Germans.

The problem for foreigners are compounded by the social isolation they face in their daily lives. Cases of prejudice, discrimination, and rejection are so widespread that many retreat into ghettoes, which produce new problems for them of adjustment to the German society. This has been especially true for the large Turkish minority that also has to face a wide cultural and religious gap. Turkish parents, dreaming about a return to their homeland, want their children to retain their native language and cultural values, but the children at school are exposed to German values, which often leads to friction at home. In addition, many have difficulty finishing school or in finding a job, and as a result get involved in petty crime and drugs.

German churches, charitable agencies, and trade unions have taken initiatives to solve some of the nearly intractable social problems, while the government in the 1980s has continued to restrict immigration and to encourage families to return home, difficult at best when unemployment there may be even higher than in the Federal Republic. The government has tried to combat the persistent attitude of moral superiority the Germans have shown toward foreign workers; with some encouraging results as social contacts between them have increased since 1980. The government has also tried to integrate foreign children in the schools and families into housing projects. The task of full social and economic integration remains a major challenge to the government and to citizens and foreigners alike.

Another challenge facing the government is to cope with the mass immigration (200,000 in 1988) of 'ethnic Germans' from the Soviet Union and other Eastern Bloc countries. Although they can almost automatically have German citizenship as long as they provide some kind of documentary evidence (that their ancestors had emigrated from Germany to the East), many do not speak German. They will also have difficulty in finding adequate employment and housing. As with other immigrants, they face problems of integrating into the fabric of German society.

Political asylum in the Federal Republic for those fleeting their homeland, many from Poland, Turkey and Iran, has become a contentious issue. The Basic Law contains a provision on asylum ('Persons persecuted on political grounds shall enjoy the right of asylum'), which is one of the most liberal in the world. The Courts must decide whether the refugees, who are housed in camps and are not allowed to work for five years, have sought asylum for *bona fide* political reasons (normally 10 per cent of the total) or whether economic opportunities lured them. In 1980 over 100,000 persons sought asylum (more than in any other European country). Parliament enacted a law two years later speeding up the administrative and judicial process of deciding whether a person can remain in West Germany permanently – a process that until then had taken as long as eight years. Those persons who have no entry permit or chance of gaining asylum normally are not allowed to remain in the country, although most of them manage to stay illegally.

The government permits a limited number of foreign refugees, especially those from Southeast Asia, entry for humanitarian reasons on a quota basis. As permanent residents, they receive economic and social assistance, comparable to those who have entered the country asking for political asylum. Yet many face the same problems of adjustment in an alien society replete with discrimination against minority groups and foreigners. To increase the civil rights for all foreigners, proposals have been made to give them the vote in local elections or to make children of foreign workers, born in the Federal Republic, German citizens at the age of eighteen. But these proposed changes have not received government support as yet.

## Societal Norms and Radical Protest

This brief survey of public order and civil liberties in the Federal Republic indicates that the rule of law and civil liberties provisions in the constitution compare favourably with those of other liberal democracies and provide minimum guarantees for a maintenance of the democratic system. Yet, in periods of crises especially, Social-Liberal and Conservative-Liberal governments have exhibited authoritarian tendencies and have attempted to repress dissenting opinions challenging the existing order, as have governments in other democratic states. Repression occurred during the 1970s and 1980s in the Federal Republic when radicals protested against the government's defence, environmental, and nuclear energy policies. As some protests turned violent, the government's overreaction (e.g., police brutality) to any breach of legality indicates that it has been intent on maintaining public order at the expense of civil liberties. The expansion of surveillance agencies and the precipitous passage of anti-terrorist legislation, including censorship of written materials, which restricted the civil liberties of all residents, is further proof that authoritarian tendencies persist. The barring of political extremists, especially Communists, from the civil service is another indication of the governments' lack of sensitivity to civil liberties issues.

These public policies reflect societal norms, in this instance a deeply-ingrained anti-communism and support for a liberal capitalist economic system. When segments of a younger generation challenged these beliefs and the governments at first paid little heed to their views, the setting for confrontational politics was at hand. In the late 1980s there has been an easing of tensions, partly because the government recognised the legitimacy of some demands and made subsequent policy changes. Yet it still must cope with radical protests and the problems concerning foreign minorities. The test of its commitment to civil liberties for all citizens and foreigners is how it balances this commitment with its legitimate need to protect the national security. If its legal restrictions are confined to the few guilty of sabotage, conspiracy, or espionage, then it maximises civil liberties for all others. But if repression is extended to dissenters who seek peacefully to create another political, economic, and social order, civil liberties will be inexorably weakened.

# 17

# Germany in the 1990s

WILLIAM E. PATERSON AND GORDON SMITH

With all the upheavals and regime changes during the first half of the century, German history could be marked off into a number of different stages. Yet there are no really sharp demarcations for the Federal Republic, but rather several phases and none really clear-cut. In the earlier years the overriding concerns were aimed at ensuring political stability, maintaining economic growth, and forging reliable international connections. These priorities have been of continuing importance, and yet – despite tangible success in all three respects – lingering doubts stubbornly persisted. Was the Federal Republic perhaps only a fair-weather democracy? What would be the political consequences of a prolonged economic depression? How would sudden increases in international tension affect the security of West Germany?

## A Look Back to *Modell Deutschland*

Even if these questions could never be definitively answered, there was nevertheless convincing evidence that particular crises could be overcome and that, as each was resolved, confidence in the republic and its institutions was growing accordingly. This formative process continued throughout the 1960s and 1970s, and after the change of power, the *Machtwechsel*, from the CDU to the SPD in 1969, the consolidation of the republic reached its long culmination during the chancellorship of Helmut Schmidt. Schmidt's style of governing epitomised the increasing self-confidence of the new Germany, and Schmidt's international stature brought a recognition that the Federal Republic was becoming an independent actor on the world stage.

The self doubts – the view that the republic still faced a 'crisis of legitimacy' – gradually receded. That the 'hump of legitimacy' had been surmounted was made evident in dealing with the residues of provocative terrorism during the 1970s: it was perceived as a specific problem, not one that could threaten to destroy the whole political fabric. In the 1970s, too, the Federal Republic successfully weathered the economic crises triggered by the oil-price shocks without any noticeable ill-effects for the political system.

On the contrary, the party system was notable in the 1970s for its rock-like stability, and the three established parties even managed to corner the electoral market with 99 per cent of the vote at the 1976 election. What of the alternatives to their cartel? The 'homeless left' found temporary havens in a variety of Marxist splinter groups, whilst the extreme right at no point appeared to be a credible force after the NPD had failed in the 1969 election. The one polarising force within the system was represented by Franz Josef Strauss, but his decisive defeat as the CDU–CSU chancellor candidate in 1980 put paid to any idea that a major party could afford to deviate from the electoral middle ground.

Seen against this backcloth, the SPD election slogan of 1976, *'Modell Deutschland'*, seemed to be more of a realistic assessment than a vote-winning strategy. The Federal Republic was a model for other countries to follow if they could, and whilst there was no certainty as to the 'secret' of German success, a decided interest was taken by outside observers in various aspects of West German institutional structures – perhaps they could be usefully borrowed. Such features as the electoral system, the federal structure, the implantation of a 'legal framework' to govern industrial relations, even the more subtle aspects of the corporate style of policy-making – all were scrutinised as possible remedies for the limping performance of other countries.

What also led to a positive reassessment of the Federal Republic was the mounting evidence that German political culture was rapidly changing. Popular attitudes and values were becoming much more directly supportive of democratic institutions, and there were indications of greater citizen-awareness and a readiness to participate. These changes showed a movement away from the predominantly subject-oriented political culture of earlier decades. Indeed, it appeared that whilst the old 'civic culture' societies, the United States and Britain, were beginning to display less stable patterns, the Federal Republic was fast developing a civic culture of her own.

All these facets of *Modell Deutschland* contributed to an imposing picture of stable strength. From the perspective of, say, 1980 it was difficult to offer any convincing scenario of what – and how – substantial change could come about. Least likely of all was a regression to a situation of political and social fragmentation that would resemble the Weimar Republic – even though that had been the usual kind of extrapolation once any serious crisis blew up. Yet, beyond making piecemeal domestic reforms and carefully adapting to changes in the international situation, it was hard to visualise just how the Federal Republic might further 'develop'. An indefinite plateau of stability was the only prospect in view, seen negatively as a kind of 'hypertrophy' of the political system.

## Changes in the 1980s

The West German experience of the 1980s differed in important respects from what would have been expected in applying the 'model'. But it is too easy to pay attention to the changes at the expense of neglecting how much its essential characteristics persisted. The West German economy compares favourably on most counts with other leading countries. Any falling-off in the rate of growth has to set against its exceptional historical performance. Although it is true that there were signs of less industrial flexibility, key indicators, such as the rate of inflation, stability of the currency and external trade position, all remained favourable, despite persisting – and historically high – levels of unemployment. There was little enough cause to see economic factors having markedly adverse political effects.

Much the same was true at the level of government. The composition of the coalition still relied on the well-tried 'formula' of the SPD or CDU in partnership with the FDP. Admittedly, the coalition change in 1982 to bring the CDU back to government for the first time in 13 years marked the end of an era for the SPD. But what of *die Wende* (change of course) that the CDU promised on its return to power? Apart from measures of financial retrenchment – a feature common to most countries throughout Western Europe whatever their political colouring – there was little evidence that the Federal Republic was changing course. What proved to be more important was the confirmation of the barriers to radical change: the political constraints imposed by the exigencies of coalition formation, the fear of an electoral backlash, and the structural conditions of policy-making in West Germany that enforce compromise and encourage a consensual outcome.

Both the continuing economic well-being of the Federal Republic and the role played by the established parties helped to impart a powerful inertia to the political system. Yet during the 1980s there were also growing signs of change, but what they signified and how they are likely to affect the stabilising factors in German society still remains unclear.

## Challenges to the *Volkspartei*

Despite their dominance in government – a grip which in one way or another is bound to be maintained – both the CDU and the SPD have shown themselves to be much more vulnerable than ever before. Their falling share of the vote, particularly evident for the SPD in 1983 and for the CDU in 1987, is by no means an indication of an irreversible decline, but they have become far less self-assured in the knowledge that they are exposed to sudden changes of electoral mood. The central difficulty of the *Volkspartei* in claiming to speak 'for the whole people' is that what it gains by casting a wide electoral net may be lost in diminished flexibility to meet new challenges. This dilemma becomes more acute when new issues suddenly arise.

In the 1970s it would have been difficult to visualise a party such as the Greens finding a secure place in the party system, and even harder to imagine it having an influential agenda-setting role. For the SPD in particular the appeals of the 'new politics' and the demands of its related social movements are difficult to counter or to absorb. The underlying reason may not relate so much to the specific issues or areas of concern – environment, feminist claims, minority rights, defence issues – but in the demands that are often latent within them, especially in the implications of the desire for 'self-realisation' and greater participation. They quickly translate into calls for direct action and confrontation. The *Volkspartei* is ill-suited to respond to these pressures. In the way the *Volksparteien* have evolved they are ill-equipped to handle the idea of a participatory democracy and much happier in dealing with well-organised and predictable interests that are firmly attached to the established structures of decision-making. Most importantly, none of the traditional parties could countenance any move away from the parliamentary-representative system.

In evaluating the 'new politics' in West Germany, a distinction has to be made between those elements that reflect the influence of post-materialist values and others that can be interpreted as a specifically German reaction to German circumstances – the governing cartel, the absence of a radical force in the political system, German environment sensitivities. If the former elements predominate, then there may be good grounds for supposing that a fundamental realignment is under way, but if it is the latter, then removal of the causes of discontent could leave the existing system relatively unscathed.

The Greens, as the chief expression of these changes in German society, are often treated as a negative and disturbing force in the body politic, and yet their contribution can be more positively assessed: as a means of assimilating social groups whose alienation otherwise from the political system would have much more damaging consequences. Even this positive view, however, has to be carefully phrased; little is gained by treating the Greens as a convenient social safety-valve, since 'assimilation' requires constructive responses from the other parties.

## The 'Electoral Shocks' of 1989

That the growing unease of the major parties during the 1980s was not at all misplaced was amply demonstrated by the outcome of two sets of elections early in 1989: the January election for the Berlin House of Representatives and the local elections in Hesse in March. The major upset in Berlin was the extent of the losses incurred by the ruling CDU–FDP coalition (15 per cent compared with 1985), a reverse unprecedented at Land or federal level. But this defeat was compounded by the sudden rise of the right wing Republican Party which, in almost 'coming from nowhere' to take 8 per cent of the vote, served notice that the two bourgeois parties now had to contend with radical competition. The Republicans drew their support from those protesting against the laxity of government immigration and political asylum policies. This signal from Berlin – 'anti-foreigner' - sent shock-waves throughout the Federal Republic with the fear that, once having gained a toehold, the Republicans and similar parties such as the NPD would serve as a focus for the rebirth of right-wing extremism using such related issues as local unemployment problems and pressures on the housing-stock to attract wider support.

This transmission did occur in Hesse where the CDU and FDP again suffered heavy losses, with the NPD becoming a credible force, despite CDU efforts to harden its line on immigration – an attempt which possibly served only to highlight the issue even more. Whilst in the earlier 1980s the problem had been only how to integrate the young, discontented left – and that was a problem just for the SPD – the new problem was how to integrate the discontented right, a task the CDU–CSU had to face, without having the benefit of Strauss still fulfilling his 'federal mission' of tapping right-wing sympathies.

Less dramatic but possibly of equal importance in its implications for future political development in the Federal Republic were the signs of emerging common ground between the SPD and the Greens. In Berlin the Alternatives, with some 12 per cent of the vote, showed that the attractions of the 'new politics' had not palled despite the factional in-fighting of the previous years. The formation of a red-green coalition in Berlin also indicated that the realist approach to parliamentary democracy had prevailed over fundamentalist rejection, and with the lesson of the failed coalition-experiment in Hesse in mind this fresh attempt could be more durable.

What are the consequences of these developments for the West German party system? With about 20 per cent of the Berlin vote going to two undeniably radical parties, the increasing vulnerability of the three established parties is underlined. For the FDP the problem has become an existential one, with the threat of being eliminated at a future federal election. For the FDP, too, questions are posed about its commitment to a continuing coalition with the CDU and – more generally – concerning its 'pivotal' function between the SPD and the CDU.

Forecasts of a movement away from the 'tight' three-party pattern of coalition-shuffling at federal level may certainly be premature, but the increasing fluidity of electoral behaviour is unlikely suddenly to stop. Parties have to consider the feasibility of new kinds of coalition alignment, and they point towards a two-bloc model for the party system, in other words towards a sharper distinction between left and right in West German politics than has been evident since the early 1950s. Such a development does not necessarily indicate a great degree of party-polarisation, but rather that the West German electorate will be in a position to make firmer choices. Whether the bulk of voters really wants to be in that position is a matter of doubt.

## A Changing International Context

A permanent priority for the Federal Republic has been to ensure stability in its external relations, an aim chiefly realised by the commitment to the Western alliance system. The ever-present question was how West Germany would fare in the event of a major flare-up between the two superpowers. Successive crises in East-West relations showed that ultimately the Federal Republic had to side with its alliance partners, that it could never act 'contra-cyclically', even if its other priority, fostering inner-German relations, had to be put on one side.

This fixed pattern has been fundamentally disturbed by the changing international context. Of all countries in Western Europe, the

Federal Republic sees itself as most affected by the changes taking place in the Soviet Union: the unwinding of the Soviet Union's defence policies and security position as well the movement towards domestic reform. Yet, despite the benefits that should accrue to the Federal Republic in this new era of detente, it is paradoxical that the evolving situation presents more problems, greater uncertainties, than when tensions were strong and clear lines had to be drawn.

Questions that had long been neglected or even suppressed have again be raised: What are German 'national self-interests', and how are they best served? Does the Federal Republic have a special role to play in central Europe, *Mitteleuropa*, which at one time seemed to be absolutely caught in the Soviet orbit? Are there not at long last realistic possibilities of achieving (in some form or other) the ultimate goal of a reunified Germany? How, in view of these questions, should the Federal Republic shape its future defence commitments?

One effect of the Gorbachev 'peace offensive' has been to convince many West Germans that the Soviet Union no longer represents a threat and that the tightness of the Western security compact is no longer essential. The increasing lack of readiness of the West German population to shoulder defence burdens – at a time when the United States is keen to begin scaling down its security contribution to Western Europe – is bound to increase intra-alliance tensions and thus also make East-West relations more unpredictable.

The issues involved have also fed into internal political debate, with security questions put onto the agenda of the 1990 election. The ailing Kohl government could not risk putting the NATO modernisation plans for short-range nuclear missiles into effect before then for fear of the harmful electoral reaction. For its part, the FDP, in danger of being squeezed by the right, has stressed even more strongly a detente-centred policy which would rule out such modernisation. These internal political pressures led Chancellor Kohl suddenly to announce, in April 1989, a basic change in the government's attitude towards NATO plans for the modernisation of short-range nuclear weapons. Kohl argued that instead the time was ripe to negotiate the elimination of these weapons – particularly threatening as they are to the Federal Republic. This *volte-face* was strongly criticised by the British government. But President Bush produced a compromise for the Brussels NATO summit at the end of May 1989. Negotiations with the Soviet Union on the elimination of short-range nuclear missiles are now envisaged, but only if the Soviet Union agrees to a series of reductions in conventional forces at the Vienna talks which would have the effect of reducing Soviet and US forces in Eastern and Western Europe to 275,000 each. One conclusion that can be drawn is that the Federal Republic, in being prepared – exceptionally – to define and insist upon her own national self-interests, has contributed to a fundamental reorientation in security perceptions for the Western alliance as a whole.

None of these developments is likely to lead to a weakening of West German alliance commitment towards NATO, and prophecies of German neutralism are misplaced, even though a future SDP-led government would certainly be inclined to push detente-oriented policies to the limit. Ultimately, the extent of movement would be dictated by the mood of the electorate. Indicative of this mood could be the appearance of the SPD–AL government in Berlin, where the allied rights in the city – once assumed to be axiomatic in guarantee-ing the security of West Berlin – have been questioned by the left. Such restiveness could be symptomatic of a changing climate of opinion in the Federal Republic as a whole. The rapturous reception accorded to President Gorbachev during his visit to the Federal Republic in June 1989 was further evidence of the fundamental change in West German perceptions and attitudes.

The questions raised earlier about German national self-interests and the future role of the Federal Republic are unlikely to recede, and during the 1990s the international dimension promises to contrib-ute further to the growing flux of West Germany's domestic politics.


## The 1990s and 'Political Stability'

By the mid-1980s it appeared that the lurking fear of slipping 'back to Weimar' had finally been dispelled. The West German Model had proved to be equal to economic challenges, and the heritage of the National Socialist past looked likely to lose much of its divisive potential with the gradual passing of those generations having experi-ence of the Third Reich. It was widely thought at the time of the *Wende* that political unrest and instability would be the consequence of organised labour no longer having favourable access to govern-ment; such forecasts proved wide of the mark.

Yet the question-mark about 'stability' has been put back again for two reasons, one intellectual, the other electoral. In the *Histori-kerstreit* conservative historians, such as Michael Stürmer and Hagen Schulze, have argued that no long-term stability is possible in the Federal Republic without an historically-grounded sense of identity. Jürgen Habermas and others have argued that precisely such a quest is destabilising: stability lies in making an identification with the Basic Law and with the West German present.

This debate showed signs of petering out when its contemporary relevance was suddenly made apparent by the dramatic swing to the right in 1989. This upsurge does relate to the historians' debate: it implies that German identity cannot be assured – and political stability ensured – if significant sections of the population find the 'present' too unpalatable.

Outside observers, however, are less inclined to put emphasis on these manifestations than on all the other indications of West German stability. The anti-immigration theme – not dissimilar, after all, from what has happened in other West European countries – should be treated as a 'warm spot' in the ice, not as a sign that the ice is thin all over. To skate round it calls for skill and nerve – political leadership, as displayed by Kiesinger and Brandt when confronted by the NPD during the time of the Grand Coalition. Germany in the 1990s will not be helped by dark talk of a Weimar syndrome. Yet it is also true that the past continues to be indigestible in the Federal Republic, and the way in which the problem of 'identity' makes its appearance in several different contexts highlights the 'otherness' of the Federal Republic within Western Europe. This legacy will be handed on to the 1990s.

# Guide to Further Reading

## Chapter 1 The German Search for Identity

There is a growing literature on this subject and related aspects of which the more controversial parts are in German. A balanced and comprehensive, if critical, account is Maier (1988) or, in German, Weidenfeld (1983). The historians' debate is also covered in most recent textbooks and journals on German history or politics. *Historikerstreit* (1987) is an excellent collection of the contending historical opinions. Nolte has spelled out his thesis more carefully in *Der europäische Bürgerkrieg* (1988). Older sources on the 'German question' tend to interpret the word to mean only the German nation in relation to the existence of East and West Germany in Europe, for example Schulz (1982), Schulz and Danylow (1985) and Weilemann (1985).

## Chapter 2 Structures of Government

Various authors deal with aspects of parliamentary government, such as Conradt (1986), Smith (1985) and von Beyme (1983). Specifically on the organisation of the executive, Johnson (1983) is a reliable text. For the structure of federalism see the references given for Chapter 3. Schweitzer *et al.* (1985) provide a wealth of material in documentary form. Katzenstein (1987) combines an assessment of structures with a firm policy orientation. Lehmbruch and Schmitter (1979 and 1982) sets German corporatism into the theoretical context, and Berghahn (1988) an historical one; von Beyme and Schmidt (1985) and Bulmer (1989) cover a wide range of policy areas; refer also to the references suggested for Chapter 8. Two older books in German, Hennis (1973) and Leicht (1974), are well worth mentioning for their discussion of the Basic Law and the parliamentary system. Jesse (1981) is a guide to the German literature, and Ellwein and Hesse (1988) is the standard German text on the institutions of the Federal Republic.

## Chapter 3 Territorial Government

Most textbooks on West German politics include an account of the origins and nature of the federal institutions (e.g., Cole, 1984a). A comprehensive account of federal institutions is contained in Johnson (1973), although this is now somewhat dated. Katzenstein (1987) captures the paradox of a decentralised state alongside a centralised society and has case studies of territorial government in operation. On specific aspects of federalism, Blair (1981) covers the importance of the law, whilst Burkett (1986) examines the role of the commentary on the constitutional provisions, and Knott (1981) gives a much more detailed account. German-language material has to be consulted on intergovernmental relations (Scharpf *et. al*, 1976) and the North-South question (Wehling, 1987). A good overall account of federalism is given by Laufer (1984).

## Chapter 4 Political Leadership

Readable accounts of several chancellors are to be found in Prittie (1979) and Dönhoff (1982). An early but useful assessment of the concept of chancellor democracy is made by Ridley (1966). For a concise analysis of the conditions affecting executive leadership, see Mayntz (1980). For cabinet structure and relationship with chancellor, see Müller-Rommel (1988). Party leadership is examined by Johnson (1982), and Paterson (1981) focuses particularly on the SPD. Boenau (1988) provides a wealth of detail on why and how chancellors have come and gone. In German, Bracher (1977) assesses chancellor democracy positively; Haungs (1986) is much more critical. Zundel (1989) summarises current debate especially in relation to Kohl.

## Chapter 5 Political Ideology

There are relatively few English-language books on this topic, though there are plenty that deal in passing with the ideological components of party programmes. These include Pridham (1977) and Miller and Potthoff (1986). The best introduction, despite its age, is still Dahrendorf (1968), first published in German in 1965. Useful information will also be gleaned from the chapter by David Conradt in Almond and Verba (1980), Baker, Dalton and Hildebrandt (1981) and the comparative data in Barnes and Kaase (1979). Much the most important works in German are Greiffenhagen and Greiffenhagen (1974), Sontheimer (1983) and Bracher (1986).

## Chapter 6   The German Voter

Kendall Baker and his colleagues (1981) provide a comprehensive overview of the evolution of German public opinion and voting behaviour from the early 1950s to the late 1970s; this research has been updated in a comparative framework in Dalton (1988). Klingemann (1985) explores the various components of volatility in German voting behaviour. Directly addressing the realignment model, Dalton (1984) and Pappi and Terwey (1982) examine the changing voting patterns of class and religious groups. Several authors provide thoughtful analyses of the particular impact of post-material issues and the Greens on the electorate (Bürklin, 1985; Inglehart, 1984, 1989). Research relevant to the dealignment model can be found in Norpoth's (1983) appraisal of the growth of partisan attachments up to the 1980 election, and Schultze's (1987) analysis of the dealignment trend since 1980. The German language literature on West German public opinion and voting behaviour is exceptionally rich and sophisticated. For an introduction to current research see the collection of edited volumes prepared by Kaase and Klingemann on the 1987 and 1980 elections (forthcoming, 1989), or the Klingemann and Kaase (1986) collection on the 1983 election.

## Chapter 7   The Party System

An excellent account of the evolution of the party system in the wider context of politics in the FRG is found in Smith (1986). Padgett and Burkett (1986) provide a textbook treatment of the historical development of the parties, internal party life and the role of the parties in the system. For more detail, especially on the minor parties see the two volume work edited by Stöss (1983). Kolinsky (1984) studies the political sociology of the parties, whilst Paterson (1987) gives a succinct account of party organisation and apparatus, both concentrating on strains and tensions in the parties. On the individual parties see Braunthal (1983) on the SPD, Mintzel (1982) on the CDU–CSU, Søe (1985) on the FDP, and Hülsberg (1988) on the Greens.

## Chapter 8   Economic Policy

The characteristics of the West German model (*Modell Deutschland*) are outlined and analysed in Dyson and Wilks (1983) and by Katzenstein (1982). On the relationship between theory and practice of the social market economy see Donges (1980) and Dyson (1982b and 1984). The complex relationships between state, banks and industry is considered in Kreile (1978) and Dyson (1985). On the role and power of the Bundesbank see Dyson (1979 and 1981). On the values and styles underpinning West German Economic policies read Dyson (1982a). The major foreign criticisms of West German economic policies in the 1980s are summarised in OECD's *Economic Out-*

*look* (1988). For insights into economic policy making by the Schmidt government see Glotz (1980).


## Chapter 9 The Politics of Welfare

A useful and still valid description of the functioning of German Social Security, as well as a brief history, is provided by Neuhaus (1979). Zollner (1989) gives a chronological history of social policy since the founding of the Federal Republic. For an analysis of the prospects for the German welfare state, expressing a largely SPD viewpoint, see Heinze, Hombach and Scherf (1987). Heidenheimer *el al.* (1983), although a cross-national study of substantive policy areas, has considerable West German coverage. Specialists are highly recommended to consult the excellent essays on poverty and social policy edited by Leibfried and Tennstedt (1985). See also Katzenstein (1987).


## Chapter 10 Foreign and Security Policy

By far the best general book on the subject is Haftendorn (1985). The domestic context of Ostpolitik is very well covered in Tilford (1975). Kaiser (1968) covers the motivations and international dimension with great skill, and still repays reading. Stent (1982) is a sound study of the interplay of trade and Ostpolitik. Moreton (1986) has some good chapters but is disappointing overall. Baring (1988) provides a stimulating, if slightly alarmist, account of recent foreign policy changes. For related references on foreign policy, see Chapters 11 and 12.


## Chapter 11 The European Dimension

The early period of West German involvement in integration is covered in Willis (1965). The period 1969–86 is examined in Bulmer and Paterson (1987), with particular emphasis on the origins of the sectorised, and occasionally, contradictory, nature of European policy. The important Franco-German relationship within the EC is covered by Simonian (1985). The essays in Morgan and Bray (1986) examine both this relationship and the Anglo-German one in the triangle of contacts between Bonn, Paris and London on European matters. Saeter (1980) explores the wider European context, including the Ostpolitik and defence. A review of West Germany and the EC, on the eve of the 1988 presidency of the Council of Ministers, is given in the conference papers edited by Wessels and Regelsberger (1988). Kirchner (1989) offers an interpretation of forty years of the Federal Republic and European integration. Of the German-language material, Hrbek and Wessels (1984) consider West German interests in most of the key areas of

European cooperation and integration, while May (1985) attempts to evaluate the costs and benefits of German membership of the EC.

## Chapter 12 Inter-German Relations

A comprehensive introduction to the development of the FRG's relations with the GDR is Griffith (1978). For more detailed accounts of specific aspects of this question, see Windsor (1971) and Tilford (1975). A particularly acute study of the changing orientation of the CDU is to be found in Pridham (1977). On the subject of CDU Ostpolitik in particular, refer to the excellent study by Clemens (1989). See Braunthal (1983) for a similarly useful general study of the SPD and Merkl (1988) for recent developments in the SPD. For developments in East Germany and between the Germanies, see McAdams (1985 and 1986).

## Chapter 13 Generation and Gender

There is no basic textbook on the issues discussed in this chapter. Baker, Dalton and Hildebrandt (1981) trace the shift towards the New Politics and show how political preferences and the salience of issues differ among generations. Bürklin (1988) focuses on the impact of value changes on electoral behaviour. The categories by Barnes, Kaase, *et al.* (1979) (especially, education and age) locate the potential sources of dissent and polarisation in the contemporary political culture. Allerbeck and Hoag (1983) present a profile of political, social and economic orientations of young people; Fischer (1985) contrasts the views and preferences of young people with those of parents. Hoecker (1987) documents representation of women in the political sphere, and Kolinsky (1989) surveys the persistence and decline of the 'gender-gap' in women's opportunities and political orientations in post-war society.

## Chapter 14 Environmental Politics

There is as yet no satisfactory account of West German environmental politics available in English. There is, however, a great deal of acute analysis and useful information in Rüdig (1986). The interface between environmental and protest movements is well analysed in Burns and van der Will (1988). On the politics of nuclear power, Campbell (1988) and Kitschelt (1986) are both exceptionally good. On chemicals, the major study is Grant, Paterson and Whitston (1988). The development of policy-making is well covered in Richardson and Watts (1985). Those who read German should consult Wey (1982) for historical background and the study by Müller (1986) which is easily the most important work to date in the area.

## Chapter 15 The Trade Unions

For recent discussions of industrial relations in the Federal Republic, see Berghahn and Karsten (1987) and Katzenstein (1987). Much of the argument in this chapter is based on the following sources: Markovits (1986), Allen (1989), Markovits and Allen (1984) and Allen (1987). More general references are Goldthorpe (1984) and Marks (1989). On West German labour law, see Silvia (1988). Streeck (1984) focuses on the car industry, and Thelan (1987) takes the case of the steel industry. Katzenstein (1989) puts industrial relations in the broader political context. Supplementary sources are Markovits and Allen (1980a and 1980b).

## Chapter 16 Public Order and Civil Liberties

Much of the literature is critical of the government's restrictions on civil liberties; some is supportive. A sophisticated analysis of the *Rechtsstaat* ('rule of law' state) is that of Krieger (1957). Among others, Jesse (1980) upholds the concept of 'militant democracy' against determined left wing critics. On the hotly debated 'Decree against Radicals' of 1972, readers may begin with Funke's edited volume (1978), presenting primarily a conservative position, and Narr's edited work (1977) for a left critique. On government surveillance, see the controversial report of the Bertrand Russell Peace Foundation's Third Russell Tribunal (1979), which warned about the growth of a 'Big Brother' society. A description of the well-publicised Baader-Meinhof terrorist group is available in Becker (1978). The pro-government Atlantic Brücke released a slim volume (1980) defending anti-terrorist legislation and the Decree against Radicals. Cobler (1978) sharply criticises government encroachment on civil liberties and warns about the dangers of a police state emerging out of the artificially-created hysteria over terrorism. Most books on foreign workers in the Federal Republic are in German; one exception is a major sociological study by an American scholar, Rist (1978).

# Bibliography

*Aktuell: das Lexicon der Gegenwart* (1984) Munich: Chronik Verlag.

Alber, J. (1986) 'Der Wohlfahrtsstaat in der Wirtschaftskrise – eine Bilanz in der Bundesrepublik seit den frühen siebziger Jahren', *Politische Vierteljahresschrift*, vol. 27, pp. 28–60.

Allemann, Fritz René (1956) *Bonn ist nicht Weimar*, Cologne: Kiepenheuer & Witsch.

Allen, C. (1987) 'Worker Participation and the West German Trade Unions', in C. Sirianni (ed.), *Worker Participation: The Politics of Reform*, Philadelphia: Temple University Press.

Allen, C. (1989) 'Trade Unions, Worker Participation and Flexibility', *Comparative Politics*, forthcoming.

Allerbeck, K. and Hoag, W. (1983) *Jugend ohne Zukunft: Einstellungen, Umwelt, Lebensperspektiven*, Munich: Piper.

Almond, G. and Verba, S. (eds) (1980) *The Civic Culture Revisited*, Boston: Little, Brown.

Andersen, U. and Woyke, W. (1986) *Wahl '87; Zur Bundestagswahl 1987*, Opladen: Leske und Budrich.

Atlantic Brücke (1980) *Civil Liberties and the Defense of Democracy against Extremists and Terrorists: A Report on the West German Situation*, Freiburg: Rombach.

Bäcker, G. and Naegele, G. (1986) 'Wende ohne Ende – Praxis und Ideologie der konservativ-rechtsliberalen Sozialpolitik', *Theorie und Praxis der sozialen Arbeit*, vol. 37, pp. 122–35.

Baker, K., Dalton R. and Hildebrandt K. (1981) *Germany transformed: Political Culture and the New Politics*, Cambridge, Mass.: Harvard University Press.

Baring, A. (1988) *Unser Neuer Grössenwahn*, Stuttgart: DVA.

Barnes S., Kaase M. *et al.* (1979) *Political Action and Mass Participation in Five Western Democracies*, Beverly Hills: Sage.

Beck P. (1984) 'The Dealignment Era in America', in R. Dalton *et al.*, *Electoral Change in Advanced Industrial Democracies*, Princeton: Princeton University Press.

Becker, J. (1978) *Hitler's Children: The Story of the Baader-Meinhof Terrorist Gang*, revised ed, London: Panther.

Beetham, D. (1974) *Max Weber and the Theory of Modern Politics*, London: Allen & Unwin.

Bell, D. (1973) *The Coming of Post-industrial Society*, New York: Basic Books.

Berg, K. (1988) 'The Inter-*Land* Treaty on the Reform of the Broadcasting System in the FRG, and the fifth decision of the Constitutional Court', *EBU Review Programmes, Administration, Law*, vol. 39, no. 2, pp 40–9.

Berghahn, V. and Karsten, D. (1987) *Industrial Relations in West Germany*, Oxford: Berg.

Berghahn, V. (1988) 'Corporatism in Germany in Historical Perspective', in A. Cox and N. O'Sullivan (eds), *The Corporate State*, Aldershot and Brookfield: Gower.

Bergmann, U., Dutschke, R., Lefèbre, W. and Rabel, B. (1968) Rebellion der Studenten, oder die neue Opposition, Reinbek: Rowohlt.

Berg-Schlosser, D. and Schissler, J. (eds) (1987) *Politische Kultur in Deutschland: Bilanz und Perspektiven der Forschung*, Opladen: Westdeutscher Verlag.

Bertrand Russell Peace Foundation (1979) *Censorship, Legal Defence and the Domestic Intelligence Service in West Germany: Conclusions of the Final Session of the Third Russell Tribunal*, Nottingham: Russell Press.

Beyme, K. von (1983) *The Political System of the Federal Republic of Germany*, Aldershot: Gower.

Beyme, K. von (ed.) (1979) *Die grossen Regierungserklärungen der deutschen Kanzler von Adenauer bis Schmidt*, München-Wien: Hauser.

Beyme, K. von and Schmidt, M. (eds), (1985) *Policy and Politics in the Federal Republic of Germany*, Aldershot: Gower.

Blair, P. (1981) *Federalism and Judicial Review in West Germany* Oxford: Clarendon Press.

Bock, T. (1982) 'Mit diesem Staat ist keine Natur zu machen' in J. Mettke (ed.), *Die Grünen. Regierungspartei: von Morgen?* Reinbek: Rowohlt.

Boenau, A. B. (1988) 'Changing Chancellors in West Germany', *West European Politics*, vol. II, no. 3, pp 24–41.

Bracher, K. D. (1977) *Zeitgeshichtliche Kontroversen*, Munich: Piper.

Bracher, K. D. (1986) 'Politik und Zeitgeist. Tendenzen der siebziger Jahre', in K. Bracher, W. Jäger and W. Link, *Republik im Wandel 1969–1974. Die Ära Brandt. Geschichte der Bundesrepublik Deutschland*, vol. V/I, Stuttgart: Deutsche Verlags-Anstalt.

Brandt, W. (1969) 'Die Alternative', *Die Neue Gesellschaft*, Sonderheft (May 1969).

Braunthal, G. (1983) *The West German Social Democrats 1969–1982: Profile of a Party in Power*, Boulder, Col.: Westview Press.

Bulmer, S. (1986) *The Domestic Structure of European Community Policy-Making in West Germany*, New York: Garland.

Bulmer, S. (ed.) (1989) *The Changing Agenda of West German Public Policy*, Aldershot: Gower.

Bulmer, S. and Paterson, W. (1987) *The Federal Republic of Germany and the European Community*, London: Allen & Unwin.

Burkett, T. (1986) 'The ambivalent role of the Bundesrat in the West German Federation', in M. Burgess (ed.), *Federalism and Federation in Western Europe*, London: Croom Helm.

Bürklin, W. (1985) 'The Greens: Ecology and the New Left', in P. Wallach and G. Romoser (eds), *West German Politics in the Mid-Eighties*, New York: Praeger.

Bürklin, W. (1987) 'Governing Left Parties Frustrating the Radical Non-Established Left', *European Sociological Review*, vol. 3, pp. 109–26.

Bürklin, W. (1988) Wählerverhalten und Wertewandel, Opladen: Leske and Budrich.

Bürklin, W. and Kaltefleiter, W. (1987) 'Die Bundestagswahl 1987: Streitfragen einer neuen Konfliktdimension', *Zeitschrift für Politik*, vol. 34, pp. 400–25.

Burns, R. and van der Will, W. (1988) *Protest and Democracy in West Germany: Extra-Parliamentary Opposition and the Democratic Agenda*, London: Macmillan.

Burnham, W. (1970) *Critical Elections and the Mainsprings of American Politics*, New York: Norton.

Burnham, W. (1978) 'Great Britain: The Death of the Collectivist Consensus?', in L. Maisel and J. Cooper, (eds.), *The Future of Political Parties*, Beverly Hills: Sage.

Campbell, J. (1988) *Collapse of an Industry: Nuclear Power and the Contradictions of US Policy*, Ithaca: Cornell.

Carr, J. (1985) *Helmut Schmidt: Helmsman of Germany*, London: Weidenfeld & Nicolson.

Clemens, C. (1989) *Reluctant Realists: The CDU/CSU's Adaptation of West German Ostpolitik*, Durham: Duke University Press.

Cobler, S. (1978) *Law, Order and Politics in West Germany* Harmondsworth: Penguin.

Cole, R. (1984a) 'Federalism: Bund and Länder', in C. C. Schweitzer, D. Karsten *et al.* (eds), *Politics and Government in the Federal Republic of Germany, Basic Documents*, Leamington Spa: Berg.

Cole, R. (1984b) 'Federalism: Intergovernmental Relations and Finance', in C. C. Schweitzer, D. Karsten *et al.* (eds.), *Politics and Government in the Federal Republic of Germany, Basic Documents*, Leamington Spa: Berg.

Conradt, D. (1986) *The Germany Polity*, New York and London: Longman.

Crewe, I. and Denver, D. (eds) (1985) *Electoral Change in Western Democracies*, New York: St Martin's Press.

Daalder, H. and Mair, P. (1983) *Western European Party Systems: Continuity and Change*, London: Sage.

Dahrendorf, R, (1968) *Society and Democracy in Germany*, London: Weidenfeld & Nicolson.

Dahrendorf, R. (1983) *Die Chancen der Krise. Über die Zukunft des Liberalismus*, Stuttgart: Deutsche Verlags-Anstalt.

Dalton, R. (1984) 'The German Party System between Two Ages', in R. Dalton *et al.*, *Electoral Change in Advanced Industrial Democracies*, Princeton: Princeton University Press.

Dalton, R. (1986) 'Wertwandel oder Wertwende: Die Neue Politik und Parteienpolarisierung', in H.-D. Klingemann, Hans-Dieter and M. Kaase (eds), *Wahlen und politischer Prozess*, Opladen: Westdeutscher Verlag.

Dalton, R. (1988) *Citizen Politics in Western Democracies*, Chatham, N.J.: Chatham House Publishers.

Dalton, R. *et al.* (1984) *Electoral Change in Advanced Industrial Democracies*, Princeton: Princeton University Press.

Dicke, H. *et al.* (1987) *EG-Politik am Prüfstand. Wirkungen auf Wachstum und Strukturwandel in der Bundesrepublik*, Tübingen: J. C. B. Mohr.

Donges, J. (1980) 'Industrial Policies in West Germany's Not So Market-Oriented Economy', *World Politics*, vol., 00 no. 3, pp. 185–204.

Dönhoff, M. (1982) *Foe into Friend: The Makers of the New Germany, from Konrad Adenauer to Helmut Schmidt*, London: Weidenfeld & Nicolson.

Döring, H. and Smith, G. (eds), (1982) *Party Government and Political Culture in Western Germany*, New York: St Martin's Press.

Dregger, A. (1988) 'Vermeidbare Sonderbedrohungen', *Blätter für Deutsche und Internationale Politik*, vol. 3.

Dutschke, R. (1980) *Mein langer Marsch. Reden, Schriften und Tagebücher aus zwangig Jahren*, Reinbek: Rowohlt.

Dyson, K. (1979) 'The Ambiguous Politics of West Germany', *European Journal of Political Research*, vol. 7, no. 4, pp. 375–95.

Dyson, K. (1981) 'The Politics of Economic Management', in W. Paterson and G. Smith (eds), *The West German Model: Perspectives on a Stable State*, London: Frank Cass.

Dyson, K. (1982a) 'West Germany: The Search for a Rationalist Consensus', in J. Richardson (ed.), *Policy Styles in Western Europe*, London: Allen & Unwin.

Dyson, K. (1982b) 'Public Policy and Economic Recession in West Germany, in A. Cox (ed.), *Politics, Policy and the European Recession*, London: Macmillan.

Dyson, K. (1982c) 'Party Government and Party State', in H. Döring, and G. Smith (eds), *Party Government and Political Culture in Western Germany*, New York: St Martin's Press.

Dyson, K. (1984) 'The Politics of Corporate Crises in West Germany' *West European Politics*, vol. 7, pp. 24–46.

Dyson, K. (1985) 'Banks, State and Industry in West Germany', in A. Cox (ed.), *State, Banks and Industrial Finance*, Brighton: Wheatsheaf.

Dyson, K. and Wilks, S. (eds) (1983) *Industrial Crisis*, Oxford: Basil Blackwell.

Edinger, L. J. (1968) *Germany: Attitudes and Processes*, Boston: Little, Brown.

Ellwein, T. and Hesse, J. (1987) *Das Regierungssystem der Bundesrepublik Deutschland*, Opladen: Westdeutscher Verlag.

Eppler, E. (1979) *Ende oder Wende? Von der Machbarkeit des Möglichen*, Stuttgart: Kohlhammer.

Eppler, E. (1981), *Wege aus der Gefahr*, Reinbek: Rowohlt.

Eppler, E., Ende, M. and Taechl, H. (1982) *Phantasie-Kultur-Politik. Protokolle eines Gesprächs*, Stuttgart: Theinemann.

Feist, U. and Krieger, H. (1987) 'Alte und neue Scheidelinien des politischen Verhaltens', *Aus Politik und Zeitgeschichte*, (21 March), pp. 33–47.

Fischer, A. (1985) *Jugendliche und Erwachsene '85: Generationen im Vergleich*, Opladen: Leske und Budrich.

Fischer, A. *et al.* (1985) *Jugendliche und Erwachsene: 1985; Generationen in Vergleich. Jugend der Fünfziger Jahre – Heute*, vol. 3, Opladen: Leske and Budrich.

Fischer, J. (1988) 'Für neue Mittelschichten attraktiv machen', *Der Spiegel*, 47/1988.

Flach, K., Maihofer, W. and Scheel, W. (1972) *Die Freiburger Thesen der Liberalen*, Reinbek: Rowohlt.

Flanagan, C. and Dalton, R. (1984) 'Parties Under Stress: Realignment and Dealignment in Advanced Industrial Societies', *West European Politics*, vol. 7, pp. 7–23.

Forschungsgruppe Wahlen e.V. (1987) *Bundestagswahl 1987: Eine Analyse der Wahl zum 11. Deutschen Bundestag am 25. Januar 1987*, Mannheim.

Forsthoff, E. (1971) *Der Staat in der industriegesellschaft*, Munich: Beck.

Funke, M. (ed) (1978) *Extremismus im demokratischen Rechtsstaat*, Düsseldorf: Droste.

Garlichs, D. and Hull, C. (1978) 'Central Control and Information Dependence', in K. Hanf and F. Scharpf (eds), *Interorganizational Policy Making: Limits to Coordination and Central Control*, London: Sage.

Gehlen, A. (1974) *Sinn und Unsinn des Leistungsprinzips*, Munich: Deutscher Taschenbuch-Verlag.

Geske, O. E. (1986) 'Konturen eines neuen Länderfinanzausgleichs' *Wirtschaftsdienst*, vol. 66, no. 7, pp. 399–403.

Gibowski, G, and Kaase, M. (1986) 'Die Ausgangslage für die Bundestagswahl am 25. Januar 1987', *Aus Politik und Zeitgeschichte: Beilage zur Wochenzeitung Das Parlament*, B48/86.

Glaser, H. (ed.) (1979) *Fluchtpunkt Jahrhundertwende. Ursprünge und Aspekte einer zukünftigen Gesellschaft*, Bonn: Hohwacht.

Glotz, P. (1980) *Die Innenausstattung der Macht*, Munich: Steinhausen.

Gluchowski, P. (1986) 'Wahlerfahrung und Parteiidentifikation', in H.- D. Klingemann and M. Kaase (eds), *Wahlen und politischer Prozess*, Opladen: Westdeutscher Verlag.

Gluchowski, P. (1987) 'Lebensstile und Wandel der Wählerschaft in der Bundesrepublik Deutschland', *Aus Politik und Zeitgeschichte* (21 March) pp. 18–32.

Gluchowski, P. and Veen, H. J. (1988) 'Sozialstrukturelle Nivellierung bei politischer Polarisierung – Wandlungen und Konstanten in den Wählerstrukturen der Parteien 1953–1987', *Zeitschrift für Parlamentsfragen*, 2/1988.

Goldthorpe, J. (ed.) (1984) *Order and Conflict in Contemporary Capitalism*, Oxford: Clarendon Press.

Grant, W., Paterson, W. and Whitston, C. (1988) *Government and the Chemical Industry: A Comparative Study of Britain and West Germany*, Oxford: Clarendon Press.

Grass, G. (1982) *Die Zeit*, (3 December).

Greiffenhagen, M. (1984) *Der neue Konservatismus der siebziger Jahre*, Reinbek: Rowohlt.

Greiffenhagen, M. and S. (1974) *Ein schwieriges Vaterland*, Munich: List.
Griffith, W. (1978) *The Ostpolitik of the Federal Republic of Germany*, Cambridge, Mass,: MIT Press.
Gruhl, H. (1975) *Ein Planet wird geplündert*, Frankfurt: Fischer.
Grunow, D. (1986) 'De-bureaucratisation and the Self Help Movement: Towards a Restructuring of the Welfare State in the Federal Republic of Germany', in E. Øyen (ed.), *Comparing Welfare States and their Futures*, Aldershot: Gower.
Guggenberger, B. and Kempf, U. (eds) (1984) *Bürgerinitiativen und Repräsentatives System*, 2nd ed, Opladen: Westdeutscher Verlag.
Habermas, J. (1982) 'Die Kulturkritik der Neokonservativen in der USA und der Bundesrepublik', *Neue Gesellschaft*, XI.
Habermas, J. (1987) 'Eine Art Schadensabwicklung', (*Die Zeit*, 11 July 1986), in *Eine Art Schadensabwicklung*, Frankfurt: Suhrkamp.
Habermas, J. (ed.), (1969) *Stichworte, zur 'Geistigen Situation der Zeit'*, 2 vols. Frankfurt: Suhrkamp.
Haftendorn, H. (1985) *Security and Detente: Conflicting Priorities in German Foreign Policy*, New York: Praeger.
Hallett, G. (1985) 'Unemployment and Labour Market Policies: Some Lessons from West Germany', *Social Policy and Administration*, vol. 19, pp. 180–90.
Haungs, P. (1986) 'Kanzlerdemokratie in der BRD: von Adenauer bis Kohl', *Zeitschrift für Politik*, vol. 33, no. 1, pp. 47–88.
Heidenheimer, A. J. (1960) *Adenauer and the CDU: The Rise of the Leader and the Integration of the Party*, The Hague: Martinus Nijhoff.
Heidenheimer, A., Heclo, H. and Adams, C. (eds) (1983) *Comparative Public Policy: The Politics of Social Choice in Europe and America*, 2nd edn, New York: St Martin's Press.
Heinze, R. and Hinrichs, K. (1986) 'The Institutional Crisis of a Welfare State: The Case of Germany', in Øyen E, (ed.), *Comparing Welfare States and their Futures*, Aldershot: Gower.
Heinze, R., Hombach, B. and Scherf, H. (eds) (1987) *Sozialstaat 2000*, Bonn: Verlag Neue Gesellschaft.
Hennis, W. (1970) *Demokratisierung. Zur Problematik eines Begriffs*, Opladen: Westdeutscher Verlag.
Hennis, W. (1973) *Die missverstandene Demokratie: Demokratie-Verfassung-Parlament. Studien zu deutschen Problemen*, Freiburg: Herder.
'*Historikerstreit'. Die Dokumentation der Kontroverse um die Einzigartigkeit der nationalsozialistischen Judenvernichtung* (1987), Munich: Piper.
Hoecker, B. (1987) *Frauen in der Politik: Eine soziologische Studie*, Opladen: Leske and Budrich.
Hofmann-Göttig, J. (1984) *Die jungen Wähler, Zur Interpretation der Jungwählerdaten zur repräsentativen Wahlstatistik*, Frankfurt and New York: Campus.
Hofmann-Göttig, J. (1986) *Emanzipation mit dem Stimmzettel, 70 Jahre Frauenwahlrecht in Deutschland*, Bonn: Verlag Neue Gesellschaft.
Hrbek, R. and Wessels, W. (1984) EG-Mitgliedschaft: ein vitales Interesse der Bundesrepublik Deutschland? Bonn: Europa Union Verlag.

Hubner, E. and Rohlfs, H.-H. (eds) (1985) *Jahrbuch der Bundesrepublik Deutschland 1985/86*, Beck/dtv.

Hubner, E. and Rohlfs, H.-H. (eds) (1987) *Jahrbuch der Bundesrepublik Deutschland 1987/88*, Beck/dtv.

Hülsberg, W. (1988) *The German Greens: A Social and Political Profile*, London: Verso.

Humphreys, P. (1988) 'Satellite Broadcasting Policy in West Germany – political conflict and competition in a decentralised system', in R. Negrine (ed.) *Satellite Broadcasting – the Politics and Implications of the New Media*, London: Routledge.

Humphreys, P. (1989) 'Public policies for the new technologies' in S. Bulmer (ed.), *the Changing Agenda of West German Public Policy*, Aldershot: Gower.

Huntington, S. (1974) 'Post-industrial Politics: How Benign will it be?', *Comparative Politics*, vol. 6, pp. 163–91.

Inglehart, R. (1977) *The Silent Revolution*, Princeton: Princeton University Press.

Inglehart, R. (1984) 'The Changing Structure of Political Cleavages in Western Society', in R. Dalton *et al.*, *Electoral Change in Advanced Industrial Democracies*, Princeton: Princeton University Press.

Inglehart, R. (1989) *Culture Shift*, Princeton: Princeton University Press.

Inglehart, R. and Hochstein, A. (1972), 'Alignment and Dealignment of the Electorate in France and the United States', *Comparative Political Studies*, vol. 5, pp. 343–72.

Irving, R. and Paterson, W. (1983) 'The *Machtwechsel* of 1982–3', *Parliamentary Affairs*, vol. 36, no. 3, pp. 417–35.

Irving, R. and Paterson, W. (1987) 'The 1987 West German Election', *Parliamentary Affairs*, vol. 40, no. 3, pp. 333–56.

Jaspers, K. (1966) *Wohin treibt die Bundesrepublik? Tatsachen-Gefahren-Chancen*, Munich: Piper.

Jesse, E. (1980) *Streitbare Demokratie: Theorie, Praxis und Herausforderungen in der Bundesrepublik Deutschland*, Berlin: Colloquium.

Jesse, E. (1981) *Literaturführer: Parlamentarische Demokratie,*, Opladen: Leske und Budrich.

Joffe, J. (1981) German Defence Policy: Novel Solutions and Enduring Dilemmas, in G. Flynn (ed.), *The Internal Fabric of Western Security*, London: Croom Helm.

Johnson, N. (1973) 'Federalism and Decentralisation in the Federal Republic of Germany', *Commission on the Constitution*, Research Paper I, London: HMSO.

Johnson, N. (1982) 'Parties and the Conditions of Political Leadership', in H. Döring and G. Smith (eds), *Party Government and Political Culture in Western Germany*, London: Macmillan.

Johnson, N. (1983) *State and Government in the Federal Republic of Germany: The Executive at Work*, Oxford: Pergamon.

Jugend '81 (1982) *Lebensentwürfe, Alltagskulturen, Zukunftsbilder*, Opladen: Leske und Budrich.

Kaase, M. and Klingemann, H.-D. (1983) *Wahlen und politisches System*, Opladen: Westdeutscher Verlag.

Kaiser, K. (1968) *German Foreign Policy in Transition*, London: Oxford University Press.

Katzenstein, P. (1982) 'West Germany as Number Two', in A. Markovits (ed.), *The Political Economy of West Germany*, New York: Praeger.

Katzenstein, P. (1987) *Policy and Politics in West Germany: The Growth of a Semi-sovereign State*, Philadelphia: Temple University Press.

Katzenstein, P. (ed.), (1989) *Industry and Politics in West Germany*, Ithaca: Cornell University Press.

Kelly, P. (1984) *Fighting for Hope*, London: Chatto & Windus.

Kerr, H. (forthcoming) 'Social Class and Party Choice', in R. Inglehart, and H.-D. Klingemann (eds), *People and their Politics*.

Kirchheimer, O. (1969) 'The Transformation of Western European Party Systems', in J. LaPalombara and M. Weiner (eds), *Political Parties and Political Development*, Princeton: Princeton University Press.

Kirchner, E. (1989) 'The Federal Republic of Germany in the European Community', in P. Merkl (ed.), *The Federal Republic of Germany at Forty*, Cambridge: Cambridge University Press.

Kitschelt, H. (1986) 'Political Opportunity Structures and Political Protest: Anti-Nuclear Movements in Four Democracies', *British Journal of Political Science*, vol. 14, no. 1, pp. 57–85.

Klatt, H. (1986) 'Reform und Perspektiven des Föderalismus in der Bundesrepublik Deutschland', *Aus Politik und Zeitgeschichte* (12 July 1986) pp. 3–21.

Klingemann, H.-D. (1985) 'Germany', in I. Crewe and D. Denver (eds), *Electoral Change in Western Democracies*, New York: St Martin's Press/ London: Croom Helm.

Klingemann, H.-D. (1986) 'Der vorsichtig abwägende Wahler', in H.-D. Klingemann, and M. Kaase (eds), *Wahlen und politischer Prozess*, Opladen: Westdeutscher Verlag.

Klingemann, H.-D. and Kaase, M. (1986) *Wahlen und politischer Prozess*, Opladen: Westdeutscher Verlag.

Kloten, N. (1987) 'Neomerkantilismus in Baden-Württemberg? Zur Regionalisierung der Wirtschaftspolitik', in R. Henn (ed.), *Technologie, Wachstum und Beschäftigung – Festschrift für Lothar Späth*, Berlin: Springer Verlag, pp. 850–68.

Knott, J. (1981) *Managing the German Economy: Budgetary Politics in a Federal State*, Lexington, Ma.: D. C. Heath.

Kolinsky, E. (1989) 'Socioeconomic Change and Political Culture in West Germany', in J. Gaffney and E. Kolinsky (eds), *Political Culture in France and Germany*, London: Routledge.

Kolinsky, E. (1984) *Parties, Opposition and Society in West Germany*, London: Croom Helm.

Kolinsky, E. (1988) 'The Greens – A Women's Party?', *Parliamentary Affairs*, vol. 40, no. 1, pp. 129–48.

Kolinsky, E. (1989) *Women in West Germany – Life, Work and Politics*, Oxford: Berg.

Kolinsky, E. (ed) (1987) *Opposition in Western Europe*, London: PSI and Croom Helm, 1987.

Körber-Weik, M. and Wied-Nebbeling, S. (1987) 'Ein wirtschaftliches Süd-Nord-Gefälle in der Bundesrepublik?' in H. G. Wehling (ed.), *Nord-Süd in Deutschland? Vorurteile und Tatsachen*, Stuttgart: Verlag W. Kohlhammer.

Kreile, M. (1978) 'West Germany: The Dynamics of Expansion', in P. Katzenstein (ed.), *Between Power and Plenty*, Cambridge, Mass.: Harvard University Press.

Krieger, L. (1957) *The German ¡Idea of Freedom: History of a Political Tradition*, Boston: Beacon Press.

Küchler, M. (1986) 'Maximizing Utility at the Polls', *European Journal of Political Research*, vol. 14, pp. 81–95.

Kvistad, G. (1987) 'Between State and Society: Green Political Ideology in the Mid-1980s', *West German Politics*, vol. 10, pp. 211–28.

Lafontaine, O. (1988) *Die Gesellschaft der Zukunft*, Hamburg: Hoffmann und Campe.

Laqueur, W. (1962) *Young Germany. A History of the German Youth Movement*, London: Routledge & Kegan Paul.

Laufer, H. (1984) *Der Föderalismus in der Bundesrepublik Deutschland*, Informationen zur politischen Bildung no. 204, Bonn: Bundeszentrale für politische Bildung.

Lederer, G. (1983) *Jugend und Autorität*, Opladen: Westdeutscher Verlag.

Lehmbruch, G. and Lang, W. (1977) 'Die Konzertierte Aktion', *Der Bürger im Staat*, September.

Lehmbruch, G. and Schmitter, P. (eds) (1979) *Trends Towards Corporatist Intermediation*, London and Beverly Hills; Sage.

Lehmbruch, G. and Schmitter, P. (eds) (1982) *Patterns of Corporatist Policy Policy Making*, London and Beverly Hills: Sage.

Leibfried, S. and Tennstedt, F. (eds) (1985) *Politik der Armut und die Spaltung des Sozialstaats*, Frankfurt: Suhrkamp.

Leicht, R. (1974) *Grundgesetz und politische Praxis. Parlamentarismus in der Bundesrepublik*, Munich: Carl Hanser.

Lipset, S. and Rokkan, S. (eds) (1967) *Party Systems and Voter Alignments*, New York: Free Press.

Livingston, W. (1952) 'A Note on the Nature of Federalism', *Political Science Quarterly*, vol. 67, no. 1, pp. 81–95.

Loewenberg, G. (1979) 'The Remaking of the German Party System' in C. Karl (ed.), *Germany at the Polls*, Washington D.C.: American Enterprise Institute.

Löwenthal, R. (1970) *Der romantische Rückfall*, Stuttgart: Kohlhammer.

Löwenthal, R. (1985) 'The German Question Transformed', *Foreign Affairs*, vol. 63, no. 2, pp. 303–15.

Maier, C. (1988) *The Unmasterable Past: History, Holocaust and German National Identity*, Cambridge, Mass.: Harvard University Press.

Mangen, S. (1985) 'Germany: The Psychiatric Enquete and its Aftermath', in S. P. Mangen (ed.), *Mental Health Care in the European Community*, London: Croom Helm.

Marcuse, H. (1969) *An Essay on Liberation*, Boston: Beacon Press.

Markovits, A. (1986) *The Politics of West German Trade Unions. Strategies of Class and Interest Representation in Growth and Crisis*, Cambridge: Cambridge University Press.

Markovits, A. and Allen, C. (1980a) 'Power and Dissent: The Trade Unions in the Federal Republic of Germany Re-examined', *West European Politics*, vol. 3, no. 1, pp. 68–96.

Markovits, A. and Allen, C. (1980b) 'Trade Union Responses to the Contemporary Economic Problems in Western Europe: The Context of Current Debates and Policies in the Federal Republic of Germany', *Economic and Industrial Democracy*, vol. 2, no. 1, pp. 49–85.

Markovits, A. and Allen, C. (1984) 'The West German Case', in P. Gourevitch *et al.*, *Unions and Economic Crisis*, London; George Allen & Unwin.

Marks, G. (1989) *Unions in Politics*, Princeton: Princeton University Press.

May, B. (1985) *Kosten und Nutzen der deutschen EG-Mitgliedschaft*, 2nd edn, Bonn: Europa Union Verlag.

Mayntz, R. (1980) 'Executive Leadership in Germany: Dispersion of Power or "Kanzlerdemokratie"?' in R. Rose and E. Suleiman (eds), *Presidents and Prime Ministers*, Washington D.C., American Enterprise Institute.

McAdams, A. J. (1985) *East Germany and Detente: Building Authority after the Wall*, Cambridge: Cambridge University Press.

McAdams, A. J. (1986) 'Inter-German Relations: A New Balance', *Foreign Affairs*, vol. 65, no. 1, pp. 136–53.

Merkl, P. H. (1963) *The Origins of the West German Republic*, New York: Oxford University Press.

Merkl, P. H. (1988) 'The SPD after Brandt: Problems of Integration in Changing Urban Society', *West European Politics*, vol. 11, no. 1, pp. 40–53.

Merklein, R. (1986) 'Den Alterskassen ein Baby schenken?', *Der Spiegel*, no. 2, 62–72; no. 3, 70–79.

Mettke, J. (ed.) (1982) *Die Grünen. Regierungspartner von Morgen?*, Reinbek: Rowohlt.

Michalsky, H. (1985) 'The Politics of Social Policy', in K. von Beyme and M. Schmidt (eds), *Policy and Politics in the Federal Republic of Germany*, Aldershot: Gower.

Miller, S. and Potthoff, H. (1986) *History of the German Social Democratic Party from 1848 to the Present*. Leamington Spa: Berg.

Mintzel, A. (1982) 'Conservatism and Christian Democracy in the Federal Republic of Germany', in Z. Layton-Henry (ed.), *Conservative Politics in Western Europe*, London: Heinemann.

Mitscherlich, A. (1963) *Auf dem Weg zur vaterlosen Gesellschaft*, Munich: Piper.

Moreton, E. (ed) (1986) *Germany Between East and West*, Cambridge: Cambridge University Press.

Müller, E. (1986) *Die Innenwelt der Unweltpolitik*, Opladen: Westdeutscher Verlag.

Müller-Rommel, F. (1988) 'The Centre of Government in West Germany:

Changing Patterns under 14 Legislatures (1949–1987)', *European Journal of Political Research*, vol. 16, no. 2, pp. 171–90.

Murswieck, A. (1985) *Health Policy-making*, in K. von Beyme and M. Schmidt (eds), *Policy and Politics in the Federal Republic of Germany*, Aldershot: Gower.

Narr, W. -D. (ed.) (1977) *Wir Bürger als Sicherheitsrisiko: – Berufsverbot und Lauschangriff – Beiträge zur Verfassung unserer Republik*, Reinbeck: Rowohlt.

Naumann, K. (1987) 'Die Normalisierung der Republik und die Zukunft der Koalition', *Blätter für deutsche und internationale Politik*, 10, 1987.

Neuhaus, R. (1979) *Social Security: How it Works in the Federal Republic of Germany*, Bonn: Friedrich Ebert Stiftung.

Nolte, E. (1987) *Der Europäische Bürgerkrieg 1917–1945*,

Norpoth, H. (1983) 'The Making of a More Partisan Electorate', *British Journal of Political Science*, vol. 13, pp. xxx.

OECD (1988) *Economic Outlook*, Paris: OECD.

Opielka, M. and Ostner, I. (eds) (1987) *Umbau des Sozialstaats*, Essen: Klartext.

Oyen, E. (ed.) *Comparing Welfare States and their Futures*, Aldershot: Gower.

Padgett, S. and Burkett, T. (1986) *Political Parties and Elections in West Germany; the search for a new stability*, London: Hurst.

Papadakis, E. (1984) *The Green Movement in West Germany*, New York: St Martin's Press.

Pappi, R. -U. (1973) 'Parteiensystem und Sozialstruktur in der Bundesrepublik', *Politische Vierteljahresschrift*, vol. 14, pp. 191–213.

Pappi, R. -U. (1984) 'The West German Party System', *West European Politics*, vol. 7 (October), pp. 7–26.

Pappi, F. -U. and Terwey, M. (1982) 'The German Electorate', in H. Döring and G. Smith (eds), *Party Government and Political Culture in Western Germany*, New York: St Martin's Press/London: Macmillan.

Paterson, W. (1974) *The SPD and European Integration*, Farnborough: Saxon House.

Paterson, W. (1981) 'The Chancellor and his Party: Political Leadership in the Federal Republic', in W. Paterson and G. Smith (eds), *The West German Model: Perspectives on a Stable State*, London: Frank Cass.

Paterson, W. (1987) 'West German Parties – Between Party Apparatus and Basis Democracy', in A. Ware (ed.), *Political Parties: Electoral Change and Structural Response*, London: Basil Blackwell.

Paterson, W. and Webber, D. (1987) 'The Federal Republic of Germany: The Re-emergent Opposition?', in E. Kolinsky (ed.), *Opposition in Western Europe*, London: Croom Helm.

Pedersen, M. (1979) 'The Dynamics of European Party Systems', *European Journal of Political Research*, vol. 7, pp. 1–26.

Pridham, G. (1977) *Christian Democracy in Western Germany. The CDU/CSU in Government and Opposition*, London: Croom Helm.

Prittie, T. (1979) *The Velvet Chancellors*, London: Frederick Müller.

Raschke, J. (ed) (1982) *Bürger und Parteien*, Opladen: Westdeutscher Verlag.

Richardson, J. and Watts, N. (1985) *National Policy Styles and the Environment*, London: Institute for Environmental Policy.

Richter, E. (1987) 'Subsidiarität und Neokonservatismus: die Trennung von politischer Herrschaftsbegründung und gesellschaftlichem Stufenbau', *Politische Vierteljahresschrift*, vol. 28, pp. 293–314.

Ridley, F. (1966) 'Chancellor Government as a Political System', *Parliamentary Affairs*, vol. 19, no. 4, pp. 446–61.

Rist, R. C. (1978) *Guestworkers in Germany: The Prospects for Pluralism*, New York: Praeger.

Roth, R. and Richt, D. (eds) (1987) *Neue soziale Bewegungen in der Bundesrepublik Deutschland*, Bonn: Bundeszentrale für Politische Bildung.

von Rothkirch, C. and Weidig, I. (1985) *Die Zukunft der Arbeitslandschaft, Zum Arbeitskräftebedarf und Tätigkeit bis zum Jahre 2000*, Nuremberg: Institut für Arbeitsmarkt.

von Rothkirch, C. and Weidig, I. (1986) *Zum Arbeitskräftebedarf nach Qualifikationen bis zum Jahr 2000*, Nuremberg: Institut für Arbeitsmarkt.

Rüdig, W. (1986) *Energy, Public Protest and Green Parties: A Comparative Analysis*, PhD, Manchester.

Rummel, L. and Wessells, W. (1983) 'Federal Republic of Germany: New Responsibilities, Old Constraints', in C. Hill (ed.), *National Foreign Policies and European Political Cooperation*, London: Allen & Unwin.

Saeter, M. (1980) *The Federal Republic, Europe and the World*, Oslo: Universtetsførlaget.

Sårlvik, B. and Crewe, I. (1983) *Decade of Dealignment*, Cambridge: Cambridge University Press.

Scharpf, F. *et al.* (1976) *Politikverflechtung. Theorie und Empirie des kooperativen Föderalismus in der Bundesrepublik*, Kronberg: Scriptor.

Scharf, F. (1985) 'The Joint-Decision Trap: Lessons from German Federalism and European Integration', *Discussion Paper IIM/LMP 85–1*, Berlin: Wissenschaftzentrum.

Scheer, H. (1979) *Parteien kontra Bürger?*, Munich: Piper.

Schelsky, H. (1957) *Die skeptische Generation. Eine Soziologie der deutschen Jugend*, Düsseldorf: Diederichs.

Schelsky, H. (1961) *Der Mensch in der wissenschaftlichen Zivilisation*, Cologne Opladen: Westdeutscher Verlag.

Schelsky, H. (1975) *Dir Arbeit tun die Anderen. Klassenkampf und Priesterherrschaft der Intellektuellen*, 2nd edn, Opladen: Westdeutscher Verlag.

Schmidt, M. (1985) 'Budgetary Policy: A Comparative Perspective on Policy Outputs and Outcomes', in K. von Beyme and M. Schmidt (eds), *Policy and Politics in the Federal Republic of Germany*, Aldershot: Gower.

Schmidt, H. (1987) 'Arm in Arm mit den Franzosen', *Die Zeit*, (27 May 1987).

Schmidt, U. (1987) *Zentrum oder CDU. Politischer Katholizismus zwischen Tradition und Anpassung*, Opladen: Westdeutscher Verlag.

Schoeck, R. (1987) 'Methoden und Ergebnisse finanzieller Wirtschaftsförderung', in R. Henn (ed.), *Technologie, Wachstum und Beschäftigung –  Festschrift für Lothar Späth*, Berlin: Spring Verlag, pp. 685–96.

Schulz, E. (1982) *Die deutsche Nation in Europa, Internationale und historische Dimensionen*, Bonn: Europa-Union Verlag.

Schulz, E. and Danylow, P. (1985) *Bewegung in der deutschen Frage*, Bonn, Forschungsinstitut der deutschen Gesellschaft für auswärtige Politik, Arbeitspapiere zur internationalen Politik, no. 33.

Schultze, R. -O. (1987) 'Die Bundestagswahl 1987 – eine Bestätigung des Wandels', *Aus Politik und Zeitgeschichte* (21 March) pp. 3–17.

Schweitzer, C. *et. al.* (eds) (1984) *Politics and Government in the Federal Republic of Germany: Basic Documents*, Leamington Spa: Berg.

Seidenspinner, G. and Burger, A. (1982) *Mädchen '82 , Eine repräsentative Untersuchung über die Lebenssituation*, Munich: Deutsches Jugendinstitut.

Silbermann, A. and Schoeps, J. (eds) (1986) *Antisemitismus nach dem Holocaust*, Cologne: Politik und Wissenschaft.

Silvia, S. (1988) 'The West German Labor Law Controversy: Struggle for the Factory of the Future', *Comparative Politics*, vol. 20, no. 2, pp. 155–73.

Simonian, H. (1985) *The Privileged Partnership: Franco-German Relations in the European Community 1969–84*, Oxford: Clarendon Press.

Smith, G. (1982) 'The German Volkspartei and the Career of the Catch All Concept', in H. Döring and G. Smith (eds), *Party Government and Political Culture in Western Germany*, New York: St Martin's Press/London: Macmillan.

Smith, G. (1986) *Democracy in Western Germany: Parties and Politics in the Federal Republic*, 3rd edn, Aldershot: Gower.

Smith, G. (1987) 'The Changing West German Party System: Consequences of the 1987 Election', *Government and Opposition*, vol. 22, no. 2, pp. 131–44.

Søe, C. (1985) 'The Free Democratic Party', in H. Wallach and G. Romoser (eds), *West German Politics in the Mid-Eighties: Crisis and Continuity*, New York: Praeger.

Sontheimer, K. (1983) *Zeitenwende? Die Bundesrepublik Deutschland zwischen alter und alternativer Politik*, Hamburg: Hoffmann und Campe.

Statistiches Bundesamt (various years) *Wahlbeteiligung und Stimmabgabe der Männer und Frauen nach dem Alter,*

Stent, A. (1982) *From Embargo to Ostpolitik*, Cambridge: Cambridge University Press.

Stöss, R. (1983) *Parteien-Handbuch: Die Parteien der Bundesrepublik Deutschland 1945–1980* (2 vols), Opladen: Westdeutscher Verlag.

Stöss, R. (1986) 'Pronazistisches Protestverhalten unter Jugendlichen', in A. Silbermann and J. Schoeps (eds), *Antisemitismus nach dem Holocaust*, Cologne: Politik und Wissenschaft.

Streeck, W. (1984) *Industrial Relations in West Germany*, New York: St Martin's Press.

Sturm, R. (1989) 'The Industrial Policy Debate in the Federal Republic of Germany', in S. Bulmer (ed.), *The Changing Agenda of West German Public Policy*, Aldershot: Gower.

Stürmer, M. (1986) 'Die Suche nach der verlorenen Erinnerung', *Das Parlament*, 36.

Tennstedt, F. (1986) 'Die Zukunft sozial Gestalten', *Zeitschrift für Sozialreform*, vol. 8, pp. 445–51.

Tilford, R. (ed.) (1975) *The Ostpolitik and Political Change in West Germany*, Westmead: Saxon House/Farnborough: Gower.

Thelen, K. (1987) 'Codetermination and Industrial Adjustment in the German Steel Industry: A Comparative Interpretation', *California Management Review*, vol. 29, no. 3, pp. 134–48.

US Information Agency (1984) *The West German Successor Generation: Their Social and Political Values*, Washington, D.C., US Information Agency.

Veen, H. -J. (1989) 'The Greens as a Milieu Party', in E. Kolinsky (ed.), *The West German Greens – Policy Making and Party*, Oxford: Berg.

Wallace, H. (1986) 'Bilateral, trilateral and multilateral negotiations in the European Community', in R. Morgan and C. Bray (eds), *Partners and Rivals in the European Community*, Aldershot: Gower.

Wehling, H. G. (1987) *Nord-Süd in Deutschland? Vorurteile und Tatsachen*, Stuttgart: Verlag W. Kohlhammer.

Weidenfeld, W. (ed.) (1983) *Die Identität der Deutschen*, Munich/Vienna: Hanser Verlag.

Weilenmann, P. (1985) *Aspects of the German Question*, St Augustin: Konrad-Adenauer Stiftung.

Weinstock, U. (1987) 'Von der Sachlogik zum Pragmatismus – Erfahrungen als europäischer Beamter', *Integration*, vol. 10, no. 3, pp. 121–7.

Wessels, W. and Regelsberger, E. (1988) *The Federal Republic of Germany and the European Community: The Presidency and Beyond*, Bonn: Europa Union Verlag.

Wey, K. (1982) *Umwelt in Deutschland. Kurze Geschichte des Umweltschutzes in Deutschland seit 1900*, Opladen: Westdeutscher Verlag.

Wildenmann, R. (1986) 'Ludwig Erhard und Helmut Schmidt, die charismatischen Verlierer', in M. Kaase and H. -D. Klingemann (eds), *Analysen aus Anlass der Bundestagswahl 1983*, Opladen: Westdeutscher Verlag.

Willis, F. R. (1965) *France, Germany and the New Europe 1945–63*, Oxford: Oxford University Press.

Windsor, P. (1971) *Germany and the Management of Detente*, New York: Praeger/London: Chatto & Windus.

Zapf, W. (1986) 'Development, Structure and Prospects of the German Social State', in R. Rose and R. Shiratori (eds), *The Welfare State; East and West*, Oxford: Oxford University Press.

Zollner, R. (1989) 'Sozialpolitik', in W. Benz (ed.), *Die Bundesrepublik Deutschland: Geschichte in drei Bänden* (Band 2: 'Gesellschaft'), Frankfurt: Fischer Verlag.

Zundel, R. (1989) 'Ein Kanzler wie ein Eichenschrank', *Die Zeit*, 2–6 January.

Zundorf, B. (1979) *Die Ostverträge*, Munich: C. H. Beck.

# Index

352